Politics in Czechoslovakia

Politics in Czechoslovakia

Otto Ulč
State University of New York at Binghamton

With a Foreword by
Jan F. Triska
Stanford University

W. H. Freeman and Company
San Francisco

Library of Congress Cataloging in Publication Data

Ulč, Otto.
    Politics in Czechoslovakia.

    Bibliography: p.
    1. Czechoslovak Republic—Politics and govern-
ment—1945–   I. Title.
DB215.5.U4   320.9'437'04   74-11106
ISBN 0-7167-0779-9

Printed in the United States of America

9 8 7 6 5 4 3 2 1

To Priscilla and Ota

Foreword

Since the Czechoslovak Spring of 1968, over two hundred studies dealing with that subject have appeared in print. I have read most of them. I have also read some which have not been published. It is my opinion that *Politics in Czechoslovakia* by Otto Ulč ranks among the best.

Although the subject of his study is Czechoslovak politics from World War Two to the present, Professor Ulč's major focus is on the socioeconomic and political developments, conditions, trends, processes, and events which culminated in the Spring of 1968 and which, in turn, led to the invasion. Professor Ulč views the 1968 Czechoslovak leadership as attempting to re-conceptualize the state into a broadly purposeful instrumentality for achieving social goals, a political system adapting to its social environment and manipulating changes for the sake of the well-being of its citizens. He examines the incipient efficiency and effectiveness of the performance in *statu nascendi* in view of the increased emphasis on differentiation and specialization of political structures and the stipulated secularization of political culture. Under what conditions, the author asks, would the new government have had the capability and the capacity to solve major problems? Professor Ulč's principal concern is thus with political change. In fact, he views the 1968 politics in Czechoslovakia as a major mechanism of change. And here, in his attempting to understand and explain political change, rests, in my opinion, the real contribution and value of this important study. For the author reminds us that the 1968 Czechoslovak experiment transcends a mere parochial theorem taking place in a far-away land. Rightly, he stresses the universality of the learning experience which this process entailed, namely, an intensive search for a new type of political system which would combine the political equality of citizens with their social equality, while meeting the organizational demands of an advanced industrial society. "The Czechoslovak aim was to combine socialism with democracy," he writes, "freedom with social security, and equality with efficiency." Unfortunately, the August intervention effectively terminated the search for better human relations and higher moral standards within a Marxist socioeconomic setting. We will never know how the Czechoslovak experiment would have come out. Still, the brief, intense interregnum gave us an unequaled opportunity to view openly a closed society. The abolishment of censorship made available a wealth of information not obtainable elsewhere in Eastern Europe. This information, together with the results of many survey research studies carried out by Czechoslovak social scientists at the time and even after the invasion, provides the solid backbone of this study. They endow it with a hardness and reliability which is rare in the literature on Eastern Europe. The author's imaginative mode of analysis, his fine feeling for the dramatic subject matter, his incisive wit as well as deep compassion—make the monograph a solid, important, professional contribution to the literature on comparative politics as well as on contemporary history of Eastern Europe.

Stanford, California   Jan F. Triska
February 1974

Contents

Preface   x

1. **State Building**   1

   Unique Opportunity and Failure. Capabilities of the
   Stalinist System. Quest for a Monolith.

2. **Nation Building**   12

   The Minorities. Czechs, Slovaks, and the Federal
   Solution. National Character and Contemporary
   Challenges.

3. **Problems of Participation**   24

   The Party. The Leading Role of the Party and Suggested
   Alternatives. Pre-Invasion Achievements. Setback to
   Pluralism.

4. **Problems of Welfare**   45

   Stalinist Redistributive Measures. Social Pseudo-
   Security. Working Class, Intelligentsia, and Equalization. A Socialist Ideal of Sorts.

5. Policy Making 59

Leaders and Leadership. Interest Articulation and Interest Groups. Interest Aggregation. Rule Making.

6. Rule Application 74

The Party and the State Bureaucracy. The New Economic Model.

7. Adjudication 85

The Roots. Roles and Structures of Adjudication. The Volume and Nature of Adjudication. Challenges and Responses. Recent Developments.

8. Political Recruitment 96

Lure of a Career. Apparatchiks and the Party College. Political Recruitment and the Young Generation.

9. Political Socialization 108

Family and School. Youth Organization. Adult Socialization. Creation of the New Socialist Man—Some Setbacks.

10. Political Communication 130

The Language of Stalinism. Information as Power. Implications of 1968.

11. The Resulting Political Culture 141

12. Conclusion 147

Notes 152

Bibliography 172

Index 177

Preface

Hemingway said, "Revolution is a wonderful thing—for a time!" This is not a naive statement, certainly not a reactionary one. It means, to put it differently, that a prolonged dictatorship of the proletariat degenerates into a dictatorship over the proletariat; that socialism can be accomplished de jure by governmental decree, but de facto only through democracy; that socialism without democracy is not possible. Well, pardon me: In a certain form it is possible. It was once with us in the world. It was called, of course, Nazism.

Josef Skvorecky, Literarni listy, April 18, 1968.

Czechoslovakia accounts for only three-tenths of one percent of the world's population, yet its impact upon international affairs has not been negligible. Most recently, the events of 1968 catapulted Prague into the role of a challenger of the Soviet monopoly of Marxist ideology and its interpretation. The aim of the Czechoslovak reformers was to combine socialism with democracy and economic security with civil liberties. Whether or not it was a realistic ambition, it represented an attempt to "bring back Marx to Europe" and eliminate Leninism as an allegedly crippling distortion of Marxism. After all, Lenin himself had acknowledged that Russia was less than ideal for testing socialist theories that had been designed with Western industrialized states in mind. Furthermore, according to Lenin, Soviet Russia would be likely to lose her political and ideological primacy in the Communist movement if Marx's ideas prevailed in another, more advanced country.

Russia, largely sequestered from the great past movements—the Reformation, Renaissance, and Humanism—was thus challenged by a society with a pre-World War II tradition of pluralistic democracy and a postwar record of compliance with the Soviet model. After two decades of Stalinist rigidity and public docility, new goals were articulated: "From totalitarian dictatorship to an open society; the liquidation of the monopoly of power; effective control of the power elite by a free press, as well as by public opinion. . . . [To be accomplished] with the workers' movement, without its apparatchiks;

with the middle classes, without groups of willing collaborators, and with the intelligentsia leading the way."[1]

Precious few, if any, ideological principles were left unchallenged. Sacrosanct values, such as the doctrine of global struggle between the socialist and capitalist camps, were questioned and rejected. The conflict between humanizing and dehumanizing forces, not the class struggle, was considered more relevant to the contemporary age. "We want socialism for the people, not people for socialism," wrote philosopher Miroslav Jodl. Touching on the possible contagion of Czechoslovak heresy, he said: "Until now, there has not been socialism of this kind either in our country or the world; but this is the socialism we want. I have not the slightest doubt that in those countries from which obviously biased critical voices have come, the people also desire it. Nor do I have any doubt that those who have become accustomed to privilege and power do not want this type of socialism."[2]

As is well known, and will be discussed further on in the text, the "tanks of August" reintroduced, at least for the time being, the old order and tranquillity in the realm of Soviet power.

This monograph is not intended as an encyclopedic undertaking on Czechoslovakia. Although the entire post-1945 period (including the formative years of the People's Democracy) is taken into account, the focus of this work is the unusual developments of the late 1960s. The temporary abolishment of censorship (indeed, of the entire image of a "closed society") provided a wealth of information unavailable in other one-party systems. This study follows the functional approach to the study of political systems,[3] and as a result certain themes appear in more than one chapter. For example, the question of a Stalinist subculture is dealt with in two separate places, as is the Party College. As befits the nature of the ruling party, it is bound to permeate the entire analysis.

The daily press and periodicals—notably the Writers Union weekly, *Literárni listy*, and the Journalists Union weekly, *Reporter*—were my most important research sources. The impact of the suspension of censorship was felt immediately in journalism whereas in book publishing there was a natural time lag. Regrettably, books produced during this period did not always reach the reader before the reimposition of ideological purity. Data for this study also include material from the post-invasion period of thorough censorship up to 1972.

February 1974   Otto Ulč

Politics in Czechoslovakia

The political system built up during the 1950s failed to solve any of the key problems and tasks of socialist democracy.

Karel Kaplan, Nova mysl, May 1968.

1

State Building

Czech history, which Marx found so contemptible, was for others like Goethe the saddest in the world. Located in the geographical center of Europe, the Czech nation suffered recurring punishments from its more powerful neighbors. In the fifteenth century the Christian world punished the Czechs for the Hussite heresy, a deviation which contributed to the breakdown of the Universal Church. In the seventeenth century—as the somewhat ethnocentric Czechs would point out—Prague again ignited Europe, causing the Thirty Years' War and inaugurating the age of nation-state building. In this case, the penalty for the Bohemian kingdom was absorption by the Hapsburgs for the next three hundred years.

World War I led to the collapse of the Austro-Hungarian Empire and the creation of the Czech-oslovak Republic in October 1918. However, its independence was twice shattered in fifty years: in 1939, with Hitler's occupation, and in 1968, when Brezhnev applied his protection against the alleged threat of capitalism. Consequently, a single genera-tion has experienced pluralistic democracy and totalitarianism of both the Nazi and Stalinist varieties. Catastrophes like these, and repeated failures to avert them, have had a lasting effect on the nation's political culture.

Unique Opportunity and Failure

Communist parties gained control in East European countries less than three years after the cessation of hostilities in 1945. The stability of any political system, with respect to the chances of successful restructuring, depends to a large extent on the types of problems faced by its elites. The proponents of change in Czechoslovakia were, it may be argued, quite fortunate compared with their counterparts in neighboring countries.

First, Czechoslovakia is the only state created by the Versailles treaty whose democratic form of government was not destroyed from within. While the East European proletariat lived in semifeudal conditions, with their leaders in jail, underground, or

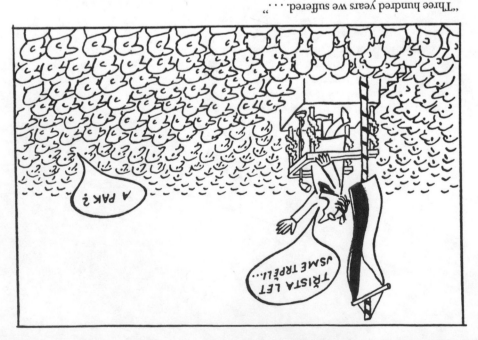

"Three hundred years we suffered. . . ."
"And then?"

(Dikobraz, October 22, 1968)

in exile, the interwar Czechoslovak socialist movement was strong and the Communist Party (*Komunistická strana Ceskoslovenska*—KSC) was a legitimate political participant. "No one had to acquaint our nation with the ideals of democracy, social progress, and internationalism by foreign pamphlets sometime late in the twentieth century . . . ," it was smugly pointed out in 1968.[1] Socialism—though not Stalinism, to be sure—was the choice of the majority, not an import imposed and supported by foreign military force.[2]

Second, the country was economically developed, with her non-Slovak part having a high level of industrialization and a high standard of living, and was only slightly scarred by World War II. Third, despite the wartime pro-Nazi puppet regime in Slovakia, the victorious powers considered Czechoslovakia an ally, with no burden of reparations or the permanent presence of foreign troops.

Fourth, the country was free of anti-Russian sentiment. On the contrary, the nineteenth-century Pan-Slavic movement had left a positive imprint. Finally, the Czechoslovak government of Benes was the only exile government of the Communist-bound part of Europe which was allowed to return, at least

[1] Notes on sources begin on page 152.

as a symbol of statehood and preservation of its continuity.

In all, the task of building a socialist political order in Czechoslovakia appeared neither arduous nor unrealistic. The resulting failure must to a great extent be ascribed both to Soviet insistence on direct copies of their institutions and the timidity of local elites, who offered little resistance to such demands. Such concepts as a *Prokuratura* (a combination of a public prosecutor and Scandinavian ombudsman) or *Arbitraz* (a quasijudicial body deciding conflicts between state economic enterprises) were transplanted in alien soil. Some indigenous structures were abolished, e.g., the administrative court, a citizen's avenue of redress against decisions of the bureaucracy. Some structures were retained in form though not in content, e.g., regular courts adopted the concept of "class justice" and explicitly rejected equality before the law. Some primarily technical institutions were retained both in form and purpose. The original revolutionary zeal was reflected in continuous reshaping of the state. However, restructuring in later Stalinist years—e.g., reduction and then multiplication of ministries—did not introduce many fundamental changes. Though an element of improvisation (generally illogical) was not absent among Czech political architects, in most instances they merely copied current experiments within the Soviet Union.

By th 1960s it had become common knowledge among the Czechoslovaks that their country had been surpassed by all its socialist neighbors in economic growth, as well as in development of the political system (or at least the preservation of its vitality).[3] This failure deserves some comment. Im-position of the Soviet system on the advanced, differentiated, and secularized Czechoslovak system indeed resulted in a transformation, but as far as "development" is concerned this was development in reverse. If secularization is understood to be a process of increased rationality in political behavior, then the imposition of a state doctrine, of monopoly of creed, of censorship curtailing inventiveness and imagination must be considered a setback. The Stalinist political system, at least in Czechoslovakia, has led to a "desecularization" of political culture.

Proceeding from secularization of culture to differentiation of structures, one can observe strains of irrationality, waste, and overextension. Instead of enhancing smooth operations, devices of mutual control result in deadlocks, overlapping, and absence of identifiable responsibility. In Stalinism it is a mat-ter of prime ideological significance to view the political system as one which is all-embracing, with legitimacy of access and substitution for any role and function, irrespective of its nature. Accordingly, the Party Secretariat is not inhibited from pondering about the political significance of sauerkraut or encroaching upon the management prerogative of the State Retail Sauerkraut Organization.

Within this political system itself uninten-tional and at times deliberate confusion reigns, leading to and emanating from the substitutability of roles and structures. Even the anti-Stalinist political elite of 1968 suffered blurred vision in these matters. Thus, it was Alexander Dubcek, the First Secretary of the Communist Party (a voluntary organization), and Premier Oldrich Cernik who signed a treaty of friendship with Bulgaria while the head of the state Ludvik Svoboda stood idly by.[4] Two decades of constitutional neglect and this long-standing inces-tual affair between the State (the father) and the Party (the mother) left many marks, from the remuneration for political engagement from the state treasury to the existence of workers militia, a private army under the sole command of the Party's First Secretary.[5] In other words, rather than enhancing

development and state building, this Stalinist variety of cultural secularization and structural differentia-tion led to a rather complex setback.

It might be helpful at this point to indicate the phases of Czechoslovak socialist development. Party historians identify three periods:

1. 1945–1948: the interim coalition, terminating in February 1948 with the Communist defeat of an-tisocialist forces. With the adoption of the May Constitution, the formative period of the People's Democracy came to an end—and so did surviving forms of pluralistic democracy.

2. 1948–1960: establishment of a People's Democracy proper, characterized by the leading role of the Communist Party, dictatorship of the prole-tariat, and class struggle, culminating in 1960 with a new constitution and promulgation of the achieve-ment of socialism.

3. 1960 to the present: socialist construction, approximating the Communist ideal, with some unanticipated ups and downs.

The end of Novotny's rule in 1968 saw the discrediting of these official categories. The following simplified phases would be more useful here:

(1) 1945–48, struggle for power
(2) 1948–1968, Stalinism consolidated and pro-tracted
(3) 1968–1969, Stalinism suspended
(4) 1969 to the present, "normalization"—period of restoration of pre-1968 political style

Various periods within the two decades of Stalinism can be identified, such as pure Stalin-ism (1948–1953), Stalinism mellowed (1953–1957), Stalinism retained and overripe (1957–1963), Sta-linism paralyzed (1963–1968). The rather arbi-trary calendar of these phases notwithstanding, they do coincide to some extent with the rule of individual Czechoslovak leaders: from 1948 to 1953 Klement Gottwald, a faithful disciple of Stalin, was President of the Republic, followed by Antonin Zapotocky, upon whose death in 1957 Antonin Novotny took over until 1968.

In 1969 the prominent liberal weekly Listy com-mented on the periods of Novotny's rule. First, his rise to power was characterized by overall cen-tralization and bureaucratization, the Czech variant of decaying Stalinism. Second, after the Twentieth Party Congress in the USSR in February 1956,

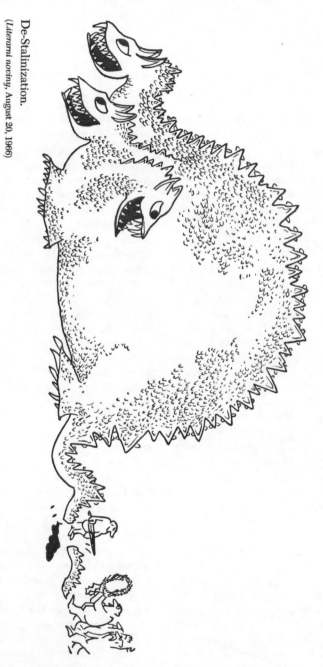

De-Stalinization.

(Literarni noviny, August 20, 1966)

an era of "deformed de-Stalinization" began in Czechoslovakia. While Khrushchev opened the gates of the concentration camps, Novotny continued to keep his charges under lock and key. An historical opportunity was therefore passed up, and the country emerged as the most conservative in the socialist camp. Political hypocrisy and camouflage were joined to the Stalinist brutality of the 1950s. Finally, in the 1960s, some room for maneuvering was secured by antidogmatic forces, although the threat of a return to Stalinization was never suspended. The personal power of Novotny, secured by the 1960 constitution, had reached its zenith.[6]

This assessment requires some comment. During the 1950s, the cohesiveness of the top political elite and its rather skillful tactics made tight control of society possible, and the dangers of de-Stalinization experienced by Poland and Hungary in 1956 were thus avoided. Although the order to remove Stalin's corpse from the mausoleum was issued in October 1961, his statue in Prague—reputedly the tallest stat-ue of Stalin ever constructed—reigned over the city's embankment until October 1962. By then, however, the Party's effective leadership was in decline. The many years of mismanaged economy, rising popular discontent, calls for overdue de-Stalinization, and the reemergence of the Slovak nationality issue caused friction and disunity among the leaders and con-sequently some concessions. However modest and deficient these concessions were, economists were allowed to work on the New Economic Model (NEM) and some especially discredited Stalinists were deposed. Political relaxation also affected civil rights, such as those concerning travel abroad. Most sig-nificantly, the Party lost its momentum; the in-strument of rule deteriorated into a defensive and ineffective tool. Its policies, it was also charged, were "improvised, unrational, unsovereign, [and] vassal."[7] Novotny's response to international (i.e., Soviet) wishes was always instant compliance while he ig-nored or repressed domestic demands. Faced with the dilemma of either repressing internal demands or undermining his authority, Novotny chose the former but was still unable to avoid the latter.

Novotny's 1960 declaration on the achievement of socialism and of an "all people's society"—imply-ing the extinction of domestic class struggle—has come under vehement attack since 1969 by post-in-vasion sources. Novotny, of all people, was accused of being soft on class approach, of confusing reality with

his own wishes, and of skipping some twenty to fifty years of socialist development toward a truly classless society. Condemned by critics as "unrealistic and non-Marxist, [and thus] creating confusion in the Party and society,"[8] Novotny ironically became as-sociated, through the sin of rightist deviation, with the liberal wing of the Party which had brought his rule to an end in 1968.

Capabilities of the Stalinist System

Stimulus toward political change may emanate from (1) the political system itself, notably its elites, (2) social forces in the domestic environment, or (3) ex-tranational political systems. These forces of change do not operate independently of each other. Rather than a monopoly of one at a given time, it is the interaction of the three elements that determines the intensity and course of such a change.

By way of an example, look at Table 1.1. Stimulus 2—economic crisis and the pressure of restive in-tellectuals in particular—led to the overdue changes within the political leadership. The liberal wings of the Party (1) then proceeded toward reformation of the system until this program was stopped by the August invasion of the Warsaw Pact forces (3). It should be stressed that the second stimulus (domestic social forces) exercised a vitally important pressure upon the political elite in the pre-invasion period as to the direction and speed of the liberalization reforms. This pressure deprived the Party of its crucial ingredient for the leading role, namely, the monopoly of initiative. In the post-invasion period, the second stimulus (nation's unity in anti-Sovietism) delayed the expected restoratory results of the third force for almost a year.

Table 1.1. Dominant Stimulus Toward Change in Czechoslovakia in 1968.

Time	Stimulus
Preceding January 1968	(2) Domestic social forces
January–August 1968	(1) National political system
Following August 1968	(3) External political systems

As suggested, the three forces are interdependent, irrespective of their varying degrees of importance or capacity for effecting change. A crisis is likely to occur if a particular stimulus, rather than being absent, is ignored. The failure of the Czechoslovak Stalinist political system can be traced to unresponsive elites misjudging, deliberately or otherwise, social groups within the nation. The demands of such social groups were sacrificed for the sake of doctrinal harmony with the cradle of world socialist revolution. The system was bound to become weakened for lack of adaptability, once elites remained committed to a foreign ideology interpreted elsewhere. An external political system (3) thus became dominant, while the other forces atrophied: 2 because of a lack of legitimacy, 1 because of a loss of integrity. This atrophy soon affected economic and social systems as well.

Present evidence is inconclusive about whether political development in Czechoslovakia after 1948 was determined more by Soviet insistence on following its model or by the willingness, even eagerness, of local elites not to deviate from the tested example. For instance, although Soviet secret police to some extent engineered the political trials in Prague in the early 1950s, Stalin allegedly admonished Czechoslovak leaders to keep the "advisors" under firm control.[9] According to some sources, the Party's early program calling for the "Czechoslovak road to socialism" prompted Gottwald to entertain the idea of establishing political opposition, with Zapotocky inclined to have this role exercised by the trade unions. However, Tito's misbehavior and the Cominform Resolution of 1948 put an end to such unorthodox thoughts. As a substitute solution, Gottwald decided to form the Commission for Party Control (KSK) which developed, ironically, into the main perpetrator of lawlessness.[10]

A clearer picture of the elites' responsiveness to Soviet demands can be obtained from their political record. The record shows that patriotism was not among the virtues of Gottwald and his lieutenants. This group, which assumed control of the Party in 1929, was characterized by dogmatic ultraleftist policies, with Moscow their only allegiance.[11] Faithful implementation of Soviet demands did not require massive recruitment of Soviet advisors. Content analysis of the Party's documents, leaders' speeches, textbooks of the Central Party School and other records reveals that in Czechoslovakia "there were no significant forces [during the early postwar period] aware of an alternative to the Marxist-Leninist [i.e., Stalinist] building of socialism."[12] On the basis of Gotwald's speeches and writings of that

period, it would not be incorrect to say that the policies undertaken after 1948 were a matter of his conviction and not outside coercion.

Czechoslovak writers delving into the subject in 1968 were virtually unanimous in concluding that the adoption of Soviet Marxism was a major disaster. Marxism, they wrote, was vulgarized in an environment which history had deprived of humanizing influences. Even Russian Christianity—the likely tie with Western civilization—was marred by caesaropapism, superstition, and overall primitivism. Hellenic man views his God with humor—Byzantine man lives his creed with deadly seriousness. Stalinism cannot be reduced to the "cult of personality," the terror of the 1930s, and the theory of the intensification of class struggle under conditions of socialist construction, just as it cannot be explained as a mere outgrowth of Tsarism and Byzantine culture. According to the 1968 Czech views, Stalinism as a political system is characterized by a subordination of the interests of the society to those of the state, a fusion of state and Party, strict centralism, bureaucratic rule, reduction of civil rights, and a rigid hierarchy of authority.[13]

All political systems based on Marxism-Leninism, it was argued, led at one time or another to lawlessness, liquidation of opponents (real or imaginary), and their subsequent rehabilitation. The faults recurrent in all the countries where the Soviet mode of government was applied could not therefore be explained by reference merely to the "shortcomings" of local leaders—the fault must be with the system. In the words of the philosopher Robert Kalivoda, this system "entirely lost its potential of becoming a realistic alternative to the modern bourgeois democracy of the European type."[14]

We shall now briefly analyze the political record of the Novotny era, characterized by one writer as a "mildly modified Stalinist model of bureaucratic-statist socialism."[15] In the 1960 constitution the Communist Party is declared the "state party" and Marxism-Leninism is declared the "state ideology." However, making the state absolute also leads to its degradation, inasmuch as it is then manipulated by forces not legally or politically accountable. In Czechoslovakia, concentration of political power in a single ruling party excluded some four-fifths of the population from political participation. Generally, the elites may either suppress or comply with demands: they may ignore them or seek a compromise. Communist elites publicly boasted about ignoring such demands, or at least complained—as has Gustav Husák since 1968—about public meddling in the decision making process, thus causing "crisis situations."[16]

Bureaucratization brings with it the total manipulation of individuals and the whole society. A former Central Committee member and noted philosopher, Karel Kosík, likened this manipulation to that of the medieval guilds: lock up the workers in factories, isolate the peasantry in villages, and confine the intelligentsia to libraries. These groups are isolated from each other and depoliticized, with their energy geared to their work, thereby fostering special interests and obscuring common interests. Above them stands the bureaucracy—the alleged incarnation of common social goals. This system of universal manipulation respects neither the living nor the dead: Babylonian monuments built for eternity are torn down, Gottwald's corpse is dressed in a general's uniform and mummified, then changed into mufti and burned, Manipulation, Kosík adds, is then joined by the metaphysics of modernity—lack of permanency and nihilism.[17]

The concept of the Party's leading rule is the root of crisis. Political roles substitute for economic administrative and cultural roles; before acting, governmental bodies request approval from the Party. This transfer of decision making eventually exempts administrators from responsibility; and the Party, because it is infallible, remains immune from the consequences of its own blunders. The Kafkaesque circle of *obezlička* (dodging responsibility) is closed. The usurpation of decision making in economic affairs by the Party bureaucracy, though perhaps justifiable in conditions of economic underdevelopment, is counterproductive in a modern industrial society.

Attendant difficulties, which occasionally surfaced during the 1950s, developed into a chronic ailment after 1960. Constant reorganization decreed from above could not provide the cure. Neither liquidation of political privilege nor the emancipation of individual structures from Party domination was contemplated. Any reform of substance would have precipitated the self-destruction of the system itself, the liberation from what Kosík called "that peculiar conglomerate of bureaucratism and Byzantinism, that monstrous symbiosis of the state and the pagan church, of hypocrisy and fanaticism, ideology and faith, the bureaucratic facelessness and mass hysteria. ..."[18]

Novotný and his group could not qualify as agents of change. Some critics such as novelist and KSČ member Milan Kundera, found this leadership an accurate reflection of a general social malaise, characterized by pettiness, timidity, envy, and primitivism. For Kundera, Antonín Novotný was the incarnation of the Czech genius for pettiness.[19]

What little is known about Novotný illustrates the style of that epoch: an ill-educated lifetime apparatchik; a friendless, conspiratorial ascetic; a faceless, glacial nonentity, unyielding and inflexible. Here was a leader who was known to occupy himself with such trivia as the closing of a Prague striptease theater or taking part in the house search of his arrested friend and Interior Minister, the rather popular Rudolf Barák, who allegedly was Khrushchev's choice for

(*Listy*, March 6, 1969)

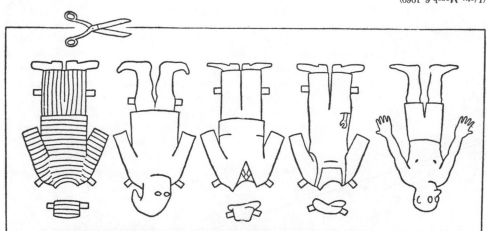

leadership in the country.[20] Novotny was perhaps aware of his own incompetence, yet he increasingly became convinced that he alone could guarantee Czechoslovak socialism and friendship with the USSR.[21] Called "the conspiracy of the below average," Novotny and his group decided important political issues during card games and occasional fistfights at their prisoner-built retreats near the Orlik castle.[22] This regime—also known as the Orlik Dynasty—was harshly described by Miroslav Jodl in these words: "Seldom in our history has there been simultaneously gathered together, from top to bottom, such incompetence and brutality, so much dilettantism and despotism, so much stupidity of initiative and lack of it, as under the leadership of Novotny. This man was politically so improvident that he even allowed the price of beer to rise."[23]

T. G. Masaryk, the first president of the Republic, resigned in 1935 because of advanced age; all of his successors left the office under conditions of defeat—Benes being twice defeated (by the Munich Treaty of 1938 and by the Communist coup of 1948), Hacha by the Allied victory of 1945. After the three bourgeois presidents came the three proletarian heads of state: Gottwald, who acquiesced in judicial murders; Zapotocky, who did not rehabilitate the innocent victims;[24] and Novotny, who could not change the inherited system because he could not change himself.

Defects in the economic system illustrate the poor performance of the policy makers. The Czechoslovak economy in 1945 was the most promising among those of the countries which would later constitute the European socialist camp. Yet its management seemed almost intent on destroying it. The American-backed plan of building up an automobile construction industry was vetoed while the European market was starving for cars and both the Italian and German competition was in ruins. The restoration of such profitable prewar foreign trade as that in porcelain, glass, and other light industry was also turned down. Tourist trade was blocked, ignoring the popularity of such famous spas as Karlsbad and Marienbad; even the proposal to build an international airport, badly needed in this geographical center of Europe, was shelved—and so, literally, were its proponents.[25]

All economic science of bourgeois vintage was replaced by political pamphleteering, and the country adopted a model of extensive industrializa-

tion based on that of agrarian Russia. Veneration of the plan and its quantitative fulfillment generated the recruitment of the idle part of the population, mainly women, in the labor process. Emphasis was placed on basic industries such as mining, steel, and heavy machinery. Investment policies ignored modernization of equipment and the development of such modern industrial necessities as chemicals, plastics, and electronics. Instead, in a country lacking the necessary raw materials, emphasis was on steel production. With only quantitative criteria of performance, the quality of products deteriorated. The opportunities for huge exports to socialist and developing countries did not provide the incentive to stop this dangerous trend. By the end of the 1950s, difficulties began to emerge in foreign trade, soon followed by difficulties in the domestic market. Stores became filled with unsalable merchandise whereas items the population desired were rarely obtainable. By 1963, Czechoslovakia had achieved a record, matched perhaps only by Indonesia: a decline in the gross national product (GNP).

Some figures revealed in 1968–1969 illustrate the depth of this failure. Compared with France, Czechoslovakia's industrial production per capita was 1.75 times higher while the average standard of living was 2.5 times lower. Czechoslovakia in 1968 had the third highest industrial output in Europe and was among the top ten in the world, yet her living standard was lower than that of her Western neighbors.[26] Another vicious circle is being spun in the 1970s: the country is dependent upon exports, yet because the prices of such goods are subsidized by the state, the higher the export volume, the higher the costs and the poorer the nation. The most optimistic estimate sees the economy's efficiency at half its potential, with 85 percent of all losses in production caused by mismanagement. Not surprisingly, of about 12,000 executives in the nationalized industries in 1963, only one-fifth were university-educated and one-fifth had not gone beyond grade school.[27] Doctrinaire investment policies led to huge assets frozen in unfinished projects; at the same time, equipment in some industries, such as breweries and sugar refineries, had to be written off by as much as 75 percent for obsolescence.

The total price was high, as can be seen in Table 1.2.[28] Novotny's political management proved incapable of curing the economy. Although a new economic model (NEM) had been worked out, presented to the Party, and formally adopted in 1965, it has not been implemented because of ideological timidity and pressure from managerial and bureaucratic beneficiaries of the old system.

Table 1.2. Change in Standard of Living of Socialist Countries.

Country	Index of per capita income	
	1950	*1965*
Poland	100	100
Rumania	48	82
Bulgaria	53	83
USSR	82	115
Hungary	104	100
East Germany	115	165
Czechoslovakia	151	144

The damage to the economy seems small compared with the moral damage inflicted on society. Honest work became synonymous with stupidity. This endemic deterioration was exemplified by two sayings: "Take it easy" and "He who does not steal from the state, steals from his own family." In this case, from a Marxist viewpoint, the economic realm (material base) did indeed determine political culture (superstructure) in this society. Some observers have argued the reverse; for example, Vladimir Kadlec, Minister of Education in 1968, declared in 1969 that an ethical crisis was the basis of the economic crisis, with the outlook for the coming years gloomy, even posing a threat to the very existence of the state.[29]

In this context, official pronouncements in 1960 about Czechoslovakia overtaking the world in per capita production—the United States included—sound quite hilarious. "Khrushchev was wrong when he claimed that socialism could produce more and do it more cheaply than highly developed capitalism. Slogans about catching up with and overtaking [capitalism] sound ridiculous to those generations which have had to contend with shortages in staple goods for twenty years."[30]

Defects in Novotny's political system were equaled by its incapacity to make the values presented by the regime credible. In the first place, the regime was discredited by the very personality of its leader. Czech cultural values include respect for, even worship of, the president. In this kind of "republican religion," as it is sometimes called, the legacy of the Czech monarchy is echoed. The presidential seat is in the "castle of the Czech kings," and the most famous photograph is that of T. G. Masaryk on a white horse. Against this tradition, then, stands the dull, uneducated, and arrogant Novotny, incapable of commanding the respect of even his closest followers.

Intensive socialization efforts by the Party for two decades did not yield the desired results and with many issues (e.g., love for the Soviet Union) its efforts were clearly counterproductive, as we shall see later. Public opinion surveys provide data on a variety of subjects. For instance, in replying to a question about equality of the sexes and the economic emancipation of women, only 7 percent of the respondents stated that they sought employment primarily for the sake of "self-realization." Only 18.9 percent of one sample of Czechoslovak citizens held Western imperialists responsible for the war in Vietnam. In another survey, not more than one-third of the citizenry knew the name of the mayor of their municipalities. And most significant, according to a public opinion survey conducted by the Czechoslovak Academy of Sciences (CSAV), the Communist Party under Novotny enjoyed the support of only 23 percent of the respondents, 48 remained distrustful and opposed, and 29 percent undecided.[31]

The system fared worst with the generation born into it. Participation in the Czechoslovak Youth Organization (CSM—Ceskoslovensky svaz mladeze—a counterpart of the Soviet Komsomol), a moribund enterprise for at least a decade before it officially expired in 1968, was largely nominal. Participation by young people in the Communist Party was even less. By the end of Novotny's era, only 15.3 percent of the Party's members were under thirty years of age. At Prague University the percentage of students who were organized Communists dropped from 10 percent in 1960 to 5.2 percent in 1967. In all, students constituted 0.4 percent of the total Party membership in 1966.[32]

Content analysis of poster slogans carried in May Day parades through Prague may give some indication of the nation's mood.[33] It should be mentioned, however, that although this affair was spontaneous and attendance voluntary in 1968, in preceding years it was a standard totalitarian spectacle, with public participation mandatory. Furthermore, in 1968 the Stalinist slogans were almost monopolized by foreign students. Overall, the most striking fact was the decline in the number of exhortatory statements characteristic of a manipulated society. This is shown in Table 1.3. Without attempting any sweeping interpretation of these figures, it could be said that the appearance in 1968 of "demands" and the disappearance of references to "Soviet," for example, was hardly irrelevant to the mood of the country. The laurel probably belongs to this poster: "With the Soviet Union forever—but not a single day longer!"

Brief mention should be made of one specific aspect of the system's distributive performance, namely, the bestowal of honorific titles—combining Hapsburgian veneration of title and Stalinist Byzantinism. Athletes, artists, scientists, and individuals with a variety of merits were arranged into a hierarchy of ranks with awkward titles, literally translated from the Russian. Political elites showed a penchant for titles of their own. The Party College satisfied this desire with the lavish distribution of "political Ph.D.'s." Not until Novotny's downfall were objections raised against this manifest negation of the egalitarian ethos of Communism.

The issue of Czechoslovakia's servility, if not servitude, to Moscow and its demands was also raised in 1968. Subjection to the Soviet economic model as well as to Soviet interests is well known. Indeed, Czechoslovakia was known to pay the USSR double the price for crude oil charged to Western customers.[34] It is in the realm of international relations, however, that the country's status becomes a caricature of mini-grandeur. As a rule, the Czechoslovak delegate to the United Nations follows the Soviet speaker and, if possible, slightly exceeds Soviet demands. Czechoslovakia is one of the most active UN members in drafting proposals. It has the second highest foreign aid program per capita (after France), and its extravagant foreign finance ventures are matched only by its widespread espionage activities,[35] which are more appropriate to a superpower. These then are the ludicrous gestures of a noisy, little, but above all, loyal man. As one Czech writer put it, there has not been the will to have a sovereign foreign policy and then pursue it; therefore this pretense of power, while the real picture is that of a country girl at a grand ball in a borrowed dress and with runs in her stockings.[36]

Quest for a Monolith

In Gustav Husak's opinion, with a sufficient amount of terror any idiot can run a country, disregarding the flow of demands into the system. Novotny's performance seems to disprove this view. In words of the philosopher Ivan Sviták:

An outstanding advantage of the [Novotny] regime was the fact that it was headed by full-blooded Bohemians, with their Austrian tradition of joviality, combined with the muddled inefficiency of a concierge (for which there is such a good German word, Schlamperei). . . . This dictatorship was rather a comic paradox. Apart from some murders, the government was as helpless in the handling of absolute power as a baby would be with a slide rule. The occasional fits of democracy, periodically introduced and then removed, never succeeded in bringing about fundamental changes, and the foundations of this system were undermined again and again by aggressive stupidity.[37]

With all the vast central power at their disposal, the leadership failed to bridge the economic and cultural gaps between the Czech and Slovak regions or even to eliminate the all too apparent differences within regions. In 1968 vast disparities were revealed, such as the depopulation and decay of southern Bohemia and the cultural deprivation in the industrial center of Ostrava in northern Moravia. Ineptitude and lack of sophistication among political elites, with their penchant for trivia, led to what political scientist František Samalík calls "universal provincialism."[38] With stagnation in both the economic and social systems, the political structure began to loosen at its seams.

To some degree this was accelerated by the organizational structure of the Communist Party itself. Although most of the members belong to Party cells at their places of employment, a minority—mainly senior citizens with a distinct Stalinist bent—belong to neighborhood cells. It was the Party units at universities and scientific institutes that became strongholds of reformism. Novotny's application of "democratic centralism" was not sufficient to obliterate this pluralization.

Less than total homogeneity of personal temperament among provincial power holders contributed to a certain horizontal diversity in political style. Even in the peak years of Stalinism, "soft" and "hard" districts existed. This polarization sharpened in 1968. Thus, in the municipal organizations of Prague and Brno (the two largest cities), the liberal wing dominated, whereas in the province of Central Slovakia (with the seat in Banska Bystrica—also known as Slovak Tirana) the conservative forces dominated. In general, however, the political landscape revealed a rather uniform pattern: the farther from an urban area, the closer to the Stalinist past.[39] A one-hour trip out of Prague was likely to move the traveler back in time by a decade. Some heterogeneity of political outlook was also found in factories. The type of industry, social composition, and percentage of nonproletarians assigned to

manual labor were among the important determinants of the political climate in a given place.

The Stalinist quest for a monolithic system of rule was handicapped above all by the multinational character of Czechoslovakia. Prague centralism was bound to offend and provoke adverse reaction in the less populous Slovak nation. Novotny's outstanding lack of tact in matters of Slovak self-respect aggravated the situation to such a degree that the Slovak branch of the Party emerged as a political force in opposition to Prague.[40] Disregard of the Slovak minority in the process of state building contributed substantially to the destruction of the Stalinist political system in Czechoslovakia. It will be the task of the next chapter to probe into the issues and problems of nation building.

Table 1.3. Types of Slogans (in percentages).

Slogans	1955	1960	1968
Exhortations, instructions ("Keep your city clean")	77.7	51.3	7.5
May First Greetings ("Long live May First")	–	–	13.0
General greetings ("Long live the C. P. of Australia")	13.1	17.1	2.5
Ethical messages ("Jesus—not Caesar")	–	–	9.5
Demands ("We demand a Party congress")	–	–	10.0
Critical opposition statements ("Democratization? Democracy!")	–	–	12.0
Political wit and innuendo	–	–	12.0
Slogans bearing on democracy ("Democracy for dissenters")	–	–	12.0
Others	–	–	13.5

Source: Reporter, May 15, 1968.
Note: Data in original do not total 100 percent.

2

Nation Building

Compared with the Czechs, the development of the Slovak nation was more difficult all around. The consequences are still all too visible in every field, except for soccer and alcohol consumption. . . .

Jan Mlynarik, Listy, February 3, 1969.

A substantial organic part of the Czechoslovak crisis, dragging on for years, has been the crisis of Czech-Slovak relations.

Jaroslav Opat, Literarni listy, July 18, 1968.

Ethnic diversity seriously handicapped prewar Czechoslovakia. According to the 1921 census, of the total population of 13.6 million, the German minority accounted for 3.23 million, Hungarians for 0.75, and Ruthenians 0.46—in all, ethnic minorities comprised one-third of the population. In 1938 the issue of the Sudeten Germans became the principal cause of the destruction of the Republic.

The defeat of Nazism in 1945 sealed the fate of the German minority, most of which was expelled, largely into the Western zones of occupied Germany. The question of the Hungarian minority was visualized as a combined program of population exchange, expulsion, and integration with the Slovaks. Finally, the incorporation into the Soviet Union of Ruthenia, the easternmost part of the country, disposed of the Ruthenian (Ukrainian) problem. Consequently, the 1948 constitution did not mention minorities at all.

The Minorities

In 1970, more than two decades after the official resolution of the minorities question, census takers counted over 800,000 inhabitants who were neither Czech nor Slovak.[1] Table 2.1 shows the ethnic population distribution between 1950 and 1970, with the exception of one important minority, the Gypsies (see p. 14). Minorities comprised 6 percent of the total population, with the largest concentration (15 percent) in Slovakia, further aggravating nationalist sentiment there.

The very survival of these minorities deserves some explanation. The two Slavic groups, the Poles and Ruthenians, are spillover populations from neighboring countries. Accordingly, Poles live in Northern Moravia on the Polish border, Ruthenians in Eastern Slovakia facing the Soviet Union. As Table 2.1 shows, these are the smallest groups. Most Ger-

Table 2.1. Ethnic Population in Czechoslovakia, 1950-1970 (in thousands).

Year	Czech		Slovak		Hungarian		German		Polish		Ukrainian		Other		Total
	No.	%	No.	%	No.	%	No.	%	No.	%	No.	%	No.	%	No.
1950	8,384	(67.9)	3,240	(26.3)	368	(3.0)	165	(1.3)	73	(0.6)	67	(0.6)	41	(0.3)	12,338
1961	9,070	(66.0)	3,836	(27.9)	534	(3.9)	140	(1.0)	68	(0.5)	55	(0.4)	43	(0.3)	13,746
1967	9,263	(64.9)	4,151	(29.1)	559	(3.9)	124	(0.9)	71	(0.5)	57	(0.4)	46	(0.3)	14,271
1970	9,335	(65.0)	4,194	(29.2)	574	(4.0)	86	(0.6)	72	(0.5)	57	(0.4)	43	(0.3)	14,361

Sources: Statistická ročenka ČSSR 1968 (Prague: SNTL, 1968), p. 93; Rude pravo, August 17 and September 14, 1968; and Svet hospodarstvi, July 13, 1971.

minority is recognized as an autonomous entity entitled to political participation but merely as a loose common denominator of atomized individuals or, at best, as an instrument of folkloristic endeavor.[5] Over the years minorities were allowed native language newspapers and individual participation in (mainly local) political bodies, and—except for Germans—were also able to form nationwide cultural organizations.

The Ruthenians, mainly a farming people living in villages of less than a thousand inhabitants, presented the KSC with a particularly sensitive problem because of kinship, both personal and linguistic, with the inhabitants on the Soviet side of the border. Prague Stalinists, assisted by the local Slovak power structure, could not do enough to comply with what they presumed were Soviet desires in fostering Ukrainian interests, even chauvinism, in Eastern Slovakia. This zeal even led the Party to "engage in the role of Apostle of the Russian Orthodox Church and Moscow patriarch."[6] Avowed internationalists and atheists, Czechoslovak policy makers promoted Ukrainian over Slovak as the language of school instruction and, as the lesser of two evils, the Russian Orthodox Church over the Uniate (Greek Catholic) Church.

The most acute postwar ethnic conflict involved Slovaks and the Hungarian minority. These two groups have a long record of grievances, uneasy assimilation, and a formidable language barrier. Hungarians constitute only 12 percent of the population in Slovakia but are concentrated mainly along the border with Hungary. Of twelve districts in the area, Hungarians are an absolute majority in two and make up half the population in four. About one-fifth of all

mans remaining in Czechoslovakia were exempted from expulsion on account of their personal antifascist record or economic usefulness—some were merely overlooked. They are the only substantially declining minority—the decline resulting from voluntary emigration and cultural assimilation of the young—and are dispersed mainly throughout the western borderland. The failure of the postwar attempt to settle the minorities issue accounts for the continued presence of the largest minority, the Hungarians, who are concentrated in Western and Southern Slovakia.[2]

After 1945 the Communist Party excelled in echoing popular anti-German sentiment. Reminiscent of prewar animosity, reference to anything German was usually prejudicial. This minority was deprived in toto of citizenship; abolition of legal discrimination in 1953 did not affect their second-class status. Although the 1960 constitution acknowledged certain ethnic minorities by name, it disregarded the Germans, who had to wait until 1968 for recognition.

Minorities, particularly the Slovaks, regarded the government's lack of responsiveness to their legitimate needs as evidence of Czech chauvinism, if not "micro-imperialism." Such an assessment was hardly accurate. The two decades of Stalinist rule from Prague were essentially as unresponsive to Czechs as to any other group.[3] However, very little is known about the past minority policies of the KSC because most of the documents have been kept secret.[4] With the notable exception of the German-speaking population, no official attempt has been made to prevent interaction between minorities and parent cultures in other countries. However, no

Hungarians in Slovakia live in exclusively Hungarian communities. In 451 communities—13.5 percent of the total number of settlements in Slovakia—the Slovaks feel themselves to be, and in fact are, a minority.[7]

The fall of the Novotný regime precipitated the articulation of accumulated ethnic grievances with the *Czermadok* ("Cultural Union of Hungarian Toiling People") and *Matica Slovenská*, a historical-cultural society of the Slovak nation, as natural antagonists. The polarization continued during the eight pre-invasion months of 1968 and reached the point of demands that the Magyar-populated areas be incorporated into Hungary.[8]

It cannot be proven now—if it ever can be—to what extent the planners of the August invasion anticipated and tended to exploit minority discontent in Czechoslovakia. Nevertheless, occupation forces from Hungary met with as much hostility among Hungarians in Czechoslovakia as they did elsewhere in the country. Moreover, Stalinist-inspired calls for separatism in Eastern Slovakia during the first hectic days of the occupation failed for lack of indigenous support.

These pro-Czechoslovak loyalties, however, were not sufficiently appreciated. Both the Czechs and Slovaks, wounded in their national pride, reacted by condemning the minorities along with invading armies. This led, for example, to the ostracism of Poles and clashes with them in Northern Moravia and Eastern Bohemia, where there was some support for Polish soldiers (on nationalistic rather than political grounds.[9]

Paradoxically, the Western-oriented German minority had to suffer from ethnic identification with East German invasion troops, who, in uniforms much too similar to those of their fathers thirty years earlier, rekindled old anti-German feelings, prompting a further voluntary exodus of this minority to West Germany.[10] On the other hand, in 1968, after almost a quarter of a century, the German minority was finally legally recognized (Constitutional Law on Nationalities, No. 144, October 1968) and was permitted to form a nationwide organization, the Cultural Association of Czechoslovak Citizens of German Nationality.

The 1960 constitution recognized the Hungarian, Polish, and Ukrainian minorities, and the Nationality Act of 1968 remedied legal discrimination against the Germans, but no official recognition has

been accorded the second largest minority in Czechoslovakia—the Gypsies. Usually lost in census statistics among "Slovaks," "Hungarians," and "Others," the total number of Gypsies in 1966 was estimated to be 221,525, or 1.55 percent of the national population. They are concentrated in the eastern part of Slovakia, accounting for 3.72 percent of the population in Slovakia, and 7.33 percent in the province of Eastern Slovakia, where they even constitute a majority in a number of villages. Primarily because of postwar immigration and a galloping birth rate, Czechoslovakia has become the Gypsy center of the world; a population of some 300,000 in 1970 is expected to reach one million by the year 2000.[11] In short, these descendants of Punjabi and Rajasthani nomads have altered the ethnic character of a Slavic state in the very center of Europe—statistical anonymity notwithstanding.

The central government approached the problem of the integration of Gypsies with considerable inconsistency, with condescension and impatience, with benevolent inactivity and calls for radical solutions. It is beyond the scope of this book to deal adequately with the issue. It should be noted, however, that the government conceived the program of integration of the Gypsies as one in which they would surrender their identity. This linguistically distinct culture was to be decreed into oblivion. A crash program of integration was tried, as well as a program of forcible resettlement; both have failed. Evidence has been gathered attesting to racial prejudice and backlash, notably in housing allocation policies and education. The Gypsies—with a high rate of illiteracy and crime—have yet to be incorporated into the socialist milieu.[12]

Czechs, Slovaks, and the Federal Solution

A crucial element in the protracted crisis of the Stalinist system was the crisis in relations between Czechs and Slovaks. Some observers even consider it the core problem replacing the pre-1945 conflict between Czechs and Germans. When the Republic was founded in 1918, the urbanized Czechs of the industrial provinces of Bohemia and Moravia found that except for proximity and linguistic affinity, they had little in common with the impoverished, agrarian, and to some degree Magyarized Slovak nation. In 1918, the Slovaks were the least mature nation in Central Europe. Ivan Dérer, a Slovak member of the interwar government, declared that only a tiny group of patriotic intellectuals stood for the realization of national aspirations against the will of a hostile or, at best, apathetic majority of its own people.[13] The Czechs, on the other hand, regarded the establishment of the Republic as merely the continuation of the Czech state after a millenium.[14]

These disparities were destined to burden the Republic from the start. Typical of people lacking a tradition of independent existence, the Slovaks were both insecure and overly sensitive about their national identity. Policies of the Prague government were often regarded as evidence of colonialization, or as missionary hypocrisy at best. With due respect to the record of the prewar Republic, federation and self-government for the Slovaks were not among its achievements. Instead, the fiction of "Czechoslovakism," i.e., of one nation speaking two somewhat differing languages, was established.

Grievances, real or imagined, along with offended pride and a not insignificant inferiority complex, energized the Slovak independence movement, which benefited from the destruction of Czechoslovakia in 1939. During the six war years an "independent" Slovakia was established under the paternalistic eye of the Third Reich. Its government, a clerical dictatorship with Monsignor Jozef Tiso as president, commanded considerable loyalty among the predominantly Catholic Slovaks. Compared with the hibernating Czechs in the so-called "Protectorate of Bohemia and Moravia," the Slovaks' exposure to the war was more direct, on the side of the Nazis until 1944, and then on the side of the Allies. However imperfect or even illusory this independence, the memory of sovereignty and a taste for independence has not been entirely obliterated.

The settlement following World War II introduced only partial change: the fiction of Czechoslovakism was disposed of and the Czechs and Slovaks were each declared distinct nations. However, this recognition was not reflected in the new political structure of the Czechoslovak Republic. Instead of true federalism, a compromise known as "asymmetry" was reached. This called for the establishment of a Slovak legislature (National Council) and executive (Board of Commissioners), in addition to the Czechoslovak governmental organs in Prague. Nominally at least, the Slovaks were in a privileged position compared with the Czechs, who had no legislature or executive of their own. In ac-

tuality, these Slovak bodies could not satisfy national aspirations, and in any case Slovak autonomy, however imperfect, has been gradually curtailed; under Novotny's 1960 constitution, the Board of Commissioners was abolished altogether.

The anti-Yugoslav resolution of the Cominform in 1948 also marked the beginning of a witchhunt for "bourgeois nationalists" in the Slovak land. According to a published accusation by Novotny in 1954, leading Communist figures—Clementis, Husak, Novomesky and others—"consorted with descendants of the Hapsburgs and with all kinds of riffraff in the service of imperialist warmongers."[15] Whereas Stalin was the prime mover behind political trials of such men as Slansky and Clementis in the early 1950s it was believed in Slovakia that the trials of Husak and other Slovak nationalists were solely a domestic affair, predominantly of Czech Stalinists.

The insensitivity of the centralist policy of the Prague rulers increased in proportion to the distance dividing them from the ruled—and Slovakia was the farthest away. Here the crucial issues of Communism in the 1950s, such as collectivization of agriculture and the class struggle against bourgeois elements, were handled with particular violence. At the same time, economic development in Slovakia did not catch up with that of the Czech provinces; pockets of perpetual unemployment persisted, along with a lack of educational and cultural opportunities. Prague, in the view of Slovak nationalists—Stalinism, in the eyes of the less passionate—discriminated against the younger brother in a variety of ways, from minor irritants to principal issues such as political recruitment. For example, as late as May 1968, of 585 appointees in the diplomatic corps, only 82 were Slovaks, and over half of all missions had no Slovak representation whatsoever. It was even charged that the man in the garb of a Slovak shepherd at Expo '67 in Montreal was a Czech.[16]

Polarization of this conflict began in the early 1960s. In December 1962, when the Twelfth Congress of the Czechoslovak Communist Party convened it exhibited less than enthusiastic response to the de-Stalinization orientation of the Twenty-Second Congress of the USSR Communist Party (the last one held under Khrushchev's leadership). Among its actions was a partial rehabilitation of victims of Stalinism (including "bourgeois nationalists") and the dismissal of at least some persons implicated in the terror of the past decade. As a result of pressure from Bratislava, the most willing Slovak tools of Prague rule were dismissed: Premier Viliam Siroky, said to be Hungarian-born, who never learned proper Slovak, and Karol Bacilek, Czech-born and head of the Ministry of Security at the time of Slansky's trial. Bacilek was removed as First Secretary of the Slovak branch of the KSC in 1963, against the vehement objection of Novotny. (Novotny was present at the crucial meeting but left without waiting for the election of Bacilek's successor, Alexander Dubcek, and has never attended a Slovak Party conclave since.)[17]

The new Slovak Party leadership created a noticeable change in the cultural climate. Censorship was eased, and the literary weekly *Kulturny zivot*, edited by Pavol Stevcek, was permitted to flourish. In the Czech provinces, Slovak became to be referred to as the language of freedom—manuscripts banned in Prague often found a publisher in Bratislava. Novotny lacked any conception of how to cope with this situation, nor could he comprehend the necessity of some accommodation to demands for structural autonomy. Until the very end of his regime he obstinately insisted on unity and uniformity in everything, whether in trade unions or schools. Novotny called for "intolerant struggle against demonstrations of any nationalism."[18] Through monumental blunders, he managed to offend and therefore to unite Slovaks, regardless of their political philosophy. The only creative idea Novotny was able to offer was his program for mass intermarriage which would obliterate Czech-Slovak distinctions.[19]

Until 1968, any call for federalization of the Republic was condemned as a threat to the entire socialist order. After the fall of Novotny, such aspiration became legitimate. Unfortunately, Slovak demands for autonomy relegated the cardinal program of democratization to a lesser order of urgency, allowing Stalinist elites in Slovakia to survive behind patriotic rhetoric. This nationalistic unity, along with the lack of a democratic tradition, helps to explain the absence of political pluralization in Slovakia and the relatively uneventful developments there under the Dubcek leadership. Even the Slovak university students were predominantly nationalists; voices echoing the demands of Prague liberals were in a minority. The liberals warned against false unity with Stalinists, who (until 1968) were outspoken enemies of federation.

Slovak intellectuals reminded their nation of its long history of servility to foreign overlords and of the missed opportunities in 1968, when nationalism overwhelmed better judgment.[20] The following criticism was published in April 1969, three days before Dubcek's replacement by Husak: "A nation that a whole year after January 1968 has still retained in official posts—in villages, districts and regions—persons who are stupid, who have successfully weathered all storms and campaigns since February [1948], and who have disqualified themselves in every possible manner—a nation like this has not yet matured into a nation."[21] Political activism among non-Communist Slovaks remained low. The advocates of democratization were to be found among intellectuals, students, and journalists, but little sympathy for reform penetrated into the higher echelons of the Slovak Party apparatus. Moreover, unlike the Czechs, the Slovak reformist forces failed to establish ties, or at least an understanding, with industrial workers.

At the same time, however, the confusion between demands for democratic reform in general and political autonomy in Slovakia did harm the Stalinists. Czech Stalinists, unable to overcome their taste for totalitarian uniformity—i.e., Prague centralism—isolated themselves from their Slovak natural allies as effectively as they were isolated from the liberal majority of the Czech nation.

The year 1968 was the year of Slovak national self-realization, accompanied by an unprecedented degree of socialization. For example, *Matica Slovenska*, the cultural organization, gained almost 200,000 new members—double the membership before 1948.[22] The commemoration of the tragic death of the great Slovak patriot of the World War I era, General Milan Rastislav Stefanik, was attended by a million of his countrymen. In an opinion survey conducted in Slovakia in March 1968, 94.3 percent of the respondents favored a new settlement of Czech-Slovak relations; 73 percent favored federalism; and only 18.1 percent supported improvement of the existing asymmetrical arrangement.[23] A similar survey among Czechs showed that barely half of those surveyed favored federalism. In a survey conducted before the August 1968 invasion, the notion that the two nations' equality was *the* important matter was maintained by 91 percent of Slovak respondents, but by only 5 percent of Czech respondents. While Slovaks identified federation as their top demand, the same claim dropped to seventh place in urgency among the Czechs.[24] These data do not prove anti-Slovak or pro-Czech orientation, but, as observers of the Czech scene have noted, the absence of nationalistic sentiment as such. The Czech national identity has not been threatened, and their leadership in the Republic has been taken for granted. One Slovak complained: "It is with mute astonishment that we in Slovakia watch this fantastic metamorphosis of young Czech thinking, in which the young are becoming accustomed to evaluating matters in European and world categories, and slowly, but surely, are forgetting not only the Slovaks, but as another phenomenon worth considering—even themselves."[25] The Soviet invasion rendered this assessment obsolete, at least for the time being. This lack of patriotism, especially among the young, was transformed into strong identification with one's country.

The Constitutional Law of Federation was promulgated on October 27, 1968, the eve of the fiftieth anniversary of the founding of the Czechoslovak Republic. Soviet leadership, cognizant of the potentially harmful effect of authentic federation on the exercise of total control, consented to the change but vetoed federalization of the KSC, thus denying Czech Communists the opportunity to organize themselves separately. Given the structural fusion of Party and state, the combination of a centralized party and a federalist state presents an unsatisfactory arrangement.

This defect notwithstanding, the initial performance of the Czechoslovak federation was one of robust energy, in no way resembling that of its anemic counterpart in the USSR. In response to demands for maximum autonomy, separate structures such as the Slovak Ministry of Justice were set up, and even dual citizenship was established: the Czechoslovak Socialist Republic (CSSR), on the one hand, and either the Czech Socialist Republic (CSR) or Slovak Socialist Republic (SSR), on the other.

Federation had to be worked out without the benefit of any precedent, fitting the conditions of two national republics, one with more than twice the population of the other. A compromise solution had to be found between parity and majority representation in federal structures. (These matters will be discussed at some length later.) An ancillary problem relating to division of jurisdiction was solved by following the Soviet pattern of three types of ministries: (1) federal only, (2) both federal and national,

and (3) national only. This transformation was expected to be a time-consuming process. In the words of Dalibor Hanes, Chairman of the Upper Chamber of the Federal Assembly, "Our entire social system is in a state of reconstruction."[26]

This process of change followed an unexpected path, however. Four years later, in 1972, Hanes was out of office, federation out of vitality, and restorative measures toward centralization well under way. As early as January 31, 1970, *Rude pravo* published an "initiative proposal" on the restoration of uniform Czechoslovak citizenship. The system of state secretaries, which had balanced the representation of both nations in the federal roles, was abolished. A constitutional amendment in 1970 disposed of the principle of equality between federal and state structures by authorizing the former to interfere and invalidate the measures of the latter. Significantly, Prague also recovered administrative control over the Slovak police.

Ironically, it was Gustav Husak—whose identification with federalism and Slovak national self-assertion had twice catapulted him to political prominence and once to a Stalinist jail—who was to preside over these developments. This militant foe of "Czechoslovakism" (the prewar one-nation concept) declared to the Slovak Communist Party Congress in 1971: "We must consolidate a common consciousness among the nationalities of Czechoslovakia, a single Czechoslovak consciousness founded on our socialist order."[27] This evidently echoed Brezhnev's view, expressed at the Twenty-Fourth Congress of the Communist Party of the USSR, that a new common entity had come into existence in the country, namely, the "Soviet people" comprising peoples of all nations and nationalities, an echo hardly suggesting that the fervent federalist Husak remained much of a free agent in the role of First Secretary of the KSC.

Recentralization has also affected the economic sphere, curtailing Slovak ambitions to expand, for example, in the automobile industry. Despite these setbacks, accelerated industrialization and preferential investment programs are closing the gap between Slovakia and the more advanced Czech regions. Whereas the share of Slovakia in total national industrial production was a mere 14 percent in 1948, in 1970 it reached 25 percent. The projected Slovak share of the GNP in the current Five-Year Plan (1971–1975) is 28 percent. The Slovaks reportedly caught up with the Czechs in earning power in 1971.[28]

In the cultural sphere, Slovakia's challenge in 1968 to the political status quo did not match the intensity of Bohemia and Moravia, but it equally avoided subsequent neo-Stalinist reprisals. This situation somewhat resembles that of the early 1960s, when Slovakia permitted a wider range of artistic expression and hence became a refuge for writers banned from publishing in Prague. In the early 1970s, outcasts fom Prague are once again publishing in Bratislava, against the protests of Czech defenders of ideological purity.[29]

National Character and Contemporary Challenges

The temporary abolishment of censorship in 1968 provided an opportunity to delve into such matters as the legacy and formation of national character. The Slovaks in their unflattering self-examination probed into the nation's unreasonable touchiness, intolerance, and tendency toward thoughtless collectivism. However, most of the soul-searching was conducted among the Czechs. Some of their conclusions were applicable of course to the peoples of both nations.[30]

The fact that the majority of the people have experienced nothing but amoral political regimes has been identified as the major cause of social malaise. The corrosive impact of three decades of oppression has been all too evident. From a deeper perspective, the train of sorrow extending from betrayal of Hus to betrayal by Husak reveals itself in the lack of civic courage and in dissatisfaction and withdrawal into petty prejudices. Alienation has led to endemic dishonesty vis-à-vis the political system. By virtue of protest and the scarcity of certain goods, pilferage of socialist property has become the most popular felony. Antisocial behavior is not always pragmatic, as the high rate of destruction of public property dramatizes. Arthur Miller, visiting Czechoslovakia in 1969, pointed to such phenomena and added, "It reminded me of the worst kind of capitalist indifference to one's life environment."[31]

Among the impediments to nation building, pettiness, servility, fear, lack of civic courage, and maliciousness were among the most often mentioned traits of Czech national character, especially servility toward the strong, arrogance toward the weak, and distortion of the concept of democracy into a form of envious egalitariansim, with little concern for civic freedoms.[32]

Contradictory attitudes, such as a yearning for freedom coupled with a lack of civic courage, were frequently pointed out. The ambivalent democrat venerates rank and title, and academic degrees serve as substitutes for aristocratic tradition. The timid man prefers tenured mediocrity to tenuous eminence. A bureaucratic role fulfills his need for an unexciting but desirable permanency. This particular trait was exploited by the Stalinist system, which, of course, instead of security produced arbitrariness with a host of uncertainties.

Their less than attractive behavioral characteristics notwithstanding, the Czechs, at the advent of independent statehood in 1918, were not terrorized, brutalized subjects of Austrian oppression. Compared with the state of affairs after World War I, Hapsburg rule will remain a nostalgic memory of a tolerant, if not particularly efficient, political order, in which German was not mandatory even as a second language in schools, censorship was unknown, and judges were incorruptible. (The courts were of such integrity that the pretender to the throne lost a civil suit against a humble subject.) In the last ten years of Austrian rule not a single criminal was executed in Bohemia and Moravia.[33] In the bourgeois Republic seven murderers were executed. The Nazi occupation and the war itself led to a sharp decline in the value of human life. It suffices here to refer to the Czech exercise in bellicosity toward the Germans in 1945, by then safely defeated by others. The forcible expulsion of the German minority, application of the principle of collective guilt, and often indiscriminate revenge contributed to the brutalization of the entire society.[34]

In the closing years of postwar Stalinism, more prominent Communists were executed in Czechoslovakia than in all the rest of the People's Democracies combined.[35] Between November 20 and December 2, 1952, the Central Committee in Prague received 8,520 hate messages, including mail from Pioneer children and letters demanding physical torture of the victims.[36] Obviously, not only were the terrified and manipulated among the signatories, but also the bloodthirsty. Low value on life was evident well into the 1960s. Of 300 respondents to a survey in that period 272 were in favor of retaining the death penalty for murder, 197 for the sexual abuse of minors, 197 for high treason, 34 for vehicular

Table 2.2.   Reaction to August 1968 Invasion (in percentages).

Issue	Yes	No	Don't know
Confidence in Dubcek	99.0	0.5	0.5
Was there any danger of counter- revolution to justify the invasion?	2.0	93.0	5.0
Will the unity of the people last?	79.0	7.0	14.0
Are you still willing to support the Action Program [Charter of liberalism]?	95.0	0.0	5.0

homicide, and three misanthropes favored death also for disturbing the peace.[37] It was not until 1968 that the shock resulting from disclosure of Stalinist crimes generated the so far unsuccessful demands for the abolishment of capital punishment.

A further element of continuity between the war years and the Stalinist era is that of officially sanctioned anti-Semitism, transformed into class animosity (without losing its racist connotation). In contrast to neighboring peoples, Czechs were not attracted to fascism in the 1930s. Fascism did not take hold with any particular social group and attracted only isolated individuals; nevertheless, a Czech fascist movement did exist.[38] Anti-Semitism surfaced in the early 1950s with the political trials and in 1968 with the attempt of the Stalinists to discredit the reformist movement.

The final period of the Novotny regime was marked by political abdication of the public. Residual patriotism was consummated on the sport fields. Schweikism—the cult of Jaroslav Hasek's literary hero Good Soldier Schweik, symbolizing the pretense of stupidity as the safest way of political survival—reached refined heights among Czechs. On the other hand, such self-mockery was also a sign of apathy and/or lack of stamina to challenge the status quo.

One hallmark of the Dubcek era was the maximum politization of the citizenry. After decades of lethargy, the speed and intensity of change in political participation was startling. However, as was noted earlier, preoccupation in Slovakia with the question of autonomy overshadowed the issues of democratization. The Czech political landscape was far less monotonous.

Supporters of the deposed order dwindled to an insignificant minority while the majority was dis-

covering a previously unknown degree of unity within the citizenry as well as within the leadership. In February 1968, one month after the removal of Novotny as First Secretary of the KSC, a survey showed 55 percent of the respondents facing the future of their country with optimism; in March this mood climbed to 75 percent. The Czechoslovak concept of "socialism with a human face," implying rejection of both past political practices and adherence to the Soviet model, was approved in a number of surveys by as much as 90 percent. A survey conducted by the Academy of Sciences (CSAV) in June 1968 revealed that not more than 5 percent of the sample favored capitalism—a surprisingly small figure in view of the previously unimpressive performance of the socialist experiment.[39]

Public response to the August 1968 invasion had two phases: first, a period of patriotic unity characterized by determination and intense political activism; second, a period of fatigue, a breakdown of unity, and finally private withdrawal known as "inner emigration." The first post-invasion survey,[40] conducted in September 1968, produced the results in Table 2.2.

Linked to these sentiments was an upsurge of anti-Sovietism. In a country unaccustomed since 1945 to the presence of foreign troops, exposure to the Red Army provoked questions of cultural affinities with the Soviet Union. The results were far from flattering. In October 1968 the CSAV conducted a survey in which respondents were asked to name the nation culturally closest to them. In Bohemia and Moravia, the people of the Soviet Union (with no distinction being made between Russians and non-Russians) were placed fifth and sixth, respectively, with 10 percent of the total sample. Among Slovaks, they were third with 18 percent of the sample.[41]

Table 2.3. Respondents Opposed to Alliance with Soviet Union (in percentages)

Survey	Age Groups				
	18–30	31–40	41–50	51–60	61 up
1968: before August 21	4.7	2.0	1.1	0.6	0.6
1968: after August 21	38.4	28.2	17.9	11.2	10.1

Surveys of that period demonstrate in a number of ways the heterogeneity of political culture. For example, Czechs and Slovaks differed in selecting the most illustrious periods and personalities in their history.[42] The Czechs chose (1) T. G. Masaryk, (2) Jan Hus, (3) Charles IV ("Father of the Country," a fourteenth-century emperor), and (4) Comenius, in that order. The Slovaks chose (1) L. Stur (nineteenth-century patriot), (2) A. Dubcek, (3) M. R. Stefanik, and (4) T. G. Masaryk, in that order (note that Masaryk is first for the Czechs but fourth for the Slovaks).

One positive result of the invasion, which has contributed to at least temporary national cohesiveness, has been the cessation of separatist tendencies in the eastern part of the country. Federalization no doubt helped to neutralize this movement. At the end of 1968, 84 percent of Slovaks sampled in one survey declared their pride in being citizens of the Czechoslovak Republic. Concerning relations with the Czechs, in a survey conducted in Slovakia in February 1969, 21.7 percent felt relations had improved, 63 percent considered them unchanged, 4.8 percent felt they had deteriorated, and 10.5 percent didn't think about it.[43]

Once federalization had been granted, Slovak public opinion reflected an appreciation, however belated, of the political liberalization advocated by Czech reformists. At the same time, the autocratic Husak, a Slovak, greatly declined in popularity.[44]

The political system of the Novotny period, despite its emphasis on the totalitarian electoral triumphs showing 99 percent unity, contained three cleavages in the population: (1) ethnic—Czechs versus Slovaks, (2) social—workers versus intelligentsia, and (3) generational—young versus old. The unique national consensus generated by the 1968 invasion merely suspended the differentiated orientation of the citizenry. Soon afterward, old divisive factors surfaced: personal political records, economic and social status, age, and ethnic identity. Social cleavage will be discussed in Chapter 4; here we shall focus our attention on generational cleavage.

In July 1968, the Institute of Political Science of the Central Committee of the KSC conducted a survey among Party members, concentrating on questions of political democratization and tolerance. Responses favoring authoritarianism were markedly higher among Slovak Communists and, significantly, increased in proportion with the age of the respondents.[45] In similar Party opinion surveys conducted since the invasion, certain trends were reportedly evident; conservatism, for example, was highest among the older generation of Communists, those of long-standing membership in the Party, Slovaks rather than Czechs, and those with little education. In comparing the results of two 1968 surveys (taken before and after the Warsaw Pact invasion), age proved to be a significant factor when respondents were asked to agree or disagree with the statement, "We shall continue to strengthen our alliance with the Soviet Union." Table 2.3 shows the percentage of respondents in each age group in disagreement with this statement.[46]

A number of Czechoslovak publicists stressed the political importance of the age variable.[47] Of the entire population at the time of the 1968 invasion, 58 percent were either born under socialism or were less than 18 years of age in 1948. By 1968, death had taken 40 to 45 percent of all manual workers alive in 1948. Less than 30 percent of the population in 1968 had lived through the Munich crisis of 1938, but all witnessed the August 1968 invasion. Not more than 42 percent of those who were adults at the time of the Communist accession in 1948 were alive in 1968. In effect, until 1968 the only significant political experience in the lives of a majority of the population had been the failure of the socialist experiment.

The subculture of the Stalinists contrasts strongly with that of the young, and the liberal forces in

"Middle Ages?"
"Of course, I remember them well!"
(*Dikobraz*, October 29, 1968)

general. Drawing up character types of those attracted to Stalinism has been a favorite pastime in Czechoslovakia. A hierarchy of ex-kings, crown princes, men in the background, and bullies, offered by Ivo Planava in *Listy*, is an example.[48] In my own classification, the common denominator of most Stalinists was the fear that their set of values and privileges were endangered by the reformist movement of 1968.

First, there were the beneficiaries of Stalinism, their core being at least 200,000 individuals who for reasons of social background and political loyalty were elevated into roles to which their merit and competence did not entitle them. These were the permanent functionaries who either had not learned or had forgotten any worthwhile skills, or as Miroslav Jodl put it not too charitably, "The aggressive, uneducated, smug, envious, avaricious mediocrities from whom the political elite were recruited."[49]

Second were the perpetrators of Stalinist crimes (judges, prosecutors, members of the secret police, provocateurs, and common murderers), some of whom had already been demoted to menial work by 1968 but who feared that the new regime would hold them criminally liable for their past actions.

Third were the so-called Old Communists, pre-World War II Party members, for whom adjustment to new times would have meant rejection of their past creed, performance, sacrifices, and, in a way, purpose in life. Wedded to outdated dogma, they often allowed themselves to be manipulated by other types of Stalinists.

Finally, there were the opportunists, individuals with authoritarian traits, and diverse types of universal misfits.

These are people who for their entire lives have been driven by two sources of energy: envy and hatred toward everything inaccessible or simply different from what they themselves are. For this reason they joined up with Communism, and not because of Marx's humanism or idea of justice. They remain disappointed, of course, because there is still enough in the world to provoke their envy.[50]

Doctrinaire black and white images do not apply in these matters. Twenty years of Stalinist experience often blurred the distinction between the society's "righteous" 90 percent and the "wicked" 10 percent. Except for a marginal group of nomadic Gypsies, everybody was likely to absorb some totalitarian traits. Even the language of the clergy resembled that of Party manifestoes.

In 1968 the Czechoslovak society was ill prepared for pluralistic political behavior. Intolerance plagued even the well-intentioned proponents of pluralistic values. Undemocratic usages and stereotypes were common in political polemics. A nation of Novotnyites turned into a nation of anti-Novotnyites. Rigid ideological behavior, although largely subconscious, nonetheless persisted. It is said that Czechoslovak hippies even started to build an organization along the lines of the Communist Party. Demands of unity and consensus appeared to some to be camouflage for a lack of civic courage. As one writer put it acidly, "In a crowd we absolve ourselves of the fear of death, especially of the death of someone else."[51]

The attempt at humanizing socialism in 1968 considerably narrowed the gap between the Party and society. Yet even among reformist Party members the legacy of Stalinism hindered the establishment of authentic civic equality. In the words of Jiri Sekera, the first and so far last anti-Stalinist editor-in-chief of the main Party daily *Rude pravo*:

> Under the conditions of the power monopoly of the Communist Party of Czechoslovakia, the Party membership did not have to provide the rank and file with any particular privileges. But it did provide them with a certain social favoritism, and thus did mark—more with one, less with another—their way of thinking and acting; it did create undesirable stereotypes and relations of domination and subordination. . . .[52]

Or, we might say that habitual Stalinism prevented "political democrats" from becoming "cultural democrats."

Citizens were forced into active political participation without being allowed much of an input into the decision making process. We may identify three modes of political expression, listed in the descending order of acceptability in a totalitarian system: manipulated participation, nonparticipation, and independent participation. Only the first is considered legitimate and a mark of proper citizenship. The second, nonparticipation, must not be confused with indifference or resignation. Exactly the opposite may be true: a great deal of courage may be required *not* to join the only sacred church or to leave the congregation and preserve one's integrity. The indifferent do not stand aside but place themselves in the very midst of manipulated activity.[53]

During 1968, nonparticipation was no longer the ultimate in political daring; instead, attempts at independent participation were made. These will be described in some detail in the next chapter. Here it should be noted, however, that because such activity posed a threat to the monopoly of the ruling Party it was the cardinal sin precipitating the Soviet military intervention.

The Russian political mind, fed by centuries of uninterrupted autocratic experience, finds instances of genuine initiative and participation not only harmful (i.e., posing a danger to the Party's monopoly of initiative), but outright inconceivable. The experience of one district apparatchik with a Soviet military commander provides an illustrative vignette:

> They asked me who had issued instructions to the townspeople to remove road signs, street names,

and house numbers. I said that no one had issued such instructions. However, the commanders did not believe me. They said that the people would not do anything without instructions. This is apparently also the reason for their constant suspicion that there is some agency of counterrevolution.[54]

This is not an isolated incident with a rock-headed soldier. Evidence attests to the same caliber of judgment among the sophisticated Soviet political elite.[55]

The 1968 invasion ruled out the eventuality of independent participation but failed at the same time to restore manipulated participation. Withdrawal became the prevailing norm of political response, and democratic spokesmen warned against letting it degenerate into apathy or compromise. A memorandum of the intellectual elite read:

> We are not and never will be willing to confess to crimes we have not committed, or to be thankful for help which is nothing but injustice. We are not and never will be willing to call a lie "truth," and injustice a "necessity." Force may liquidate a people, but not their ideas. In a single century we in the Czech lands have three times witnessed the collapse of monolithic systems, so that the truth could once again be heard. The 1950s remain a warning to us that conscience is not an empty concept. We love our lives but more precious to us is the legacy we want to leave to our children.[56]

With the ascendancy of Husak in 1969, such voices of defiance were effectively silenced. The high hope of 1968 was followed by deep disillusionment. In one survey, 78 percent of the respondents viewed the coming year 1969 as one promising grave difficulties (as against 12 percent expecting prosperity).[57]

In a CSAV survey, conducted in December 1968,[58] respondents were asked, "What is your most frequent reaction when thinking about the present situation in Czechoslovakia?" The results are given in Table 2.4.

A traumatized society is not likely to plunge into a dramatic challenge of a status quo that is maintained by an outside force. Yet on the other hand the outside force may be unable to impose manipulated participation on the members of that society. Evidence available from the period of four post-invasion years supports the conclusion that in Czechoslovakia participation has been reinstated in form only; with skin-deep commitment on part of the

Table 2.4. Reactions to Situation in December 1968 (in percentages).

Response	Czech Rep.	Slovak Rep.	CSSR
Oppression, helplessness	20	25	22
Uncertainty, lack of information	19	24	20
Disappointment, betrayal	15	9	13
Depression, fear	10	17	12
Pessimism, skepticism	14	5	12
Dissatisfaction	3	4	3
Other negative responses	8	3	6
Trust and hope	4	7	5
Other positive responses	2	1	2
Others	5	5	5

drafted audience. The Party leadership realized the magnitude of this passive resistance and in 1970 offered a compromise modus vivendi by granting political legitimacy to nonparticipation. Echoing an earlier maxim of the Hungarian leader Janos Kadar, "He who is not against us, is with us," Husak was somewhat less generous, declaring that "He who is not against us is our potential ally."[59]

It should be stressed that this concession is neither universal nor permanent. Impunity for nonparticipation by blue-collar workers does not apply to white-collar workers; a lack of activism, although tolerated among postal clerks, is not tolerated among college teachers; furthermore, what is considered to be proper political behavior today may be denounced tomorrow. This shrinking range of legitimacy of nonparticipation is exemplified by a definition of the duties of the socialist artist which appeared in *Rude pravo* in 1972 (two years after Husak's declaration)· "Not to oppose socialism was one of the first steps in the consolidation effort in the cultural sphere. Today, no honest artist can find this sufficient. Today's task is to march, to get involved, to fight for the future by transforming the present."[60]

The specter of opposition haunts Czechoslovakia.

Pavel Kohout, Literarni listy, *May 16, 1968.*

Problems of Participation

One-party rule restricts the citizen to the role of a subject-participant, requiring him to support actively a set of policies he has had no part in formulating. He is called upon to implement decisions of a small circle of the power elite. Since "unity" and its "strengthening" are perpetual socialization requirements, lobbying by special interests is not permissible. In fact, the existence of pressure groups is neither acknowledged nor tolerated, yet the process of allocating resources is hardly free of conflict. The Party, the ultimate arena of settlement, is also prone to reflect the ethnic, cultural, and economic diversities of society. This plurality of interests may surface through a variety of channels: the mass communication media, "voluntary mass organizations," and even puppet parties.

At times the Czechoslovak rulers seemed to consider unresponsiveness to popular demands as an indication of wise, unyielding statesmanship and as proof of Bolshevik integrity. As the Slovak Communist writer Zora Jesenska put it:

The supreme body of the ruling Party could boast that no one had exerted any pressure on it, that it had not listened and did not want to listen to the opinion of others, that none of the Party members and of the fourteen million inhabitants of this state had any influence, and that no one should even dare to imagine that he could have any influence.[1]

The Stalinist variant of the socialist experiment poses the dilemma of either maintaining its unresponsive posture and thus generating alienation and inefficiency throughout society or legitimizing participation and broadening access to influence, thus forfeiting its totalitarian quality. From the beginning, the Prague leadership tried to enjoy the best of both worlds, but after two decades the project finally collapsed—in January 1968.

Those who advocated the reform and rehabilitation of the political system urged that three aspects of the political process again be granted legitimacy:

(1) participation, (2) dissent, and (3) the possibility of a choice among political alternatives. Foreign force intervened, however, and crushed the plan altogether.

In this chapter we shall examine the formative years of monopolized decision making, the later inflexibility of this monopoly, and, finally, its disintegration in the face of the challenges of 1968. Attention will be given to various political alternatives proposed within Czechoslovakia, including those offered by the prominent Communist reformers.

Before turning to the Communist Party as the core of our analysis, we will offer some information regarding the formative years of postwar political development as well as the two decades of manipulated (subject) participation.

In the period between May 1945 (the reestablishment of sovereignty) and February 1948 (the Communist coup d'etat), prewar political practices were not restored. Only a handful of political parties were licensed, all of which were at least rhetorically sympathetic to socialism and the Soviet Union. They joined in a broad coalition called the National Front. Any political participation outside this circle was prohibited. There were marked regional differences in these developments. Four political parties—the Communist Party, the Czech Socialist Party, the People's (Catholic) Party, and the Social Democratic Party (listed here in the order of their 1946 electoral strength and all with a history of prewar political participation)—existed in Bohemia and Moravia. In Slovakia, because of less political differentiation and the somewhat punitive effect of the wartime pro-Nazi Slovak state separatism, only two parties were allowed—the Communists and the Democrats.

Only the Communists were authorized to organize throughout the country whereas their National Front partners were confined to either Czech lands or Slovakia. The Communists were similarly privileged in the allocation of ministerial offices, obtaining control of such vital agencies as the police and the propaganda apparatus. On the other hand, command of the mailmen was entrusted to the minor parties of this uneasy coalition.

In May 1946 the first, and last, postwar contested election took place, and the Communists won a plurality though not a majority—35 percent of the total vote, the highest (42 percent) being in Bohemia. By contrast, the Communists in Slovakia lost to the Democratic Party by two to one. Based on the system of proportional representation, the Communists received 114 of the 300 seats in the National Assembly. In local government, however, the Party's representation was far in excess of the electoral gain. For example, the Communists obtained 128 out of the 163 chairmanships of District People's Committees.[2]

In the postelection period the Communists launched a campaign to gain a "51 percent majority." This drive for majority support was accompanied by attacks on the Democratic Party in Slovakia, accusing it of collaboration with the Nazis, and by the establishment of two new Slovak political parties. "Divide and conquer" was the strategy, one which had been successfully tested in other People's Democracies, e.g., Hungary.

Without delving into the history of the February 1948 coup, it should be noted that the Party's realization of the impossibility of obtaining an electoral majority contributed to its decision to seize control of the government. As a result of this takeover, the Communist Party was vested with absolute power. The fate of the defeated parties varied; the Czech Socialist Party and the People's Party were demoted to puppet status, with membership limited to a few thousand each. In Slovakia the Freedom and the Rebirth parties were also mummified as nominal minor partners. The rest were total casualties: the Social Democratic Party was merged with the Communist Party, and the Slovak Democratic Party was disbanded.

Gottwald decided to retain the concept of the National Front in a modified form, as a politically harmless but useful propaganda device.[3] Whether a coalition of political parties, an organization in its own right, or a facade for nothing, its structure has never been clearly defined.[4]

Be that as it may, in 1948 the National Front became an arm of the Party, its agent, and a multiple transmission belt, an intermediary vis-à-vis the society. A single slate of National Front candidates would also assure the ritual 99 percent victory. Membership in the National Front was diluted by the admission of several dozen transmission belts of Stalinist machinery—organizations such as trade unions, youth movement organizations, women's societies, and various friendship societies. This arrangement not only eliminated genuine political

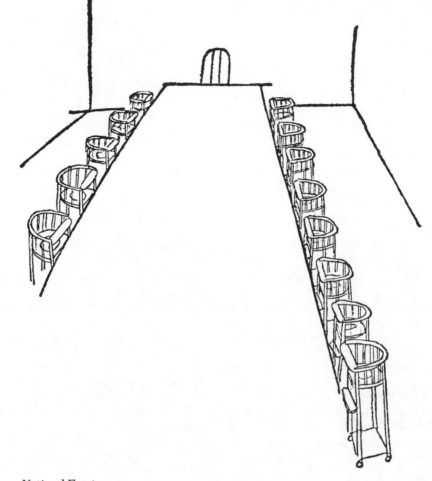

National Front.
(*Literarni listy*, August 8, 1968)

contests in which alternatives were present, but also led to multiple representation of the Communist Party. Deputies for the social organizations were Communists, as a rule, and therefore their prime loyalty and responsibility was to the Party. It was not until 1968 that the issue of conflict of interest was publicly raised.

Paradoxically, the puppet parties were over-represented. Their miniscule membership did not warrant the charitable allocation of their seats in the Parliament, but they were generals without an army and without a say in matters of command. Illustrative was the view of Josef Plojhar, an excom-municated Catholic priest, head of the People's Party, and member of both the Parliament and the cabinet for twenty years. When asked to describe the activities of his party, he referred to voluntary work in school cafeterias and repair of a cemetery wall.[5]

The extinction of democratic processes proceeded simultaneously in the ruling Party, the National Front, and society at large. The Party, a key component of this political system, experienced the standard sclerosis of Stalinization: notably, the elimination of responsiveness to the demands of lower components of the Party structure and the rank and file, the growth of Party bureaucracy to the detriment of elective bodies, and the reduction of the circle of actual decision makers. This development was supplemented by some specifically Czechoslovak features, the effects of whose impact have not yet been eliminated.

The Party

Although Gottwald had chosen the course of electoral victory over revolutionary takeover as part of the "Czechoslovak road to socialism," the victory did not materialize and the Party did gain power by extralegal means. Yet this development did not dispose of an important legacy of the pre-1948 experimentation: mass Party membership (see Table 3.1). The foremost characteristic of the Czechoslovak Communist Party has been its *lack of elitism*.

Table 3.1. Communist Party Membership in Czechoslovakia.

Date	Total membership
Before 1945°	80,000
March 1946	1,150,000
November 1948°	2,500,000
January 1051	1,077,000
January 1968	1,691,000
January 1969	1,672,000
December 1970°	1,200,000

Sources: Rude pravo, November 20, 1948, and February 27, 1951; *Zpravodaj KSC,* No. 16, a supplement to *Zivot strany,* April 29, 1969; and *Rude pravo,* December 15, 1970.
  ° Estimated.

The drive for a mass party was contrary to the Leninist concept of elitism; the continuation of this policy after coming to power must be regarded as blunder of the first magnitude. Whether because of the euphoria of February 1948 or an attempt to legitimize the Party's power through the display of membership enrollment figures, the gates were opened to a wide variety of candidates, among whom the timid and opportunistic were most prevalent. Almost 50 percent of all Czech intelligentsia joined the Party.[6] Before the end of the victorious year 1948, the Party's total membership was second only to that of the Soviet Union and was unsurpassed in its recruitment record of one out of every three adults.

Overzealousness in recruitment was recognized as early as 1949 but was never fully remedied.[7] A purge did reduce the membership from 2.5 million in 1948 to 1.6 million by 1951, but this number remained constant for almost two decades. Among the causes for this stagnation was the fact that the goal of improving the social composition of the membership by recruiting more proletarians was frustrated by a lack of responsiveness to this effort. Thus, in five years—between the Ninth Party Congress in 1949 and the Tenth Congress in 1954—only 83,154 new members were added. Despite this slowdown in growth, 18 percent of all Czechoslovak adults and 12 percent of the total population were registered Communists—roughly one out of every five adults belonged to the ruling party in 1954.[8]

Absolute and relative figures of enrollment and voting patterns would indicate that Italy, for example, is "more strongly Communist" than Ireland. Once a party becomes the monopolist of political power, it invalidates the correlation between the strength of membership and the nature of the society. The direct opposite may come closer to the truth: the larger the party, the more diluted and less elitist and, in effect, the less suitable an instrument of totalitarian rule. In such a situation the party is endangered by the tendency of reflecting the heterogeneous interests of the broad membership. Inflation of membership may be cured either by a purge or by dual elitism: a minority of authentic participants and a majority of nominal participants.

> Party organizations became so numerous that it was impossible to direct them and they were led into action only with the greatest difficulty. The Party colossus was becoming politically immobile and unmaneuverable. The demands of practical politics required that, in the framework of such a mass Party, a more active, politically more experienced and ideologically stronger *aktif* be formed (Party committees, officials, etc.).[9]

Not surprisingly, among the first post-invasion demands by the Soviets was that KSC membership be reduced to about 300,000, a figure equal to the estimated strength of the so-called Novotny *aktif*, the Stalinist core of the Party. More will be said about this in Chapter 8.

Table 3.2.   Communist Party Membership Among Laborers.

| | January 1, 1962 | | January 1, 1966 | |
	Total	%	Total	%
Industrial laborers	554,084	33.4	551,917	30.2
Farm laborers	43,741	2.6	46,082	2.7
Retired workers	158,425	9.6	216,542	12.8

Absorption of the Social Democratic Party brought a large group of reformists into the KSC. As if this ideological Trojan Horse were not dangerous enough, the open recruitment also created a threat to the proletarian image of the Party: 57 percent of blue-collar workers prior to February 1948 sank within a little more than a year to 45 percent.[10] Since then, the Party has not achieved its desired improvement in social composition despite several moratoria on the recruitment of white-collar workers and fresh drives for new proletarian members. The failure in this effort has been camouflaged in Party statistics by utilizing the category of "workers by origin." This inclusion of various beneficiaries of the Stalinist system meant that 62.5 percent of all Communists in 1966 were of allegedly proletarian ancestry. The membership figures for actual laborers are quite different.[11] (See Table 3.2.) The frequency of Party membership among manual laborers varied, however, according to the type of industry. In the preferential branches under the "iron concept" of socialism—such as energy production, mines, heavy industry, steel mills—20 percent and even more workers were organized Communists compared with 11 percent in the construction industry.[12] Putting functional differentiation aside, there has been a steady decrease of worker membership and activism in the Party, caused to some extent by the retirement and death of the old Bolsheviks.

Age is also a factor. The Czechoslovak Communist Party is not only nonelitist and nonproletarian; it is also aging. The stoppage of recruitment for over a decade—as a substitute for a drastic purge—produced an age disparity between the Party and society. The high average age of the Communist stratum impedes smooth communication, particularly with the younger generation.

In 1949, 14.5 percent of the KSC membership was under twenty-five years of age. The age spread of the Party in 1966 is shown in Table 3.3.[13] The aging of the Party is most profound in rural areas, partly due, of course, to the higher age composition of the rural population. In 1966, 300,000 Communists organized in village cells consisted of these age groups: up to 26, 5 percent; 35, 9 percent; 45, 16 percent; 60, 29 percent; and over 60, 40 percent.

Table 3.3.   Party Membership by Age, 1966.

Age	Membership	Percentage total membership
Up to 26 years	152,812	9.0
27 to 35	309,053	18.2
36 to 45	452,901	26.7
46 to 60	487,486	28.7
Over 60	295,750	17.4

Party members under the age of 30 accounted for 16 percent in 1967 and 15.3 percent in 1968. The local Party cells in the country total 45,000. Of these, 20 percent had only one member under 25, and 36 percent had no members under that age. At the 1969 annual meetings of the KSC, 260,000 members were elected to the committees. Of these, 3.3 percent were under 25, 9.3 percent were between 25 and 30, 30.3 percent between 30 and 40, 33.7 percent between 40 and 50, 16 percent between 50 and 60, 7.4 percent over 60. By 1966 only 0.8 percent of all members had joined the Party before 1945, leaving the remaining 99.2 percent suspect of opportunism as their motive for joining. By the end of the 1960s prewar idealists and young recruits remained marginal fringes of what was, essentially, an aging body of the class of 1948.[14]

Between 1948 and 1968 the KSC also suffered a

decline in membership among women. Although females accounted for a full third of the membership in 1949, this dropped to 27.4 percent in 1966.[15] An even greater decrease in women's participation in political roles was evident.

In Slovakia the violation of the elitist principle of the Party was less profound. Of a total of 2,311,066 members and candidates in 1948, only 236,432 (10 percent) were in the Slovak branch. Twenty years later the figure stood at 311,656 of a total of 1,671,637. This increase did not obliterate the elitist and fairly homogeneous complexion of the Slovak Party structure.[16]

By contrast, Czech Communists in 1968 exhibited a wide spectrum of political temperaments, ranging from advocates of liberal democracy to defenders of Stalinist terror. Accordingly, one came across a variety of political labels in the Czech press: such as Communists-democrats, hesitant liberals, timid liberals, dogmatists, old dogmatists, and Stalinists.[17] With the vitality of the totalitarian monolith exhausted, this diversity, hidden under the old-fashioned one-party umbrella, was found untenable. It was argued that unity in everything is immoral and that unity of everyone is unachievable.

The Party apparatus, too, has changed since 1948, and improvements took place in the education and consequent sophistication of its personnel. Considerable credit belongs to the Party College, as we shall see in Chapter 8. It has been reported that of the total of 4,733 professional Party workers (as of September 1968) 16 percent were in provincial offices and 72.5 percent in district and factory posts. Of them, 36.1 percent had graduated from universities. Among the apparatchiks of the Central Committee in Prague, the percentage was reported as high as 69 percent and the percentage in Bratislava was even higher (77 percent).[18] Even allowing for the deflated value of the flashy academic title RSDr (Doctor of Social Sciences), the contrast with their semiliterate proletarian predecessors is by no means negligible.

Many apparatchiks were recruited from among the activists in the youth movement of 1948 and the early 1950s.[19] Although veterans of political infighting, these educated, middle-aged Party bureaucrats nevertheless did *not* form (at least in 1968) a bastion of Stalinist reaction. In fact, at one time or another some of the most imaginative minds and creative articulators of Marxism, such as Professors Milan Hübl in Prague and Miroslav Kusy in Bratislava, were associated with the Central Committee apparatus.

However, as the political scientist Frantisek Samalik, a prominent KSC intellectual, has pointed out: "Since the age of Babylonian bureaucratism, we know that the main impulse toward change in the Party apparatus cannot come from within, but from without."[20] Communist reformers affiliated with universities and research institutes, assisted by some of the inner elite of the Party, were such external forces that accelerated the breakdown of the old political structure.

The mass character of the Party impeded implementation of commands from above, as well as strict uniformity in response from below. This problem was aggravated by the prevalence of the functional principle in the Party's organizational structure: A member's primary connection with the Party was in his place of employment, not in his residential area. In 1966 there were 35,470 local cells (74 percent of the total) in places of employment, excluding agricultural cooperatives; 3,419 (7.1 percent) in agricultural cooperatives; 6,581 (13.7 percent) in villages; and 2,469 (5.2 percent) in urban neighborhoods, this last category being composed largely of housewives and pensioners.[21] Although the neighborhood cells echoed the Stalinist sentiments of their senior members, the much more numerous factory and office cells manifested diverse positions. It was very unlikely that the local cell of the secret police in the Ministry of the Interior and the local cell of Communist intellectuals in the Economic Institute of the Academy of Sciences would subscribe to identical values. Communists of the philosophy department of Charles University in Prague passed a resolution calling for reexamination of the Party's role in society;[22] it would have been most unlikely for Communist guards at Ruzyne prison to do so. Reformers within the inner elite were also aided by intellectuals outside the Party's ranks, by the mass communication media, and, in a way, by the manifold crises that beset the Stalinist system. The debate over the role of the KSC was a contest over the very nature of the political system.

The Leading Role of the Party and Suggested Alternatives

In 1960 a new constitution was adopted to symbolize passage from a transient stage of a people's democracy to an era of accomplished socialism. The class struggle, it was said, had ceased to dominate the internal affairs of the country although it continued in the global arena of the contest between capitalism and socialism.

> The moving force of our internal development is no longer the class struggle of antagonistic forces but a common interest and increasing solidarity of social classes and groups. . . . The social composition of society will necessarily retain for some time a class character. . . . Also we must not overlook the existence of sharp class struggle on the international scale, the reflection of which finds its very concrete demonstrations inside our socialist society.[23]

This standard Party rhetoric, pregnant with qualifications, pledging commitment to everything and yet to nothing, was also characteristic of the Party's approach to the issue of its monopolistic role. In 1967, the last year of Novotny's rule, many sacred concepts were subjected to reexamination. Still, in matters of the Party's exclusive power, the old-fashioned uniformity of views seemed to prevail. For Jiri Hendrych, chief ideologist and number two man in the country, "the fundamental principles of the Party's leading role have retained their full validity and cannot be modified."[24] According to his opponent Josef Spacek, an advocate of democratization, "our point of view is based on the principle that there exists in society no sphere whatsoever in which the Party would not enforce its leading role."[25] The main theoretical organ of the Party, *Nova mysl*, in an editorial in the first issue of 1968 found no inconsistency in stressing both the passing of the class struggle and a need to strengthen the Party's leading role in society.

The reformers within the inner ruling elite in 1968 were attempting to cure the Party's body and mind, not to destroy it with reckless experiments. None of the members of the pre-invasion politburo, with the possible exceptions of Frantisek Kriegel or Central Committee Secretary Zdenek Mlynar, could envision any legitimate alternative to the Party's rule. The position of Josef Smrkovsky, a liberal leader who was very close to the top on Moscow's hate list, is illustrative of the limitations of Communist progressivism. Smrkovsky, conceding that it was unfortunate to have the leading role of the Party anchored in the constitution, nonetheless objected to the establishment of political opposition on two

grounds. First, the machinery of checks and balances to the ruling power could be secured by other means. Second, the Party deserved to lead because of its superiority in skills and experience. To Alexander Dubcek, too, an oppositional party made no sense because "we don't know of any better party than the Communist Party."[26]

Instead of allowing pluralism with open contests of political forces, the Communist reformers seemed to believe that the democratization of the political system was completed with the democratization of the Party. The new Party statutes—the draft of which was published a month before the invasion[27] but was never implemented—were to provide the framework of permissible change. The draft forbade formation of "factions" but called for *oponentura* (a custom-made term, not previously known in the Czech language) to fill the role of devil's advocate and for the protection of minority rights. In addition, the rules concerning the incompatibility of offices and rotation in office were designed to prevent the concentration of roles in the hands of only a few as well as tenured political power.

This plan of replacing the compromised with the compromising, the unyielding with the attentive, did not dispose of the core problem of civic incapacitation of the vast majority of the ruled and their lack of political choice. Under the program of reform, although the Communist Party's leadership was not to be imposed but was to be gained and maintained through daily work and good example, the KSC was not to be supplanted: that was the gist of Dubcek's reformism. The Communist Party had to earn rather than usurp the leading position in society, but the Party alone would sit in judgment over its own performance.

Those opposed to this arrangement argued that the concept of the Party's leading role had no theoretical support in Marx, that it was invented by Lenin, institutionalized by Stalin, and found its rationale in the backward Russia of 1917. There the Party bureaucrats had to assume the revolutionary role that the numerically weak, illiterate proletariat could not fill, but similar measures were scarcely necessary in industrial Czechoslovakia. The "legitimacy of dissent" and the legitimacy of an alternative remained as different as *voda* (water) and vodka, as did "democratization" and democracy.

The frustration over the delayed de-Stalinization in Czechoslovakia was matched in 1968 by the intensity, number, and diversity of suggested alterna-

"I'm a modest man! I'd be content with constitutional monarchy. . . ."
(*Reporter*, May 1, 1968)

tives to the totalitarian system. At times, it was reminiscent of traditional experimentation, with ideas and voices canceling each other. All blasphemous, according to Moscow standards, some of them may one day be hailed as gems of a creative Marxist spirit. The proposals included the so-called British two-party solution, the Yugoslav solution, the separation of State and Church (i.e., the Party) approach, the revival of direct democracy. A pedantic typological analysis is not called for here, but some of the main trends of thought may be identified and roughly divided into two groups: one seeking inspiration in past or present practices of non-Stalinist political systems, and the second offering untested models.

Among the key proposals in the first category was the blueprint presented by the young playwright Vaclav Havel, reflecting to a considerable degree the thinking of the Circle of Independent Writers, a non-Communist branch of the Writers Union.[28] Basically, this was a call for a pluralistic system, close to a liberal parliamentary democracy. Havel arrived at the need for a two-party system by eliminating all other conceivable alternatives. Individuals running for office as independents—as some student groups advocated and as some enthusiasts were already doing—were engaged in a futile exercise. Because of their helplessness and hopelessness, the Establishment would welcome such an atomized, penniless challenge. Special-interest groups were discounted because of the conflict of loyalties of their representatives, most of whom were members of the Communist Party and thus bound by its discipline. Revival of the National Front and of the puppet parties, to which Havel referred unflatteringly as "these mummified remnants of pre-February 1948 political forces," was unlikely. Totally discredited through twenty years of servility to the Communists, they would be incapable of regaining public con-

fidence within the reasonable future, and conditions made time a precious commodity.

According to Havel, democracy makes sense only when attainable political alternatives exist. Therefore, he proposed a two-party model, based not on the class struggle but on a "new type of coalition and cooperation" and bound by consensus to the fundamental aim of both parties: "the humane, socially just and civilized self-awareness of the nation through democratic socialism."

One-party monopoly excluded the majority from participation. Even a reformed KSC would remain—given its sordid record under Stalinism unacceptable to a great number of people. Furthermore, the Party would be unattractive to those who felt uneasy about its inadequate emphasis upon the democratic, humanistic essence of socialism. Thus, as a counterpoise to the Communist Party with its emphasis on socioeconomic transformation, a Democratic Party should be founded, which would give more attention to democratic principles, both parties contributing to the establishment and maintenance of democratic socialism. *Klub* 231, the organization of former political prisoners, many of whom had suffered under Stalinism because of their premature advocacy of such values, was suggested as capable of becoming the nucleus of the new party.

Havel's dismissal of the potential of the special-interest groups and of the old non-Communist parties was too sweeping. As subsequent events proved, the representatives of the special-interest groups, such as the trade unions and artistic organizations, clearly demonstrated by their opposition to KSC directives a primary loyalty to their group. Similarly, not all non-Communist parties had prostituted themselves during the Stalinist period, if for no other reason than the lack of opportunity to do so. The dissolved and banned Czech Social Democratic Party and the

Slovak Democratic Party were cases in point. A further question about the maintenance of a two-party system may be raised, namely, the likelihood of its disintegration in a country with a tradition of a multiparty system and proportional representation.

The basic concept of a two-party system put forth by Havel, who was not a member of the Communist Party, was endorsed, even if indirectly, by such influential Communists as the District Secretary in Prague, Milos Nemcansky, and Central Committee member Karel Kosik. Among their proposals was the formation of two Communist parties—a modern one, adhering to humanistic Marxism, and the traditional one, of the Bolshevik type. Another proposal suggested that the Catholics constituted the only force able to counterbalance the Communist Party's organization and *Weltanschauung.*

On the whole, Havel's model reflected the sentiment of a large proportion of the population with no ties to the ruling party. Other reformers were more cautious in their use of non-Soviet precedents and focused instead on the period of transition between 1945 and 1948, implying that the February 1948 seizure of power was an unnecessary mistake. Political scientist Michal Lakatos, a member of the KSC until his expulsion in 1969, was among the main advocates of this model.[29] He argued that the decision makers faced only two alternatives: preservation of the unworkable monolithic system or the revival of the pluralistic system based on the platform of the pre-1948 National Front. Within the National Front every social interest would exert its influence in the policy making process. Political parties and mass organizations would both function as agents of interest aggregation. Demands and pressures upon the political system should be recognized, and the emergence of autonomous associations based on the common interests of their members should not be regarded as injurious to the interest of the Communist Party.

Lakatos conceded some weakness in his model—weakness stemming from the disparate political experience and culture in the Czech and Slovak areas. The mass character of the Communist Party in the former contrasted with its elitist character in the latter, and the puppet parties in Slovakia were purely artificial structures. Because they were thus disqualified as potential partners of the Communist Party in Slovakia, Lakatos suggested that this role be played by the trade unions.

Perhaps for tactical reasons, this model left unanswered the pivotal question of the tenure of the Communist Party's rule. Whether inhibited by strategy or timidity, Lakatos did not call for the revival of the Slovak Democratic Party, the strongest pre-1948 organization, or for the Catholics to assume the balancing role that he assigned to the trade unionists.

Conservative Communists rejected Havel's model as a reactionary plot and Lakatos's model as an unnecessary regression to the beginnings of the struggle for socialism. A more exacting task was to demolish proposals that were not handicapped by unrespected precedents but were presented instead as authentic contributions to creative modern Marxism. Among the authors of such proposals were Petr Pithart and Zdenek Mlynar, both young political scientists and members of Dubcek's brain trust.

Pithart touched upon the agonies of explorers of untested courses, the tragic solitude of the Czechs when most of the socialist countries could not or did not want to understand what they were trying to do. Even among the sympathizers, the degree of understanding was limited: in Rumania the Communist Party remained merged with the state, and in Yugoslavia the notion of a second political party remained taboo. Pithart referred to autonomous political parties, contested elections, and freedom of the press as the minimal bases of a workable democracy. At the same time he warned against overestimating the competitive multiparty system as the guarantee of democratic political processes. The novelty in Pithart's model was the involvement and mobilization of the mass communication media to assist in transforming formal democracy into real democracy.[30] Radio and television stations would continue to be owned by the state, but their administration should be made autonomous, and the enforcement of the press law was to be put under the control of independent courts. In addition, the Workers Committees for the Protection of the Freedom of the Press (organized before the invasion and silenced after it) would provide a guarantee of grassroots political expression.

In 1968 the mass media proved their capacity for independent action, and during the August 1968 abduction of the political leadership they functioned as an underground government, preventing chaos, disintegration, and immediate surrender.

The most elaborate and innovative model for restructuring the political system was prepared by a theoretician of high political standing, the Secretary of the Central Committee and Moscow University graduate Zdenek Mlynar.[31] He did not veto the variant of a two-party system functioning on the basis of socialism, but he offered several caveats: the weaknesses of Western parliamentarism, the danger that the mass media might be dominated by power groups, and the likelihood of a hostile reaction from the less innovative socialist countries. In addition, Mlynar brought up a point of great importance, one that everyone else seemed to disregard: the havoc that would follow the electoral defeat of the Communists. A society that had been frustrated and tormented for two decades would in all likelihood seek sweet vengeance against the party of former rulers.

Mlynar's model of pluralism used the National Front as its basis, and among its elements he included interest groups (unlike Havel) and new political parties (unlike Lakatos). Access to political participation was to be granted to organizations other than political parties, notably to interest groups formed along functional lines (trade unions, farmers organizations, professional groups), generational lines (youth, senior citizens, women), and economic lines (producers). In order to realize this goal, a formal structure of several chambers was to be established. A Political Chamber, consisting of deputies from the Communist Party, from other parties, and from politically nonaffiliated groups, would be controlled by four other chambers: (1) Industry and Commerce, (2) Agriculture, (3) Science and Technology, (4) Culture. Representatives to the four chambers were to be elected from their place of employment and were to be in no way identified with political parties. According to Mlynar's outline, deputies to these four chambers were to be elected directly whereas deputies to the Political Chamber were to be chosen indirectly. In the Political Chamber the political parties would function as proxies for the electorate. In the other chambers the deputies would be direct representatives of the basic social interests of the society.

This is very likely the most nonconformist reform model ever produced by any secretary of a Central Committee in a Warsaw Pact country. Mlynar, who left politics after the 1968 invasion and turned to entomology, presented his model without the customary inflexibility or intolerance of a Communist bureaucrat. Aware of flaws in what he termed his "socialist parliamentarism," he conceded that his attempt at direct democracy might deteriorate into double representation and confused corporativism.

It should be added that in 1968 distrust in representative government and calls for direct democratic participation were not infrequent. Philosopher Robert Kalivoda wrote, for example, that the "Marxist model of socialism is vitally tied to the development of direct democracy."[32] This goal might be approached in a variety of ways, e.g., by interaction between the leadership and the populace through the mass media, by a process of "socialist syndicalism" in the trade unions, or by direct participation of the Workers Councils.

The innovative reformers were opposed by the sterile conservative forces, who had little more than abusive language to offer. Only the Jodas group—named after a previously obscure Party veteran, Josef Jodas—came forward to defend Stalinism. In 1968 this miniscule sect of prewar Communists presented a gloomy portrayal of the country in which the fate of socialism was said to depend upon the outcome of the conflict between two forces, the elite of power (EP) and the elite of influence (EI). Painting thick conspiratorial designs with the Stalinist brush, the group maintained that in the 1960s hostile forces had penetrated the Party ranks as a result of open recruitment of nonproletarian elements and had formed a revisionist Fifth Column. The Party College in Prague became their center, with the graduates intruding into all levels of the KSC apparatus and the mass media. Challenge by these elements came into the open in 1968: "There is the elite of power and the elite of influence. The writers, newsmen, artists are the elite of influence but they possess no power . . . ," and the warning was issued that the EI would strive to usurp all the power.[33]

It is difficult to envisage power without influence, since the latter is presumably inherent in the former. Perhaps categories such as "paralyzed power"—a conflict between government and an alienated society, and in post-totalitarian circumstances a conflict between a society awakened by its writers, newsmen, and artists and the alienated (i.e., rejected, bankrupt) Stalinist power structure—may be employed.

With Stalinist intellectual counterattacks in short supply, the mass media in other socialist countries assumed the defense of the discredited cause in vitriolic polemics. The only rejoinder by a Czechoslovak Stalinist, namely Vasil Bilak, a member of the Politburo, appeared, of all places, in the New York *Daily World*.[34] Bilak wrote that the Czechoslovak working class was guilty of anti-revolutionary decrepitude and of an inability to distinguish between right and wrong. Incidentally, Bilak was rated in a Czechoslovak public opinion poll as the most unpopular politician in the country.[35]

Pre-Invasion Achievements

The Action Program of April 1968 did not promise that the leading Party role was to be decided in a popularity contest; it visualized instead a modification of the bureaucratic model of socialism as well as increased public participation in the political processes under the paternalistic eyes of self-appointed rulers. Notwithstanding these limitations, the non-Communist forces took considerable advantage of the thaw. They may be listed in four categories: existing puppet parties, aspiring parties, "mass" organizations, and mass media.

The Puppet Parties.   It should be stressed that the democratization of 1968 was confined primarily to the Czech lands and that in Slovakia neither the old non-Communist parties nor new organizations showed any noticeable signs of life. With a grand total of 248 members in the Freedom Party and 364 members in the Rebirth Party, these were meaningless organizations, incapable—unlike the Catholic Church—of developing into a counter-balancing political force.[36]

In the Czech lands the People's (Catholic) Party and the Socialist Party shared with their Slovak counterparts a humiliating record of servility, but they also differed on some significant points, notably, the tradition of their pre-1948 political existence, some membership base, and an expressed dissatisfaction with their inferior status. In the words of *Svobodne slovo*, the main daily of the Socialists, "it [the Socialist Party] considers it not only a right but a duty to bridge over the humiliating existence during the ill-famed twenty years (when one's activism was measured by the number of hours spent in voluntary unpaid work, and kilos of collected raw material or expressions of devotion and faithfulness)."[37]

Moreover, the changed circumstances restored the potential of the two minor parties to attract new members. The strength of the People's Party was reported to be 21,362 in 1966 (compared with 483,725 in January 1948). The Socialist Party had suffered an even greater decline—from 652,000 members in 1947 to 3,792 in 1949 and 10,705 in 1967.[38] Reduced to sad symbols of defeat, these organizations had been prohibited from recruiting new members for almost a decade. Even after the ban was lifted in 1956, the membership did not change significantly because there were no incentives to join. The parties exercised greater influence through their press. The People's Party daily *Lidova demokracie* and the Socialists' *Svobodne slovo*, each with an average circulation of 200,000, became the favorite papers of noncontroversial news (e.g., capitalist strikes, Hollywood scandals), in contrast with the repetitious propaganda of the Communist publications. In 1948, each puppet party was allocated twenty seats in the National Assembly and one or two seats in the cabinet.

The demise of Novotny also led to the dismissal of the puppet parties' leaders. Their successors' record of servility and opportunism were not strikingly better, but their misdeeds were at least not public knowledge.[39] Subsequently, some of the new leaders managed to vindicate themselves. The head of the Socialist Party, Bohuslav Kucera, as Minister of Justice in 1968 pursued a consistently liberal course. Kucera and his non-Communist colleague Vladislav Vlcek, sitting in the cabinet for the People's Party, were the only ministers to join the Society for Human Rights, which was banned in 1969 as antisocialist.

The two parties communicated their resumption of political life through their dailies. These papers avoided direct polemics against the Communist media and even against individual Stalinists. This task was formidably performed by special interest periodicals, in particular by journals of the Writers and Journalists Unions and by the students' weekly *Student*. Of course, innuendo was rather common, as in this reference to the international discipline of the Communists: "I have an advantage which the members of the Communist Party do not have. I am an ordinary citizen, whose view is just his own. Therefore, I want to speak up clearly and frankly." The writer then declares that he prefers "John Amos Comenius to Ivan the Terrible, and, therefore, socialist democracy to the cult of personality."[40]

In general, the editorial policies of the non-Communist parties' press were not characterized by recklessness but rather by measured probing in the direction of respectable political self-expression. This search for equality of political partnership alongside a realistic appraisal of the configuration of power led to what might appear as schizophrenic responses. On the one hand, the minor parties conceded that the KSC, by virtue of its brilliant minds and other superior resources, was predestined to run the country at this time. On the other hand, they protested against their role as mere transmission belts and resented the fact that the Communists brushed aside with insincere jokes their questions about true pluralism in political life.[41]

Even for the reformist Communist leaders who favored participation of the non-Communist groups, the notion of opposition and, indeed, the word itself (*oposice* in Czech) smacked of subversive, antistate behavior. Advocates of pluralism, therefore, resorted to a semantic solution by coining the word *oponentura*. In short, *oponentura* equaled *oposice* minus its destructive connotation. This semantic strategy is illustrated by the following excerpt from an interview with Bohuslav Kucera, in the West German weekly *Spiegel*:[42]

Q. How do you visualize the role of the Socialist Party within the National Front—against the Communist Party? The Communists have maintained the leading role. Do you accept it?

A. The leading role of the Communist Party is a reality; whether we accept it or not, it does exist. However, this does not preclude the eventuality of confrontation. [The Czech term *konfrontace* carries no bellicose, challenging overtones.] We want such a confrontation, we want *oponentura*.

Q. An opposition?

A. *Oponentura*. . . . We have our own program, differing from other programs.

The mini-parties, indeed, engaged in their own political thinking. The People's Party endorsed Christianity and its progressive ecumenical spirit; the Socialist Party endorsed socialism but not the Marxist doctrines of class struggle, economic determinism, and historical inevitability. Instead, the humanistic philosophy of T. G. Masaryk and Czechoslovak patriotism were emphasized. These programs were not heralded as a challenge to the dominating creed but were kept in discreet obscurity under the modest title "Draft of Ideological Principles."[43]

The non-Communist parties did not engage in rivalry with one another, but neither did they openly cooperate, although cooperation would appear to have been logical and salutary for two groups of compatible orientation, mutual interest and goals, a common adversary, and the identical predicament of imposed inferiority. The reasons for this lack of interparty cooperation—whether it was solely a delaying tactic or compliance with an order of the Communist Party against fraternization, or something else—are not apparent to the outside observer. Except for occasional informal meetings of their leaders, we also know nothing about possible cross-national ties between non-Communist parties. Theoretically, at least, some cooperation between the Czech and Polish Catholics, for example, would seem logical.

Given the tarnished image of the minor parties, their recruitment achievements in 1968 were considerable. Their soft approach carried tones of Churchillian prose: "We can offer you no executive posts or other sinecures, but only work, hard work, and risks."[44] According to scattered evidence, each party's membership had reached 20,000 by the time of the invasion, climbing shortly thereafter to some 50,000 for the Socialist Party and to some 60,000 for the People's Party. In January 1969 the latter reported a total of 77,566 members, organized in 1,744 cells, with a final monthly gain of 2,367, a figure exceeding the recruitment of the Communist Party itself.[45]

The Communist Party report, prepared in August 1968 but not released until a year later, noted certain differences in the resurgence tactics of the two minor parties. The Socialist Party recruited mainly in Bohemia and in urban areas, particularly among the intelligentsia and highly skilled workers. The People's Party was mainly oriented toward the villages, appealing to practicing Christians. The Catholics managed to capitalize on their pre-1948 influence in several towns. Unlike the Socialist Party, the People's Party tried to build up a broad organizational network in the greatest possible number of communities, and their meetings were less openly anti-Communist. Both non-Communist parties, however, suffered from a shortage of qualified cadres.[46]

In fact, both concentrated on building up an organizational base rather than mass membership. Instead of building a leaderless mass army, they decided to create an officer corps without an army—a decision that prompted some worried Communists to point to the ominous precedent of the Reichswehr in the Weimar Republic, which had formed the nucleus of a large army under the strictures of the Versailles treaty. Only this effort to build up their organizational bases (or a self-deluding desire for grandeur) can explain the puppet parties' establishment of political schools, district conferences, and sections and departments ranging from ideological to agricultural.[47]

Time prevented many of these plans from materializing. Another handicap was that none of the leaders of the minor parties gained national recognition and stature. Perhaps the best known member of the Socialist Party was pop singer Waldemar Matuska, whose decision to join the ranks in 1968 was met by the Communists with displeasure and even something akin to jealousy. As a rule, however, uncommitted first-rate persons in the arts or sciences tended to form and join new organizations that reflected new ideas.

Aspiring Parties.   Three rather different structures appear under this heading. Of them, the Social Democratic Party was no newcomer; it was the oldest socialist party in the country, co-founded by the father of the second Communist president, Zapotocky, and dissolved in 1948 through merger with the Communist Party, a maneuver common throughout Eastern Europe. With representatives in exile, jail, or compromised by their embrace of Stalinism, the Social Democratic leadership had been decimated, morally as well as literally. In 1968, former officials and members demanded restoration of their party —and they appeared to have a strong case. Zdenek Fierlinger and other fellow travelers who had merged with the Communists had violated the bylaws that required consent of the rank and file for such a move.[48] The result, which was thus legally null and void, could be rectified by reviving the party. This demand, backed by a number of prominent Czechoslovak intellectuals, posed a touchy problem of prime significance; the precedent it would set would be intolerable to other Warsaw Pact coun-

tries. Accordingly, the Central Committee of the Communist Party and the National Front refused to consider the revival of the Social Democratic Party, claiming that it would be injurious to proletarian Marxist unity.

The re-establishment of the Social Democratic Party was feared primarily for ideological reasons, but a major headache affecting practical politics was caused by KAN, the Czech acronym for what is variously translated as the Club of Non-Party Activists, The Club of Committed Non-Partisans, or Club of Engaged Non-Communists. Some 150 intellectuals with ties to the Academy of Sciences established KAN in 1968 for the purpose of "offering citizens without party affiliation the possibility of active participation in political life." The long-range goal was to "secure for its members who have no political affiliation a position in their work equal to that of members of the Communist Party of Czechoslovakia, especially in view of the fact that there is no organization associating citizens who are not politically organized."[49]

In its official statements, KAN studiously avoided identifying itself as a political party. One manifesto read: "We want to be an independent political force of an entirely new type, representing the interests and views of unaffiliated people," and to be neither against nor under but alongside the Communist Party.[50]

These protestations were not convincing. With the exclusion of Communist Party members, KAN appeared for all practical purposes to be a "Party of non-Party men," a multifunctional structure engaged in the customary activities of a political party. KAN announced its intention of having its own candidates run for elective offices, and began to concern itself with all phases of the political process. Its ideological commission was engaged in the preparation of various position papers. Using the United Nations Declaration of Universal Human Rights as its reference, attention and demands were directed toward the National Assembly. KAN was energetic in these activities, notably in its pressure on the legislative commission drafting a new election law.[51]

The KAN program calling for political emancipation of the non-Communist majority of the nation and open electoral contests was met by a positive public response. It was reported that as many as three-fourths of the adult residents of some communities applied for membership.[52] The KAN's May

First slogan, "There Are Six Million of Us," while perhaps not a statement of fact, was a plausible prediction of future numerical superiority over the Communist Party. Unhandicapped by discredited leaders, presenting fresh people and fresh ideas, KAN received thousands of applications for membership.[53]

However, at that time, KAN was little more than an idea. Its founders at first restricted membership and concentrated on building up the basic structure of the organization. Admission of KAN into the political arena was regarded as a test of the Communist Party's sincerity in abandoning its totalitarian persuasion. During the pre-invasion period this test was merely postponed.[54] KAN's Preparatory Committee applied for registration with the appropriate authority, which simply failed to act within the thirty-day limit prescribed by the law (Act No. 68 of 1951). The Minister of the Interior neither permitted nor prohibited KAN—or any other emerging political organizations—leaving it in an indeterminate state and preventing it from using funds received from public contributions.

An organization which generated a similar degree of official hostility was the association of persons who had been political prisoners during the Stalinist period, called *Klub* 231 (in reference to Act No. 231 "On Protection of the Republic" of 1948). Owing to its restricted membership K-231 aspired to become not a political party but merely an interest group. To the credit of K-231 and the alarm of the KSC, this new group appeared elitist not only in quantity but also in quality. No other organization in the country could boast such a high percentage of war heroes and men of distinction from all walks of life. (Paradoxically, with a preliminary membership of 80,000, this exclusive club was larger than the legitimate non-Communist parties.) In addition to the individual respectability of the members of K-231, the common tragic experience of political persecution added a special quality of cohesiveness to the organization.

Representatives of K-231 had to reassure the worried Communist Establishment that their members were not a militant phalanx determined to drown the country in blood. The stated aim of the group was to press for belated justice and to promote rehabilitation, not retribution or revenge. Furthermore, it explained, by exposing criminals and sadistic officials (a task which ought to have been carried out by the state in the first place), it would

benefit all of society. But such statements, though restrained and conciliatory, failed to placate the ruling Party.[55]

All three emerging political participants—the Social Democrats, KAN, and K-231—were occupied with the problem of whether or not to join the National Front. They had to assess, in other words, the realistic range of dissenting and even alternative political action. This dilemma was premature, however, because all three aspiring forces were ultimately prevented from entering the political arena.

"Mass" Organizations. In accord with Soviet practice, social organizations in Czechoslovakia had served as transmission belts for the policies of the ruling Party. The 1968 drive for autonomy was accompanied by new sets of demands, generated by centrifugal tendencies within existing structures and by the pending federalization of the country.

Greatly affected by these developments was the numerically strongest and politically one of the most compliant and conservative groups, the trade unions, officially listed as the Revolutionary Trade Movement (ROH).[56] A centralized structure and a servile tool of the Party, the ROH actively assisted in abrogating the workers' participatory rights that had been introduced in 1945. The absence of a secret ballot and the procedure whereby outgoing trade union committees nominated and installed their successors led to the perpetuation of Stalinist control.

At the April 1968 plenary session the conservative trade union leadership was removed and new statutes were adopted. A massive wave of political awakening among the workers accompanied this change. Non-Communists increasingly began to participate in the labor movement. In some factories a situation developed in which Communist Party membership effectively disqualified a candidate from election to the trade union council.[57] Post-invasion developments reversed the trend but failed to impose a status quo ante immediately. By March 1969 Communists held between 55 and 80 percent of the offices in the central organs of the unions. Composition of the factory committees varied widely, however, with 500 committees (out of 26,000 in the country) still functioning without participation by Communist Party members.[58]

In January 1969 the Constituent Congress of the Czech Trade Unions declared that the ROH would not serve as a transmission belt for government policy and that it would become a political force though not a political party. The term "interest group"—illegitimate in the Stalinist lexicon—was explicitly used to identify the unions' new role. They vowed to play the role of a "constructive opponent" and to "fight against the misuse of power and to control this power,"[59] in blatant disregard of the warning issued by Moscow *Pravda* on the opening day of the Congress against anarcho-syndicalist tendencies penetrating socialist countries. Prominent among the specific tasks the trade unions pledged to perform was that of acting as a watchdog over trends in the standard of living.

Reorganization by the unions of their internal structures did not go beyond adjustment to the federation pattern introduced in Czechoslovakia in October 1968. Centrifugal tendencies were present, however. The Czech locomotive crews battled for a year for their independence but were ultimately forced to rejoin the unified ranks.[60]

By 1972 the conservative restoration in trade unionism was fully accomplished. The reformers were replaced by neo-Stalinists. Measures adopted in the 1968–1969 period were declared null and void. In June 1972 the Eighth Trade Union Congress convened to sanction total restoration of a centralized system in the service of the Communist Party.

The second largest mass organization was the Czechoslovak Youth Union (CSM). Since more will be said about this structure in Chapter 9, only a few observations are in order here. In contrast to the more cautious action of the trade unions, the CSM leadership in 1968 presided over the dissolution of this moribund organization. The young people restructured the CSM not only along ethnic lines, by setting up separate Czech and Slovak organizations, but also along functional lines. The appeal of these new autonomous organizations for high school youth, university students, industrial and agricultural youth, campers, Scouts, and the like, led to a correspondingly high rate of recruitment and socialization. The university youth in particular contributed to the democratization movement in the country.

Professional organizations, which had previously been dormant or nonexistent, also increased their activities significantly in 1968. The Union of Czechoslovak Lawyers, the Czech Medical Society, the Architects Union, and other professional groups began to assert themselves and to demand recogni-

tion of the social utility of professional work.[61] Various other associations, such as those representing senior citizens or members of agricultural collectives—groups unacceptable in conditions of totalitarian uniformity—also began to form.

Mass Communication Media. Though structurally entirely different from the groups demanding a participatory role in the political process, the media during this period exercised a liberalizing influence that was far from negligible. According to conservative Communists, the mass media must bear most of the responsibility for the damage done in 1968 to the monopoly of the Party's rule.

The activities of writers, artists, and scientists in 1968 "obliterated the distinction between politics and culture."[62] Both Communists and those with no party affiliation became in effect the political counterforce. The Writers Union, for example, planned to run for five seats in the National Assembly.[63] It was also suggested that a new daily paper be published which would "demonstrate its independence primarily by the wealth and breadth of its information and commentaries and by taking its own position within the framework of socialist *oponentura*."[64] The media encouraged at least indirect political participation by such means as televised political debates, public opinion polls, exposure of Stalinist crimes, and responsiveness to letters to the editor. During that period the media also served as the corrective mechanism in Dubcek's post-totalitarian machinery. Moreover, all the state-owned radio and television stations as well as the press won the right (in a conflict not unknown in Western democracies) to establish editorial policies that diverged from the owners' views. Even the editors of the Party's main daily, *Rude pravo*, prevailed in obtaining primacy for their editorial prerogatives over the previously undisputed authority of the publisher.

In conclusion, we may perhaps characterize the political structure of this pre-invasion period not as a two-party system but as a two-force system. On the one hand, there was the Communist Party, a force of essentially centrist orientation, as a result of the compromise between the progressive and conservative wing. On the other hand, the mass communications media constituted a force of clearly reformist persuasion, with resources—talent and mass support—that exceeded those of their opponents. The media temporarily deprived the Party of its monopoly of initiative. A more permanent contribution, however, was the awakening of the citizenry.

Setback to Pluralism

Public opinion polls in 1968 reflected the process of public awakening. The data in Table 3.4 indicate the extent to which citizens abandoned the values imposed upon them during twenty years of Stalinist rule. Respondents were asked: "Do you consider the present electoral system of a single slate of National Front candidates satisfactory?"; and "Do you wish equality of political parties?".[65] Similarly, according to a *Rude pravo* poll, the creation of opposition parties was favored by 90 percent of respondents who were not members of the Communist Party, and by more than half of respondents who were Communist Party members.[66]

Table 3.4. Reactions to Soviet Type of Rule (in percentages).

Respondents	Accepting a single slate	Favoring equality of parties
All respondents	34	81
Those with grade education	41	78
Those with higher education	20	87
Age groups		
26–39	29	86
40–54	35	81
over 55	41	75
Communist Party members	47	71
Not members of the Communist Party	30	85
Members of the Socialist Party	7	100
Members of the People's Party	5	100

These data reflect a trend prevalent in other surveys: the higher the level of education and the lower the age of the respondent, the greater was the

likelihood of antitotalitarian attitudes. Particularly significant was the finding that the majority of Communist respondents were willing to risk their party's monopoly in an open contest of political forces. This response also reflected the refusal of the rank and file to be held responsible by the nation at large for the failures of policies over which they had had little influence. Jiri Hanak echoed such sentiments in his polemical article in *Reporter* against an obscure Stalinist, Bohuslav Chnoupek (future Czechoslovak Minister of Foreign Affairs):

If someone says, "I am the leader," he must certainly consider all failures as well as all successes as his prime responsibility. He is concretely responsible for a sufficiency or shortage of housing, for the functioning or malfunctioning of transportation, for the great or small stature of our country in the world, for high or deplorable working morale, for feelings of legal security or insecurity. . . . Without the help of any sociological survey I would dare to say that an absolute majority of the readers will agree that failures predominate; it has been clear for some time that we really have not enough housing, no functioning transportation, no hard currency, no weight in the world, no competitive products, no feeling of legal security, and many things which we ought to have. . . . The author of these lines is a Communist, who, years ago, joined the Party without any reservations, and who has derived no advantage from his membership—apart from the one advantage that, as a Party member, he was always right, even if he was wrong. This advantage I should like to be free of. . . . [67]

The issue of participation boiled down to the issue of the incompatibility of democracy and a one-party system. It was pointed out that the entire concept of a single party was a contradiction in terms, both linguistically—a party being a part, hence requiring another party to create the whole—and politically. The best self-control is a poor substitute for control by someone else. A pledge of democratic rule and sovereign statehood by one party with a monopoly of power and binding international commitments to other single-party states was said to be both hypocritical and unrealistic.[68] Continuation of the previous statement by Hanak can give us the gist of the issue:

Entrance for non-Party people.
(*Literarni listy*, April 18, 1968)

Comrade Chnoupek is also somewhat taken aback by "the strong movement in other parties toward increased activity." What, then, are these parties good for if not for political activity? Or does Comrade Chnoupek perhaps believe that the Communist Party of Czechoslovakia has a lease for all time on this country? ... Let us assume for a moment that some eight million people in the country do not wish to be led by the Communist Party but by a monarch of the dynasty of the Premyslides. What then? Would it mean that the rule would be applied that revolutions do not give way and that a country once won for Communism must always remain Communist? ... I am convinced—and you will no doubt agree with me—that if there are two makers of ice cream in a town, people are likely to prefer the one who makes the better and cheaper product. This makes the other fellow try to make his ice cream even better and cheaper than his competitor. Nobody has been able so far to convince me that this simple rule is not applicable to the sphere of politics.

The discourse over the legitimacy of participation and political alternatives did not entirely deteriorate into a dialogue between the deaf but rather into one between those with impaired hearing in an environment of Kafkaesque logic. Their political appetite whetted, those who had no say in the political process may have believed that their demands for participation would be granted. Meanwhile, the May 1968 Plenary Session of the Central Committee concluded that "loyal minor partnership" was the maximum concession. That is to say, various groups might be permitted a quiet voice as long as they remained small and their loyalty to the regime was unquestioned. The future of the KSC was visualized as one in which it would enjoy the spontaneous support of most of the population—a support they would not be entitled to terminate. The Party would remain the sole judge of whether or not it retained public confidence. As Cestmir Cisar, one-time favorite of the students and their candidate for president put it, the Czechoslovak experiment would be called off the moment an antisocialist opposition was formed.[69]

To sum up, the pre-invasion period was one of upsurge in expectation, experimentation, promises, and hopes—all pervaded with an aroma of unreality. The badly needed laws—the electoral law and the National Front law in particular—were not enacted. The inherited structure was suspended but not destroyed. In retrospect, and with some cynicism, it might be asserted that the invasion by foreign troops saved the leadership from embarrassment and charges of bad faith. After August 1968 the unfulfilled promises of extended political participation could be blamed on an outside force.

The pluralistic trends may be viewed as a series of concentric circles: The inner circle consists only of the ruling Communist Party. The middle circle represents the confines of the National Front, i.e., all authorized structures outside the Communist Party. The outer circle includes all other, if any, political groupings.

Membership in the National Front is a precondition for admission to the middle circle, and the applicant has to scale several barriers in the process. An organization seeking to be approved must first obtain a legalization permit from the Ministry of the Interior. In the pre-invasion period the Ministry used delaying tactics to sabotage demands for increased participation, and by June 1968, out of seventy new associations that had petitioned, only one (the Society for Human Rights) was accredited.[70] Accreditation itself does not ensure participation because the National Front holds the power of the

purse. After admission, the National Front as a whole decides what proportion of state subsidies, office space, and printing facilities become available to the new member.

The National Front is essentially a vehicle for manipulated participation. The organization applying for membership pledges good behavior in exchange for toleration and material amenities. A suspected troublemaker is denied membership, as was the Federation of Locomotive Crews; a misbehaving member is expelled, as was the Union of Film and Television Artists. Thus groups that aspired to independent participation in the political system found themselves involuntarily in the outer circle of political outcasts. Of the groups eligible for membership only the Czech University Students Association refused—unlike its Slovak counterpart—to join the National Front, and inevitably, the organization was banned.[71]

Among the first acts of the post-invasion regime was the elimination of the three most prominent components of the outer circle—the preparatory committees for the Social Democratic Party, KAN, and K-231. Having banned them as "voices of counterrevolution," the Ministry of the Interior further ruled that because KAN was political in character its program did not meet the criteria for a voluntary organization. The K-231 was liquidated with an equally bizarre argument, namely, that no need existed for such an organization.[72]

After the virtual elimination of the outer circle, the purification drive extended to the middle circle, i.e., to the non-Communist parties and mass organizations in the National Front. A rule of proportion was established: the less political the organization applying for accreditation (the first step toward admission into the National Front), the fewer obstacles stood in its way. Accordingly, the Ministry of the Interior declined to accredit the Christian organization called Work of Council Revival (DKO) but had no objections to the establishment of the Czech Union of Teetotalers.[73]

Shortly after the invasion the puppet parties enjoyed an unexpected boost. Having languished for two decades in obscurity, they were honored by hostile publicity in a 14,000-word statement in *Pravda* (August 22, 1968) justifying the invasion. The minor parties were accused of aspiring to equal status with the Communists. In another Soviet publication the writer remarked:

> The Czechoslovak People's Party and Czechoslovak Socialist Party, which, as members of the National Front, had recognized the special status of the Communist Party of Czechoslovakia as the leading force throughout society, began to demand the same position and role in the administration of the state; they began to express an effort to form a legal opposition.[74]

This exaggeration not only provided the puppet parties with an unwarranted appearance of courage, but also inspired the local conservative Communists to polemize against them. A year earlier the Party press would have considered it beneath its dignity to acknowledge even the formal existence of the non-Communist parties; now it joined the attack. They were accused of attempting to form their own People's Militia and of other counterrevolutionary stratagems.[75]

Husak, too, contributed to this public display of hostility. In his inaugural speech in May 1969, he observed that the leading role of the Communist Party was an "historically inevitable attribute of a socialist society" and that Czechoslovakia was characterized by "a closed political system."[76] In this explicit repudiation of Dubcek's call for "an open system," Husak declared that no organization desiring to participate in political life could have a legal basis outside the National Front and that the puppet parties had sinned by reverting to ideas and concepts of a pre-totalitarian vintage. He further admonished them to follow the example of the KSC in purging their own ranks.

These developments helped the minor parties regain some self-respect and public recognition for an honest try. They could not, however, assume an autonomous political role, and within less than a year after the invasion they had returned to a position of subservience.

With the components of the outer circle

eliminated and those of the middle circle brought to obedience, the Communist Party circle became the focus of purification. As mentioned earlier, the developments of 1968 provided the opportunity for the pluralistic tendencies in this mass party to surface, even to the extent that proposals were offered to create two Communist parties—one reflecting the modern trends of democratic socialism and the other adhering to the traditional Bolshevik pattern.[77] New political parties do not simply arise out of nowhere, it was pointed out; they are a result of either the unification or the division of existing structures. As 1948 had been the year of unification, 1968 was to be the year of division. Failure to establish a second Marxist party, it was asserted, would cause the majority vote in the country to go to the political Right.

The invasion rendered these worries immaterial but did not remove the consequences of the 1968 differentiation within the Communist Party. Several public opinion polls confirmed that nine-tenths of both the nation and the KSC membership supported the reform policies that had led to fraternal military visitation and the status of limited sovereignty. Dubcek's successors regained the confidence of the Soviet leaders only to lose the confidence of the Czechoslovak people themselves, including most of the Communists. This was in part conceded by Husak when he referred to the dualism of the existing "oppositional KSC" and the "governmental KSC."[78] The major share of the blame was placed on the municipal Party organization in Prague—termed in the Stalinist parlance the "Second Center"—which had allegedly attempted to usurp total power in the party and the state.[79]

Challenges from within all of the three circles were curbed, if not eliminated, and the mass media were effectively purified through preliminary censorship. Husak's concept of a closed system stipulates that political participation is legitimate only within the KSC-dominated National Front. This vehicle with a collective membership of fifty organizations[80] has become increasingly a meeting place of special interests attending to matters of somewhat less than devastating importance. Teetotalers and beekeepers are not expected to be an effective substitute for the outlawed Social Democrats.

In Chapter 2 we referred to three types of political participation: manipulated, noninvolved and independent. Listed in the descending order of acceptability, the third alternative has been outlawed —it was, in fact, never fully legalized. A year after the invasion, outlets for independent participation were closed, with the nation standing aside, observant but not applauding. The proponents of the imposed order have become enamored of a quaint kind of revivalism, trying to breathe new life into socialization structures that have been defunct for more than three decades, such as the Left Front of the intellectuals and the prewar variant of the Komsomol youth movement. These nostalgic exercises have produced no noteworthy results.

The 1968 attempt to foster independent participation in the political processes was short-lived, more potential than real. The government continues to be controlled by one party and by people of a single type on all levels of public engagement and responsibility. The ruling party reasserted its monopoly, failed to provide the citizen with an alternative political choice, and consequently reinstituted the conflict between citizenship and partisanship. The legitimacy of different paths to socialism—sanctioned by Lenin, stifled by Stalin, revived by Khrushchev, and smothered once again by his successors—seemed in the Czechoslovakia of 1968 to be ready for qualitative refinement: the legitimation of different paths to socialism *within* one country.

The post-1968 reckoning with the Party's revisionist ventures has been gradual, but the severity of applied measures was greatest at the apex of power. Notably, the purge did not reduce the Party to an elitist group of pure militants, but did result in a drastic turnover in the membership of the Central Committee and the Party apparatus.

Denunciation of the errant vanguard of the proletariat was very explicit. *Tvorba* accused the Communists of having "simply merged with their environment," thus forfeiting their leading role. According to another accusant, the leadership "managed to achieve the monstrous metamorphosis of the Party as a Marxist-Leninist revolutionary organization into a some new sort of nationalistic, socialist *baracnictvi*" (an untranslatable term: an old-fashioned neighborhood association).[81] It was also charged that tens of thousands had joined the Party only because of their sympathy for Dubcek and disapproval of the Soviet military entry and that as Communists they were total failures.[82]

The euphoria created by national unity in 1968 was dissipated by the subsequent traumatic events, and differentiation within Party ranks and society at large set in. Pavel Auersperg, an apparatchik of the KSC Central Committee, reportedly classified party membership into five groups: (1) the incurably ill, (2) the ill, (3) the temporarily incapacitated, (4) the healthy, and (5) the excessively healthy comrades.[83] The fourth type, officially known as "the healthy core," is the ideal: the conservative wing loyal to the present Party leadership and the Soviet Union. The fifth category denotes the "Ultras": the unrepentant Stalinists, the nostalgic revivalists, the perpetrators of the sordid misdeeds of the 1950s. A major issue of the purge was whether the recuperative powers of the second and third groups—the "ill" and "temporarily incapacitated" comrades—were great enough to restore them to "health." The figures that follow indicate the extent of the problem.

On February 3, 1970, *Rude pravo* printed a lengthy "Letter of the Central Committee of the Communist Party of Czechoslovakia to All Primary Organizations and Party Members Concerning the Exchange of Party Cards." A total of 70,217 purging committees with 235,270 members (the loyal core of the Party) had been established. The result of their labor was reported at a Plenary Session of the KSC Central Committee in December 1970 by Husak: 67,147 were expelled, 259,670 lost their membership by cancelation (a milder form of punishment). This meant termination of Party membership for 326,817 individuals, 21.67 percent of the total at the time the purge commenced. However, the decline in membership since January 1, 1968, was 473,731 or 28 percent. Husak was less specific about the number of remaining comrades, referring only to the existence of "approximately 1.2 million members."[84] In Slovakia, where the bacillus of revisionism was less virulent, the toll of the purge was only 18 percent of the existing membership, i.e., 63,000 out of a total of 350,000.[85]

The purge did not eliminate the mass character of the Party, nor did it change its social and age composition. According to a twenty-two-page pamphlet published by the KSC Central Committee, industrial workers accounted for 26.4 percent of the total membership and cooperative farmers a mere 5.3 percent. The worker-peasant bloc of 31.7 percent comprised some 380,000 members (of 1,200,000), whereas in 1962 these two basic classes of socialist society constituted 42.4 percent, i.e., 704,200 members (of 1,657,000). Younger members, irrespective of their class profile, were more frequent casualties of the purge than were their elders. Consequently, the average age of KSC members increased to 47.9 years.[86]

The likelihood of expulsion increased with the political importance of the individual: the closer to the top the more frequently did the lightning strike. Of the 115 Central Committee members elected at the Fourteenth Congress of the KSC in May 1971, only eight had been elected for the first time at the Extraordinary Fourteenth Congress, held underground in August 1968 (and later declared illegal). Only 26 members elected in 1966 at the Thirteenth Congress were reelected in 1971, further attesting to the high degree of discontinuity in the elite roles.

Among the rank and file, developments were less monumental. The Party that emerged from the purge is still nonproletarian, aging, and nonelitist. As will be elaborated later in the text, the "healthy core" of reliable Party members, identified with the interests of the Soviet Union and the current Czechoslovak leadership, is estimated to be between 200,000 and 300,000. The rest of the Party, i.e., the majority of almost one million, belongs largely to the category of the "temporarily incapacitated" who hailed Dubcek and cursed the invaders along with the rest of the nation. The "healthy" militant core has expressed doubts about the genuineness of the repentance of the majority of the Party and considers the purge an unfinished undertaking.[87]

Pro-Soviet members of the KSC are also worried over the fact that they are outnumbered by *former* members of the KSC. Since 1945, Party membership has been terminated for some 1.3 million. Although death has no doubt accounted for some of this total, many ex-members are alive, especially from among the 470,000 who left the Party during Husak's term.

The core issue is not one of number but the existence of a potentially cohesive group sharing a common experience, political outlook (i.e., preference for humanized socialism), organizational skills, common bitterness, and, in many cases, hardship caused by current disfavor. Former Party members of the Dubcek era have not been completely isolated from one another and are potentially an entity capable of offering alternative political leadership should such an opportunity arise.

On the eve of the Fourteenth Congress in May 1971, the issue of bipolarity of the Czechoslovak Communist movement was raised in a letter to the Central Committee by Alfred Cerny, a former member and reformist apparatchik from Brno. Cerny used the term "Party of the Future"—a community of people without organization but with the power of critical thinking and rank solidarity—in contrast to the "Party of the Past," meaning the neo-Stalinist establishment.

> The Party of the Future cannot consist only of the present and past members of the Communist Party of Czechoslovakia. For two decades now young new forces have been coming forward, and they cannot be pushed aside any longer. . . . They have many justified doubts about the Communists, seen from this or that angle, but the year 1968 has shown that they can march alongside us and we alongside them.[88]

Cerny concluded with an appeal for "the formation of all avant-garde forces of Czechoslovak people." He was arrested in January 1972 and in August 1972 sentenced to a three-year term for the felony of undermining the Republic.[89]

In 1968 reformers suggested the establishment of two Communist parties. Before such a model could be tested, outside force interfered. The process of differentiation was too advanced, however, and with *the aid* of the purge a virtual two-party arrangement came into existence three years later: the official organization and its hibernating, reformist alternative.

Problems of Welfare

In this chapter we shall examine the distributive practices of the political system and their impact upon the structure of society and the performance of the economic system. The major theme as well as the major cause of the failure of the Stalinist system in Czechoslovakia is the too literal application of the Soviet model in alien territory—an environment already industrialized and a society already modern and safely out of the feudal period.

Before 1938, Czechoslovakia was the sixth largest industrial nation in Europe and the first in the Danubian sphere. Its foreign trade was four to five times that of any of the fourteen countries of East-Central Europe—Finland, Greece, and Turkey included. The industrialized state had also introduced some redistributive measures in the hope of precluding an eventual revolutionary ferment. The land reform of 1919 fixed the maximum amount of arable land which could be owned by an individual at 150 hectares (1 hectare = 2.47 acres). Compulsory social insurance covered all wage earners. Differences in levels of wealth were much smaller

than, for example, in neighboring Hungary or Poland.

History also contributed to social tranquility. For reasons going back three hundred years before the creation of the independent state, the Czech nation had almost no aristocracy of its own and had gradually developed from one class, the peasantry. The bourgeoisie was of comparatively recent origin.

Twenty years (1918–1938) of Czechoslovak independence furthered the development of a pluralistic society while avoiding the extremes of social polarization. A study of Czechoslovak social composition as of 1930 divided the total population of fourteen million into five classes:[1]

(1) An upper class (120,000 or 0.85 percent of the total population), composed of capitalists, intellectuals, and bureaucrats.

(2) An upper-middle class (810,000 or 5.8 percent), including the same types as the upper class but differing in the degree of prominence, power, and wealth.

(3) A lower-middle class (4,150,000 or 29.6 percent), mainly merchants, farmers with 2 to 30 hectares of land, entrepreneurs with 1 to 10 employees, and among the intelligentsia mainly teachers in schools of basic education.

(4) An upper-lower class (3,490,000 or 24.9 percent), mainly peasants with small farms, retail traders, artisans, white collar workers with low qualifications, and skilled industrial workers.

(5) A lower-lower class (5,430,000 or 38.8 percent), the semiskilled and unskilled industrial workers and farm laborers.

For historical reasons the relations between the social classes in Czech lands and in Slovakia differed. Bohemia and Moravia were described as the provinces of the "little man," fond of his privacy and his family, proud of his occupational skills, middle class in his style of life, and democratic in his outlook. In Slovakia, egalitarian attitudes were confined to the lower class. The rural population was less educated and poorer, the bourgeoisie less numerous and highly class-conscious. In short, the Hungarian feudal tradition was not extinct there.

The Nazi occupation ended the socioeconomic tranquility. Not only were repressive measures directed against racial groups and political adversaries, but authorities also took over "Aryan" property, especially large banks and industrial establishments. Under the pressure of the war economy, thousands of industrial plants were either closed or converted to other production. An effective supervisory system curtailed the enterprising autonomy of Czech industries, and the war-deformed economic structure of the state has not been remedied since.

Changes in the society reflected political subjugation and economic exploitation. One effect of the partial elimination of the social and economic elite was to reduce the social distance between classes. In fact, industrial workers, essential for wartime production, were the only Czechs the Germans tried to win over as a class. Forced labor and rapid bureaucratization were introduced in that period.[2]

The socioeconomic mobility of the war years was given new impetus after 1945. Three million Germans expelled from the Sudetenland left sufficient property to accommodate any applicants and, in effect, to neutralize much of the eventual social discontent. New land reform was promulgated. In its

first phase, about three million hectares of land—roughly 23 percent of the Republic's total area—were confiscated and, in part, handed over to individual applicants.[3] Settlers were also given the private possessions of German traders and artisans. As for industry, confiscation led to nationalization rather than redistribution into private hands. By the end of 1945, about 65 percent of all industry (in terms of manpower and output) was owned by the state.[4] This nationalization signaled the end of the remaining industrial upper class. Compensation for seized property, although promised, never materialized.

Further redistribution measures were undertaken by the pre-Communist regime between 1945 and 1948. The next step in land reform was to set a limit of fifty hectares on private ownership. Enforcement of the law was delayed, however, until after the February 1948 coup. Despite its beneficial political effect, this measure led to an economically unsound fragmentation of land. Private property in industry and trade was further curtailed by nationalization of plants with more than fifty employees, and in some industries of all plants regardless of the number of personnel.

In 1948 there were 383,000 commercial establishments, of which 173,000 were engaged in production and the remainder in buying and selling. Altogether, they employed 904,000 persons. In the same year 2.2 million people were engaged in agriculture.[5] The capitalist sector was weak and unimportant, owing to the gradual process of liquidiation since 1939. Because of land reforms, the "farmer-capitalist" existed largely in the minds of the Party ideologists eager to imitate the Soviet struggle against the kulaks.

Stalinist Redistributive Measures

Faithful to the Soviet pattern, Czechoslovak Marxists declared that their country, like Russia, in moving from capitalism to socialism included three economic sectors and, correspondingly, three social classes: (1) a socialist sector, the proletariat; (2) a sector of small-scale production and trade, the petty bourgeoisie, but mainly the peasantry; and (3) a capitalist sector, the bourgeoisie.

The period of the dictatorship of the proletariat and rigorous application of the doctrine of class struggle resulted in a thorough transformation of the composition of Czechoslovak society.[6] (see Table 4.1). This was a transformation enforced from above

Table 4.1. Social Composition of Czechoslovakia, 1950–1967.

Social groups	1950		1961		1967	
	in 1,000s	%	in 1,000s	%	in 1,000s	%
Workers	6,950	56.4	7.738	56.3	8,319	58.3
Other employees	2,028	16.4	3,834	27.9	4,212	29.5
Collectivized farmers	2	–	1,466	10.6	1,186	8.3
Other cooperative producers	–	–	164	1.2	166	1.2
Small (private) farmers	2,510	20.3	484	3.5	332	2.3
Independent professions, craftsmen, entrepreneurs	470	3.8	51	0.4	45	0.3
Capitalists	378	3.1	–	–	–	–
total	12,338	100.0	13,746	100.0	14,271	100.0

rather than generated from within the nation. The main shift took place immediately after the seizure of power in 1948. By 1953, coinciding with the death of Stalin and Gottwald, a major part of the state's goal had been accomplished. Most affected were capitalists, who were eliminated as a class, and the peasantry, the majority of whom were collectivized. Of the Marxist trinity of economic sectors and social classes, the third sector, the capitalist, was completely done away with, and the second, the small producer, was reduced to a politically and economically negligible entity.

It is beyond our limits here to discuss fully the doctrinal riddles and Stalinist practices demonstrating that a change in economic status is not necessarily followed by a change in class identification. The claim that transformation of class identity will lag behind a change in economic status serves a twofold purpose. First, protraction of class struggle against the defeated and pauperized provides rationalization for further arbitrariness and disregard for the rule of law. Second, ostentatious preference for and identification with the victorious proletariat serves as an excuse for maintaining the spoils system and discriminatory recruitment, and as a shield for unqualified bureaucrats of working class background.

The forcible vertical mobility whereby some 300,000 loyal and largely unqualified proletarians replaced the holders of positions of authority in both the political and economic system, was accompanied by a thorough restructuring of the economy. A brief

mention was made in Chapter 1 (page 8) about this goal, known as the "Iron Concept of Socialism," that is, an emphasis on heavy industry and a corresponding neglect of light industry—in particular, consumer products. This preference, in effect, sacrificed lucrative foreign markets in the hard currency areas. Although the Soviet Union and the rest of the forming socialist camp absorbed only 19 percent of Czechoslovakia's exports in 1947, a year later this percentage had jumped to 39.6 percent and had reached 78.5 percent by 1953.[7] In 1969, among the Warsaw Pact countries (except for Bulgaria), Czechoslovakia had the lowest share of foreign trade with the West. The restructuring of the national economy and reorientation of foreign trade led to, among other things, inefficient production, loss of competitive spirit, decline in the quality of products, and attendant export difficulties.

The economy was further impeded by the heavy demands of the military. In the short period 1950–1952 armament demands quadrupled.[8] Very little data are available on this sensitive matter, but it is common knowledge that Czechoslovakia has developed into a major arms supplier. Guerillas throughout the world brandish Czech machine guns.

The structure of the economy, an erroneous foreign market orientation, inefficiency, obsolescence, neglect of agriculture, neglect of services and the infrastructure in general, overemployment, a decline in morale at work and in the standard of living, and other negative aftereffects were the price

"Thanks to the continuous development of socialism, we became a developing country."
(*Dikobraz*, July 30, 1968)

of Stalinism. The emphasis on quantitative expansion of the national economy resulted in 75 percent of investment being allocated to production, and a mere 25 percent to service industries. In comparison, the ratio in the USSR was 65.4 : 34.6, in France 58.3 : 41.7, and in the United States 38.4 : 61.6.[9] Czech Premier Stanislav Razl admitted in 1969 that the economy suffered from reckless concentration on superficial goals and neglect of the country's real riches and potential.[10] Pursuit of the unachievable went hand in hand with neglect of the achieved. For example, in the last thirty years, no new machinery has been installed in the factories of Bata, the famous prewar shoe manufacturer. According to Premier Razl, housing in particular exhibited signs of neglect and deterioration: 50 percent of all housing units in Czechoslovakia were forty or more years old, and 12 percent more than a century.[11]

Stress on quantitative expansion was accompanied by a steady increase in employment. Rather than modernizing equipment and management practices, the government decided on a labor-intensive economy, adding women and the aged to the labor force. This state of affairs has lately been criticized as "overemployment." In the Czech provinces half a million pensioners are employed at least part time, and nearly half of the total labor force consists of women, allegedly a world record (see Table 4.2). According to figures for 1966,[12] in Czechoslovakia women constituted a majority of the labor force in agriculture (51.2 percent), municipal services (54.3 percent), communications (51.1 percent), education and culture (60.4 percent), retail trade and restaurants (71.7 percent), and health and social services (77.5 percent).

Table 4.2. Women in the Labor Force of Czechoslovakia.

Year	Employed (in 1,000s)	Percentage of labor force
1955	1,852	42.7
1960	1,994	44.0
1965	2,214	46.3
1968	2,328	47.1
1969	2,366	47.2

Source: *Tribuna*, March 10, 1971, No. 10.

If we then consider deterioration of services—in the short period 1966–1969 the network of retail outlets in the country was halved[13]—the lot of an employed mother and household provider is hardly enviable. The price for the state neglect of proper services is an enormous amount of unproductive time wasted by the populace in a search for the necessities of daily life, a hectic style of life that leads to collective fatigue, low matrimonial stability, and a low birth rate.

The shadow cast by the iron concept of socialism is long. In 1965 there were some 23,000 public dining places in the nation, less than half of the prewar number. In comparison with the 676,578 hotel beds in neighboring Austria (population 7.1 million), Czechoslovakia (14 million inhabitants) had only 117,277 beds. Not surprisingly, the annual hard currency earning in tourist trade in Austria was $59.50 per capita; in Czechoslovakia it was $2.80.[14]

Autocratic movements usually stress physical

fitness, but Czechoslovak Stalinism seems to have ignored the muscle building aspect of socialism. By 1967 most schools had no gymnasium, and approximately half of the military draftees failed the physical fitness test.[15]

Owing to a myopic preference for heavy industry, large complexes such as those in Ostrava, Kladno, and Plzen were favored with subsidies, a preferential wage scale, political prestige, and widespread publicity. In contrast, light industries, such as textile manufacturing, languished, prompting this query: "Does the lady cabinet member know that our mothers sleep on the floor of the textile factories during the night shift? Oh, my dear, this is a superfluous question. We have got the Iron Concept."[16] Even among the employees of the shoe manufacturing giant Bata, the long-established tradition of loyalty to the firm vanished. Annual turnover of personnel was between 50 and 60 percent and in some years reached a full 100 percent.[17]

Industrialization of Slovakia narrowed the gap between it and Bohemia and Moravia but did not close it. By the end of the 1960s the industrial output of the Ostrava region alone exceeded that of the entire Slovak Republic. However, the emphasis on industrial progress was not matched by attention to other needs. Thus, Ostrava, the industrial heart of the country, deteriorated into a polluted, crime-infested, culturally underdeveloped region. The city even acquired the reputation of being a "mammoth house of correction."[18]

So far, little has been said about the classic victim of socialist construction, agriculture. Though by no means approximating the terror of the 1930s in the Soviet Union, the prolonged, irrational and highly arbitrary class struggle ill affected the Czechoslovak peasantry. According to some sources, forced collectivization delayed the postwar recovery in agriculture by three decades. The farmer subsidized the Iron Concept to a considerable degree.[19]

In 1968, with censorship lifted, the issue of forced collectivization and its injustices came under public scrutiny. It was even implied that the uncritical imitation of far less developed Soviet agriculture was perhaps not entirely a matter of blind loyalty but part of a shrewed Machiavellian calculation: the country's agricultural self-sufficiency collapsed, making her dependent on the Soviet Union for food.[20]

In the year 1968 the surviving remnants of private peasantry consisted of 160,000 farmers cultivating less than 9 percent of all agricultural land, mainly in inaccessible (and for big farming unsuitable) areas.[21] The rural section was little affected by the reform movement of 1968. The socialist foundations of agriculture—the Uniform Agricultural Cooperatives (JZD)—were not challenged. Apparently the cooperatives, once despised and never admired, have been accepted as an inevitable way of life, preferable to the risks a challenge to the status quo might generate. This lack of engagement in the political whirlwind of 1968 did not go unnoticed by the conservative post-invasion leadership. Politburo member Oldrich Svestka, commenting on the failure of the industrial workers to resist the lure of revisionism, said: "It is not without interest that cooperative farmers as a whole did not succumb to the hysteria generated by the news media last year and this year and that in general they represent a very important part of the sound forces of the Party."[22]

The reason for this apparent loyalty was not that the regime was strong and popular but that the peasantry was largely old and feeble. The flight of the young from villages to the cities is a universal phenomenon, but in Czechoslovakia it has reached extreme proportions. In some areas over half the remaining farmers have passed the retirement age in private farming, 67 percent of the farmers are over 60. In addition to a decrease in the number of youth, agricultural areas also lack qualified personnel. Little improvement in large-scale farming and managerial skills can be expected from the cooperatives, 60 percent of which are run by individuals with only a grade-school education. Cooperative farming carries a stigma; JZD members are even embarrassed to reveal their vocation for fear of ridicule.[23] This, too, can be considered a legacy of the Iron Concept.

Social Pseudo-Security

Socialist construction, it has been charged, has forsaken the individual man, the supposed beneficiary of all the effort. It seems that socialism of the Stalinist variety is bound to be insensitive to the poor and needy. Scarcity, of course, precludes generosity, and the maxim "to each according to his merits"—unlike the maxim "to each according to his needs"—means that magnanimity is both ethically and ideologically unsound. This principle insulates the fat, contented socialist from feelings of guilt over the misery of his undernourished fellow citizen.

In strange contrast to the totalitarian insistence on uniformity, the promulgation of the 1948 Social Security Act ended the existing system of uniform social policies. The Ministry of Labor and Social Welfare was abolished and its jurisdiction divided among various agencies. It was not until 1968 that the ministry was resurrected, as part of an attempt to restore a uniform, efficient, and just social policy.

A narrowly conceived concept of merit justifies neglect of senior citizens, who, after all, now contribute little to the new political order. Paradoxically, the generation which had the most to do with the victory of the Stalinist cause in 1948 has reached not only retirement age but also socioeconomic degradation, the foundations of which they themselves laid in their more august days of robust revolutionary selfishness. Too feeble to protest or be heard, the average beneficiary among the 2.8 million pensioners is believed to exist at the poverty level.[24] Harrowing facts were revealed in 1968 concerning this matter. Perhaps the most severe indictment of the system was the humiliating lot of the physically handicapped.[25] The Stalinist system also applied the "class approach" to social security. As Igor Tomes, an authority in the field of social legislation and welfare, pointed out, insistence on class differentiation abolished the very principle of citizens' social equality: what resulted was political aristocracy at one end and political outcasts at the other, and the mass of the nation in an uncertain center. Social security was degraded from a legal right to a political award, subject to ex post facto whims of the state. As Tomes put it, "Citizens could not have enjoyed any social security because they did not know when and where someone would get an idea and take away what the state had once guaranteed."[26]

As the construction of socialism proceeded, social insecurity increased. In 1956 a principle was openly promulgated relating one's retirement benefits to his record of contribution to the socialist cause. A further step was taken in 1958 when local people's committees were authorized to cut a recipient's social benefits if they felt that he had committed political sins. Benefits for orphans of politically suspect parentage were also subject to reexamination. These prerogatives of local committees remained in force until 1967.[27]

Stalinism has never been in favor of philanthropy.

In 1968, the practice of charity was restored, not as a substitute for social welfare but as a humanizing supplement, enriching both the recipient and the donor. The State Secretary in the Federal Ministry of Labor, Dr. V. Brablcova, stressed that cooperation and assistance had always been a part of proletarian solidarity in the past and should be brought back, though in a revised form.[28] Several other demonstrations of human solidarity appeared in Czechoslovakia after Novotny's fall, such as revival of the prewar tradition of voluntary contributions under the so-called Christmas Tree of the Republic and the Austrian practice of S.O.S. villages—named after international distress signal—for abandoned children.

The social policies of Stalinism affected the old and the young with particular severity. Benefits for newlyweds, such as state loans and grants, were abolished. The high employment rate among women contributed to a record low birth rate.[29] According to a survey conducted by a women's weekly, *Vlasta*, the 8,500 female respondents considered motherhood the eighth most important function in marriage. Desirability of motherhood appears to be inversely proportional to education, but even among the less educated there has been a constant decrease in the birth rate.[30] Liberal policies of legalized abortion have had considerable impact throughout society. A further deterrent to motherhood has been a lack of state child care centers. Again, the Iron Concept is responsible for neglect in this field; only one out of ten children could be accommodated.[31]

The housing situation among newlyweds was reported in 1966 to be as follows: 59.1 percent lived with parents, 20.5 percent had separate living quarters, and 4.1 percent lived with other families.[32] To the low priority given housing development, some oddities of economics and law have been added. The average rent paid in Czechoslovakia covers only about half of the maintenance costs. The private owner of a house does not always possess a legal title to full use and benefit of his property. Many landlords are forbidden to collect the rent (deposited in a frozen, state-administered account) though they are held responsible for maintenance. The waiting period for the award of housing by the state depends on several variables, such as family size, present living conditions, and political merit of the applicant. On the average, a wait of seven years is not considered unusual.[33]

The disappointing record in housing construction

has had other results of a rather different nature. On the positive side, the low rate of construction has saved the country from overurbanization, congestion, and disruption of established patterns of settlement. Thus, contrary to trends in other countries, the population of the capital, Prague, has remained stable. Of the total population of Czechoslovakia, 5.2 percent lived in Prague in 1921, 6.06 percent in 1930, 7.56 percent in 1950, and 7.23 percent in 1960. The projected figure for 1980 is 6.5 percent. Static population is also reported for the provincial capitals. According to the census of March 1966, no less than 42.5 percent of the total population still lived in communities with under 2,000 inhabitants.[34]

One negative aspect of this situation is an enormous commuting problem for the employed population. National fatigue is the price for the failure to build socialist residences near places of socialist employment. One-half of all employed males and one-third of all employed females have jobs in communities away from their place of residence.[35] The problem of commuting is compounded by the peculiar Czechoslovak practice of starting work early: 6 A.M. in factories and between 7 A.M. and 8 A.M. in offices. For a considerable part of the nation, life begins at 4 A.M.

In 1969 cabinet member Leopold Ler assessed the legacy of the Stalinist Iron Concept as "the problem of the existence of the Czech nation. Therefore, I cannot imagine a Czech government which would be concerned, say, with figures on steel output or with the electrification of railroads, and not whether the Czech nation will exist at all in ten, twenty, or thirty years."[36]

Working Class, Intelligentsia, and Equalization

In a spell of frankness, the KSC admitted in 1968 that its policy toward the working class was an outstanding failure. Not only had promises failed to materialize, but also the worker—the presumed beneficiary of the effort to build socialism—had changed.[37]

Since 1948, there had been a substantial increase in the industrial proletariat, reflecting the expansion of the economy. This development was hailed as a valuable political achievement. Reminiscent of the Czechoslovak preference for a mass character of the ruling Party, rather than an elitist one, the emphasis on quantitative expansion of the working class

generated the establishment of so-called "political enterprises," industrial undertakings in socialization rather than economically rational production. As a result, there was a dilution rather than a strengthening of the proletariat and its revolutionary consciousness.

This consciousness suffered with the departure of the most militant segment of the working class to fill positions in both the political and economic systems. An estimated 300,000[38] members of the working class were elevated, leaving their former jobs to be filled by their class enemies, who as casualties of the revolution were assigned to manual labor, further weakening Party spirit at the point of production. Along with the demoted bourgeois elements, the working class was augmented by recruits from a politically harmless but nonproletarian milieu, in particular by housewives and rural people.

It was perhaps the young who caused the Party's greatest disappointment. Those who were not "welded into one front of class solidarity in the fight against capitalist oppression" have gradually become the majority of the working class, leaving the prideful and nostalgic identification with the 1948 change to the growing ranks of the retired senior citizens.[39] Ironically, then, of the three components of a socialist society—the workers, the farmers, and the intelligentsia—the workers are biologically the youngest, and the Communist Party—their alleged embodiment—is mainly the preserve of aging former workers and nonproletarian officialdom. It would be very difficult to exaggerate the importance of this disparity or the fact that the young industrial worker is beyond the reach of the KSC. These were also the thoughts of Vasil Bilak, who complained in the American Communist press of the political immaturity of the Czechoslovak proletariat and its lack of resistance to counterrevolutionary lures.

These unsavory developments in the working class have worried the KSC leadership for years. Increasingly passive, this group, theoretically amenable to easy manipulation, has become difficult to move toward the designated goal of an ideal society. Ideological assessment of the social classes has generated endless questions and the need for reevaluation. Even Novotny himself ventured into the field of creative Marxism by enriching the Thirteenth Congress of the KSC in 1966 with a thesis about the convergence of the intelligentsia and the working class, with the former becoming part of the latter.[40] It was implied though that this "broader concept of the working class" would require greater subtlety and intellectual refinement for its implementation. The same Congress reasserted that this new concept did not invalidate the old premise of the leading role of the proletariat in society. For Czechoslovak Stalinism the ideal man was engaged in hard, physical labor, highly motivated, and politically engaged. Every worthy citizen was expected to approximate this goal, given, of course, the deterministic limits of his class identity. As we shall examine in some detail in Chapter 8, the concept of class struggle, with privileges and discrimination, introduced a system reminiscent of feudalism. Upward social mobility was restricted to one class only, with multiple adverse consequences.

It was commonly agreed in Czechoslovakia that, of all the socialist countries, it was the country that treated her intelligentsia the worst. Part of the problem was that the Czech intelligentsia did not enjoy the advantage of being scarce. A highly placed official in Prague told this writer in 1958: "The Poles pay their professionals well because they haven't got enough of them. The East Germans have to pay even better so that not all will defect to the West. In our country we abound with intellectuals who, incidentally, have nowhere to flee. Hence we can afford to mistreat them with impunity."

Primitive glorification of the proletariat was heralded in 1948, along with the imposition of collective guilt on just about everyone else, except for the KSC bureaucrats who had imposed such procedure. The Czech intelligentsia, despite their traditionally leftist orientation, became a scapegoat for all seasons, a whipping boy to be held on short lead in an environment in which the values of the more primitive part of the proletariat were made binding on all. For many of the uneducated political elite, including Novotny, this militant anti-intellectualism was the expression of their rather substantial feelings of inferiority. The intelligentsia, as one writer put it, "had to continuously defend themselves against the presumption of hostile and even quasi-subversive activity, and their fate was often decided by people with an instinctive hatred of everyone who surpassed them in education."[41] To underscore their precarious status, the term "intelligentsia" is preceded by the epithet "working" (*pracujici*), in spite of the fact that, given the conditions of the Czechoslovak economic and legal order, a "non-working intelligentsia" would be difficult, indeed, to imagine.

The "class criteria" deteriorated into what political scientist Frantisek Samalik, himself a former industrial laborer, calls "social racism"—a primitive feeling of superiority compensating for gratifications the revolution promised but did not deliver.[42] From the viewpoint of the Stalinist bureaucracy, the implantation of social racism in the consciousness of the proletariat has been an important political achievement. Their insulation from and the consciously engendered antagonism vis-à-vis their natural ally—the intelligentsia—enhanced the tenurial prospects of the ruling Party.

It should be noted, however, that the anti-intellectualism of the working class was not a pure Stalinist creation but also a reflection of the traditional Czech understanding of democracy. The "little Czech man" has habitually professed plebeian egalitarianism as an excuse for envy and social jealousy. Stalinism successfully exploited this attitude.

Marxist socialism became, rather than a model for human emancipation and self-realization, a tool for the so-called *nivelizace*, or "equalization of income." The lifetime earnings of highly trained specialists are lower than those of laborers with average skills. For physicians, lawyers, and teachers to earn less than such semiskilled laborers as streetcar conductors has become commonplace in Czechoslovakia. Even instances of voluntary occupational "demotion" for the sake of financial gain, for example, a dentist becoming a taxi driver, have been reported.[43] Brian Abel Smith, a British economist prepared for the World Health Organization a comparative study in which Czechoslovakia was rated first by many indices, such as the number of physicians, hospital beds, and nurses per patient and population, but next to last (followed by the then Tanganyika) of seventeen countries compared, in remuneration of medical personnel.[44] In 1964 the ratio of average incomes among bluecollar workers, technicians, and white collar workers was 100 : 130 : 84.[45] The data from other countries show a far greater income differentiation.

Proponents of economic reform were well aware of the debilitating impact of this policy. Material incentives were recognized as a necessity in order to energize the economy. It was pointed out, for example, that in the Trinec steel mills, 93 percent of each worker's wage was fixed and secured by his mere physical presence at the plant. Only the remaining 7 percent was determined by the worker's initiative and actual performance. As a result, even ambitious individuals would avoid undue exertion, relying instead on either overtime or the employment of other family members for extra money.[46] The ambitious found another solution in the so-called "black deequalization," meaning work done illegally for private customers, using illegally acquired material from state inventories. This activity served to meet public needs which the socialist services could not satisfy.

Income equalization progressed throughout the years of Novotny's rule. In 1959, 75.6 percent of all employees in the country earned between Kcs 1,000 and Kcs 2,500 per month (Kcs = *Koruna*), and in 1964 the proportion had grown to 81.8 percent.[47] (The exchange rate of $1.00 for Kcs is: officially, Kcs 7; tourist, Kcs 15; and domestic, Kcs 35.)

A thorough in-depth study of the income pattern of the nation was completed in 1967.[48] Among the first conclusions of the authors (a scientific team led by Pavel Machonin) was that the tripartite division of society into workers, peasants, and working intelligentsia was antiquated. "Czechoslovak society is vertically differentiated according to the type of work, education, and leisure activity.... This is all the more surprising since we had anticipated ways of life to be far more uniform." The surprised authors revealed that the leveling of incomes did not lead to leveling the ways of life. The latter remain largely determined by one's type of work and education.

The vertical social differentiation of the Czechoslovak population was presented as a six-layer pyramid. From top to bottom these are:

(1) A total of 2.3 percent. Engaged exclusively in white collar occupations, with professionals from industry heavily represented. The majority live in cities in Czech provinces rather than in Slovakia. The largest age group is 31–45 years old. Seventy-five percent of this category are KSC members.

(2) A total of 8 percent. Predominantly white collar employees. Composition is similar to that of the first category but includes a greater proportion of small-town residents and younger persons. Half of the group are KSC members.

(3) A total of 15 percent. Of this group, 40 percent are technicians: skilled workers and young workers are also represented. Residents of urban areas predominate.

(4) A total of 26.2 percent. This group represents the "national average." Largely skilled labor and white collar employees, residents of nonmetropolitan urban areas.

(5) A total of 30.4 percent. The worker-peasant stratum. Forty percent are Slovaks and other minorities. Largely small-town and village residents. Seventy-five percent are not KSC members; 80 percent are not politically active.

(6) A total of 18.1 percent. Composed of unskilled laborers and peasants. Largely rural stratum and the aged. Only one in seven are KSC members, and only 6.4 percent have a political role.

This Machonin report was embarrassing to the ruling elite because it is explicit about the disparity between the high level of income and the way of life of the uneducated elite and because it reveals this group's effort to block the advancement of the qualified younger generation into their preserve. In all, one-fifth of the labor force is engaged in work other than that for which they are qualified.

The report expressly stated that the study did not include the political elite. However, some information (albeit inadequate) is available from other sources. For example, the retired members of the political elite collect so-called "honorary" or "personal" pensions, which are well above the social welfare standards and regulations. To add insult to injury, the nation learned that princely sums are paid to retired Stalinists whose often illegal acts have been euphemized as faithful service to the Party. The pension of Karol Bacilek, Minister of Security at the time of the Stalinist trials, is Kcs 2,500 a month, about double that of a university professor after thirty years of teaching.[49]

In addition to special pensions, the elite reap certain amenities, such as the purchase of mansions or construction of summer retreats at extremely low prices. In an economy of scarcity, privileges such as renting homes or purchasing goods without the ordinary waiting period are particularly important. What were standard luxuries among the political elite to some degree became the privilege of the official artistic, intellectual, and industrial elites by way of following the Soviet tradition of Byzantine pomp of titles and decorations. It has been suggested that the practice of state awards served to mend damaged relations between the leadership and the intelligentsia. For instance, the preferential right to purchase an automobile—the socialist status symbol—without being left for years on a waiting list was reserved for holders of the "Golden Star of a Hero of the Czechoslovak Socialist Republic, the Golden Star of a Hero of Socialist Labor, the Order of Klement Gottwald, the Order of the Republic, the Order of the Red Banner, the Order of the Red Star, the Order of Labor, and the Laureates of State Awards."[50]

A Socialist Ideal of Sorts

After this rather unflattering account, it may come as a surprise that this welfarism was viewed by a majority of the Czechoslovak people as synonymous with socialism and worthy of continuation. Among numerous writers who touched upon the subject in 1968 was a young economist, Vaclav Müller. In his article "What Is Socialism?," Müller found Czechoslovak society rife with economic, political, and moral crises.[51] Increased production does not generate better living conditions. Under conditions of more realistic economic planning, the existing overemployment would become unemployment. Although in capitalist systems mechanisms have been developed for averting long-term recession and technical stagnation, in socialism such mechanisms, however badly needed, are absent.

For Müller the political crisis is self-evident, and he states that he will "never again believe that the domination by one Party offers a guarantee of democracy." The moral crisis, in his opinion, is the heaviest burden. Stalinism was a system of mediocrity "in which average people ruled and the below-average played havoc," permitting unworthy individuals to compensate for their deficiencies through officially condoned abuses of power. Yet despite the sorry record of two decades of socialism, the Czechoslovak people have not basically rejected this experiment. Müller finds the explanation in the nation's mass preference for socioeconomic security.

Factories and other enterprises of the state are the only sources of livelihood. Employment and income, once essentially economic categories, have taken on the qualities of a guaranteed social pension. In pursuit of "tenured citizenship," the man in the street is likely to prefer economic security to an order of law and civil rights. Such a concept of security becomes an obstacle to economic progress and, after the moral stimuli of the revolution have been exhausted, leads to the extinction of all stimuli to further progress.

The next step is economic stagnation, bringing with it the impossibility of guaranteeing even the social security for which the other aims were forgone. The insecurity thus engendered was felt in Czechoslovakia mainly by senior citizens and young married couples.

The debilitating effects of welfarism have been experienced in a number of countries. A Czechoslovak specialty is the national preference for equalization of incomes and a readiness to settle for less, provided that everyone's lot is no better. Müller put it in these words: "The unique aspect of our situation is our willingness to be satisfied with low wages—on the assumption that other people's income will not rise beyond certain limits either. This way of thinking has grown in our country to absurd proportions."

In addition to economic security and egalitarianism, a gentle pace of work is another characteristic of Czechoslovak socialism. Contrary to the glorification of Stakhanovites (champion shock-workers) in the early Stalinist era, the malaise of tardiness has spread: "to exert only as much energy and effort as have been accepted tacitly and with absolute solidarity in a given place of work [is] a kind of collective norm. As a rule, it is not the able and efficient who raise to their level the average and below average workers, but vice versa: it is the mediocre who set the norm. . . ."[52]

Actual performance is far below potential performance. According to a UNESCO report, the Czechoslovak morale at work is one of the lowest in Europe. For example, rational utilization of working hours in West Germany and Japan is three to four times greater.[53] The following episode was reported in the Czech press: "A certain Western businessman, who had visited several of our industrial plants, when asked about his view on Czechoslovakia's standard of living responded: 'Considering the way you work, you live exceedingly well, indeed.' "[54] It is customary for a worker to save his energy for after-hours work for illegal profit, something which he considers a legitimate supplement to the income received from the state.

This malaise was recognized even in Novotny's era, although perhaps not to its true extent. It became difficult to overlook the increasing indifference of industrial workers to the time factor which, in contrast to the hurried pace of the modern age, is characteristic of the attitude of traditional

(*Hospodarske noviny*, October 7, 1966)

societies. A tendency also developed "to harvest but not to sow, . . . to resist the exertion of one's energies . . . to maintain the attitude of a mere spectator . . . ,"[55] in other words, a trend whereby under the conditions of decaying totalitarianism the subject-participant participates less and less and the system is incapable and/or unwilling to resort to coercive measures to break his passivity.

In other societies, notably in the German Democratic Republic, totalitarianism did not lead to endemic apathy, stagnant economy, low-quality products, or miserable services—all evident in Czechoslovakia. Czechoslovak workers, with a Hapsburg-tested genius for accommodation, stripped Stalinism of its most oppressive qualities, which were paramount in Russia and other countries with a history of despotism. As far as job discipline was concerned, Czechoslovak Stalinism allowed, or failed to prevent, practices economically injurious to any industrial society. No doubt a result of the Czech plebeian heritage, democracy has been practiced at the wrong time with the wrong issues. A plant manager attempting to enforce work rules was in danger of being accused of "antiproletarian arrogance," or adherence to the "cult of personality manners,"[56] for which alleged shortcomings he would be hounded from his post, generally with the active support of eager would-be-successors. Diminishing respect for the political system affected other systems. With the factory foreman's authority at its lowest point, production became a matter of the workers' good will. Instead of taking a stand against the workers, managers resorted to lobbying at the respective governmental agency for surrender to, or at least compromise with, the demands of the "toiling masses." Here we detect a unique feature of Czechoslovak totalitarianism: fear of antagonizing a symbolic worker.

The 1968 invasion, at least in the short run, did not lead to noticeable change. In May 1969 the then Premier of the federal government Oldrich Cernik complained: "In offices, institutes, and some factories work ends at noon on Friday, and thus the working week is not five days, but often only four and a half, four and a quarter, and so on. . . . In the first quarter of this year wage increases in industry were three times as high as the increase in productivity. With such results we will not get far."[57]

Apparently, the average man considers permissiveness in job discipline as a foretaste of the socialist Nirvana. In the early part of 1968, conservative forces fighting the reformist tide exploited the workers' attitudes by pointing out that liberal reforms, including the New Economic Model and the revival of a market economy, would endanger individual economic security (implying also security from undue exertion).[58] Industrial labor in particular was not unresponsive to this strategy. In a public opinion poll conducted by the Academy of Sciences in February 1968, i.e., a month after the dismissal of Novotny and exactly at the time of the twentieth anniversary of Communist rule in the country, democratization of the political system came out seventh in importance, trailing far behind issues of economic improvement and housing. Only 4.9 percent of the sample considered liquidation of totalitarianism the top priority![59] A valiant socialization effort by intellectuals and the mass media in 1968, aided by the counterproductive effect of the invasion, substantially changed the priority of values of the average man, a change which is discussed later in this book.

Let us now examine some data relating to the standard of living, which in Czechoslovakia's case was occasionally described as an imitation of that of an affluent society. Pauperization and a simultaneous increase of freely distributed services, draconic taxation and spectacular subsidies, a warped scheme of priorities, overemployment, and Czech petty bourgeois craving for material possessions as status symbols—all these contributed to a pattern quite different from that in countries with a similar level of industrial development.

Enormous distortions in price structure resulted from the way the turnover tax was applied: in 1966 retail prices varied from wholesale prices in a range extending from minus 60 percent to plus 1,700 percent.[60] The national daily average intake of calories is 3,150 calories, thus exceeding by 250 the intake in other industrial societies and by 350 the level recommended by health experts. According to 1972 data, the population is substantially overweight. In Prague, the majority of males are too fat, and the average resident of the countryside is even fatter: only 25 percent of rural women are not above optimal weight.[61] Czechoslovak culinary habits are reminiscent of a major characteristic of Stalinist economy—emphasis upon quantity rather than quality. The average citizen eats plentifully but not well. Seventy-seven percent of the population suffer from deficiencies in protein, no doubt as a result of high prices for animal products. A thousand calories

in flour cost a mere Kcs 1.0 and in sugar Kcs 2.23, but for eggs the price is Kcs 12.04 per thousand calories and for meat it is Kcs 14.29. In 1962 the average Czech diet, in which starches predominate over protein, accounted for—together with alcohol and tobacco—51.6 percent of the population's total expenditures.[62]

The Czechoslovaks hold the world record for beer consumption: 129 liters (one liter = 1.06 quarts) annually per capita, followed by West Germans with 127, Belgians with 122, and Australians with 120.[63] The rise in consumption of alcohol since the start of socialist construction attests to the escapism rather than the hedonism of the nation. Since the early 1950s—when, incidentally, on orders of the then powerful Rudolf Slansky, the Anti-Alcoholic Union was banned and its propaganda ceased for some seven years—the consumption of alcohol per capita rose 1.5 times. Of the total population, 200,000, i.e., 1.5 percent, are classified as alcoholics.[64]

The Soviet invasion added to the nation's hangovers. According to *Svobodne slovo* (December 7, 1968), "As of late, there has been a distressing increase in alcohol consumption. This trend is in part ascribed to the political situation we got into recently." The article quotes figures for Northern Bohemia where, between October 1967 and October 1968, consumption of alcohol, excluding beer, jumped from 3,370 to 5,320 hectoliters of wine, and from 1,890 to 2,600 hectoliters of hard liquor.

The average citizen also smokes a great deal—2000 cigarettes is the annual average for persons over fifteen years of age. He buys four pairs of shoes annually, and his rent represents less than 2.5 percent of his spending! This particular saving is offset by the housing shortage. The housing situation in the country has deteriorated to such a degree that there are less than ten square meters of living space per person. Only 10 percent of all apartments are centrally heated and only one-third have private baths.[65] Poor housing contrasts with impressive cultural opportunities in urban areas.[66] For example, a state-subsidized repertory opera house is standard in every province.

But it is the automobile which best exemplifies the Czechoslovak imitation of an affluent society. Since 1953, the year of monetary reform—which in practice meant annulment of private savings and a fresh start for the pauperized nation—new car sales were: 1953, 74 cars; 1954, 211; 1957, over 20,000; 1961,

Table 4.3. Automobiles in Socialist Countries, 1966.

Country	Number of cars	Population (in 1,000s)	Population per car
East Germany	661,600	17,011	25.7
Czechoslovakia	521,163	14,240	27.3
Yugoslavia	237,200	19,511	82.2
Poland	234,100	31,420	134.2
Soviet Union	1,000,000	230,508	230.5
Hungary	40,000	10,146	253.6
Romania	29,000	19,027	704.7
Bulgaria	11,000	8,144	740.4
China	17,400	686,400	39,448.3
United States	78,672,100	194,583	2.5

29,500; 1966, 47,500; 1968, 75,000; and an estimated 100,000 in 1969, with 200,000 potential customers on the waiting list.[67]

The number of automobiles in socialist countries by the end of 1966 appears in Table 4.3.[68] The distance between the two industrialized countries and the rest—with the Chinese added, it appears, with tongue in cheek—is quite substantial. Yet in Czechoslovakia, the privately owned automobile is an unreliable measure of the standard of living; it is rather a reflection of the craving for a status symbol for which other amenities of life have to be sacrificed. Miroslav Holub, a well-known poet and scientist, after a prolonged sojourn in the United States, touched upon this theme. "[It is a] paradox that whereas for an American property is rather a utilitarian tool, for us property—a cottage, an icebox, a car—is a value in itself, a value measured not by advantages to the man but by all the hardship required for the sake of its acquisition and maintenance."[69] The price for this petty-bourgeois Czech folly is the struggle to accumulate a sum equal to five times an average annual income, living on an inferior diet, denial of the rest of worldly pleasures, and the anxiety of spending several years on a waiting list. After such austerity, the socialist bliss of owning a car is attained. However, maintenance is often beyond the means of the proud owner, and the automobile becomes a rather immobile status symbol. Social value prevails over economic value in this environment, more reminiscent of Emperor Franz Josef than Stalin Josef.[70]

According to a 1969 opinion survey, Kcs 3,153

was considered a decent monthly income for a family with two children of school age. Data on earnings in 1969 are not available, but in 1966 this level of income was reached by only 2 percent of the population.[71] Dissatisfaction, of course, is a universal human trait. It has been charged that the average Czechoslovak citizen fails to appreciate the value of what he receives as "free income." The expenditures for health services reached Kcs 7.7 billion (5.5 percent of the national budget), Kcs 11 billion (7.5 percent) for education and culture, and Kcs 29 billion (20 percent) for social welfare.[72]

The Czechoslovak system of social welfare proved to be vulnerable to abuses: endemic misuse of sick benefits is a case in point. Under the Novotny regime many loopholes in social legislation and practices were closed. The state retreated further from its original position of magnanimity. For example, after February 1, 1967, treatment not mandatory for health, such as cosmetic surgery, was excluded from insurance coverage. Alcoholism was also excluded.[73]

The Dubcek regime declared improvement of the senior citizens' lot to be one of the country's most urgent issues. In 1968 there was an unprecedented shift in allocation of resources, from the industrial to the social and cultural sphere. Cuts in subsidies for industrial development allowed for almost a doubling of the allocations for social services in the 1969 budget. Steps were also taken to dispose of the crippling policy of egalitarianism in earnings, and the first step was to increase the salaries of employees in health services and education.[74]

The success of these plans will be determined by conditions in both the political and economic system. So far, there is little available information about measures intended to remedy erroneous structural features of the economy, technical obsolescence, managerial incompetence, and low morale at work. Husak, who ascended to leadership in April 1969, has enunciated policies that reject both the reformist experimentation of Dubcek and the permissiveness of the feeble Novotny order. Within a few months the Labor Code was amended, introducing a score of punitive measures against the recalcitrant labor force.

So far, the new leadership appears to have succeeded in establishing the flow of an adequate supply of consumer goods to the market. This improvement, reportedly helped along by massive Soviet aid, has been acknowledged even by observers very critical of the post-invasion regime.[75] The Institute of Public Opinion Research of the Czechoslovak Academy of Sciences reported that 67 percent of respondents in a poll conducted in November 1971 regarded the economic situation as improving, compared with only 37 percent of positive responses in 1970. As for the future, optimism is dominant,[76] as Table 4.4 indicates.

Table 4.4. Future Economic Predictions (in percentages).

Prediction	1969	1970	1971
Improvement	20	54	68
No change	40	23	15
Deterioration	33	11	4

The mass media in the employ of the post-invasion system do not inspire much confidence, in view of their past record. A source which identifies the midnight entry of an uninvited foreign armed force of half a million as "fraternal assistance" is bound to damage its credibility, particularly in the case of messages favorable to the imposed order.

However, it may well be significant that the results of no public opinion surveys touching upon political issues have been published. "Consolidation" in the economic system seems to outweigh expected developments in the political system, irrespective of the 99 percent electoral victory in 1971. This particular feat will be discussed in the next chapter.

5

Policy Making

In a monolithic state the ruling party performs manifold roles which in a pluralistic system are diffused through various structures: associational interest groups, each articulating its own special interests; political parties, each representing an aggregation of reconcilable interests; executive and /or legislative power components engaged in resultant rule making. However, in Czechoslovakia not even the most vigorous form of Stalinism managed to achieve a total monopoly of policy making capable of disregarding forces outside the small circle of rulers. During the Novotny regime, the political system became increasingly vulnerable to such pressures. These ideologically illegitimate inputs contributed to the breakdown in 1968 of whatever was left of the original monolith. Hidden conflicts surfaced, accompanied by differentiation within the ranks of the KSC. Within the mass organizations docility and uniformity of opinion gave way to pluralistic tendencies, converting what had been mere transmission belts into semiautonomous participants in the political process. They also attempted to exert influence on the legislature, as we shall discuss in the closing part of this chapter.

Leaders and Leadership

Producers of totalitarianism are also its products. In Chapter 2 we touched upon the Stalinist subculture and the elites who, insulated from public scrutiny, were in Czechoslovakia justly described as constituting "the conspiracy of the below average."[1] Stalinist rulers, it may be argued, feel ill at ease with the people. The "cult of personality" implies a cult of the inaccessible, of the deified. (In this respect, the populist Khrushchev was further removed from the image of a totalitarian ruler than most of the other Soviet potentates.) The grim idol demands symbolic popularity only; distrustful and contemptuous of the ruled, he finds genuine popularity as suspect and as unnatural as informal behavior in public. Czech Stalinists apparently became aware that they could not impose their standards upon an ironical and intelligent nation. Their mode of communication with society deteriorated, and the issuance of prohibitions became the norm.

Stalinist elites combined cultural primitivism with considerable skills in political survival. Masters of Byzantine intrigue, they were accustomed to duplicity of all sorts and were well versed in the rhetoric of ideological disputation. In situations with no tested precedent, where detached rational judgment was required, they often exhibited the subtlety of a hippopotamus. The practitioner of complex manipulation was frequently ineffectual in matters of ordinary human relations.

The fear of losing the monopoly of political initiative was likely to lead to neurotic reactions among the elite. The closer to the top, the greater the accumulation of uncertainty, unpredictability, and fear. Multiple and not always compatible pressures from a society that was deprived by the monolithic system of its legitimate outlets, were reaching the topmost elite. It has been said that, paradoxically, the most powerful man is the one most fearful for his position and most dubious about his achievement.[2] Not surprisingly, he dramatizes the slightest deviation from his command as a mortal danger to the system.

The first concrete sign in 1968 for the Czechoslovak people that more than just an exchange of a mediocre, distrustful, and dull elite for another was taking place was the personal style of the new leadership. Josef Smrkovsky, instead of sending cartoonist Hadak to jail, sent him a bottle of cognac. Dubcek felt no threat to his authority in making public details of his private life. Insecure and unenlightened despots constantly worry about their authority:

> While Dubcek was not afraid to appear in public in swimming trunks, a despot does not dare, even among his faithful, to take off his iron gloves. Because of the awareness of his own unpopularity, there is no one, in the emptiness surrounding him, to lean on; he is constantly suspicious of everyone; and he finds moments of happiness only in artificially manufacturing enemies, whereby he confirms his suspicions.[3]

The man in the street was not completely immune to romanticism: the veneration of John F. Kennedy was profound in Czechoslovakia. However, the arid years of Stalinism—the years of domination by uninspiring bores—conditioned the society to expect little from its political elites. The basic decency of the noncharismatic, antihero apparatchik Dubcek was sufficient to earn him widespread popularity and gratitude.[4]

This change in style could not obscure the background of this Stalinist-reared generation of political elites. The KSC reformers of 1968 found it difficult to accept the prospect of losing the monopoly on political initiative. They abhorred opposition, or any loss of Party control over the political process. Their rejection of old values without having new values to replace them, made their improvisation in the transitional period often grotesque and embarrassing. Writer Jiri Mucha commented on these developments:

> For thirty years there has been no true governing in the Czech lands: even less was there a chance for political personalities to develop. It does not come as a surprise, therefore, that the government does not know how to deal with the public, that it consistently confuses authority with power and accuses the public for its own failures. It is like a case of a poor violinist complaining about the audience's bad musical taste.[5]

Many KSC reformists appeared to be prisoners of their own *Weltanschauung*, distrustful of compromise and fearful of dissent. Interest articulation along non-traditional channels appeared to them to be motivated by sinister forces, striving for the ultimate destruction of the socialist order. To such a way of thinking, responsiveness was a weakness, caused either by the ebbing strength of the political system or by the growing power of destructive forces. The members of Dubcek's political generation, as Czech student leader Lubos Holecek charged in 1969, "were not capable of ideas of their own; they were political amateurs."[6]

A good example of the wavering and indecision of the reformists in 1968 is the crucial conflict between supporters and adversaries of change over the fate of the old political appointees in the Party apparatus, government, and industry. These bureaucrats were the bastion of conservatism, and interpreted all attacks on their privileges as attacks on the socialist foundation of the state. The failure of the political system to provide for the opportunity to retire gracefully—implications of which will be discussed in Chapter 8—no doubt fortified their resistance. Widespread public demands for the removal of these impediments to democratization failed to convince the reformist leaders. Dubcek did not respond to such pleas as that made by writer Jan Prochazka, himself a member of the KSC Central Committee: "People who systematically erred in the past should not be given the democratic chance to commit new errors. It may be possible to put a corpse into a sitting position . . . but it would be foolish to expect a corpse to reform the alphabet. Sentimentality in personnel policy is the most expensive luxury."[7] By the end of March 1968, about one-third of all local cells of the KSC demanded convocation of the Fourteenth Congress to cope with the cadre issue and remove the Stalinists, especially from the Party apparatus and Central Committee. In a classic maneuver, in which the interests of a few were identified with the interests of society (and which, further, violated Party rules), Dubcek's leadership refused to convene the congress and even attempted to conceal the entire affair.[8] The leadership was fond of its popularity and public support, but it had not abandoned its autocratic temperament.

Behind the disguise of the political elite's uniformity, contrary trends could be detected even before 1968. These trends toward nonconformity were partly attributable to the fact that the members of the Party belonged to different generations. First, there were the prewar members, many of whom joined the movement because of such traumatic experiences as the Great Depression and the Munich Settlement. By 1968, these were senior citizens, at the end of their economic usefulness and numerically a minute fraction (less than 1 percent) of the total Party membership. Second, there was the absolute majority of the membership—the generation of February 1948. Unlike their elders, this middle-aged group was vulnerable to the charge that joining the cause had been motivated by self-interest. Third were the far from numerous very young Communists. As witnesses of the Stalinist system's failures throughout their life, they were the most likely to aid the reformists.

It would be inaccurate to regard only prewar Communists as opposed to democratization and characterized by "envy, hatred, anti-Semitism and primitivism."[9] During the 1960s, the middle-aged generation had penetrated the top power elite in substantial numbers—and later became the backbone of the pro-Soviet restoration in the country (witness the performance of such men as Alois Indra,

Drahomir Kolder, Oldrich Svestka, Vasil Bilak, and Lubomir Strougal).

The closing years of Novotny's rule were characterized by substantial changes, both personal and generational. Some figures may illustrate this. The Twelfth Congress of the KSC (1962) elected 97 members to the Central Committee. Four years later, at the Thirteenth Congress, 65 were reelected and 32 were not. With 45 new faces, the Central Committee had 110 full members. In addition, 56 alternate members were elected, of whom 43 were new. In August 1968, in the wake of invasion, the underground Extraordinary (Fourteenth) Congress convened. This gathering elected 144 members to the Central Committee of whom 119 were newcomers and only 25 were members of the old Central Committee.[10]

This large turnover is further dramatized by the fact that of the 25 reelected members, only 9 held their seats before 1966. In other words, the term of over 90 percent of all Central Committee members was less than two years. Of 28 elected to the Presidium of the Central Committee in 1968, only 2, Dubcek and Cernik, were incumbents. Under Soviet pressure, the results of the Extraordinary (Fourteenth) Congress were invalidated, and successive purges removed the advocates of reformism. The vacancies were filled by second echelon middle-aged apparatchiks of conservative outlook, like their predecessors under Novotny.

In 1966, at the Thirteenth Congress, the elected Central Committee included some better educated individuals, more enlightened and more difficult to manipulate—especially several courageous women.[11] Before 1966 the Central Committee was no place for dissent. According to Jan Piller, a middle-of-the-road member of the Presidium, between 1963 and 1965 he was denied the opportunity to address any plenary sessions of the Central Committee. The floor was reserved for "conflict-free speakers," and the discussion period was always prematurely closed.[12]

Rapid developments in 1968 further polarized the ranks of the Central Committee.[13] Differentiation within the Party occurred also vertically, between the central and provincial, district, and local tiers of the KSC, and horizontally, between the Czech provinces and Slovakia.[14] Prague and Brno were the centers of the reformist movement. Democratization was an urban affair, and a short excursion into the countryside soon revealed the familiar features of the

"God Almighty's high in heaven, Dubcek's too far, and the district secretary's too close. . . ."
(*Rohac*, August 21, 1968)

Stalinist landscape. Local potentates continued to rule their districts with the firm hand of medieval dynasts.[15] It was easier to criticize the President of the Republic than the village mini-Stalin. The latter also proved more durable and more dangerous to the man-in-the-street. Low-level Stalinist functionaries survived the 1968 challenges with the least difficulty.

The notion of plebeian democracy also contributed to political differentiation and affected the responsive capacity of the elite. In any dictatorship, the degree of political participation of the public is relative to the good will of the power elite, i.e., its willingness to take outside voices into consideration. The Czechoslovak leadership listened to the nation as long as it confirmed their judgment—and this happened quite often. Such support served as a kind of psychotherapy for the elite, even though the confirmation of the rightness and the righteousness of their actions came from persons of no greater intellectual capacity than their own. Novotny was more inclined to listen to unsophisticated Party officials in industrial suburbs than to the Academy of Sciences. Endemic amateurism and lack of inhibitions against meddling in tasks beyond one's qualification added a peculiar twist to the Czech plebeian democratism: debates between equally unqualified partners who preferred quasi-plebiscitary assent to a solid scientific analysis.

This plebeianism had an impact on the functioning of the entire political system. Ludvik Vaculik, author of the "2,000 Words Manifesto," touched upon this when he wrote: "The ministries were usually afraid of the districts. . . . In this state of ours it was the districts which ruled, and therefore the politics of the central government, too, had the sophistication and intelligence of the districts."[16]

A practice has also developed whereby individual citizens, if not encouraged, are at least not discouraged from approaching various political authorities directly with their demands. This is not interest articulation in its generally accepted meaning; rather it is most often an attempt to obtain favors in predominantly personal matters. The citizenry increasingly fail to consider final and binding an unfavorable ruling by any state organ. For many years the central authorities have been inundated with requests of this nature.[17] This is surprising in a country lacking the tradition of a *Batushka* Tsar, the ultimate just arbiter. Hundreds of thousands of complaints and requests reached Prague, in particular the Office of the President of the Republic. The practice of approaching the president directly became popular at the time of Zapotocky and continued under the less accessible and certainly less popular Novotny. Others frequently approached were the KSC Central Committee, district secretariats, and law enforcement agencies—the police, prosecutors, the courts, organs of state control, and the like.

Even in the peak period of Stalinism, common human frailties, such as petty animosity or bidding for popularity, eventually affected the conduct of political elites. The case of Vaclav Talich provides an example.[18] This famous orchestra conductor had been accused of collaboration with the Nazis, and further suffered because of a personal vendetta by Zdenek Nejedly, a music scholar and Minister of Education. However, because of Talich's great prestige in artistic circles, Vaclav Kopecky, Minister of Propaganda, managed to restore the conductor's honor and nominate him as a National Artist.

It would be perhaps useful to comment on the citizen's relation to his lawmaker. We shall not delve into oddities such as the absence of the secret ballot for the voter and the exercise of the secret ballot by his representative in Parliament. What interests us here is the heterogeneity of styles and responses by the deputies to their constituents. Data published in 1968 amply document this unintentional deviation from totalitarian uniformity. Contributing factors were a deputy's political weight, engagement in other roles, the degree of his aloofness, his vanity, and the nature of the demands. For example, a report in *Rude pravo* on the activities of Deputy Ondrej Sulety, member of a puppet Slovak party, is a pathetic account of rustic peregrinations and missionary fervor.[19] By contrast, Jiri Hendrych, second to Novotny in power and deputy for Southern Bohemia, did not visit his constituency for an entire year and did not bother even to acknowledge letters from his voter.[20]

Another member of the National Assembly, Jan Sejna—beneficiary of Stalinism, "political general" in the army, pro-Novotny plotter and ultimately, defector to the United States—conceived of his duty to his constituents in a way that at least added color to Czech totalitarian values:

The voters liked him, they often turned to him for help, and he was always taking care of something. But he would never do it the legal way or through proper use of his parliamentary mandate, but exclusively through his acquaintances, nepotistic ties, and a complicated exchange of favors. If, let us say, a village voter would ask him for help in the matter of allocation of cement, it would never occur to Sejna to think of a lawful way. Instead,

quite naturally, he would start to search for information about where and how one could get cement on the black market. Then he would send to the supplier a bottle of cognac from the supplies of the Ministry of National Defence, and order the stolen cement delivered in the Tatra limousine to the voter in question.[21]

The eventful year of 1968 provided a rare test of the representative system. In several areas, voters took the constitution seriously and decided to recall their deputy. According to the constitution, a petition for recall signed by at least one-third of the registered voters in a given constituency would require an election within one month after formal filing of the petition. Such steps were taken both before the Soviet invasion (against M. Pastyrik, the former trade union head) and after (against D. Kolder, a Central Committee apparatchik). However, both deputies, as befitted their concept of a political role, refused to surrender their seats, and this became the final decision.[22]

A deputy's only legitimate loyalty is to the KSC, not to his constituents. Accordingly, Deputy Marie Mikova was stripped of her mandate because she took the parliamentary oath seriously.[23] In late 1969, legislative amendments calling for expulsion of numerous deputies and cooption of new Party nominees further degraded this representative system. The only form of dissent left to the deputies was physical absence from Parliament. The call for totalitarian restoration was aptly expressed by Deputy Bozena Machacova in the 1969 Federal Assembly: "Never again must the parliament be allowed to degenerate into a political arena. . . ."[24]

Interest Articulation and Interest Groups

Decision makers occupy themselves with considerations of the consequences of their rejection of or compliance with particular demands. The interests of Stalinist rulers and the ruled are likely to be in fundamental conflict, and nonresponsiveness to demands is among the preconditions of the perpetuation of such a political system. To a Stalinist mind, particularly one sensitive about the leading role of the Party, compliance with outside initiative would appear as a surrender, a confession of weakness. However, in Czechoslovakia the abyss separating decision makers from the populace was crossed by a suspension bridge, on which heavy traffic of demands of a personal nature took place. License to petition

Deputy Kolder responding to his hostile constituency: "What kind of democracy is this when there are so many of you against me."
(*Dikobraz*, October 1, 1968)

the leadership contributed to an illusion of accessibility.

The fall of the Novotny regime, and the consequent widespread though not complete emancipation from fear, introduced a measure of frankness into the political sphere. Progressives referred to this development as "healthy participation"; the Sta-linists condemned it as "moral terror." A national debate took place on all levels. In September 1968 the KSC conducted a survey among its members in Northern Moravia. The pollsters asked, "As a member of the Party, have you been attacked during the past month because of the Party's policies? Among the respondents 7.8 percent had been attacked once, 21 percent more than once, but the remaining majority had been left alone. The most frequent targets of attack were Communists of pre-1947 standing, followed by those who joined the Party in 1948.[25]

Such spontaneous political acts as riots, demonstrations or assassinations have been very rare in Czechoslovakia's history and quite alien to the political temperament of the people. Realization of the counterproductive consequences of such measures has also helped to deter acts of violence. Perhaps only one event between 1948 and 1968, the Plzen revolt of June 1953, may be considered a serious disturbance. This industrial city erupted into violence in reaction to a monetary reform, and immobilized the power of the State. Out-of-town forces restored order, and repressive measures followed.[26]

Spontaneous actions during the 1960s were confined almost solely to Prague youth, who resorted with traditional regularity to antiestablishment protests on May Day, following the annual government sponsored parade. The most serious incident of this type was the so-called Strahov incident (named after an area in Prague). A peaceful student demonstration in the fall of 1967 protesting deplorable living conditions in dormitories was brutally suppressed, but rather than being counterproductive, the protest accelerated the downfall of Novotny.

In August 1968 the entire nation faced the occupying forces as a homogeneous entity, exhibiting a solidarity that was later described by the Stalinists as "false unity." An extraordinary state of affairs generated extraordinary actions, exemplified by the self-immolation of student Jan Palach in January 1969. Two months later, elation over an ice hockey victory over the Soviet Union precipitated a public demonstration of anti-Soviet sentiment, which was repeated in August 1969, on the first anniversary of the invasion. These two events were counterproductive in that they served as a pretext for further purges and repressive measures.

As a rule, the Czechoslovak leaders, though not always heedful of the public's interests, did not consider articulation of interests by an individual citizen as a danger to the political order. Isolated persons were not viewed as potentially dangerous as was any organization other than the ruling Party. If an organization exhibited any sign of an effort toward achieving autonomy, the price was extinction. The system of "transmission belts" developed. During the

protraction of Stalinism in the 1960s, squeaks, friction, loose nuts, and occasional breakdowns plagued this transmission mechanism.

In a totalitarian system the mass organizations are characterized by docility and uniformity. In Chapter 1 we referred to three types of participation: manipulated, nonparticipative, and independent. Corrolaries to these categories, listed in the descending order of political acceptability, may also be identified: (1) the ideal of totalitarian unity, (2) differentiation and autonomy, and (3) authentic unity, which was briefly and defiantly realized in 1968.

The history of the Czechoslovak Youth Organization (CSM) illustrates the point. This organization, uniform for all youth, and mandatory for students, had existed for two decades. Despite demands for differentiation and decentralization, the KSC remained adamant. As late as 1967, Novotny decided to preserve the uniform structure, disregarding all evidence of increasing ineffectiveness of the CSM.[27] In 1968 the totalitarian ideal of manipulated unity was rejected and the CSM was dissolved. Instead, eighteen autonomous organizations reflecting age, vocation and special interests were formed. Nevertheless, all of these groups joined together after the Soviet invasion in an expression of nonmanipulated unity.[28] This defiance brought the younger generation on a collision course with Stalinist forces. In order to avert the danger of authentic unity, the Party decided to support the lesser evil of differentiation. Although as late as 1967 this had been regarded as a mortal sin, it was adopted as a desirable short-term tactic that would lead ultimately to the restoration of totalitarian unity. The Party then called for the establishment of a new organization, the Leninist Youth Union, to be the nucleus of a future unified youth organization. Subsequently, this tiny Leninist group of pro-Soviet sympathizers was absorbed by the Socialist Union of Youth, a newly formed mass organization. The emergence of a new unity was hailed, while previous attempts at differentiation and autonomy were condemned:

The act of discrediting and destroying the unified youth organization after January 1968 was a crime against young people and also an attempt to divert the youth from socialist perspectives. . . . After a pause of almost two years, a unified organization has once again been created—the

Socialist Union of Youth [SSM]. It has inherited the lesson learned from past mistakes but, above all, it has the opportunity to restore the correct ideological, political, and organizational principles of the [defunct] Czechoslovak Union of Youth.[29]

By early 1972, of a total of some six million Czechoslovaks between the ages of six and thirty, 600,000 had joined the SSM and 750,000 of those under fifteen had joined the Pioneer Organization (PO).[30] As in the defunct CSM, the membership of the SSM consists predominantly of high school students eager to secure admission to universities.

In the same period, several other mass organizations traversed a similar circular route, which led from manipulated unity and participation through differentiation and semiautonomy right back to the starting point—manipulated participation and enforced unity.

The emphasis on the leading role of the Party and its monopoly of initiative relegated other forces to the role of supporting actors. Organizations that would have been referred to in a pluralistic system as associational interest groups were known as "voluntary mass organizations," and became instruments for socialization and control of the non-Communist majority. Gradually, however, the adjective *zajmovy*, or "interest," did lose its satanic connotation and was reluctantly reintroduced into the political vocabulary. On the other hand, the expression *natlakova skupina*, or "pressure group," remains synonymous with the subversion of socialism.

In the Novotny era the Party distinguished between obedience and passivity. Mass organizations were quite frequently requested to comment on proposed legislation. The Party also solicited the judgment of scientific institutions on pending policy measures.[31] However, there was neither an obligation nor the inclination to follow such advice.

Of all the transmission belts, the trade unions came closest to articulating special interests. In the early years of the People's Democracy the regime entertained the notion of the withering away of the state and the transfer of its functions to nongovernmental organizations. Accordingly, the trade unions were entrusted with co-administering social welfare, a right that was poorly utilized, as this trade unionist self-criticism reveals: "The trade unions were the initiators of social laws. But their deputies in the National Assembly acquiesced to all the objections raised against such bills by the government and other state organs. They were quite willing to listen to state bureaucrats and ministers while turning a deaf ear to factory workers."[32] Leadership of the trade unions included some of the most notorious Stalinists in the country. They put great effort into preventing differentiation in the labor movement; the interests of physicians and garbage collectors were expected to be identical.

The professional organizations that did exist existed only in name. The Union of Czechoslovak Lawyers (JCSP) is a case in point. Its function did not extend beyond the preparation of public relations handouts for the political system, addressed to capitalist countries. Dissatisfaction among the rank and file was unlikely for the excellent reason that the JCSP, which was classified as a "voluntary selective organization," appeared to have no membership whatsoever although it had a full complement of officers. In the late 1960s the JCSP tired of its pseudo-existence and declared its determination to become a true professional organization open to all law school graduates, regardless of their actual occupation. The new program of the JCSP was concerned with the fight for economic, political, and social improvement for the legal profession and included demands for substantive changes in the legal system.[33] As in other professional organizations, these developments were short-lived. In February 1970 the JCSP called a special conference, at which its reform programs and demands were completely repudiated and the leading role of the Party declared inviolable.[34]

The medical profession was subject to the same frustrations. For several reasons—in particular, because of the Iron Concept of socialism and the timidity of unfrocked priest Josef Plojhar, the Minister of Health for twenty years—the health services personnel received little socialist attention: trade union effort on behalf of physicians was nil. In 1968 the autonomous Union of Czech Physicians was founded for the purpose of defending and furthering the interests of the 23,000 physicians in the Czech provinces.[35] The union also addressed itself to general sociopolitical issues, exemplified by their demand for the abolition of capital punishment. In February 1970, the Ministry of the Interior outlawed the union.

During the brief period of reform following

Novotny's fall, some established associational interest groups gained in stature. For instance, the all but dormant Czechoslovak Scientific and Technological Society became a member of the National Front and a consultant for the government on matters affecting the material and social interests of the intelligentsia in technical fields.[36] The Society of Human Rights, established under Dubcek (and banned by Husak in 1969), is an example of an interest group which, despite its marginal political recognition and the stigma of fostering "bourgeois class appeasement," exhibited surprising political agility. The organization attempted to influence legislative action and even submitted its own recommendation on the proposed law for rehabilitation of victims of Stalinism, and in an effort which can be described as a classic case of lobbying, managed to have the Minister of Education order the inclusion of the United Nations' Declaration of Universal Human Rights in the school curriculum.[37]

The confusion over what constituted legitimate expressions of special interests is evident in a 1968 interview with Bohumil Simon, head of the municipal Communist Party organization in Prague.[38] His rejection of "pressure politics" and acceptance of "interest pressure," without explaining the difference between the two, is symptomatic of the reformers' lack of terminological and conceptual clarity in these untested matters. The interview centered on the housing shortage in the capital, the city's obsolete communication system, and the need for priority funding from state coffers.

Q. Isn't a demand for these funds considered an expression of so-called pressure politics?

A. To articulate reasonable demands and to forward substantiated proposals to higher organs for the solution of problems which are beyond the power of the city, district, or province, cannot, I hope, be considered an expression of pressure politics. . . . The appropriate Russian word is *nazhimat*, and it is likely to be most often used in this context.

Q. Was this something you learned during your recent stay in Moscow?

A. Yes. It seems the Moscow Party organization [exerts] *nazhimat* on central agencies frequently and effectively. This can be confirmed by—among other things—two facts. In the capital of the USSR no solid fuels

are used any more (only gas, oil, and electricity)—and herein is the secret of Moscow's clean air—and housing construction is four to five times greater than in Prague.

Q. Thus, we, too, will *nazhimat* more strongly . . . . But to understand each other properly: Do you or do you not exclude the existence of interest pressure from below, represented by individual interest groups?

A. I do not exclude the existence of such interest pressure; on the contrary, I consider it an inseparable part of politics.

The centrifugal trend toward differentiation and autonomy was marked by ideological uneasiness among the reformers, amateurishness among spokesmen for emerging special interest groups, and by considerable disparity in their activism. In contrast to the energetic action of some of the professions, that of other groups, notably the peasantry, was timid and hesitant.

The most important intellectual force in the early post-invasion period—and second only to the trade unions in their effort to avert conservative restoration—was the mobilization of what is stiltedly referred to as the "creative intelligentsia." Associations of writers, composers, architects, television and movie artists, and the like formed a Coordination Committee—an institutional form of what has been called the "Elite of Influence." However, the reimposition of censorship in 1969 severed their channels of communication with the rest of the nation. Artistic associations in the Czech provinces, unlike their counterparts is Slovakia, persevered in their defiance, forcing the new Party leadership to employ a different strategy in dealing with them. In the words of Miloslav Bruzek, Czech Minister of Culture: "The goal in the Czech provinces is to gradually widen the circle of those who are prepared to commit themselves to this aim [i.e., docility] while in Slovakia the goal is to get rid of those in the artists' associations who, by their opinions and attitudes, hinder the accomplishment of ideological political tasks."[39]

By early 1971 the unions of composers, graphic and plastic artists, architects, theatrical artists, film artists, and writers were all outlawed.[40] Of these, the Writers Union had been the most prestigious and had had the greatest impact on policy making. Accordingly, post-invasion criticism of the writers was very hostile: "The Union not only succeeded in having some secretaries and heads of departments of the Party's Central Committee recalled but even nominated its own candidates to fill the vacancies. The Union's local KSC cell generated public pressure for an immediate recall of the highest state officials."[41] The writers also appeared the least willing to recant and endorse the new regime (in exchange for the amenities that the establishmentarian artistic elite are usually accorded). The essence of the conflict was succinctly expressed by Jaroslav Seifert, chairman of the Writers Union, in a talk with Party chief Husak: "You want us to support your policies because you know that we enjoy moral authority in the nation. But should we support you, we would lose this authority and in such a case we would be of no use to you."[42]

A strange vacuum has developed, surpassing even that of World War II. Unlike the period of Nazi occupation, the early seventies have been characterized by a ban on all literary journals, by the disappearance from the market of books by the majority of contemporary Czechoslovak authors, and by oppressive measures affecting their private lives. At the same time, a protracted effort has been made to establish a new organization of writers, one that would pledge loyalty to the regime. The results so far have been embarrassingly meager. A handful of fifth-rate scribes make up the new Writers Union, and conciliatory gestures of the KSC addressed to the silent majority of writers have so far met with little success.[43]

A severe lack of information prevents full examination of interest groups based on kinship or local and ethnic ties. They are not even granted the right to articulate their identity. Spokesmen for such causes face suspicion of "local patriotism" or, more ominously, "bourgeois nationalism."

One such movement emerged in 1968 as an organized associational interest group. As mentioned earlier, the Slovaks demanded federalization of the country and the Czechs unenthusiastically consented to comply. However, the inhabitants of Moravia —one of the two "historical provinces," or "Czech lands", the other being Bohemia—opened a drive for tripartite federation.[44] The movement reflected the energetic spirit of Moravian patriotism and was by no means an impractical romantic venture. Some 100,000 copies of the draft of the plans for tripartite federation were published. Demands included a plebiscite to decide the organizational

structure of the state, official recognition of Moravian tradition, and the resignation of high Czech officials unfriendly to the cause. However, the movement succumbed to the more mundane pressures of post-invasion existence.

Some data are available about institutional interest groups, and these will be discussed in the next chapter in connection with the outlook and behavior of industrial managers.[45]

A strong esprit d'corps is evident among the first wave of proletarians who took over roles in the state apparatus (such as the judiciary) shortly after February 1948 and have held these positions ever since. They constitute a homogeneous conservative force, and were prominent among those who attempted to block the reforms of 1968.

Some of the most notorious institutional symbols of Stalinism, such as the Workers' Militia and above all the Secret Police (STB), have developed cohesiveness and their own institutional personality. In 1968, attacks upon the STB—denounced in the reformist press as "the largest illegal organization in the history of Czechoslovakia"[46]—put the secret police on the defensive. Though such attacks demoralized them, social ostracism and the fear of retribution for past crimes solidified their ranks. Thus, unlike the early 1950s, when one group of STB thugs was prepared to liquidate another, the late 1960s found the organization turned into a kind of mutual protection society. A belief that its very existence as an institution was in danger led the STB to arrange for quiet dismissals of its more compromised members, providing them with sinecures either as pensioned invalids, as nominal employees of research institutes, or better still, as instant diplomats who could be dispatched abroad. The 1968 invasion averted the threat to the existence of the organization, but, given the conspiratorial nature of its work and the degree of public hostility toward it, the cohesiveness of this institutional interest group is likely to continue.

Interest Aggregation

The function of converting demands (from whatever sources) into policy alternatives is called interest aggregation. In a Communist system, the formulation of general policy alternatives is limited to the central group of Party leaders. In Czechoslovakia the 1960 constitution gave legal sanction to this practice, denounced in 1968 as "Novotny's system of personal power." The growing scope of government responsibility after 1948 generated an increase in the bureaucracy; it also led to a reduction in the number of actual participants in decision making. By the end of the Novotny regime about one dozen comrades—the Orlik Dynasty—constituted this power elite.

In a noncompetitive political system, the Party aggregates interests in a manner similar to that of large bureaucracy. Consequently, the Party apparatus gains both in size and authority. A rare insight into these sacrosanct matters was provided by the *Reporter* in 1968 in an interview with Miroslav Mamula, Novotny's protégé and head of the Eighth Department of the Secretariat of the Central Committee.[47] This apparatchik was in charge of what was innocuously labeled the Department of State Administration. In 1960 this structure was solely concerned with defense and security; in 1961 supervision of the courts and the prosecutors came under its jurisdiction; in 1963 the Workers' Militia was added.

Not surprisingly, Mamula complained about the difficulty of managing and coordinating such a vast machine. An ineffective instrument of rule was bound to be an ineffective instrument of oppression. Typical was this comment about the overloaded totalitarian machinery:

> In the final run, the growing apparatus even failed to serve its own goals of power because of its lack of effectiveness and purpose. The social engine malfunctioned, but neither did the Party apparatus function properly. Perhaps this was also due to specific conditions and national uniqueness. I can imagine Orwell's 1984, the year of total manipulation of the people and history by the central power of Big Brother, but I cannot imagine this happening in Czechoslovakia.[48]

The overburdened elite was unresponsive and inefficient. The style of policy formation, whether in trivial or substantial matters, was subjective. Both the *Weltanchauung* and political centralism tended to magnify the importance of any issue: to the ideological mind anything may become a matter of principle. Often, however, under the camouflage of esoteric language, substantial realistic bargaining took place. Czech Premier Stanislav Razl conceded this, advising the managers of the national economy to change their tactics. "Let us realize that with the

gradual implementation of economic reform we will no longer be able to conduct battles for wages and the development of our plants at the level of the ministries. . . ."[49]

One novelty of the 1960s was the professionalization and increased sophistication within the decision making structures. The beginning of this trend can be traced to the last years of the Novotny regime. Sociology and psychology were "rehabilitated" as respectable and acceptable disciplines. For example, a thorough analysis of the lives of railroad employees was undertaken in 1966.[50] One million bits of information on a quarter of a million punched cards were assembled in order to combat the lax morale of this part of the labor force. Considering the long-term ban on sociology and the imposed isolation of Czechoslovak sociologists from their foreign colleagues, the techniques employed in this study showed a surprising degree of sophistication.

The usefulness of social sciences has mainly been advocated by the reformists, who have become increasingly reluctant to give any credence to analyses not supported by solid background data. A Slovak youth organization, for example, rather impudently admonished the Party to commission thorough research on the problems of young people before passing any definite judgment in the matter.[51]

This new concern generated appropriate differentiation within the Party apparatus. In 1968 an autonomous department was established in the Secretariat of the Central Committee and in February 1969 was renamed the Unit of Political-Professional Services (UPOS). Its position in the Secretariat was unique in that it had no authority to direct the executive or controlling organs of the Party, horizontally or vertically. It was described as a "solely professional, centralized service in the fields of analyzing and synthetizing information, computer programming, sociology, psychology, rational utilization of work for Party organs, intelligence, and editorial activities."[52] In order to secure maximum objectivity in its services, the UPOS was given a quasi-independent status, insulated from interference from other Central Committee agencies.

The UPOS contains three branches. The most important, which is concerned with interest aggregation and policy formation in general, is the Institute of Political Analysis and Synthesis. This agency gathers data from KSC and non-Party sources, both individuals and organizations, analyzes a variety of proposals, complaints, and resolutions, and on the basis of its analyses attempts to predict and anticipate short- and long-term trends in political development. Alternative courses are presented to the decision making Politburo.

According to Jan Kaspar, head of UPOS, the temporary emancipation of economic and social structures from Party tutelage in 1968 enabled the KSC to concentrate on restructuring its apparatus. This required the development of a highly qualified servicing center for the elected bodies of the Party. The task of the UPOS was to establish a network of data banks. Kaspar realized that "with the growing information explosion we are increasingly witnessing the fact that the capacity of every system working with information decreases in relation to the total volume of information." Traditional methods of work had to be discarded, and the work of UPOS became increasingly computerized: the analysis of district KSC conferences alone yielded 2.5 million bits of information. Kaspar pointed out the significance of his office to interest aggregation and policy making in that every decision of a higher Party body required prior information on the relevant political relations and variants of solution, to serve as alternatives for the decision making, justification of the choice of the given alternative, and, finally, the anticipated positive and negative aspects of the chosen variant.

The second branch of the UPOS is the Inter-Party Intelligence Service, which handles the estimated 10 percent of all the data that is restricted for the use of the inner circle of the apparatchiks. Presumably, data on the popularity and prestige of individual functionaries would fall under this category. The third branch is the Scientific and Technical Service, engaged in work on organizational models of Party structures.

From the standpoint of the average citizen, this trend toward differentiation and sophistication in the decision making process is regrettable. It does not guarantee increased responsiveness but does have the potential for increased effectiveness of repressive and controlling measures, which were almost absent during the idylic impotence of the later years of Novotny's regime.[53]

Rule Making

According to Marxism-Leninism, at least in its tested Stalinist variety, the state is the organ of violence of the ruling class. In such an understanding, objectivity of laws is rejected as an impossible, hypocritical notion.

Accordingly, the legal system in Czechoslovakia underwent numerous changes, resulting in deterioration of the clarity, binding force, and jurisdictional boundaries of the rules. With the impatience of a revolutionary and the carelessness of an amateur, the ruling Party established a set of rules abounding with exceptions and escape clauses. The constitution, instead of being a framework of fundamental rules, became a device for deception and rationalization. This verbose document, which explicitly decrees that the Communist Party is the ruling force in the country, and enshrines Marxism-Leninism as the only form of orthodoxy, is very vague about civil rights. In any event, even the imperfect constitutional guarantees were negated by political practice. Thus, Catholicism was not outlawed but Catholics were persecuted if they insisted on exercising their constitutional right of "freedom of conscience."

If the shift from traditional to constitutional restraints on political action is considered one of the most important turning points in the development of political systems, then the transformation of the pluralistic society of prewar Czechoslovakia into a totalitarian one must be considered a great leap backward. In this instance, as in several others, totalitarianism represents a force reversing the process of secularization. Improvisation and substitution have been among the outstanding qualities of the system. A plumber substitutes for a lawyer and a lawyer takes the role of a plumber. In internal Party processes, a miner is appointed to represent the local organization of writers; a writer becomes the delegate of the miners' Party cell.

An overlapping of functions leads to their fusion, and confusion. In the early 1950s, Gottwald, when asked where the state's principal authority for rule making resided, answered that it was neither in the Powder Gate (KSC headquarters) nor in the Straka Palace (the premier's office) but in Hradcany Castle (the residence of kings and presidents, Gottwald included).[54] After Gottwald's death in 1953, and the official denunciation of the cult of personality, the center of decision making gravitated toward the Powder Gate. Jurisdictional boundaries were once again blurred in 1957 when Novotny, First Secretary of the Party, also became the President. A decade later, in 1968, the two offices were separated: the

Party (and through it the First Secretary) was vested with the principal political power and the President retained little more than the splendor of representing that power in public.

An abundance of rule makers and the absence of constitutional restraints contributed to a high output of rules. After the number of rules reached what was considered an intolerable level, periodic summary repeal was called for. For example, after a house cleaning at the end of 1965, of some 4,500 economic regulations only about 150 were left, and some 1,200 administrative decrees were reduced to 135.[55] (The ensuing legal uncertainty is discussed in Chapter 7.)

A peak production of rules was not evidence of a flexible, rational system; rather it was indicative of fumbling, impatient, doctrinaire amateurs. Their rules were as plentiful as they were short-lived and little respected. In 1968 a serious attempt was made to introduce some order into the rule making process. Changes affecting the legislative structure were symptomatic of the entire climate of the posttotalitarian transformation. The remainder of this chapter will be devoted to this theme.

At the beginning of 1968 the National Assembly was a prominent symbol of the deposed order. Shielded by parliamentary immunity, the legislature remained a Stalinist preserve. Bohumir Lomsky, to mention one of many, lost his role as Minister of Defense and resigned his seat on the Central Committee of the KSC, but he continued to hold the position of an unassailable member of parliament. This was also the destiny of many prominent personalities of the Novotny regime—except for Novotny himself—such as Jiri Hendrych, Bohuslav Lastovicka, Jaromir Dolansky, Otakar Simunek, Zdenek Fierlinger, Alois Neuman, and Josef Plojhar. The National Assembly of 300 deputies elected in 1964 became a Stalinist white elephant in the pre-invasion period of 1968.

Josef Smrkovsky, one of the most prominent Communist reformers, became Speaker of the Assembly. This body, after two decades of mortifying unanimity in all matters before it, began to experience the polarization which was already underway in the Party and society at large. The public and the mass media began to pay attention to what had been prematurely written off as a worthless relic. Whether on account of conscience, conviction, expiation, strategic calculation, political self-realization, or simply as a bid for popularity, tranquility vanished from under the parliamentary roof. What

had been a political cemetery was turned into a battleground of opposed forces, whose polarization had little to do with allegiance to the KSC. Thus, Communist deputy Vilem Novy, an exponent of the most primitive kind of Stalinism, would cross swords with Communist deputy Gertruda Cakrtova-Sekaninova, a proponent of liberalization. The puppet party deputies, too, took this opportunity to shed the stigma of servility. Among the most energetic was Jan Subrt, a deputy from the Czech Socialist Party. Together with the Communist Cakrtova-Sekaninova, he sponsored (but failed to have passed) a bill on legal prosecution of persons guilty of Stalinist terror in past years. Subrt also openly endorsed the "2,000-Word Manifesto," a document branded by General Samuel Kodaj, a fellow lawmaker, as a call for a counterrevolutionary uprising.[56] The same deputies who unanimously adopted a new censorship law in 1967 rescinded the act in 1968 by a vote of 184 to 30, with 17 abstentions (of a total membership of 300).[57]

In view of such changes, many deputies were accused of hypocrisy and schizophrenia. However, after August 1968, even the most vociferous critics of the Assembly referred to it with a respect that was tinged with disbelief. During the occupation of Prague the Parliament went into uninterrupted session in a gesture of patriotic defiance.[58] Female deputies, some with an impeccable record of pro-Soviet conformism, and army generals, no doubt humiliated by the surprise of the fraternal invasion, were particularly noticeable for the change in their stand.

Of course, this defiance was short-lived. Nevertheless, a rather permanent structural change affecting rule making was introduced. On January 1, 1969, the Czechoslovak Socialist Republic (CSSR) became a federation of two states, the Czech Socialist Republic (CSR) and the Slovak Socialist Republic (SSR). Accordingly, the legislative structure was changed into a bicameral Federal Assembly. The old National Assembly was retained on the federal level as the Chamber of the People, but a Chamber of Nations was added, in which the Czechs and the less numerous Slovaks would be equally represented. A unicameral legislature was to be formed in both the CSR and SSR.

The way these supposedly representative new bodies came into being was regrettable. The old National Assembly, its mandate long expired, selected the members of the Czech National Council (CNR). The CNR and its Slovak counterpart (the SNR, in existence since 1945) reciprocated by selecting the second federal chamber, the Chamber of Nations, exclusively from their own ranks. Petr Pithart, a young political scientist and member of Dubcek's brain trust, compared this method of selection to an incestuous marriage: "We watch and comment disrespectfully, and therefore we have to be prepared for a couple of slaps because one ought not to peep into the bedroom. Thus we are left only with a platonic worry about the quality of the descendants. Children from incestuous marriages are not likely to be among the most illustrious."[59]

Otto Wichterle, academician and member of the CNR, frankly admitted in an interview that except for the Stalinist leftovers from the former National Assembly, the deputies in all the chambers were fully aware of the absurdity of the situation.

> "Pre-January" or "post-January" [January 1968, when Dubcek replaced Novotny], none of us is a regular deputy.... The only correct procedure is to recall all deputies and call for a new election. Honestly speaking, I do not know whom I am supposed to represent. I was recommended by the National Front. But to tell the truth they did not tell me where I should look for my eventual constituents—whether in Dejvice [a Prague suburban district] where I live, in scientific circles, or among the non-Communist constituents. Apparently, I have a choice.[60]

The late 1960s had more than their share of irregularities. For example, Slovaks in the old National Assembly participated in the selection of the CNR, the exclusively Czech body. Three different types of electoral districts were set up. Further confusion was avoided quite neatly—by constitutional amendments postponing all elections.[61]

An interesting though short-lived by-product of this incestuous procreation is worth mentioning. Although events of the spring of 1968 led to differentiation within the old National Assembly, federalization caused differentiation between the new legislative bodies. The complicated genealogy that began when the old assembly begot the state legislatures, which in turn begot the second federal chamber, contributed to this differentiation. The conservative nature of the Chamber of the People contrasted with the relatively progressive stance of its offspring, the Chamber of the Nations. The confirmation of Dubcek as Speaker of the Federal

Assembly—after his political defeat and removal as First Secretary of the KSC—demonstrates this difference. In the Chamber of the People the vote for confirmation was 184 to 61, with one abstention, whereas in the Chamber of Nations the vote was 122 to 7, with one abstention.[62] The difference in political conservatism is expressed in the negative vote.

The Czech National Council began by pursuing a consistently liberal course. Of a total of 150 members, only 85 were members of the Communist Party whereas the rest were affiliated with the minor parties or had no party identification.[63] The CNR demonstrated a parliamentary vitality that would have been inconceivable under the more sedate conditions of one-party rule. To give just two examples, an important bill concerning acquisition and loss of citizenship was defeated on the floor, and the CNR, with great emphasis on civil rights, established a special committee to probe into the activities of the judicial and police structures.[64]

Perhaps the most illustrious expression of legislative independence was the clash between Czech legislators and Minister of the Interior Josef Groesser, regarding his alleged Stalinist sympathies. Groesser was summoned to answer sharp questions and the inquiry resulted in a mild censure, publicized throughout the nation. Deputy Wichterle, when asked about this affair, responded on behalf of the CNR: "There is nothing worse than when the people are afraid of the Minister of the Interior."[65]

Federalization, which led to pluralization of structures, also increased the likelihood of discord in the decision making process. Thus, different drafts of an important bill concerning the status of socialist enterprises were produced by the CNR and the federal assemblies.

By the advent of the 1970s the danger of diversity had been averted. About one-third of all deputies were summarily dismissed and replaced by tested conformists. The constitutional deadline for holding elections for legislative bodies expired in June 1968 and was extended twice, until the end of 1971. "Normalization" also required the abolishment of the 1967 electoral law—which had reflected a cautious democratization effort with respect to the selection of candidates—before it was ever tested. The new 1971 law revived the standard Stalinist technique whereby candidates are chosen by the Party.

The results of the November 1971 election were thus not a surprise. Some 190,000 *agitacni dvojice* (teams of two engaged in door-to-door canvassing)

reportedly reached each household in the country at least twice. All but 0.55 percent of registered voters fulfilled their electoral duty. Of all votes cast, the single slate of National Front candidates received between 99.77 percent (in the election of deputies for district committees) and 99.94 percent (in elections for the Slovak National Council).[66]

Of the 700 deputies to the Federal Assembly, 614 are newcomers. Of 86 recognizable names, 56 are conservative holdovers from the Novotny era, and 30 are considered to be opportunists who are willing to adjust to any regime.[67] Imposed unanimity in the legislative process is once again the practice, despite formal differentiation of the rule making structure.

6

To govern well means to govern less.

Stanislav Razl, Czechoslovak Life, *March 1969.*

Rule Application

In view of two decades of centralization, bureaucratization, and attempts at total control of the citizens, the words of Czech Premier Razl sound strange indeed—more reminiscent of the country of Barry Goldwater than that of Klement Gottwald. But strange or not, this dictum, based on the failure of totalitarianism in Czechoslovakia, was never put into practice.

At the close of the 1960s, Czechoslovakia was a country with policies that turned the docile conformist into a daring socialist innovator, a heretic, and, ultimately, a victim of a punitive military expedition. Volatile policies generated a high turnover in personnel. For example, within less than a year, Razl was twice succeeded in office.

The whirlwind of events is perhaps best illustrated by the revolving door that led to (and from) federal offices. Replacing Jozef Lenart, Oldrich Cernik headed the government from March 1968 until January 1970, when he was replaced by Lubomir Strougal. Cernik appeared four times within a year before the parliament with a new cabinet and new program: in April 1968 it was antitotalitarianism, in September 1968 a state of limited sovereignty, in January 1969 federation, and in September 1969 a purge of the reformists and their ideas. Finally, in January 1970, Cernik succumbed to a purge.

Under the impact of both policy and personnel changes the stability of institutions was bound to suffer. Under neither Gottwald nor Novotny had this stability been spectacular. Endless restructuring of political and economic institutions was taking place—now reducing, now increasing their numbers, redrawing jurisdictions in accordance with the latest swing of the Soviet pendulum from centralization to decentralization and back again. A full account of all ministries and other central offices created, reorganized, and abolished eludes the capacity of ordinary mortals. It is certain, however, that the move toward federalization in 1969 involved the creation of more ministerial offices and cabinet seats than ever before. A country of some 14 million inhabitants acquired 68 cabinet members—28 in the federal, 21 in the Czech, and 19 in the Slovak government. According to the calculations of the youth daily *Mlada fronta*, this meant one minister for every 1,881 square kilometers of land, or 4.53 ministers for each million citizens.[1]

Federalization ended the nationwide pattern of local administration by People's Committees (*Narodni vybory*), the equivalent of Soviets in the USSR. Prior to 1969 the three-tier structure consisted of 10,565 local People's Committees (MNV), 118 district People's Committees (ONV), and 11 regional (provincial) People's Committees (KNV). On the average, a region consisted of 10 districts, with each district encompassing 100 communities (i.e., 1,000 villages constituted one region).[2] After federalization, the Slovak Republic, as one of its first orders of business, disposed of its three existing regional People's Committees, thus creating a direct link between the thirty-seven Slovak districts and the capital of Bratislava. In the Czech Republic the three-tier system was retained, but with the proviso that its future would be decided only after a nation-wide debate.[3]

Here, we shall examine a few of the issues arising between the bureaucracy of the KSC on the one hand, and the bureaucracies of government and industry on the other. Particular attention will be paid to the issue of expertise—the conflict between professional competence and political loyalty—as a catalyst in the political polarization of 1968. We shall also examine the long-heralded but never fully implemented New Economic Model (NEM).

The Party and the State Bureaucracy

The growth of the KSC bureaucracy, distinct from government bureaucracy, led to frequent usurpation and/or fusion of roles. Stalin's theory of the continuous aggravation of class struggle became the rationalization for the growth of the Party apparatus, which attracted ambitious individuals anxious to find careers for themselves quickly. According to their critics in 1968, they were mediocrities with a lust for power; both autocratic and insecure, they rationalized their self-interest into the interests of "socialism," condemning any criticism of their performance as an attack on the foundation of the political system.[4]

This apparatus survived the reformatory efforts of 1968 without great damage, just as it had managed to survive earlier attempts at change. Before January 1968, there had been continuous, though half-hearted measures to modernize the bureaucracy through reorganization and reduction. Focused on the state rather than the Party administration, these steps were inconsistent and had little effect, despite official statements to the contrary. Whereas in 1958 there were 132 administrative officials per 1,000 employees, this ratio had declined in 1963 only to 126, and in 1965 only to 117. In 1958 the state administration employed 13.2 percent of the entire labor force; in 1965 the share was 11.7 percent.[5]

Data that were made available showed both decreases and increases in the bureaucracy. This contradiction sometimes reflected the practice of shifting personnel "from office to office, from one type of work of little use to the same work elsewhere, or to work even more superfluous."[6] By the end of 1966 a total of 640,585 individuals were employed in what was called the "directing apparatus" (*ridici aparat*). Of these, 19,967 (3.1 percent) worked at ministries and other central offices, and 41,525 (6.5 percent) at the People's Committees (especially in the districts). The overwhelming majority (512,646, or 80 percent) were engaged in work concerned with the economy.[7] According to the trade union daily *Prace* (April 12, 1970) the staff of a certain administrative unit had grown from one director and 150 to 200 administrative officials in 1947 to one director general, 7 other directors, 30 deputy directors, and almost 2,000 minor officials. Another union source claimed that in 1970 there was one administrative employee for every three workers.[8]

Given that it is the nature of totalitarianism to demand total control and to generate structures and roles for the achievement of this ambitious and impossible demand, any attempt at debureaucratization without detotalization is illusory. Professor Miroslav Kusy, an outstanding Slovak Communist reformer, commented on this problem:

In the course of the last twenty years we tried to cope several times with the plague of this bureaucratism. Naturally we always failed, because in this struggle the etatist basis of the matter was not attacked. After every reduction and transfer of white collar employees to productive factory work, the bureaucratic state apparatus would grow once again, achieving a quite miraculous recovery. This was natural and logical. The all-embracing and all-administering

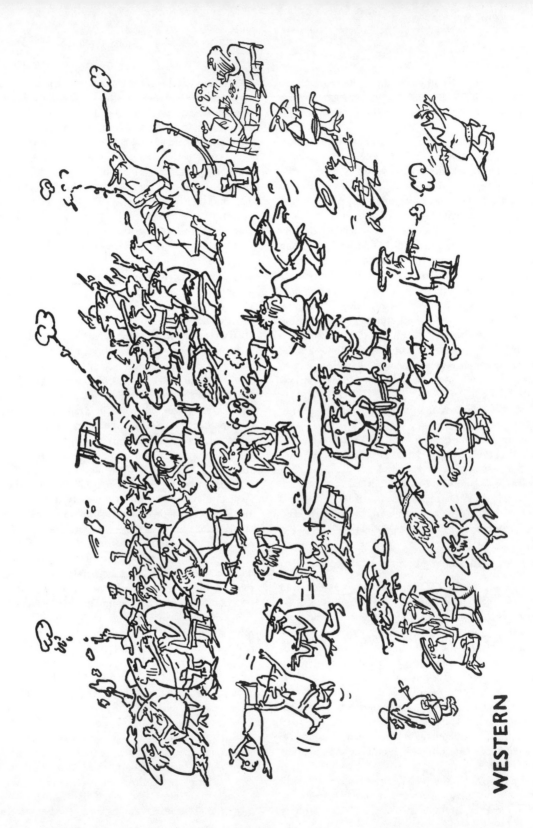

WESTERN

EASTERN

(Literarni noviny, April 3, 1965)

mechanism remained the same, the number of roles was not reduced, but rather increased, and therefore the apparatus fulfilling these roles could not be reduced. And this disproportionate growth of the state apparatus stemmed from the concentration of political power. The Party moved into a position of power, directing all areas of social life. and, as a consequence, had to adjust its own structure to the etatist model. The apparatus of the Party became the mirror image of the apparatus of the State. For every component in the hierarchy of the state structure there was an equivalent in the hierarchy of the Party structure, directing the former. . . .

The totalitarian [*direktivne*] management of a modern civilized society is a superhuman task. Under these circumstances the center of political power could do nothing more than generally direct the Party apparatus and issue only broadly formulated demands and regulations. The Party apparatus gave these real life, adding flesh and blood to these general rules and regulations. This way it became all-powerful and indispensable. . . . It reached a maximum of bureaucratization. Its omnipotence and omnipresence led to the ill-famed *obezlichka*: no one took a political step or made a decision without prior consent of the Party apparatus. For all this was convenient and without any risk. The Party apparatus assumed actual authority without anyone being able to invoke against them formal responsibility. And so, no one was responsible. This was the period when the reflexive pronoun "it" started to flourish: "it was decided," "it was agreed upon," "it was set to work," "it was in error." . . . There are errors and guilt, but no one is erring or guilty.[9]

In theory, the Party was immune from human fallibility. In practice, human beings hid their fallibility under the shelter of the Party.

The Action Program of the Dubcek regime expressed the intent to change the existing relation between the state and the Party. Its aim was not a final divorce but, in the words of Vaclav Slavik, a former teacher of dancing and a reformist apparatchik of the first rank, "a rather substantial separation of the Party from the state."[10] Among the demands for democratization was abolishment of the

so-called shadow departments (*stinova resortni oddeleni*) in the Party structure.[11] (However, this alter ego machinery was never abolished.)

After the Soviet invasion the trend toward weakening the role of the Party apparatus was halted. Instead, a policy of *status quo ante* was called for, with a return to the old structures and functions and a purge of officials with liberal leanings. For instance, the notorious Eighth (Mamula) Department was resurrected, though under a different name and head.[12] In 1969 the Secretariat of the Central Committee included 17 structural components (see Table 6.1): the hierarchical relation of these agencies, their political power, or their staff strength is not known. In addition to this structure there are so-called Standing Commissions of the Central Committee. Staffed by apparatchiks or by merited outsiders, they serve in an advisory and consultative capacity. It is asserted that the departments and the commissions all have equal rank. The Secretariat of the Central Committee directs all departments and "guarantees the implementation of the organizational and technical aspects of the committee activities."[13]

Table 6.1. Agencies of the Central Committee of the Czechoslovak Communist Party

---

Department of:
   Political Organization
   Ideology
   Education and Culture
   Party Work in Mass Media
   Economics
   Party Work in Industry, Transportation, and Communication
   Agricultural Policy
   State Agencies
   Social Organizations
   Defence and Security Policy
   International Policy
Unit of Political-Professional Services
Economic Management Administration
Secretariat of the Central Committee
Secretariat of the First Secretary
Main Staff of the Workers' Militia
Central Controlling and Auditing Commission

Source: Zivot strany, March 19, 1969, No. 12, pp. 1–2.

Lower in the hierarchy, the structure of the KSC is bound to be less differentiated. The spirit of reorganization and change also affected district and regional apparatus. The adoption of a five-secretary model was recommended for both levels: Leading (First) Secretary, to whom were subordinate secretaries for Political Organization and Information; Ideology; Economy; and Agriculture. Commensurate with the secretaries in stature was the chairman of the Controlling and Auditing Commission. Each district and regional apparatus was to consist of ten branches, covering political organization, ideology, industry, agriculture, public administration, economic-technical administration, information, and the Workers' Militia.[14]

The Secretariat of the Central Committee is located in Prague, on the Kiev Brigade Quay. This imposing building also housed an odd creation resulting from the Soviet invasion, the Central Committee Bureau for Party Work in the Czech Provinces. This bureau, consisting of ten departments, was formed in November 1968 under the leadership of Novotny's former Minister of the Interior, Lubomir Strougal.[15] It was disbanded in 1971. Its main purpose was to prevent establishment of an autonomous Czech Communist Party, and thus to undermine the federalization of the country.

As mentioned earlier, until 1968 Czechoslovakia was a unitary state of the so-called asymmetrical type. Under this arrangement the administration of the country was centralized in Prague, although some Slovak affairs were left to Bratislava. This semiautonomous status of Slovakia was also maintained in the Party. Nevertheless, the Slovaks felt (not without justification) discriminated against by the Czechs. Although the Czechs possessed no political organs of their own, they nonetheless controlled the Czechoslovak statewide machinery. Federation in 1968 disposed of this imbalance by creating a government for the Czech part of the country to complement the existing Slovak governmental structure. While Moscow reluctantly consented to the federation scheme, the proposal for establishing a semiautonomous Czech Communist Party was rejected. A need for Communist unity and the lack of precedent for a federalized Party provided the formal justification for the decision, but the real reason was probably fear that a Czech Party would become dominated by reformist, disobedient elements.[16] Instead, the Bureau for Party Work in the Czech Provinces was established. Given the fusion of state and Party, with one of the Siamese twins federalized and the other not, the bureau appeared to be an inconsistent and inadequate solution.

But this solution was short-lived. Strougal's predominant task as the head of the bureau was to purge the regional and district apparatus of the KSC. Once this purge was largely accomplished, Strougal was replaced by Josef Kempny, under whom the bureau gradually withered away, until it was tacitly dissolved at the Fourteenth Party Congress in 1971. Thus, after an interlude of less than three years, the old asymmetrical structure of the KSC was fully restored.

In 1960, the year of the new constitution, a new law on the People's Committees was adopted. Reflecting the Khrushchevian populism of that period, preference was declared for elected rather than appointed officials. The Party call for debureaucratization also included an increased engagement of volunteers and a corresponding demotion of the administrative apparatus to an essentially advisory capacity. Soon afterwards, however, this move toward democratization was declared premature, especially as it affected the higher echelons of the People's Committees.[17]

Many of the 1960 innovations were criticized. It was charged, for example, that the establishment of a system of "people's control" encroached upon and to some degree duplicated the functions of the People's Committees and fostered meddling in the activities of the economic structures.

The People's Committees were conceived of as filling two nearly incompatible roles, one as representatives of "the people," the other as representatives of the state. The structure of the People's Committees as set up, in 1960 was changed by a new law on People's Committees that was passed in 1967, the last year of Novotny's rule. However, this reorganization did little to improve the malfunctioning system, staffed largely by aging, poorly trained personnel. There were few university graduates in the committees, and the majority of the employees were women—a reliable indication of an unattractive career. Underpaid and understaffed as they were, their performance was anything but efficient. In Brno a single employee was in charge of a social welfare program covering an area with a

Arch of Triumph.
(*Literarni noviny*, March 19, 1966)

population of 75,000.[18] Dysfunctionality and poor utilization of manpower were prevalent.

Under the 1967 law, all industrial enterprises were to pay a 1 percent tax on their gross earnings to the People's Committees.[19] Given the host of responsibilities of local administration, such as housing, health, and culture, the inadequacy of such subsidies can be easily appreciated. A temporary improvement was registered in the late 1960s: the concept of local government was officially endorsed, and "self-government" ceased to be a priori incompatible with the notion of socialism.

In all, the People's Committees have remained handicapped by amateurism and arbitrariness. Health services are a case in point. Each hospital is subject to two authorities. Vertically, in professional matters, it is responsible to the Ministry of Health; horizontally, i.e., mainly in matters of financing, it is responsible to the district People's Committee. But in the committees laymen rather than individuals with medical training are in charge. Against this administrative control even the Ministry of Health is powerless. Exasperation prompted one physician to remark: "On the one hand, there is an incessant stream of orders given; on the other, they are obviously not fulfilled. But once sound judgment is on the retreat everywhere in the administration of the state, why should health services be any different?"[20]

Undoubtedly, implementation is the test of the value of any rule. In post-1948 Czechoslovakia the standards of interpreting and executing the rules deteriorated. Amateurism and proletarization of ranks masqueraded under the disguise of revolutionary zeal and necessity. Ignorant and disrespectful of the law, the bureaucrat became contemptuous of the citizen whom he supposedly served. Few other facets of socialist existence continue to be criticized with such a persistent vehemence and manifest lack of success. One Czechoslovak scientist, referring to his experiences in the United States, observed:

> If there is anything which can be solved in our country well and fast, it is often not because of the existing rules but despite them. . . . An average Czechoslovak citizen is being perpetually dragged back and forth by bureaucratic manipulation and lives a very tiring life. If an American had to live through this for a single week, he would sue the institutions twice a week.[21]

The New Economic Model

Czechoslovakia in the 1960s provided a good example of the interaction and mutual conditioning of political and economic systems. The stultifying inefficiency which was characteristic of the political environment spilled over into the economic realm.

The nadir was reached in 1963, the year of decline in industrial production. In the fall of that year a nationwide discussion on the national economy opened up. This exchange of views—which appeared to be one way, with the economists proposing and the practitioners disposing—centered on the issues of the command system; whether to replace the central plan, the main economic determinant, by the market system; and whether to grant autonomy to the economic subjects. This challenge to the outdated model threatened the bureaucracy which the command system sustained and which in turn sustained the command system. Termination of both appeared to be the price for economic recovery.

With great reluctance, the political elite consented to economic experimentation. In 1964 a draft of the principles of reform were made public and in early 1965 were adopted by the KSC Central Committee. Meanwhile, economists proceeded with detailed work on the NEM. The year 1966 and early 1967 were the period of "the start of the NEM and creation of conditions for its full functioning."[22]

The 1960s were also a period of intellectual awakening and emancipation from dogma and docility. Sacrosanct values were openly questioned. Pivotal in this respect was the work of a team from the Academy of Sciences headed by Radovan Richta, whose conclusions were published in 1966 under the title *Civilization at the Crossroads*. The authors rejected as nonsensical the optimistic Khrushchevian predictions about Communism catching up and surpassing capitalism. Instead, the authors insisted that the gap was widening and that a permanent revolution was taking place in science, but not in politics. Accordingly, it would be science and the scientist which would substantially affect success or failure in the political as well as economic system.

Novotny's regime was caught in a dilemma. Enemies of the NEM by conviction and its temporary allies out of necessity, they realized that sincere implementation of the reform would render the current mode of governing impossible. On the other hand, total boycott of the NEM would aggravate the economic crisis and bury them all under failure. Therefore, the leadership settled for a compromise of selective implementation of the less substantive measures, but did not allow the thorough structural and functional transformation that alone could guarantee the success of NEM. Procrastination and half-hearted enforcement of economic reform contributed to the fall of the Novotny regime. The new leadership showed in the Action Program of April 1968 its determination to put the economy on a rational, market-oriented foundation.[23] The program promised gradual removal of domestic protectionism and subsidies to bring prices closer to those of the world market, and to decentralize the management of the economy.

In 1968 a new dimension was added to the NEM issue, namely, democratic participation and a form of co-management by the employees. Various reformers proposed the establishment of Workers Councils (*rady pracujicich*), to be elected by the employees and designed to function over and above the management. In July 1968 the trade unions incorporated the proposal into the draft of their new charter.[24] The preparatory work on the Workers Councils and their establishment in several plants was under way—but the pre-invasion time was running out.

Simultaneously, a complex debate erupted among the advocates of change. Although they were in agreement about the necessity of reducing the authority of economic planners and increasing the importance of the market, they differed profoundly on other issues, in what could be summed up as a conflict between the democratic and technocratic school. Some reformers seemed to argue as if civil freedom and economic efficiency were mutually exclusive. Civil rights advocates feared perpetuation of dictatorial practices while others pointed out that democratic *Schlamperei* would not feed or clothe a nation. At times, the polemics over the virtues of a technocratic, managerial solution as opposed to the democratic approach through self-government reflected differences in degree rather than irreconcilable points of view.[25]

Western observers of the Soviet and East European economic scene usually view the existing conflicts as those between Party bureaucrats and rational, well-educated, competent technocrats. Such a view, however, is hardly applicable to Czechoslovakia. The issue of the NEM has never been a clear-cut conflict between managers as advocates of economic reform and apparatchiks as its foes. As a result of the recruitment pattern of the past twenty years, the rate of purge, promotion policies based predominantly on political merits, and the frequent interchangeability of political and economic roles, managers and apparatchiks—by vir-

tue of their background, training, and political motivation—have to be considered close relatives, not
hostile neighbors. The conflict has not been between
the standard type of "political managers" ("po-
litocrats" rather than technocrats) and the apparatchiks, but rather between an informal coalition
of these two groups and an emerging group of bet-
ter-trained professionals who challenged the former's
qualifications for leadership in both political and
economic roles. To put it differently, the conflict
over the NEM has not been one of economics versus
politics but one of competence versus political
loyalty.

According to data published in 1966, only 2,822
out of 11,941 factory directors and their assistants
were university educated; 2,265 had attended only
grade school. On the whole, not more than 45 percent had the qualifications required for their jobs.[26]
Educational qualification was inversely proportional
to managerial rank: the higher the position, the
greater the probability that the job holder would
have an inadequate educational background. Thus,
only 29.7 percent of the top executives in industry
had the necessary educational requirements whereas
among their assistants the ratio was as high as 48.4
percent. Of the managerial stratum in the country,
only 11.9 percent were university trained. A final
tally of the Party's preference for loyalty over
competence shows that of the 657,000 Czechoslovaks
with higher education who were between the ages
of twenty-five and fifty-nine (sixty being the mandatory retirement age for males) only 11.3 percent
held management positions appropriate to their
training.[27]

The reluctance of the economic bureaucrats to
improve their educational qualifications contrasts
with their eagerness for political participation. According to a 1965 survey, higher echelon managers
held an average of three political roles, requiring six
hours a week; factory directors, spent nine hours a
week in this type of political involvement.[28] Survey
data for 1967 show that the majority of Czechoslovak
managers were also Party functionaries. Only 21.57
percent of the respondents did not belong to the
KSC; another 21.9 percent, though members, filled
no political role.[29] This symbiosis and multifunc-
tionality of roles present the typical economic
bureaucrat as being also a Party activist.

Considering this profile of the executive, a drive

for changing the economic system from within was
rather unlikely. Instead, economic bureaucrats engaged in conflicts confined to allocation of resources
and production plan requirements in a single industrial sector under the jurisdiction of one ministry. As
mentioned in Chapter 4, the manager, rather than
face hostile workers, undertook a pilgrimage to
Prague to fight with the ministry for undeserved
subsidies. A great deal of energy was also spent in
searching for production material and spare parts in
a market of perpetual scarcity. Individuals with a
talent for extralegal ways of providing the desired
items—practitioners of what the Russians call
Blat—were eagerly sought by socialist management
rather than confined in socialist prisons.[30] Occasionally, competition for resources spilled over the jurisdictional boundaries of one ministry and reached
public attention. This was the case, for example, in a
conflict over funds for fireproof clay in mines, a conflict which required the personal intervention of two
cabinet members.[31]

In one public opinion survey, 80 to 90 percent of
the respondents, from all walks of life, favored
abolishment of all discrimination against non-Communists and the introduction of professional competence and education as the sole criteria for cadre
work. The only group disagreeing were the
managers, prompting the question of whether "this
tendency is not prevalent only among those officials
in the economy who feel threatened in their careers
by the introduction of such criteria."[32]

Managers were also hostile toward the idea of
worker participation in management.[33] In 1968 the
antagonism gained new momentum. Numerous
strikes and other pressures were aimed at removing
incompetent or unpopular executives. Not in-
frequently, the Party intervened to reinstate deposed cadres.

Stalinist managers could offer neither democracy
nor efficiency. In a significant twist of irony, the
Workers' Councils, whose creation the bureaucrats
had called a pseudo-democratic trick and a threat to
efficiency, became vehicles of rational changes,
demanding an end to dilettantism in management
and the establishment of professionalism. In these
councils, elected by popular vote, the ratio of
specialists and trained professionals was higher than
in management![34]

Under the old economic model it was impossible

for a producer to find out whether he made a profit or suffered a loss. The system was a haven for irresponsibility and ineptitude, aided by a merry-go-round of cadre changes and structural reorganization. As Ivan Holy, one of the well-known captains of Czechoslovak socialist industry prior to his incarceration in the early 1950s (on a false charge), pointed out, bureaucratization of the economy transformed enterprises into bureaucratic institutions and the enterprising spirit into a crime.[35]

It was not the intention of the Workers' Councils to duplicate or substitute for the management but rather to formulate the basic orientation of the given enterprise. This function was explicitly compared with that of a board of directors in a capitalist firm. In an Academy of Sciences poll, the idea of the Workers' Councils was favored by 53.3 percent of the respondents and only 9.9 percent were opposed.[36] The negative response corresponded to the estimated strength of conservative sentiment in the country. The most resolute hostility toward the councils was demonstrated by high-level executives of the so-called "general directorates." They either forbade council elections or refused to acknowledge the validity of such an election.

By the time of the Warsaw Pact invasion, only 15 percent of the future total councils had been established. Despite the hostility of the Soviet Union to this innovation, by October 1968 Workers' Councils had been formed in 70 enterprises and preparations were in an advanced stage in 267 others. By March 1969, the councils functioned in 114 Czech and 6 Slovak enterprises.[37] The political and economic significance of this novelty was underscored by the importance of the industries involved. Key industries, including those dear to the Stalinist Iron Concept (such as Skoda Industries in Plzen) were the most active council builders, rather than less important industries, such as a marginal textile factory with underpaid female employees in a borderland province.

At Skoda in Plzen the new director general was chosen in an open contest, publicized in classified ads, all in violation of twenty years of *nomenklatura* cadre restriction and the monopoly of the Party over appointments of this magnitude. Also at Skoda, members of Workers' Councils from 182 enterprises, representing a labor force of 900,000, assembled for their first nationwide conference.[38]

This was also the last conference, but before censorship could be effectively restored, a report from the Institute of Technology in Prague reached the public.[39] Prepared by a team of industrial sociologists, it was based on a study of 95 Workers' Councils with a total of 1,421 members, who had been elected from among 3,622 candidates. The average voting participation was 83 percent, and totalitarian monopoly of nomination had vanished. Instead, 42 percent of all candidates were nominated by trade union committees, 25 percent by workers' collectives, and 8 percent by management. The rest were scattered among other organizations and individuals, with the KSC presenting no more than 10 percent of the candidates!

Despite this manifest abdication of the leading role by the Party, the labor force did not run amok. First of all, the voters expressed confidence in senior employees. Of those elected, over half had worked in the same place for more than fifteen years; 72 percent overall, and 86 percent in the metal industries, had been employed in one place over ten years. Only 4 percent had a record of less than five years of affiliation with the place where they were elected.

Among the council members in the study, 71 percent were 35 to 49 years old. *Technici*, i.e., personnel with technical training, accounted for 70 percent of the council seats; laborers constituted 25 percent. Among the latter, not a single unskilled laborer was elected. University graduates constituted 30 percent on the councils; 28 percent were high school graduates.[40]

These figures are clearly an indication of the success of the socialization effort in 1968. Reformist intellectuals, from the economist Ota Sik to the philosopher Ivan Svitak, managed to breach the wall erected by the Stalinists between the intelligentsia and the proletariat and to convince the latter that bureaucratism and primitivism were enemies of both. The proletarians realized that amateurism and dilettantism, in the name of proletarian virtue, constituted a smokescreen for an unqualified bureaucratic elite and cast their vote for co-workers with professional training.

Also surprising were data on the political affiliation of the elected members. Among eighty-three councils, a majority of those elected were members of the Communist Party, except in the construction industry and agriculture.[41] In the absence of anything approximating an electoral contest of political parties, this remains a rare piece of evidence of the Party's resurrection and its regaining public confidence under Dubcek and his program of "socialism with a human face."

In short, elections to Workers' Councils were characterized by emphasis on competence, with no traceable class or political bias. The idea of the councils gained further acceptance in the nation, and by March 1969 opponents of the councils dropped to a mere 3 percent in one survey sample.[42]

In the meantime, the popularity of the experiment grew in inverse proportion to the probability of its implementation. The post-invasion leadership, because of Soviet pressure and also because of their own genuine preference, changed from an unenthusiastic onlooker to a force patently hostile to workers' participation in management. First, the Party declared further exploration of the idea undesirable and forbade formation of new councils—without, however, dissolving the old ones. Next came various drafts of the Socialist Enterprises Act, which was viewed as an attack on the emancipation of the labor force. With the ascendancy of Husak to power, work on the law, and thus ratifica-

tion of the legitimacy of the councils, was postponed indefinitely. By the end of 1969, the purge of liberals among the trade union leadership was accomplished, and the experiment with the Workers' Councils was denounced as a demagogic, rightist, and antisocialist stratagem.[43] All the councils were disbanded, and the democratically chosen director general of Skoda Industries was dismissed.

In a policy statement, Husak vowed to return to the decisive role of state planning in the management of the economy and to abandon what he labeled "romantic notions" about the omnipotence of the market. The NEM was condemned in terms unheard of in Novotny's time. The Party's main daily, *Rude pravo*, even published a statement to the effect that no NEM had ever existed.[44] Another source of totalitarian restoration condemned Ota Sik and all those who had fought against the rule of a dysfunctional bureaucracy in the economic sphere. It was charged that by denying the decisive role of the state in the economy, Sik and his school had destroyed its socialist character.[45] The call for restoration of orthodoxy in the economic system was explicit and unabashed. Both the democratic and the technocratic reformers lost.

7

Adjudication

At the time of the breakdown of Novotny's regime, the legal order was about as decrepit as the economic order. During twenty years of Stalinism the structures and functions of adjudication had deteriorated as much, if not more, than those of the other socialist countries, none of which were particularly distinguished for a tradition of democracy and the impartial rule of law.

The willingness of the Party in 1968 to allow revelation of its past crimes is probably unprecedented among ruling elites anywhere, dwarfing the de-Stalinization process in the USSR and even surpassing in candor the Germans' postwar effort to face the facts of the Nazi era. The evils of the Stalinist period in Czechoslovakia were manifold. In the early 1950s there were 422 jails and concentration camps, no mean figures for a country with a population then of 13 million.[1] A new generation of political prisoners had been born (estimated at well over 100,000), as well as a first generation of indigenous torturers and murderers.

Stalinism often meant protection of the guilty

and punishment of the innocent. Though under prevailing practice the Party elite were granted immunity from prosecution (following the *nomenklatura* system, according to which prosecution of an officeholder down to the district level was contingent on approval of the Party apparatus), a great many Communists landed in jail, and some perished on the gallows, for crimes they did not commit.

Liquidation of political opponents in the "judicial way," as legal theoretician Michal Lakatos pointed out, "is not at all typical of our national tradition. . . . [it] is exclusively an extreme political measure of rather backward countries, not of a progressive industrial society."[2] Yet the notorious show trials—which began in Czechoslovakia only after similar spectacles in other People's Democracies had ended—rendered a toll of corpses probably exceeding the combined total in all neighboring countries.[3] Czechoslovakia was the first country in the postwar period known to execute a woman, former member of Parliament Milada Horakova, for a (nonexistent) political offense.

Information was released about horrors in "socialist" concentration camps, off-limits to the International Red Cross, about physicians administering experimental drugs to prisoners, about torture chambers, and the like. From army officers to alleged kulaks, from tradesment to intellectuals, in groups or individually, citizens from all walks of life felt the arbitrary punitive hand of Stalinism. For example, a tally of the known facts shows that 6,174 monks and nuns spent a total of 32,016 years in prison, yet these figures are far from complete.[4] Even General Ludvik Svoboda, Novotny's successor as president of the country, was put under arrest, until Stalin—unaware of his plight—chanced to make a favorable remark about him at a diplomatic reception in Moscow, thereby saving him from a long prison term or a worse fate.[5]

These revelations resulted in numerous analyses of the causes behind the collapse of the legal order. The law, instead of being a shield for the weak, had been turned into a club for the strong, leading to nationwide disrespect for any rules. Judges became tools of the apparatchiks, inasmuch as the entire country was the tool of the Party. For the citizen, obedience to the law was an enforcible duty: for the state, it was at best a moral obligation that could be suspended at will. Some writers suggested, rather blasphemously, that the main task of the law ought to be to curb the power of the state. Such ideas were typical of the frank style of reexamination of the political system in 1968.[6]

Ten days before the August 21 invasion, Bohuslav Kucera, Minister of Justice, wrote:

> If we were to evaluate the past period from the standpoint of the position and role of the law in our state, we would be forced to characterize it as one of serious violation of the law. These days, our citizens learn with astonishment about the extent and depth of the deformations of legality, and they justly inquire after the roots of all this. . . .[7]

The main blame for what were rather tenderly termed "improper methods in the cult-of-personality era" was declared to lie with the political system and not with its implementors.

The Roots

The legal order in pre-totalitarian Czechoslovakia resembled the French system. A four-tier court structure independent of other structures, with tenured judges, a jury system, and the Continental emphasis on codified law, maintained general jurisdiction over both criminal and civil matters. The courts had a reputation for integrity and competence.

After 1948 an attempt was made to duplicate the Soviet legal system. The results were not entirely satisfactory. The Soviet codes, dating back to the 1920s, were obsolete, neglected, and moribund through prolonged disuse. In the absence of guiding precedent, the Czechoslovak lawmakers settled for a compromise by retaining, in essence, the form of the inherited bourgeois code and infusing it with the spirit of proper Bolshevik interpretation.

Adopted Soviet structures and practices included the system of *Arbitrazh* and *Prokuratura*, the concept of "people's assessor," the authority of the Supreme Court to annul verdicts of lower benches, and, most fundamentally, the Marxist-Leninist doctrine of law. This doctrine rejects the objectivity of laws as impossible and hypocritical. Instead, it is maintained that the state, as "an organ of the oppression of one class by another," employs for the promotion of its interests both the laws and the judicial machinery. The law is a political directive, and to quote N. V. Krylenko, the People's Commissar of Justice in the early years of the Soviet state, "a club is a primitive weapon, a rifle is a more efficient one, and the most efficient is the court."[8] In the 1930s, A. Y. Vyshinsky, the Prosecutor General, became the unsurpassed practitioner of this dictum.

Prague disciples of Stalin emulated the Soviet example with enthusiasm. Alexej Cepicka, Gottwald's son-in-law and Czechoslovakia's first Communist Minister of Justice, expressed gratitude for "the inestimable importance of the help and experience of the USSR . . . how to fight the class enemy and how to destroy him."[9] Legal scholars were equally uninhibited in expressing their gratitude. Even Ferdinand Boura, the moderate dean of the law school of Charles University in Prague, announced that "discovery of the class substance of the law signifies a fundamental change in legal theory—the change from metaphysical jurisprudence to legal science."[10]

This class substance of the law, never satisfactorily defined, sanctioned the dichotomy of legal and extralegal measures, regarding law not as equal but ancillary to political interests, and exempted the state, though not its citizens, from its binding force. Anything was possible and permissible with the help of the definition supplied by Jan Bartuska, Czechoslovak Prosecutor General of long Stalinist standing: "Socialist legality is an important factor in and a method of protecting and strengthening the dictatorship of the proletariat. The dictatorship of the proletariat and socialist legality create one dialectical unity. To ignore this fact means not to understand the class nature of socialist legality."[11] Accepting the standard definition of the dictatorship of the proletariat as "rule unrestricted by any law," we arrive at a dialectical masterpiece: socialist legality is an order and set of laws unrestricted by any laws.

The basic quality of this legal system is its ambiguity: it is the conditional "law if"—what the right hand giveth the left hand taketh away. Both the rule and its exceptions, the right and its eventual negation are sanctioned. For example, the 1948 constitution guaranteed individual property rights up to a certain limit, and at the same time authorized the state to restrict and expropriate this property with or without compensation. By the same token, "all citizens are equal before the law" (1948 Const., Sect. 1, Para. 1), yet offenders from among class enemies are to be punished more severely than the toiling masses. Individual rights have been annuled whenever the courts found them incompatible with clauses relating to "law," rules of socialist community life," "fulfillment of the economic plan," "common interest," or "important common interest." The codes abound with such words and phrases which are left undefined.

Such ambiguity is an elementary ingredient of what is termed the "class concept" of justice. A theoretical framework explanatory of the interaction of politics and law may be of some assistance.[12] "Class-oriented adjudication" may be viewed through a model incorporating three types of bias that impede the rule of law—bias in the law itself, bias in interpretation, and bias resulting from outside pressures. The first is the bias that is implicit (through fundamental doctrine) and also explicit (ranging from escape clauses to outright discriminatory provisions) in the law, including both substantive and procedural codes. The second is the "legitimate" (i.e., officially required) bias of the judge as the interpreter of the law and as decision maker. Finally, the third is the "illegitimate" (i.e., tolerated but not

publicly sanctioned) distortion of law by outside intervention into adjudication. These three biases may be illustrated as follows: (1) "the law protects socialism" (Criminal Code, Sect. 1); (2) a judge is required to punish with particular severity those offenders "who manifest hostility toward the people's democratic order" (Criminal Code, Sect. 20); and (3) a prevailing climate of "legal nihilism" that enables political elites to force a judge to make a manifestly illegal decision.

This triad comprises concepts of varying scope of applicability and unequal acceptance by the regime. The government has always readily admitted the practice, desirability and, in fact, inevitability of the first type of bias (on the assumption that "law without inherent class bias is bourgeois nonsense"). On the other hand, the third type of bias, implying direct Party interference in adjudication and even the extreme case of verdicts being drafted by apparatchiks, has never been recognized as legitimate. The most controversial, and the most crucial for the understanding of "class justice" and degree of legal uncertainty in the present period, is the second type of bias, that exercised by the judges. The legitimacy of its applicability was almost unchallenged until 1968.

Before proceeding further with the issue of "class justice," we should briefly note how the system identifies its victims. The designation "class enemy" has been left vague enough to be a threat to any individual. The Marxist criterion for class identification—i.e., the relation to the means of production—did not suffice, so additional labels of "state of mind" and "heritage" had to be introduced. In all, three empirical categories of class enemies appear:

(1) Classic enemies (notably, owners of the means of economic exploitation, members of former ruling classes, or anyone actively opposed to the regime).

(2) Ideological enemies (both infidels and heretics).

(3) Hereditary (derivative) enemies (any expropriated, incarcerated, or otherwise disgraced individual of the above categories, his family, and descendants).

The criteria of "ownership," "state of mind," and "heritage" are neither defined nor mutually exclusive. A single person may qualify on several counts: by being, for example, of bourgeois extraction, of revisionist leaning, and a son of a former prominent Communist with a record of anti-Party conspiracy. The degree of assumed enmity toward the political system ranges from the manifest hostility of a saboteur to mere guilt through involuntary association, like orphans with a traitorous family background. It is not unreasonable to assume that the more inactive (or nonexistent) enemies the state persecutes, the more oppressive the state is. In Czechoslovakia, in contrast with other People's Democracies, the emphasis on class warfare against hereditary enemies has been particularly strong and enduring.

Class identification may be the sole criterion for determining the guilt or innocence of a defendant. For example, during the punitive drive against so-called *kulaks* (a Russian word used in Czech to denote "rich farmers"), the Criminal Code of 1950 provided the courts with three different definitions covering such activities as failure to deliver harvest quotas to the state, loss of livestock, or abandonment of agricultural property. Whereas any of these offenses would ordinarily be one or the other of two minor felonies (Sect. 135, 136), the same offense by a kulak would be considered sabotage (Sect. 85). By means of this threefold classification, perpetrators of the same crime might be subject to different penalties, ranging from only nominal punishment to execution—depending mainly on the determination of the defendant's sociopolitical status. Characteristically, no official definition of a kulak has ever been furnished. The "class approach" was applied also by the civil law courts.[13]

The declaration of achieved socialism in 1960 implied extinction of the last hostile class, thus jeopardizing the logic of further pursuit of class justice. However, the KSC refused to surrender this tool of arbitrary power. Enemies had been annihilated and class antagonism had ceased to exist, but class discrimination against non-existent enemies had to continue. The extinct exploiting classes were replaced by "remnants of exploiting classes." Once the "remnants" became too microscopic, the Party reached for a further semantic improvement. "Remnants of bourgeois mentality" were conjured up, and since their survival was partly conditioned by the "existence of the capitalist part of the world," the enemies became candidates for longevity, if not

immortality.[14] The achievement of socialism and class harmony notwithstanding, scores of discriminatory rules continued to be enacted and enforced. This was also the case of Governmental Ordinance No. 124 of 1964. Under the title "Adjustment of Benefits of Some Persons," District People's Committees were authorized to cut the pensions of beneficiaries politically prominent before 1948, former exploiters, and former oppressors of the people (e.g., policemen). The reduction was also applicable to the benefits of the surviving members of their families.[15]

Shortly after the seizure of power in 1948 the so-called Two-Year Legal Plan was promulgated, during which period all basic laws were replaced by hastily concocted substitutes. After 1960 these People's Democratic codes were replaced by acts of fully socialist character. Furthermore, throughout the entire post-1948 era, adjudicators were also bound by legal norms of lesser order, such as ordinances and ministerial instructions, which were often unpublished and hence unknown to parties to whom they were applicable. Although it had taken three generations to produce one civil code, a single generation of Czechoslovak totalitarians managed to produce three civil codes![16] The criminal code was changed five times in fifteen years.

Laws became numerous, short-lived, arbitrary, ambiguous, and, with the deteriorating respect for law throughout society and the government, not very effective. Strict adherence to the law was brushed aside as "bourgeois formalism." The result was, in official terminology, "legal nihilism," an endemic disregard and disrespect for the rules as such. If a "political loyalty report" submitted by an anonymous janitor could determine the outcome of a trial, it is no wonder that the affected citizen felt no respect for such a legal order. Computation of social security benefits was often based not on lifetime work but on political whim. State insurance conditions could be changed at will, and ex post facto contractual terms were added with no redress available to the individuals affected. It was not the occasional execution of political victims on trumped-up charges but this continuous legal uncertainty that was the dominant cause of legal nihilism. As one commentator put it, "these little, unimportant violations of the law reached truly Homeric proportions under Novotny, so that the feeling of legal certainty fell completely apart."[17]

Roles and Structures of Adjudication

A court decision could be:

(1) lawful and just,
(2) lawful but unjust,
(3) unlawful but just, or
(4) unlawful and unjust.[18]

The very concept of class justice seriously impeded the applicability of the first alternative. Similarly, the official ban on outside intervention minimized the likelihood of the fourth alternative. "Lawful but unjust" decisions were very frequent during the Stalinist period. Therefore the criticism of Czechoslovak reformers referring to the 1950s as an era of rampant illegality does not seem accurate. Because the political system had abolished the binding force of law, it would have been impossible to violate this non-existent phenomenon. Forced-labor camps were established on firm legal grounds, as was prolonged incarceration of political suspects. The zeal of an individual interrogator who exceeded the norm of permitted blows, though a violation of rules in itself, is less important than the fact that the legal system allowed the existence of physical violence in the first place.[19]

The third kind of decision (unlawful but just) occurred rather seldom and was dependent on a judge's courage, professional reputation, political vulnerability, skill in rationalizing his decision, and the political significance of the immediate issue. Such a stand, while risky for a judge, was not particularly effective, given the remedial measures open to the opposing party (be that an individual, an institution, or the state).

> According to [the playwright Bertolt] Brecht, an age which requires heroes is to be pitied and a paraphrase occurs to me, about a pitiful legal order which requires heroism of its judges. . . . Judicial independence is not a privilege of judges, but the constitutional guarantee of civil liberties. . . . Let us surround judges with the aura of inaccessibility which their work requires.[20]

The state of adjudication further deteriorated as a result of a high turnover of judicial personnel. A special training program was set up, the so-called "Law School of the Toiling People" (PSP), whose graduates soon dominated the Ministry of Justice, the Office of the Prosecutor General, the Supreme Court,

and the provincial courts. Among an estimated total of 1,350 judges in the country, PSP graduates, invariably former manual laborers and Party activists, constituted the privileged group. PSP judges, in particular, excelled in "good judgeship" when this distinction was determined by a judge's output exceeding the national average of death penalties.[21] In contrast, graduates from regular law schools, lacking experience in manual labor and in most cases of nonproletarian birth, were relegated to politically less sensitive judicial roles.

Judges, particularly those from the PSP, did not challenge the political system which elevated them. The majority, either personally implicated in Stalinist misdeeds or demoralized because of the opprobrium descending on the entire profession, faced the 1968 changes with a noticeable lack of enthusiasm, at best adopting a wait-and-see policy.[22]

Another important factor in the decline of professional standards in the judicial process was the adoption of the Soviet practice of "lay assessors," also referred to as "people's judges." Save for insignificant exceptions, a team of three judges handled criminal and civil cases in the courts of original jurisdiction. The professional presiding judge was joined by two laymen who sat on the bench in addition to holding their regular occupations. This new system replaced the jury system and was designed as a guarantee of the proper socialist spirit in the work of the courts. Thus, the law stipulated equality of votes, making it possible for the two amateurs to outvote the single professional judge.

The economic status of the legal profession was commensurate with its lowly political status. In 1968 the salaries of judges and other legal personnel were below the national income average.[23] Legal nihilism left still other marks. After 1948, between 3,000 and 4,000 lawyers were forbidden to engage in their profession and, in most cases, were assigned to manual labor. This purification of the legal profession resulted in the state being unable to fill over 3,000 positions requiring a legal background. It was also noted that, whereas in Western Europe the average ratio was one law school per two million inhabitants, in Bohemia and Moravia, a single law school (Charles University in Prague) was supposed to suffice for a population of ten million. Well behind Yugoslavia, Hungary, Poland, and the German Democratic Republic, this meager ratio was matched only in Bulgaria. According to the spokesmen for the

Academy of Sciences and Charles University in 1968, there has been a stagnation of legal studies in Czechoslovakia for fully thirty years—i.e., since the Munich Pact of 1938—and first rate graduates could not be expected for five years (i.e., before 1973).[24] This estimate was offered before the Soviet invasion; it will hardly be attainable under the status of limited sovereignty.

Of all the components of the legal machinery, attorneys-at-law (advokati) fared worst: they were collectivized and thoroughly purged. In a Stalinist system of justice, which emphasizes the punitive role of the state, the concept of adequate defense for the accused appeared old-fashioned. Of a total of 2,144 attorneys in 1949, only 756 were left by 1965. The decline was even more drastic in Slovakia, where of some 1,000 only 175 were left and 60 percent of these were of retirement age. In Czech cities, the number of lawyers varies from one per 5,000 residents in Prague to one per 35,000 in provincial capitals. In total number of advokati, Czechoslovakia, with 756 attorneys, was found to be far behind Poland (about 6,000) and even behind the less populous Hungary (about 1,800).[25]

Functional changes were matched by changes in adjudication structures. Substantial differentiation led to the establishment of specialized branches and a corresponding decrease in the jurisdiction of general (common) courts. Among the first structural innovations after the seizure of power in 1948 was the so-called State Court. This court, with branches throughout the country, took over the judicial prosecution of alleged political offenders. It became a household synonym for Czechoslovak terror and was abolished following Stalin's death, when adjudication of political cases was shifted to newly formed special branches of the regular courts in the provinces. In comparison with the State Court, their decisions were less harsh and the resulting number of executions was lower.

In the sphere of nonpunitive actions, a considerable share of the judicial load was taken over by Arbitrazh, panels of arbiters copied from a Soviet model. These panels, in proceedings which were more administrative than judicial, were vested with jurisdiction over disputes between enterprises in matters related to fulfillment of the economic plan and to economic life in general.

On the other hand, the Arbitrazh were not authorized to handle actions between socialist en-terprises and private citizens, such as labor disputes. If no settlement of a labor dispute was reached before the trade union employment commission, the next step was to approach the court with general jurisdiction. The volume of such cases rose steadily during the 1960s. In 1964 the courts decided a total of 22,081 labor disputes. Political interference was rare; of 14,092 litigations in the first half of 1965, only 3,231 were decided against the plaintiff.[26]

Some jurisdictional authority of the regular courts was also transferred to the People's Committees. Under the Administrative Penal Code and Administrative Penal Code of Procedure of 1950, the Committees were authorized to adjudicate all misdemeanors. Although the maximum penalty for these minor offenders was two years imprisonment, the committees earned a deserved reputation for arbitrariness and harshness, with little concern for the letter of the law. Through the practice of draconic fines and confiscation of property as supplementary punishment, they assisted substantially in the drive for economic liquidation of private farmers, tradesmen, and entrepreneurs. After Stalin's death the necessity of curbing the pseudo-legal undertakings of the People's Committees was recognized, and their authority to impose imprisonment was withdrawn. Gradually, their punitive calendar stabilized to the degree that not a class enemy but a noisy drunk became the typical target of their attention. In 1966, People's Committees decided 156,000 cases. Over 84,000 related to "violations of socialist community of life and disturbance of the peace" and 15,000 were for petty theft.[27]

It should be stressed that Czechoslovakia never emulated the Soviet practice of the 1930s of in camera administrative trials. The Secret Police (STB) has never been authorized to apply this form of physical liquidation. The only remote resemblance to this Soviet practice was the activity of the short-lived Security Quintets, established in every district of the country. This Bolshevik Mafia of local apparatchiks, secret police, and other security officers orchestrated class struggle expeditions against kulaks and other elements. Their chief task was to initiate repressive measures of a political nature and to exercise duress on the judiciary but neither to take over nor duplicate its role.

The Novotny regime adopted some of Khrushchev's innovations while disregarding others. There was no Czechoslovak counterpart to the

Soviet auxiliary judicial agency known as the Antiparasite Assembly. The Comrades' Courts were adopted with modifications. Rooted in the early revolutionary belief in the withering away of the state, these "instruments of the people," designed to use social pressure as their main force, were revived in the era of Khrushchev's populism. In the late 1950s Comrades' Courts were established both in places of employment and residence. The state gave these collectives of laymen authority to adjudicate minor matters. They did not get off to a very good start. Intended as instruments of reeducation, prevention, and deterrence, they often became sources of manifest violation of the law (e.g., this writer recalls that a reprimand was the only punishment for a working class rapist, whose case did not belong before that tribunal in the first place) or of such communal merriment as was aroused by trials of adulterous couples caught in *flagrante delicto* during working hours.

With this as a prelude, a strange retrogressive compromise was introduced. In 1961 the Comrades' Courts were renamed "Local People's Courts," declared "organs of the state," and integrated into the judicial structure, although the judicial roles in these odd hybrids, continued to be filled by unpaid laymen who retained their regular occupations. These new courts, it was declared, were not intended to constitute an additional punitive branch; instead, the Local People's Courts were to be "an instrument for the further participation of the working people in the judicial process . . . , to combine elements of state authority and elements of social pressure and influence, and thereby make manifest the integration of the socialist state and the working people and their organizations. . . ."[28]

With jurisdiction over "minor offenses and simple property disputes," the courts were authorized to issue warnings, reprimands, fines, or reductions in salaries but not to impose imprisonment. The number of citizens tried by these tribunals, both in factories and communities, increased from 35,287 in 1962 to 57,458 in 1967. In order of frequency the charges were offenses against socialist community life, socialist property, and personal property.[29]

This innovation continued to be praised throughout the rest of Novotny's rule. With the fall of his regime, public demands were made for the abolishment of what was considered pseudo-democratic nonsense. The courts were abolished as of

January 1, 1970, and their jurisdiction returned to the regular courts.

In the 1962 Criminal Code of Procedure a new populistic feature was introduced—the presence at a trial of a "community prosecutor" (*spolecensky zalobce*) and/or a "community defender" (*spolecensky obhajce*). These are individuals familiar with the accused who are invited to appear in the court to participate in either the prosecution or defense (depending upon their attitude toward the defendant). However, neither replaces the officials empowered with the prosecution or defense but functions as kind of *amicus curiae*. An additional innovation of the 1962 Criminal Code of Procedure allows organizations to "sponsor" defendants. If the court accepts a sponsorship pledge, the accused is remanded to the reeducative tutelage of the sponsor without further trial. This sympathetic device has so far affected only a fraction of the accused. In 1965 (the only year for which data are available) the courts accepted 2,161 offers of sponsorship by trade union chapters and 300 submitted by other organizations. Over 800 offers were turned down.[30] Unlike the Local People's Courts, these practices have met with no major criticism or call for abolishment.

The Volume and Nature of Adjudication

Despite the differentiation within the judiciary, the regular courts—District Courts and the appellate Regional Courts—remain the most significant structures of adjudication in their sociopolitical impact upon the citizenry. Contrary to the ideological premise that socialism generates conflict-free human relations, the volume of civil litigation in Czechoslovakia has not declined in recent years (see Table 7.1). Rather, the opposite is true. In 1962, 52 civil cases per 10,000 population were adjudicated, and in 1967 this ratio climbed to 69. Considerable disproportion was registered among different provinces. Prague lead with 120 per 10,000 population followed, rather oddly, by Eastern Slovakia, the least developed part of the state, with 110. At the opposite end, Southern Bohemia appeared to be the most harmonious province (36:10,000).[31].

These findings caused no particular sorrow. It was the issue of crime and criminality which upset the Party ideologues. Their disappointment was preceded by confident statements of characteristic Stalinist sophistication:

Table 7.1. Volume of Civil Litigation in Czechoslovak Courts, 1965–1967.

Type of litigation	1965	1966	1967
Family affairs	193,269	208,509	201,373
Divorce	(21,794)	(23,150)	(22,730)
Labor litigation	25,794	27,065	22,457
Social security	10,266	11,843	9,542
Housing	11,052	10,838	10,196
Torts	14,705	14,702	13,930
Others	42,212	49,293	72,962
Total	297,298	322,250	330,460

Source: Statisticka rocenka CSSR 1968 [Statistical Yearbook of the CSSR, 1968] (Prague: SNTL, 1968), p. 126.

In capitalism the causes of criminality are poverty and unemployment, as attendant phenomena of the exploitation of man by man. In our country poverty and unemployment do not exist, and, t. erefore, criminality is caused by the remnants of capitalism in the consciousness and behavior of the people. The existence of remnants of capitalism in the consciousness and behavior of the people is a demonstration of the influence of law on social consciousness failing to catch up with social existence and is aggravated by the penetration of hostile ideology from the capitalist orbit, in particular through foreign movies, literature, and tourism. With the continuing construction of socialism, the incessant growth in the standard of living and culture of the toiling masses, and the merciless struggle against ideological diversion, criminality will decline continuously until it completely disappears. As far as individual moral infractions are concerned, society will settle these through the comradely influence of the collectives of fellow employees, citizens, and social organizations.[32]

Dogmatic minds refused to acknowledge reality for almost two decades, and it was not until the late 1960s that the issue was approached with some frankness. According to Federal Minister of Interior Jan Pelnar, the number of crimes had doubled between 1960 and 1967.[33]

Reportedly, crime in Czechoslovakia dropped after 1945 to a mere half of its prewar total and well below the average of Western European countries.[34] The Communist takeover in 1948 led to a high incidence of so-called political crimes. However, data concerning political offenders have never been released: not even during the democratization drive in 1968 was the number of political executions since 1948 made public. In the late 1950s, coinciding with the period of Novotny's elevation as president, a decline in criminality was once again reported.

The year 1960 was one of change and historical irony: "achievement of socialism" was promulgated, an era of social harmony was declared—and the crime rate started to spiral. The increase was greatest in juvenile delinquency and crimes of violence.

This development was symptomatic of a malaise affecting the entire society. The oppressive, dysfunctional, and infinitely dull political system of the Novotny era produced "socialist alienation," most evident among the uninhibited young. Any attempt to relieve the tedium was condemned as the "building of one's own private imaginary world and flight into this substitute for true self-realization."[35] In such a spiritual vacuum it is no wonder that a moral crisis accompanied the economic crisis, and that pilferage of socialist (i.e., state or cooperative) property became the most popular felony, constituting one-fifth of all criminal activity.

In 1969 it was reported that, on the average, every third violator of the law remained undetected: for pilferers of socialist property, the percentage was

44.7.[36] Crime in Czechoslovakia has been largely a male affair. In 1967, of all sentenced criminals 89.5 percent were male. Females were convicted mainly of such felonies as illegal flight from the country, crimes against property, and those which fall into the category of "parasitism." Violation of the law was most frequent among the young; seventeen was identified as the age most prone to crime. Recidivists, i.e., repeated offenders, committed 40 percent of all crimes, thus attesting to the poor rehabilitation record of penal institutions. Half of all crimes in the country were committed under the influence of alcohol.[37]

Some data on the educational background of the law violators have also been published. The person in Czechoslovakia most likely to commit a crime is a poorly educated teen-age male acting under the influence of alcohol. In 1967, of the total number of persons under indictment, 82.2 percent had not gone beyond grade school, and only 1.8 percent had attended (without necessarily completing) a university.[38] The most frequent crime of the latter was illegal exit from the country.

A psychological study of inmates of Pankrac prison in Prague was conducted in the early part of 1969. Of the total prison population, "economic delinquents" constituted the most numerous category (18.1 percent). In contrast, only 0.8 percent were labeled "political offenders." The average sentence in this institution was five years. The group with the lowest average IQ (90) comprised those individuals guilty of "crimes against youth and family" (including sex crimes), the next lowest consisted of perpetrators of crimes of violence. At the opposite end of the spectrum were political offenders, with an average IQ of 126, and economic delinquents, with an average IQ of 121.[39]

The reader may be justifiably surprised by the low percentage of political offenders. It is indeed remarkable that the upheavals of 1968, the most turbulent year since 1948 (if not since the creation of the state in 1918), did not produce a new generation of political prisoners. At the end of 1968 there were only 82 political prisoners reported out of a total of 11,020 convicts in the country.[40]

However, the situation worsened in 1969. Following the anti-Soviet riots in March and August, several thousand persons, mainly young people, were arrested.[41] Occasional press items began to appear referring to trials of a clearly political nature.[42]

Although lack of adequate data obscures the scope of judicial retribution, one thing is certain; these political trials were not confined to the capital. For example, in 1970 the court in Ceske Budejovice tried a man for the felony of "terrorism." His crime consisted of writing threatening letters to pro-Soviet citizens. In 1971, a group of six citizens who in the invasion days had mistreated the wife of a Stalinist politico were sentenced by the court in Kosice to a total of 39.5 years of imprisonment.[43] More ominously, after the November 1971 election (in which more than 99 percent of the vote was cast for candidates of the National Front) the regime ordered a wave of political arrests and trials. In 1972 several prominent reformist politicians and intellectuals were sentenced to long prison terms.[44] Moreover, the tens of thousands of citizens who have left the country since the invasion are likely to be considered political felons and tried in absentia. Special punitive legislation in 1969 and presidential amnesty further blur the picture.

Presidential amnesty requires some comment. Several declarations of amnesty have been published: in 1953, 1955, 1956, 1960, and several times in the following decade. Some 100,000 individuals benefitted from the 1968 amnesty.[45] As a rule, presidential pardon has favored the common criminal over the political prisoner, though in the later years of Novotny's rule, as a gesture of de-Stalinization, some categories of political prisoners were freed. On the whole, prison inmates benefitted at least as much from the numerous amnesties as from the rather liberal parole system. One is tempted to detect a peculiarly Czech quality of reconciliation behind this inflated presidential generosity, as if it were calculated to moderate the formal record of draconic punishments. The low life expectancy of political values also helps clarify the reasons for frequent pardoning. For example, it could hardly be considered in the best interests of the system for a person convicted before 1953 for villifying Stalin to share a cell in 1956 with someone who had been sentenced for praising the despot, although such Kafkaesque paradoxes are not uncommon. Cases have been reported in which secret police officers, imprisoned for torturing and extracting confessions from the innocent, were pardoned and released before their victims.[46]

Attempts to restore totalitarian practices in adjudication will be hampered by the revelations of

1968, when the public learned about the degree to which the law had been violated by those purporting to enforce it. Accordingly, the citizens now say to one another:

> Today we already know. A prosecutor who would lend himself to such trials will no longer be able to pose as a victim of Party duress, but will be a judicial murderer. A functionary who would like to feather his own nest is no longer a naive zealot, but a false witness. A consenting Party member will no longer be a poor deceived wretch, but equally guilty. And guilty will be all the silent and timid.[47]

The post-invasion political elite possess the power to fill the empty prisons but their use of that power is impeded by the revelations that have shown how "justice" has been administered during the last twenty years.

Challenges and Responses

The Stalinist pattern of adjudication was challenged several times in Czechoslovakia. The first attempt, following the Twentieth Congress of the Communist Party of the USSR in 1956, was short-lived and confined to a few individuals from the legal profession, without ever reaching public attention. Far more significant was the open questioning of the virtues of socialist justice from 1963 through 1965.[48] This campaign was actually initiated by Novotny as part of a whitewash of the regime's past treatment of the law, but it went out of control, considerably exceeding the bounds of suggested criticism. The Stalinist legal theory, the class concept of law, the subordination of legal to political interests, the connection between the leading role of the Party and the judicial process, the low quality of judges, and the dilettantism of the entire legal profession were topics that were publicly discussed. Illustrative of the soul-searching in this period is a statement by the writer Ivan Klima, attacking class discrimination:

> The hypertrophic application of the principle of "class" did not only cause immediate damage by disqualifying able men and preferring incompetent ones but, first of all, instead of promoting real values it promoted fictitious ones, independent of man, of his work, of his thinking. Awareness that in society there exist fictitious values and

privileges that determine a man's destiny at birth (whether these are proprietary, racial, or class values), always denigrates the category of freedom and stifles the energy of every man.[49]

These champions of de-Stalinization, however, were characterized by an absence of concreteness. Charges were manifold and specific, but the elaboration of sins was not accompanied by an identification of the sinners. The challenge did not even reach the dimensions of a dialogue between the deaf. The KSC did not bother to respond, and once the ammunition of the challengers was spent, business as usual proceeded on its tested course.

The third and last challenge, in 1968, was entirely different. This time, not the consequences but the causes, not the deviations from the system but the deviousness of the system, were rigorously examined and rejected in toto in specific, concrete terms. This indictment was not formulated by a mere handful of individuals. In an act of belated and not too sincere penitence, the whole judiciary jumped on the bandwagon. Documents prepared by the Prague Law School, the Supreme Court, and the Ministry of Justice presented a thorough analysis of the state of legal affairs and offered remedial measures toward restoration of judicial independence and integrity.[50] Prominent among the demands were abolishment of the Party's supervisory power; reduction of the prosecutor's role from "guardian of socialist justice" to one of public accuser; reintroduction of tenure for judges, or at least extension of their electoral term; curbing of the influence of the lay element in adjudication; increased jurisdiction for regular courts and corresponding restrictions on administrative authorities and various arbitration tribunals; abolishment of the amateur Local People's Courts.

These and similar proposals were not so much innovation as a call for the *status quo ante*. Restoration of the three-level court system, abolished in 1948, was proposed in 1968. Such was also true of changes in the Criminal Code or the transfer of prison administration from the Ministry of the Interior back to the Ministry of Justice. The demand for separation of common criminals from political offenders, with preferential treatment for the latter, was also a demand for the return to an earlier practice.[51]

The Rehabilitation Act of August 1, 1968, was, in the words of the new president of the Supreme

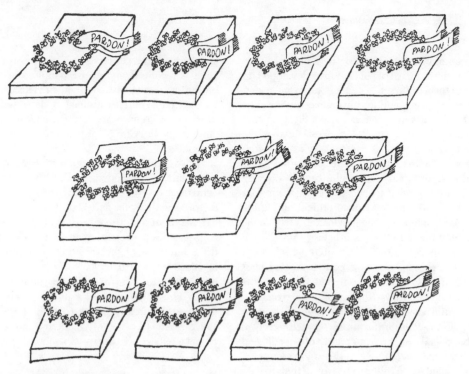

(*Literarni listy*, April 18, 1968)

Court, Otomar Bocek, "without precedent in judicial history anywhere"[52] and is the most remarkable document of that period. By its enactment, the entire punitive record of the state for the past two decades was thus submitted to review. Any person, or his relatives or heirs, could challenge an original court decision, and the claim would be handled in an abbreviated procedure by a panel of three judges. Any judge who had been active in the period concerned was disqualified from participation. The review court was to annul the original verdicts in the event that it found violations of substantive law (e.g., false evidence), violations of procedural law (e.g., use of violence in the pre-trial phase), the presence of "provocation" (e.g., the formation of an espionage ring by an impostor in the pay of the STB), and so-called "notorieties" (e.g., an apprehended border crosser convicted of espionage and high treason on the presumption that had he succeeded in leaving the country, he would have engaged in subversive activities). Particularly significant was the provision of the law which absolved the claimant of the burden of proof and ordered the court to reexamine ex officio the propriety of the original trial in all its aspects. The law affected thousands of citizens. However, within the one-year deadline for submitting the petition, less petitioners came forward than expected. Of the cases submitted, the overwhelming majority were decided in favor of the claimants.[53]

After Novotny, the regime exhibited a good deal of inconsistency in coping with the issues of an unpleasant past. Readiness to offer legal rehabilitation contrasted with reluctance, no doubt economically motivated, to offer compensation to the victims of judicial and administrative persecution. The leadership appeared least willing to prosecute those guilty of Stalinist crimes. Against the wish of the overwhelming majority of the nation and protests from distinguished lawyers, Stalinist brutes were granted immunity from prosecution with the help of numerous presidential amnesties and the statute of limitations.[54] Unless a person was charged with murder—in which case the twenty-year statute of limitation would not have run out—he could not be brought to trial.

As far as is known, only one trial of Stalinists was held. Seven secret police officers—including Josef Cech, the head of Novotny's personal guard, and M. Pich-Tuma, a Communist member of parliament—were accused of the murder of two men, whom they had gunned down "in the name of revolutionary justice" and secretly buried. Given the failure to prosecute anyone from the deposed political hierarchy, this unique trial of Stalinists developed (in the eyes of the nation) into a trial of Stalinism—a kind of little Nuremberg and an anticlimax to Slansky's trial. The Reports and comments on the trial that appeared almost daily in the press stimulated the emergence of great soul-searching questions concerning such matters as the limits of revolutionary arbitrariness, criminal responsibility for obeying criminal orders, and the conflict between superior Bolshevik morality and universal ethical principles. The accused, including the lawmaker Pich-Tuma, did not deny the murders; nonetheless, they did not seem to grasp the raison d'etre of the trial. They rejected the proceedings as a contrivance of class enemies and insisted that the only law they had ever known and honored was "the law of class struggle." These faithful executors of a Party order—murder voted for in the Politburo—quite justly felt betrayed and abandoned in this moment of need, and demanded that notables of the old hierarchy, Novotny included, be called to testify on their behalf. Without this request being granted, the only trial of Stalinism ended in June 1969. As a sorry epitaph to the 1968 determination to cope with the crimes of past era, the defendants were set free on both substantive and procedural grounds.[55]

In his inauguration speech in April 1969, Husak tried to dispel any doubts about the future rule of law: "In our country we shall very strictly maintain legality, strictly protect the people's rights, but also strictly enforce the laws. And all the rumors about political trials? We don't want and we shall not tolerate fabrication of such cases. Nothing good can be built on falsehood, quite the contrary. . . ."[56] Husak promised a kind of socialist *Rechtstaat* with guarantees of legal security though not political freedom. Let us briefly examine this pledge against Husak's record in matters of revelation, rehabilitation, and retribution—these three R's of the Czechoslovak reform movement of 1968.

First, strict censorship, the closing of journals with a liberal bent, and massive purges among journalists, all contributed to the ending of revelations about Stalinism. Instead of further analyses, a gradual whitewash of the totalitarian past began.

Second, in the summer of 1969 the deadline for submitting petitions for judicial review of earlier trials expired. In August the first anniversary of the Soviet invasion precipitated riots that caused

authorities to introduce various repressive measures. Husak's regime denounced rehabilitation as an opportunistic, revisionistic maneuver. This charge, and the call for a halt to judicial reviews was not articulated by some obscure dogmatic propagandists only, but by the CSR Minister of Justice, Jan Nemec, as well.[57]

Third, retribution for Stalinist crimes, after its lame start, crash-landed, and all the incriminating debris was carefully swept away. As pointed out by the press in the brief period of its freedom, it is easy to rehabilitate a victim if he is dead, even easier if the culprit is dead, and easiest of all if both parties are dead. But many of the architects and implementors of injustice are still alive, and many of them hold positions in the security apparatus, judiciary, and the Party. Thus, the Central Committee's investigation commission—already the third one, chaired by Jan Piller, a rather conservative apparatchik—has failed to make public or to act upon its final report.[58]

Recent Developments

The prospects of a socialist *Rechtstaat* soon became dim, as evidenced by developments immediately following Husak's assumption of leadership in April 1969. Within the first hundred days under this former victim of Stalinist persecution, a number of progressive members of the judiciary were removed, and the demand for a strict adherence to law was called a new tactic of political enemies.[59] Zdenek Zuska, a newcomer to the top rank of the Party apparatus, and in charge of law and order in the Czech provinces, offered the chilling observation that "the principle of equality before the law has often been overused."[60] In response to the anti-Soviet riots on the first anniversary of the invasion, the Presidium of the Federal Assembly produced literally overnight an extraordinary repressive decree. This manifestly unconstitutional measure, promulgated on August 22, 1969, suspended the remaining civil rights (free choice of residence, and protection against arbitrary termination of employment because of "loss of trust"), increased by one-half the maximum penalties for eleven offenses in the Criminal Code, and gave the police detention powers in excess of anything known before.[61] The only mitigating feature of the decree was its proclaimed temporariness. Valid only until December 31, 1969, the total life expectancy of this harsh measure was four months and one week.

However, in a not unexpected breach of legal commitment, the decree was made permanent by its incorporation into the Criminal Code, effective January 1, 1970.

Altogether, eight laws affecting adjudication were promulgated on the eve of the seventies.[62] Structural innovations included changes in the federal framework and redefinition of jurisdictional boundaries. Changes of this nature also applied to regional and district courts. The term of office for elected judges was extended from four to ten years, and the role of lay assessors in both criminal and civil proceedings was curtailed. The Labor Code was amended to facilitate the removal of politically undesirable employees. Other laws in this group introduced new offenses, such as exporting or importing printed material deemed injurious to the state. This particular law (No. 150/69) conflicts with the United Nations Covenant on Civil and Political Rights signed by Czechoslovakia in 1968 and further illustrates the vigor of authoritarian restoration.

The legislative output is hardly the best example of the changing times of the 1970s. To obtain a feel for the imposed sociopolitical transformation in Czechoslovakia, it may be useful to turn to the Party-controlled mass media, which embarked on an ambitious but not too realistic venture of turning black into white, and vice versa. For example, the veteran journalist Vojtech Dolejsi denounced the 1968 policy of rehabilitating victims of Stalinism and implied that their suffering was justified. Jaroslav Kucera went even further than this; according to him injustice, terror, and murders did not exist under Stalinism but were characteristic of the year 1968. Judicial murders were annulled by being referred to as "so-called judicial murders," and Stalinist henchmen became "so-called compromised judges."[63]

CSR Minister of Justice Jan Nemec seems to breathe the same Stalinist fire. According to Nemec, "the judiciary was slow to embark upon the path of consolidation [i.e., *status quo ante* 1968], starting only in the second half of 1969, and that was much later than in other branches of government."[64] Nemec reported the following causes of this retarded development: (1) the Ministry of Justice had for a number of years failed to live up to its responsibility for supervising adjudication; (2) wrong ideas about judicial independence became predominant; (3) the Supreme Court in 1968–1969 played politics to the neglect of its duties; and (4) a number of writers had publicly stressed the primacy of individual rights over the rights of the society. Minister Nemec reflected, "the cause must be found in some sort of dove-like nature of the Czech nation."[65]

On another occasion, Nemec castigated judges for promoting judicial independence, including independence from the Communist Party.[66] The judiciary, it was also charged, failed because of its liberal attitudes and stress on the rehabilitative rather than repressive function of the courts.[67]

Identification of deviant tendencies was soon followed by identification of their perpetrators. By the end of 1970, more than one-third of all chairmen of provincial and district courts had been removed.[68] The purge seems to have become a permanent process, in view of the occasional press releases briefly announcing the recall of dozens of justices.[69] There are not enough recruits to fill the vacancies; the old generation, including individuals implicated in the most sordid judicial murders, have been called back to the bench.[70]

In addition to the replacement of personnel, different adjudication policies have also been demanded: in particular, the restored subordination of the courts to the Party tutelage, a class approach in both criminal and civil matters, and abandonment of the policy of the early 1960s favoring rehabilitation over retribution. According to the CSR Chief Justice, Josef Ondrej, the punitive record of the courts has improved. Whereas in 1969 nonprobationary sentences amounted to 21 percent of all verdicts in the CSR, this figure increased to 30.1 percent in 1970, and to 35.3 percent in the first quarter of 1971.[71]

In view of these developments it may be concluded that the tendencies toward judicial autonomy have been thwarted and the leading role of the Party restored, with all the attendant side effects harmful to due process of law.

The next speaker stated that, according to the regulations, only the best of the best, people truly dedicated to socialism, should be elected to the committees, and how could he, a poor man, guarantee this if the secret ballot were introduced, which would enable the people to elect whomever they want?

Reporter, *April 3, 1969.*

8

There is a growing conflict in society, caused by the attempts of ill-qualified people to maintain their control over the well qualified.

Reporter, *March 27, 1969.*

Political Recruitment

Political recruitment—defined as a function by means of which the officials of the political system are selected—has been the sole prerogative of the Communist Party in Czechoslovakia since 1948. This power has extended from the political system to other systems (notably the economic).

Elsewhere in this book we have noted the high price Czechoslovakia has paid for its docile imitation of a less developed country. Class discrimination from cradle to grave and a primitive hostility toward the educated strata have been costly effects of the dictatorship of the proletariat. The nature of the political system ruled out universal criteria for recruitment: either popular choice (election) or proof of ability (competitive examination). Instead, particularism, promoting individuals of desired class purity and political maturity, has become the norm. The higher and more desirable the position, the more restricted the selection. Thus, while a working class background and a record of Party activism would suffice for acceptance in the police apparatus, it would not secure an entry into diplomatic service,

where additional "merits," notably nepotistic ties, are required.

High turnover among office holders is not a standard procedure under a one-party monopoly but it is often the consequence of such a crisis as a struggle for power or a purge. New blood thus enters the weakened but purified body of the political system. However, a purge often tends to become unmanageable, seeking victims indiscriminately and sparing no groups, its own architects included. On the other hand, some purges are merely formal, symbolic affairs that do not endanger or revitalize entrenched forces.

Except during the Stalinist purges of the early 1950s, a political career in Czechoslovakia has been a low-risk occupation and certainly not a health hazard. In contrast to Soviet Russia, littered with corpses of liquidated comrades, the most notable quality of a Czechoslovak political office holder has been his durability. The "cadre ceiling" has insulated the closed, self-appointed elite from the danger of competition and other challenges. This has been es-

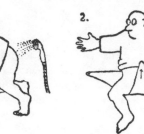

(*Listy*, May 15, 1969)

pecially true among the higher *nomenklatura*, in dividuals selected for office by a higher Party agency and hence unassailable from lower Party echelons. "There exists a type of Party members who possess the so-called *duvera* [confidence of the KSC] and who are therefore destined to hold a variety of leading roles."[1] They pass from one position for which they are not qualified to another for which they are equally unqualified. It is not unusual for the Party to establish some ad hoc structure in order to accommodate virtually unemployable comrades.

An additional character of recruitment under the KSC monopoly is the not infrequent lack of motivation in the prospective candidate. Instead of seeking office, he is drafted, and the Party obedience that is his foremost qualification prevents him from protesting. These are then "the faithful soldiers of socialism," the officer corps of "garrison socialism," as Czechoslovak Stalinism has been called.

The Party maintains that its criteria for recruitment are based on merit in its purest form. In unconcerned inconsistency, qualities independent of human will and achievement—such as historical class predestination, proletarian origin, kinship with a distinguished revolutionary, and the crudest nepotistic lies—are regarded as "merits." Similarly, little attention is paid to complaints about restricted social mobility, more akin to feudalism than socialism, and to protestations such as, "Government by a single Party is a biological absurdity, for it means, genetically, government by people of a single type, from top to bottom. . . . Imagine the kind of people who join the ruling Party: Most are guided by pure self-interest."[2]

Despite their overall prewar leftist orientation, the intelligentsia, including professionals from workers' families, were treated with suspicion after 1948. The Party-imposed and -enforced social mobility resulted in the replacement of about a quarter of a million officials[3] in government and economy by individuals who except for pedigree and political conformity had little to offer. In a great many cases, a working class background is the crucial credential and an inexhaustible source of political capital. Illustrative of this, the Party's First Secretary in the Nymburk District has been a full-time apparatchik for over twenty years, yet he identifies himself as a "tailor-worker."[4] Needless to say, such a self-styled worker has little in common with the real working class.

Ex-proletarian protégés of the Party are characterized by dilettantism and a definite lack of qualification for their roles. Professional competence and political maturity have been treated as two separate, almost mutually exclusive, categories. A corollary notion has been the widely held theory that a person could be taught anything irrespective of talent.[5] The management of nationalized industries was entrusted to *delnicti reditele* (literally translated, "proletarian executives") who had no previous experience or training.

This recruitment pattern left a damaging legacy of vested interests that blocked the challenge of the better educated young generation.[6] As noted in Chapter 6, the resistance of the entrenched forces was one of the major causes of the failure to implement the New Economic Model. Pledges from the Novotny regime that political loyalty would no longer provide job security for the incompetent have not been kept.[7]

Not even the most determined reformers of the Dubcek regime succeeded in breaking the closed, particularistic recruitment system. In the pre-invasion period the notorious system of the "cadre ceiling," blocking career advancement for non-Communists, was not abolished, and there is nothing to suggest its abolition since. Cadre questionnaires, requiring information on the political activities of distant relatives, on travel abroad, and residence data for as much as thirty years, have withstood campaigns for repeal with the force of a law of nature.[8]

Lure of a Career

In "garrison socialism" any loyal, disciplined comrade—the kind who refers to himself as a "soldier of the Party"—is likely to be drafted to fill a position for which his only qualification is the confidence of the Party. Sometimes he may choose between alternatives, for example, between the Party apparatus and the security forces.

These ranks contain not only draftees but genuine volunteers and mercenaries as well. It was precisely this that provided the basis for the attempt to whitewash and exculpate the proletarians, and the working class in general, from complicity in Stalinist crimes. In the protracted juggling over responsibility for the corpses of former comrades, the Trojan Horse

theory was coined, according to which guilt lay with former Gestapo men who had penetrated the state security apparatus.[9] This whitewash theory was demolished by referring to the facts: although a handful of individuals, such as V. Kohoutek, the prominent investigator of the Slansky group, had been in Nazi employment, the majority of the STB were dedicated Communists with the most impeccable proletarian credentials, obeying only the will of the Party.[10] Stalinism also offered an opportunity for engagement and purposefulness to persons who had so far been failures. For many, it was not so much "humble origins" as much as "humble achievement" that propelled them into involvement with the totalitarian cause. Mysanthropes of all persuasions also found an opportunity to settle their accounts with the world. It is not without interest to discover that many Stalinist recruits had once had occupations in which one's self-respect may suffer. Waiters, barbers, hairdressers, shoe salesmen, traveling salesmen, and others subject to long and degrading experience with customers' whims—so typical of Central Europe—were frequent candidates for totalitarian roles.[11]

Writing on the attraction of Stalinism, one Czech observer pointed out that "whenever uncivilized political manners have been introduced into a society, there has been an influx of hordes of unbalanced people in public life."[12] "Perpetual students," deserted husbands, embittered spinsters, sexual failures, the physically handicapped, unfrocked priests, and dropouts of all types hurried into political engagement.

Inferiority complexes are often accompanied by immaturity and the longing for submission to authority: individuals with a disciplinarian upbringing may find a totalitarian career highly attractive. The totalitarian careerist not only obeys but also issues order. Servility to superiors and arrogance toward subordinates—this traditional pattern, characteristic of the former domains of the Austro-Hungarian Empire, required only minor adjustments to fulfill the yearning of the "Party soldiers" for uniformity and conformity. In its latter years the Novotny regime increasingly favored political recruitment of this type of person. It should be noted that key themes in the defense of the implementers of totalitarianism for the last twenty years have been "fidelity," "faithfulness," and "obedience." Similarly, the adjective "honest" was always used to defend an incompetent comrade.[13]

Prolonged engagement in political roles made it next to impossible for individuals to return to "civilian life." Their skills were nil, obsolete, or long forgotten. But, as one writer argued, it would be a mistake to interpret the reluctance of the Stalinists to surrender their political roles as solely a concern for the preservation of their material well-being.[14] It is not only the *job* but the *life* itself—i.e., its purpose—that is threatened, and aggressive responses and rationalization are used to defend the endangered values. The dogmatic mind does not seek truth but confirmation of its beliefs. Objective reality is either ignored or treated in a way which psychologists call "false projection," a reaction similar to that of a child who when hurt by a protruding corner of a piece of furniture slaps the object.[15] Czechoslovak Stalinists, instead of doubting their historical destiny, have for years been searching for pieces of furniture to slap. The most prominent targets, especially in the post-invasion period, have been artists and the mass media.

Instead of engaging in rational dialogue, the Stalinist embarks on a verbose flurry noted for its lack of any concrete content. Reference to hazy socialist goals of a distant, undefinable future is the standard response to any logical argument. This inability to communicate anything but abstract platitudes has been particularly evident among the older generation. They demand from the young allegiance to archaic dreams and illusions; disappointed with the response, they invoke own experience and sacrifices and issue reprimands for ingratitude. It has been said that these conservatives resemble the realists of medieval Catholicism. These defenders of the faith, too, thwarted all criticism by pointing to the fundamental, and hence undisputable, holiness of the Church.[16]

An even less charitable interpretation of the behavioral pattern of the Stalinists has been offered by referring to their exceptional mediocrity. A poverty of intellect, above anything else, it was said, prevented them from rational dialogue in the censorship-free year of 1968.[17] Dogmatism, antiintellectualism, primitivism, and intolerance were frequently cited characteristics of this political subculture. The Stalinists-by-persuasion were joined by Stalinists-by-necessity—mainly, opportunists too discredited to be acceptable for roles of comparable stature in the posttotalitarian system.[18] This community of mutual interests made bedfellows of

"proletarian executives" and the ex-bourgeois Party members of 1948 vintage, with both in solid opposition to reformist Party forces.

Estimating the numerical strength of the Stalinists is a favorite pastime. Given the nature of the subject, no accurate data are obtainable, if any exist at all. However, it has been established that at the end of the 1960s the so-called Party *Aktif*, which has remained under the Stalinist spell, maintained a strength of between 200,000 and 400,000, i.e., between one-eighth and one-fourth of the total KSC membership.[19]

It seems a safe though somewhat trite observation that man's resistance to change, irrespective of his true political temperament, is in direct proportion to the hardship such a change would effect. In Czechoslovakia, such an attitude has been hardened by the failure of the KSC to effect an orderly exchange of cadres. Once recruited, a person becomes established within the circle of the chosen. Miroslav Kusy, the prominent Slovak reformer, pointed out: "There has been no normal return of the power elite into the community at large. If someone violated the rules of the game, or proved totally incompetent (which was practically impossible), or had to be sacrificed, there was only one possible way of leaving: departure by scandal."[20] With or without impeachment and trial, the degree of disgrace was influenced by the notoriety of the person involved and type of work he did. Unlike some other agencies of the state, the secret police apparently knows how to provide a smooth transition from power to obscurity for its former officials.[21]

The lack of orderly cadre exchange did not jeopardize the totalitarian system of self-perpetuation before 1968, but proved to be a great handicap in the following period. Reform could not be carried out by conservative functionaries, and their reluctance to abdicate was complemented by the reluctance of Dubcek's regime to force them out. Dubcek's credo was that "Party ethics demanded that people be dealt with in a humane, dignified, humanistic way."[22] Anxious to avoid the semblance of a purge, the emphasis was on persuasion, appeal to good will, and the prospect of a comfortable retirement. As we know, there were few takers, the majority biding its time and thirsting for revenge. Both desires materialized.

In 1968 "horizontal demotion" became widely practiced, consisting largely of exiling the old guard

(*Rohac*, June 5, 1968)

to diplomatic posts. After the Soviet invasion this cadre movement was applied along the lines of political geography. Totally discredited conservatives like Politburo member Drahomir Kolder went to Bulgaria, and prominent liberals like Jiri Hanzelka and Jiri Pelikan were dispatched to the safety of Oslo and Rome, respectively.

Federalization of the country was also exploited as a pretext for reshuffling politicians hostile to the reform program of 1968. For example, the conservative Vasil Bilak, no longer acceptable in Slovakia, was assigned to Prague to represent his hostile constituency in the Politburo.[23]

Although the turbulent last two years of the 1960s endangered the conservative political cadres, and many officials were temporarily suspended, the majority were ultimately restored to their sinecures.

Apparatchiks and the Party College

The performance of the KSC apparatus may be viewed as a magnification rather than a mere reflection of the malfunctioning in other spheres of the totalitarian system. In matters of exaggerated urgency, overloading, secrecy, *obezlichka*, improvisation, and maximum bureaucratization, the leading example of the Party has been truly established.

The leadership emulated their Soviet counterparts in introducing innovations and prescribing the subsequent remedies. Prague engaged, with an equal

lack of success, in the Khrushchev-inspired populist effort at debureaucratization of the Party apparatus. It appears that the burden imposed on the unpaid activists was too heavy for them to carry. The majority of the activists were functionaries 2.5 times over, spending an estimated eighty hours a month in political activity, in addition to their regular employment.[24] As a result Party work and/or the Party worker suffered.

This shortcoming—known as "formalism" in the official catalog of sins—was evident among Party professionals as well. The apparatchiks were further handicapped by frequent shifts of their assignments. No rational system of rotation existed; haphazard transfers and whimsical reshuffling were prevalent. It was revealed in 1969 that 72 percent of the workers in the Party's central apparatus had been transferred an average of six to ten times.[25]

Since 1948 a record of service in the Party apparatus has become a precondition for a career in a (nominally) elective Party office, or for a significant position in the government (e.g., as minister or commissioner). Only rarely have these offices been filled by individuals without any earlier service in the Party apparatus. The Secretariat of the KSC Central Committee, as the hub of power, has retained for its own use what it considered to be the best cadres. Assignment of Party workers to government posts has often been viewed as a disgrace and punishment. Miroslav Kusy, an insider with top Party rank in

Bratislava, commented in 1968 on this subject:"This way we have created a special system of punishment: if you turn into a failure in the Party apparatus, you are assigned a function in the state administration, or we send you to a diplomatic post."[26]

Not even Party bureaucrats can remain forever youthful. By the end of the 1960s, the generation of recruits from the immediate postwar period had reached middle age. The younger generation that will eventually replace them are, on the whole, much better educated. The proletarians recruited straight from the assembly line are being challenged by a new breed of better trained Party bureaucrats. In 1969 it was reported that over a third of all apparatchiks had graduated from a university.[27] Distribution of the graduates has been uneven; more of them are found among departmental heads than among secretaries of the KSC apparatus. Importantly, the educated apparatchiks are not monopolized by the secretariat of the Central Committee in Prague but many are being dispatched into the districts. (However, specific data on this distribution is not available.)

The alma mater of the majority of the educated apparatchiks is the Party College in Prague. This institution has been renamed several times—in 1972 it was known as the "Higher Political School of the Central Committee of the Communist Party of Czechoslovakia." Along with the label, the school itself has changed (at least temporarily) from an uninspiring propaganda center to perhaps the most significant political institution in the country. Westerners know of FAMU, the famous college of cinematography in Prague, but Easterners have heard much more of the Party College, the source of revisionism during the 1960s. What writers, intellectuals, and journalists did for democratization of the political system in the society at large, teachers and graduates of the Party College have done for the strategic centers of Party power. Milan Hübl, a brilliant young scholar and the president of the Party College in 1968 commented on the subject:

I know of no other institution of higher learning in Czechoslovakia whose entire faculty was so politically engaged and took all the risks involved. . . . Don't forget that a considerable number of the "Men of January" [i.e., the progressives] at the center as well as on the regional and district levels are graduates of this school. There is no need to give names here, but if there were any persons

within the Czechoslovak Communist movement actively striving for change, these were to a large degree people who came out of the gates of Veleslavin [i.e., the school]. The political university has therefore been subjected more than once to harassment and criticism.[28]

The Party apparatus has traditionally been distrustful of sophisticated interpreters of the official ideology, as a great numbers of teachers of Marxism-Leninism in Eastern Europe would testify.[29] During the 1960s, much of this hostility was focused on the Party College. By supplying graduates for the Party apparatus, the school presented both an ideological and existential threat to entrenched forces.

Since its inception, there has been no love lost between the Party College and the state institutions of higher learning, and for a variety of reasons, such as conflicts over allocation of resources, disdain of traditional schools for the newcomer, and the issue of academic degrees that are so dear to the Czech political culture and mentality. In 1953, despite massive opposition throughout the country, doctorates were abolished and replaced by descriptive unabbreviated professional titles. (Since they make little sense in Czech, we shall dispense with the attempt to translate them into English.) The national feeling was that the law abolishing them was a primitive act of an envious, uneducated ruling class. In the course of the years, with more apparatchiks enrolling in and graduating from the Party College, they themselves developed a taste for the forbidden academic fruit. Allegedly, by 1966 there were enough apparatchiks who were qualified for "political Ph.D.s," so that the law was changed and the awarding of traditional academic degrees gradually restored.[30]

Along with its title, the Party College has also frequently changed its structure and affiliation, at one time being both a state and a Party school. This temporary fusion occurred: in the early 1950s, as a result of a Stalinist witchhunt, the state social sciences institution was abolished. (Its present descendant is the School of Economics in Prague.) Thus, the Party College functioned as a sort of school of political science, the only such school in the country. An alternative solution was to send students to Moscow to either the Soviet Party College or the Institute of International Relations.

The transformation of the Prague Party College from a mere propaganda center to a crucible of revisionism was a long process. The conflict between dogmatism and progressivism was exemplified by the differences between Vilem Novy, a Stalinist of ultra-conservative temperament and long-time president of the school, and Milan Hübl, his temporary successor, and the majority of the faculty. Periodic purges of the faculty took place under Novy, as in 1964, when the legal theorist Zdenek Jicinsky, the historian Milos Hajek, and the economist Karel Kouba were removed.[31] After January 1968, Novy was one of the few Stalinists forced to resign. After the invasion, it was Hübl's turn for involuntary departure, along with many of his colleagues.[32]

Some figures attesting to the failure of the "ideological front" were offered by Gustav Husak at the Fourteenth Congress of the KSC in May 1971: "One hundred out of 170 lecturers on Marxism-Leninism had to be fired, and half of the Party secretaries in charge of ideology dismissed, and whole institutes of political learning have had to be closed or restructured."[33] According to Jan Fojtik, Secretary of the Central Committee, the Party College had recovered its Marxist spirit by 1971. The regular school program now requires four years. After completing an introductory (uniform) curriculum, students specialize in one of three fields: philosophic-historical, economic, or social studies. The Party College is also expected to guide provincial Party schools and even district training programs.[34]

In addition to the regular courses, a number of special programs are listed. In the school year 1967–1968 there were nine kinds of short-term courses and two kinds of one-year courses: cultural politics for Party workers in regional and district offices and in the mass media, and also, sociology and the theory of management for apparatchiks and teachers of Marxism-Leninism.[35] In the school year 1968–1969 qualified applicants could take a two-semester postgraduate course in management theory and Marxist sociology. (A qualified applicant has a minimum of five years of Party membership, preferably with experience in the Party apparatus, has completed the university, and is under thirty-five.) An outline of the courses refers to such topics as "Mathematical Models of Decision Making Processes," "Sociological Theory of Organization," "A Cybernetic Approach to Management," "Applied Sociological Research," all clearly alien to earlier Stalinist thinking.[36] However, it is very likely

that the post-invasion "normalization" of the faculty was also matched by gradual "normalization" of the curriculum.

The disease of revisionism also penetrated other institutions of political recruitment. At the Klement Gottwald Military-Political Academy thirty scholars allegedly failed in a test to define existing contradictions between socialism and capitalism. The Party diagnosed the ideological decrepitude as fatal and had the school closed in 1969.[37] The Central Committee's Institute for Political Sciences, set up in 1967 for the purpose of assisting the Party in political and social analysis, was also closed in 1969 and its director, Vaclav Slavik, expelled from the Party. Further restoratory measures in 1969 affected all universities in the country; for example, all social science departments were ordered to be replaced by "Institutes of Marxism-Leninism." The Institute of Social-Political Sciences in Prague, along with its branches in Brno and Bratislava, was closed and replaced by the Institute of Marxism-Leninism attached to the Party's Central Committee. Bourgeois disciplines such as sociology and political science were once again brushed aside in favor of the "three classic Marxist disciplines," i.e., dialectical materialism, historical materialism, and scientific socialism-communism. An integrated, uniform program of ideological instruction was to be fully implemented at all institutions of higher learning in the school year 1970–1971.[38]

Political Recruitment and the Young Generation

The charge that Czechoslovak Stalinism at first discriminated against only some youth, and later against all youth, is not entirely inaccurate. The emphasis on class warfare made family background the main criterion for college admission, and registrars were openly hostile toward anyone not from the working class. Over the years this hostility became generalized. The "class instinct" gave way to a blend of political and generational hostility against the entire younger generation, who, though born under socialism, did not seem to accept the values of their elders.

At the outset, the KSC openly and even proudly announced its policy of preventing children with undesirable political or social family backgrounds from having access to higher education. This bias reached its peak in the early 1950s. Often, the majority of a graduating *Gymnasium* class would be assigned to manual labor whereas the students who came from families with impeccable Party records were forced to continue studies for which they had neither the interest nor talent. This experiment failed miserably. Many of the "recruited students" did not succeed, and most of the political rejects, after some years of wasteful detours through fields and workshops, managed to be admitted to the school of their choice. As a result, statistics on the social composition of university students reveal the percentages in Table 8.1.[39]

Table 8.1. Social Composition of University Students (in percentages).

School year	Workers	Children of Peasants	Others
1949/1950	27.6	9.9	62.5
1963/1964	37.9	8.3	53.8

Among other things, these figures revealed the continuing importance of the family's influence on offspring. The low percentage of youth of working class background led the Party to admit reluctantly in 1966 that "since 1948 we have not succeeded in balancing the share of youth from workers' families in university studies with the share and role of the working class in society."[40] Although 93.4 percent of children of university-educated parents expressed a desire to attend a university, this dropped to 42.8 percent among children of parents with only an elementary school education. Among families in which both parents did not go beyond grade school, no less than 60 percent of the offspring failed to reach a higher level whereas in families with at least one parent better educated, the probability of children reaching a higher level increased to 70 percent.[41] Official acknowledgement of facts, two decades too late, read: "Facts show that the system of selecting for higher education children with a so-called working class background [a euphemism for families with an elementary school education] has not been properly worked out. The administrative method of selection has helped neither the children nor the state."[42] Irrespective of proclamations about

achieved socialism in 1960, class discrimination in education, employment, and opportunities in general continued. It was not until April 1968 that the last (1962) discriminatory regulations were (at least *pro tempore*) abolished.[43]

In the 1960s the Novotny regime liberalized the system of mandatory job assignment for university graduates. Prior to that, type and place of employment for each graduate were specified in a so-called "assignment order" against which there was no legitimate appeal. In 1965 free manpower recruitment was tried with 23 percent of the university graduates. In 1966 47 percent of the graduates were given the privilege of selecting their employment, and it was planned to make this practice universal.[44] In the meantime, improvement was made in the surviving practice of employment assignment—some attention being paid to individual preference.

Some changes also occurred in political recruitment. In the Novotny era the channels of political advancement in the Party were clogged. At the same time there was little real challenge to aging office holders by the younger generation. The Czechoslovak Youth Organization (CSM), unlike its model, the Soviet Komsomol, played no significant role as a recruitment agency or as an avenue to a political career. CSM was unsuccessful with young people, commanding mainly the loyalty of its full-time employees. Since CSM membership was a prerequisite to higher education, whole *Gymnasium* classes joined as formal, nonparticipating members. The organization failed in even nominal recruitment among youth in industry.

Although CSM membership was the rule among students, Party membership was not. A belated effort was made to rejuvenate the Party; to accomplish this the leadership in 1966 abandoned the Soviet practice of "candidacy" as the first step toward full admission. In this very atypical demonstration of independence, the Czechoslovak leaders calculated that doing away with trial membership would simplify the paperwork in the local organizations, would be welcomed by the present members, and, above all, would rejuvenate Party ranks. The first two objectives were realized, the third not at all.[45]

Political recruitment has been pursued also outside the KSC. In the 1960 elections for People's Committees (local, district, and regional) almost a quarter of a million individuals were elected. Of these, less than 12,000 (less than 5 percent of the total) were under twenty-six.[46] Moreover, the absolute majority of these young deputies were elected to local committees. Among the eighty committee members of any average-sized district in Prague, two to four were young deputies. Often encountering misunderstanding and even hostility by their elders, in 1965 they began to organize Young Deputies clubs for the protection and advocacy of the interests of their generation. These clubs were reportedly established throughout the country.[47]

Very few of the young held Party offices. In 1968 there was not a single member of the Central Committee of the KSC under thirty-five![48] In becoming a member of the Communist Party a young person separated himself quite substantially from his own generation without, however, getting any closer to the older generation of the Party. This predicament was articulated by young Party functionaries at the university in Prague who stated that a dialogue with the rest of the KSC was simply not possible. For the young, the Party is merely a means; for the old, it is an end in itself. It was emphasized that the price for political engagement by a young person was total isolation.

The danger of losing contact with one's own generation without gaining anything in return has been a considerable deterrent to political engagement. In an opinion survey among university students in 1968—the one and only year of genuine popularity of the Party—the majority (roughly four to one) indicated a willingness to engage in political work, but *outside* the Communist Party. Only one-fifth of the respondents said they would join the Party if invited to do so.[49] Given the widening gap between the Party and society at large in the post-invasion period, the generational difficulties that beset political recruitment were bound to worsen.

The 1968 Draft of Party Statutes attempted to cure and prevent a relapse of several of the ills described thus far. First, acquisition of both Party and state offices by an individual was to be gradually eliminated; second, a set of guarantees would prohibit any one person from holding several significant Party offices; third, tenurial privileges and ossified self-perpetuation in office were to be eliminated by restricting the Party functionaries to two terms of two years each. Any exception to this rule would require a two-thirds majority vote by the members of the appointing authority.[50]

Eleven days after publication of the draft the Soviet invasion of Czechoslovakia took place, aimed at ending just such revisionist experimentation. Since then, gradual reintroduction of the closed, particularistic pattern of recruitment has taken place.

Data on the 1969–1970 purge of Party ranks are included in Chapter 3. In all, membership declined by some 470,000 (28 percent) to a new low of 1,200,000. Turnover in Party offices has been even more substantial. No comprehensive data reflecting all the political and career changes have been made public. However, the following examples indicate the magnitude of the turmoil among the careerists.

During 1968, 57.8 percent of all officers under thirty left the army at their own request. The Party, unable to replace the depleted officer corps, called three years later for the establishment of a two-year emergency military academy.[51] By 1971 almost half of all school supervisors had been replaced.[52] And by 1972 almost 40 percent of all journalists in the country had been dismissed.[53]

Nomenklatura appointments, which required consent by the Party Secretariat (of the district, regional, or central committee, depending on the importance of the position), amounted to over 100,000 in the post-invasion period. This valuable information comes from Vaclav Pelisek, a former apparatchik in the Central Committee Secretariat and a one-time Novotny adviser. According to Pelisek, hundreds of thousands of additional positions were filled by "cadre departments" and "cadre officials" whose decisions were primarily political.[54]

Spokesmen of the post-invasion regime warned against repetition of past errors. "Unfortunately, we tried to make Communists out of generals so to speak, and not the other way around. This broke the moral integrity of many. . . ."[55] Predictably, the most blame was placed on such liberal tendencies as the selection of cadres in open competition (a so-called *konkurs*). Some Party Secretariats (Prague's First District and the district of Uherske Hradiste) we..t so far as to announce a *konkurs* for the position of apparatchiks in charge of ideology, in blatant disregard of the required *nomenklakura* selection process.[56]

In 1969–1970 both members and nonmembers of the Communist Party were subjected to "loyalty reviews" (*proverka*). For this purpose, the discriminatory clause of the labor law on termination of employment for "loss of trust," which had been invalidated in 1965, was reenacted. Evaluation of political loyalty was declared an integral part of the personal file of every employee in the country, and views doubting the legality of this measure were vehemently rejected.[57]

Other evidence of a return to discarded political practices was provided by changes in the requirements for admission to Party membership. Conditional membership ("candidacy"), abolished in 1966 at the Thirteenth Party Congress, was reinstituted in 1971 at the Fourteenth Congress, with reference to the numerous instances of immature entrants and the need for more thorough screening procedures. Allegedly, Party members willing to sponsor new applicants are in great demand.[58]

The most reactionary feature of the new recruitment process affects the younger generation. Once again, the irrational concept of social class background ("identification through breeding") and the attendant penalizing of children with the wrong kind of parents have been revived. A spokesman for the Ministry of Education announced that the 1970 school rules were invalid because of their emphasis on students' classroom performance. The so-called

"complex evaluation" was introduced instead, combining merit with such factors as birth and family political record. The elementary schools (grades one through nine) prepare a "complex evaluation" of every pupil who applies for admission to a secondary school. In turn, the secondary schools prepare similar evaluations of students applying to universities. This practice has reportedly already yielded a change in the class composition of university student bodies. In the fall of 1971, of 13,000 students admitted to the universities, more than 40 percent came from families of workers and farmers, as opposed to 31 percent for the 1968–1969 period.[59]

To sum up, the post-invasion purge of the KSC members with a reformist orientation spread from the political system—and the Party apparatus in particular—into other systems and the society at large. Stalinist features of recruitment were reintroduced, often to the benefit of office seekers who were failures even in Novotny's time. The price of this purification drive, aimed with particular vehemence at the Party intelligentsia, will not be negligible.

9

Political Socialization

We concluded earlier that the legacy of bourgeois democracy to some extent tempered the harshness of the totalitarian mode of government. The Stalinist ideal of stern, inflexible, intolerant, and highly ideological political behavior remained out of reach for most Czechoslovaks. Verbal bravado and hypocrisy often camouflaged deficiencies of revolutionary dedication. Two decades of socialist construction undoubtedly left their imprint on the value orientation and behavioral pattern of the citizenry. However, the results were neither desired nor anticipated, particularly with respect to the younger generation.

Political socialization is a process by which political cultures are both maintained and changed. This process continues throughout the life of an individual. The demands upon him differ in different societies, and no modern political system has been more demanding than totalitarianism. The Herculean task of creating the "new socialist man" calls for an approach without patience and subtlety. Universality and intensity of indoctrination are among the outstanding features of totalitarian socialization. No aspect of human existence is fully exempt. Doctrinal dedication demands that facts often be sacrificed at the altar of ideology. The frequent price for this manipulation is the vanished credibility of the message.

The process of inculcating an identical ideological outlook in society is a strenuous, costly undertaking where the danger of diminishing returns is ever present. Boredom and fatigue were perhaps the most outstanding phenomena produced by Czechoslovak Stalinism. The poverty of the system's economic performance was matched by its ideological sterility, which was incapable of responding to the cumulating crises of the 1960s. Since the start of de-Stalinization in the socialist camp in 1956, the KSC under Novotny had not been able to demonstrate that it had the ability to cope with changing times. The Party lost its initiative in society, failing as an agent of effective socialization and reconciling itself to the role of a (not too effective) brake.

In the 1960s a new generation of artists (writers in particular) emerged. Bohumil Hrabal, Vaclav Havel, Ivan Klima, Milan Kundera, and Ludvik Vaculik, to mention only a few, represented a force challenging simplistic socialist realism as the recipe for cultural creativity. This new wave also contributed to the rehabilitation of the writer's profession. During the 1950s the Writers' Union was one of the main citadels of Stalinism. Artists publicly glorified the execution of political prisoners, pledging greater poetic enthusiasm in exchange for more hangings. In the popular understanding, a writer was tantamount to a secret police informer.[1] In contrast to this sorry record, the Fourth Congress of the Writers, held in July 1967, presented a most audacious indictment of totalitarianism.[2] As in the Czech national awakening in the nineteenth century, the artists once again assumed the political role of articulating the demands of the citizenry. The heavy-handed reaction of Novotny accelerated the demise of his regime.

The new generation of "creative intelligentsia" established immediate communication with the young, who were not scarred by experience with Stalinist terror. Artistic experimentation provided a starting point for toying with nonconformism and even outright philosophical and political heresies. Benefiting from looser censorship, the mass media carried fresh messages to a wide audience. Broadcasts such as the program "Club of Committed Thinking," in early 1967 could well pass for training in democratic thought.

These developments were complemented by ferment and change within the community of scholars. The Czechoslovak Academy of Sciences had a reputation as a bastion of Stalinism, and often bestowed unearned academic honors on political opportunists and intellectual nonentities,[3] yet during the 1960s, a number of talented Marxist scholars from the Academy and the universities emerged with fresh views. They regarded Marxism as an "open scientific system," not a collection of sacrosanct and increasingly irrelevant formulae. Simultaneously there was a demand that the social sciences be rehabilitated and freed from Party interference and servility to dusty dogma.

Sociology evinced the most notable recovery of all the academic disciplines. Sociology in prewar Czechoslovakia had gained the respect of other European scholars but did not survive the Communist ascendancy to power. (Sociology courses were dropped from universities after the school year 1949–1950). The entire discipline was buried under a tombstone erected by the Stalinists. After the Twentieth Congress of the Communist Party of the USSR in February 1956, the Poles were the first in the socialist camp to return to sociological study and research. The Czechoslovaks maintained their typical wait-and-see policy. Although some empirical works in the field were published in the late 1950s, it was not until 1964 that a lecture on sociology was given at Charles University in Prague. In the 1965–1966 school year this discipline reappeared in the curriculum. In 1968 there were seventy-six graduate sociology students in Prague.[4]

Fifteen years of international isolation and neglect can not easily be overcome by the popularity sociology has enjoyed in Czechoslovakia in recent years. Reminiscent of the early days of totalitarian rule when academia swarmed with self-appointed experts on "features of dialectics and materialism," the mushrooming vogue for sociology was marked by regrettable superficiality. According to a self-congratulatory statement, in the late 1960s the size of Czechoslovakia's society of sociologists was second only to that of the United States. At the same time, the new Institute of Public Opinion Research at the Academy of Sciences—described by its director as "a variant of the famous Gallup Institute in the U.S.A."—consisted of only nine professionals and no facilities whatsoever.[5]

Social scientists, some of whom have risen on the political ladder as high as membership in the Party's Central Committee, presumably have convinced the political leadership of the usefulness of sociological research. It was argued that such research, far from being a form of bourgeois trickery, could produce results that might well serve Marxist-Leninist decision makers. Characteristically, one of the first sociological projects sanctioned by the KSC in the 1960s dealt with the deficiencies of Marxist indoctrination in the universities. A 287-page report, under the title "The Qualification Composition of Teachers of Marxism-Leninism at Institutions of Higher Learning in Czechoslovakia," exempted only the dogma itself from criticism.[6] Topics of other early projects reflected the concern of the Party with the younger generation: social profiles of school age children and youth, career preferences, interaction of the family and the school as agents of socialization, and the role of teachers.

The more conservative elements in the political leadership viewed these innovations with suspicion, if not outright hostility. Scientific analysis posed a danger to easy doctrinal assumptions and primitivism in general. Insecure comrades also warned that this was both ideologically and practically a dangerous trend since it encroached upon the leading role of the Party. (This sentiment echoed the Stalinist dictum of the late 1940s: "We don't study public opinion, we create it.")

A sociological project undertaken in 1965 illustrates the threat to the entrenched conservative forces posed by objective analysis. This study was concerned with socialization in the armed forces and, in particular, with the role of political officers. Following the Soviet practice, the concept of "Deputy Commander for Political Affairs" (ZVP) was introduced into the Czechoslovak armed forces. In the early years of revolutionary Russia the political officer had a dual role: first, as a watchdog of political propriety among the officer corps (whose loyalty to the Bolsheviks was often doubtful), and, second, as an agent of political socialization. Owing to the low literacy level in the Red Army, the basic form of indoctrination was oral communication.

Such activity, appropriate in a predominantly illiterate society in the early decades of this century, now provided a great number of individuals in a country with one of the highest rates of literacy in Europe, with a comfortable, parasitic career. The 1965 survey also covered political socialization of career officers. (Of these, 21 percent had completed a university education, and 45 percent had graduated from the so-called Evening University of Marxism-Leninism or had an equivalent political education. Seventy-five percent of the officers were members of the Communist Party.)[7] The survey revealed that the impact of the mass media was three times as great as direct oral communication, i.e., the function of the ZVP corps, as the main source of information. It was established—to the substantial consternation of the ZVP officers, whose function was thus placed in jeopardy—that the more advanced the education of the professional soldiers the greater their reliance on the mass media.[8]

Sociological findings were bound to upset several categories of beneficiaries of the system. Most of the sociological work was made public in 1968. In this period there seems to have been little political interference with the publication of the data, and the public was thus given some opportunity to explore previously (and subsequently) inaccessible subjects.

Milos Kalab, a one-time Stalinist and in the late 1960s an innovative social scientist, stated that "the sociological basis of the entire post-January [1968] development is in the acknowledgment of the existing interest differentiation within the socialist society. Against the thesis of the existing identity of interests of individuals, groups, and the entire society under socialism . . . the existing interest differentiation is being recognized."[9] The post-invasion leadership vehemently rejected such heretical assertions. Accordingly, sociological findings of political relevance have become very scarce.

Family and School

The family is the first socialization structure in one's life, and among the many primary attitudes it implants are those toward the political system. Regimes with revolutionary ambitions regularly attempt, by a variety of devices, to prevent the continuity of generational socialization and the transmission of traditional values.

The most drastic method of achieving this would be the abolition of the family and physical separation of children from their parents. In modern times no consistent effort has been made to attain this goal. The Soviets followed the policy of cultivating the allegiance of children from families presumed to be hostile to the regime on class, economic, ideological, or other grounds, but did not break up the families. Stalin's dictum that the parents' sins should not be visited upon their children, although not always followed, has never been officially discarded.

In Czechoslovakia, the degree of original intolerance was such that instead of attempting to indoctrinate the children of class enemies, they were condemned along with their parents. This policy was all too visible in the discriminatory standards for admission to institutions of higher learning and in the occupational opportunities offered them. According to a 1954 circular of the Ministry of Education, "The applicants from families of former capitalists and the village rich may be admitted to higher education only in exceptional cases deserving special attention and then only with the permission of the Ministry of Education."[10]

The Party employed several devices in order to create a loyal younger generation. Most crucial was compulsory attendance at schools that articulated the desired values of the day. In the Stalinist period this articulation was complemented by fear of expressing unorthodox opinions, thereby inhibiting frank and open parent-child communication. Concern for family well-being led to political schizophrenia—talk of nothing but loyalty when children were present and expressions of authentic hostility when children were absent.

Both those who controlled the system and the parents underestimated the perceptiveness of the generation born into Stalinism, and in consequence failed to anticipate the attendant results. The young grew up despising the system for its lies and their own parents for cowardice in not challenging them. Confessions like the following appeared even during the Novotny regime:

> I completed my studies in 1960 and have experienced personally the contradiction between the textbook ideal and reality. In civics I was taught fairy tales about the agricultural cooperatives while my mother slaved in the fields for five crowns a day. "Subscribe to the Pioneers' newspaper, join the Pioneers' organization if you want to get to a university," etc. From childhood one was taught hypocrisy. So why should anyone be surprised nowadays that youth is hypocritical, skeptical, and sometimes even cynical, often without a deep regard for our regime?[11]

Czechoslovak totalitarians have never seriously attempted to promote institutional over family upbringing. The main reason has not been ideological but economic. Under the Iron Concept of socialism little money was left for social welfare, even for projects that would foster political welfare. Child care facilities have always been inadequate.[12] I recall from my own experience in adjudicating family law cases how difficult it was to place a child in the care of the state. The widespread image of heartless commissars tearing little angels from the maternal bosom has never been true in Czechoslovakia (although we in the judiciary, witnesses to household deprivation, sometimes wished it were so).

Economic necessity, too, left a substantial imprint upon the socialization capacity of a family. As noted in Chapter 4, a high employment rate among women and the housing shortage were the two factors that substantially damaged family stability. In an opinion

survey among females of child-bearing age, motherhood rated as eighth in order of importance in family life.[13]

In contrast to the trend among advanced industrial societies, there has been a general demand in Czechoslovakia to raise the legal age limit from eighteen to twenty-one. In one opinion survey, 93 percent of the respondents favored this change for boys and 58 percent for girls.[14] Another departure from the pattern of advanced societies is the preservation of multigenerational households. Under conditions of high employment and low housing opportunities, the Czechoslovak grandmother—a permanent babysitter, cook, maid, and shopper—functions as a vital component of the family. Multigenerational households contrast strangely with the mounting rate of divorce and broken homes.[15]

The family has remained the center of the social life of adults in their spare time, despite a massive effort by the state to promote other outlets, particularly in places of employment. A survey among employees of an electronics factory in the medium-size Bohemian town of Pardubice revealed that their most frequent social contacts were 24.33 percent with relatives, 15.58 percent with friends outside the place of employment, 13.64 percent with nobody, and 8.35 percent with co-workers.[16] The Party gradually realized the failure of its effort to promote the factory as the chief place of socialization.

There were 2.2 million in the age bracket between fifteen and twenty-four in 1966. Of these, 101,000 were students in SVVS (equivalent to a high school in the United States and a poor replica of the pre-Communist *Gymnasium*); 188,000 attended technical (trade, vocational) schools; 90,000 attended universities; 361,000 were enrolled in apprenticeship programs; and 1,460,000 were gainfully employed.[17]

These statistics require some comment. First, unlike other socialist countries and developing countries in general, Czechoslovakia's exercise in Stalinism began with a populace more than marginally literate. Universal compulsory education in the Czech provinces (though not in Slovakia) is over a century old.[18] The Party inherited and did not create the educational infrastructure, as is apparent from the fact that 78.6 percent of all school plants in Bohemia and Moravia (48 percent in Slovakia) were constructed before 1945.[19]

Second, increases in the number of students (see Table 9.1) were not accompanied by increases in educational standards. The total of university students for 1967–1968 was 137,497, i.e., almost 1 percent of the population of Czechoslovakia. The same source of these data acknowledged deterioration in the quality of the education. For one thing, class struggle entered the classroom. When a student's classroom performance becomes secondary to his political activism and the reputation of his parents, ascriptive criteria generating discrimination and undeserved privileges jeopardize the educational process. The "class criteria" were not mere aberrations, to be terminated with Stalin's death, but after a pause in the 1960s, they were reintroduced in 1970. Thus, the entire—and the first—young socialist generation has been affected.

Table 9.1. University enrollment in Czechoslovakia.

School year	Bohemia/ Moravia	Slovakia	Total
1936/1937	24,810	2,258	27,068
1945	54,378	7,412	61,790
1956/1957	54,016	23,681	77,697
1965/1966	96,528	49,462	145,990
1967/1968	89,264	48,233	137,497

Sources: Marie Hulakova, *Nova Mysl*, July 11, 1967, pp. 8–12; and *Statisticka rocenka CSSR 1968* (Prague: SNTL, 1968), p. 491. *Tribuna*, July 8, 1970, No. 27, p. 12, gives a total university enrollment for the school year 1969/1970 of 62,000 in the CSR and 38,000 in the SSR. If these figures are correct, they reveal a substantial enrollment decline.

Furthermore, the traditional, differentiated, and (in the opinion of foreign observers) superb educational structure was abolished and replaced by the Uniform School System. The then Minister of Education, Zdenek Nejedly, was a virulent imitator of everything Russian. The Soviet pedagogue Anton S. Makarenko became the most quoted (though little read) authority, and Russian was elevated as the only mandatory foreign language, beginning with the fourth grade.[20]

With mediocrity the ideal norm, the educational endeavor was geared toward discouragement of individual excellence. Talents were frowned upon and at the same time the teachers were held responsible for the failures of poor students. The Iron Concept of

socialism penetrated the school system with a heavy emphasis on technical education. Concentration on the natural sciences left little for the humanities, and the social sciences dissolved into propaganda exercises. The university admission quotas favoring technical education have been a lasting legacy. According to 1969 estimates, over half of all university students in the country were engaged in technical studies, notably engineering, in contrast to 30 to 45 percent in other socialist countries, 25 percent in Western Europe, and a mere 10 percent in the United States.[21]

In the absence of the regulative mechanism of supply and demand, governmental intervention in matters of admission to universities seems unavoidable. Otherwise, the country would run the risk of graduating more movie directors than agronomists. However, once a university education becomes to a considerable degree a matter of draft rather than choice, the price is wasted talent, low motivation, and a high rate of dropouts. The widespread practice of arbitrarily reassigning applicants from one field to another, from one school to another, only for the sake of meeting some recruitment plan, eventually led to a general decline of interest in higher education. Unlike education-hungry youth in the Soviet Union and other socialist countries, in the school year 1965–1966 there were only 1.46 applicants for every vacancy in Czechoslovak universities; and in technical fields the number of applicants per vacancy was as low as 0.87.[22] Since then the picture has not changed. In the 1972–1973 school year 20,140 applicants competed for 14,795 university openings in Bohemia and Moravia whereas the institutes of technology received 1,000 fewer applications than the total 6,685 openings.[23] An additional factor discouraging the pursuit of advanced studies may be traced to *nivelizace*, an exaggerated concept of egalitarianism, which financially penalized the professional man.

The Stalinist maxim "One's love for the Soviet Union is the yardstick of one's political maturity" applied both to adult life and to the socialization of the young. The Soviet model has been followed with unimaginative, disciplined consistency, whether in copying the Pioneer Organization or Khrushchev's short-lived school reforms in the late 1950s. Only after Novotny's fall was independent thought applied to education.

By then, however, the damage was done. The

LENIN
CHRUŠČOV
STALIN

UŽ SOUDRUH LENIN ŘEKL...

"It was Comrade Lenin, Stalin, Khrushchev, Lenin
who said . . ."
(*Literarni listy*, May 2, 1968)

continuous diet of black and white images turned the involuntary recipient of these undigestible comestibles into a person indifferent, contemptuous, and even hostile toward the Soviet Union. Uncritical admiration of everything Western was a frequent corollary to this posture. In the words of the Stalinist pedagogue Bretislav Dejdar (complaining about the failure of many students to master the Russian alphabet after five or more years of study), "Genuine Russophiles have almost disappeared, and instead an obnoxious toadying to Western ideas has erupted. . . ."[24]

Education in Marxism-Leninism also yielded counterproductive results. Vladimir Kadlec, the liberal Minister of Education, confessed in 1968 that "dogmatism and one-sided interpretation of social problems bored plenty of people, and that cannot be overcome all at once." Kadlec reminisced about his teaching career, "when I felt I was a preacher. I would finish my lecture and nobody would get up to ask me anything. I saw in the eyes of the students that they were not convinced."[25] (I was one of Kadlec's students in that period and can confirm the accuracy of this.)

Distortion of facts (e.g., "Stalin is our greatest benefactor and Masaryk attempted to assassinate Lenin") was not the sole vice of Stalinist education. Perhaps more damaging was the fundamental hostility toward factual knowledge of any kind.[26] The earlier *Gymnasiums* were often criticized for forcing students "to know but not to think." Under Stalinism, the school standards deteriorated to the point that neither of the two achievements was found particularly desirable. The uniform curriculum in the SVVS (the high schools) allotted the following amounts of time in geography courses: North America, four hours of instruction; Latin America, five hours; Africa, six hours; the nonsocialist part of Europe was worth 200 minutes. Not surprisingly, a survey among fifteen-year-olds, who were asked to identify certain cities on a world map, rendered this toll of failures: Delhi, 60 percent; Varna, 65 percent; Johannesburg, 90 percent; Teheran, 100 percent. In another test not a single student knew that 1918 was the year Czechoslovakia was founded. The neglect of factual knowledge affected also the realm of required political knowledge, resulting in such incredible lapses as the failure to identify Antonin Zapotocky or even to place the October Revolution of 1917 in the twentieth century.[27]

All this is a symptom of a general malaise of knowledge. Ill-educated political elites and numerous purveyors of Stalinist socialization set the style and norm of thinking. The source of the above data assessed the situation:

> Most of the time, concrete images were replaced by superficial, meaningless sentences. . . . A cult of the approximate and the inaccurate was established. . . . Namely, the fundamental time sequence of facts is missing; the data fall under the table in the deluge of generalities. . . . Phrase-mongering, superficiality, half-truth, and ignorance is the almost indestructible weed. This all is due to babbling [zvaneni, a very derogatory term denoting empty, primitive chatter] in classrooms, newspapers, or radio, and from public tribunes. . . . It will be difficult to create democratic socialism with semiliterate, indifferent, people . . . The ideal of the average began to approximate dangerously the ideal of the below average.[28]

A preference for quantity over quality also characterized the field of applied knowledge. A total of 2,000 persons were engaged in research in 1950; by 1954 the number reached 14,000, and within fifteen years swelled to almost 130,000. At the same time, in research institutions the proportion of personnel with a completed university education declined to 30 percent on the average, and in some institutions the figure was as low as 10 percent. In a sample of successfully defended doctoral dissertations in the natural sciences, over two-thirds would have failed to meet the pre-Stalinist criteria.[29] In what then passed for "social sciences," the results would presumably have been no more encouraging.

Criticism of education came to a head in 1968 when educational uniformity was wholly rejected. Reestablishment of the traditional Gymnasiums was demanded, and it was charged that individual talent could no longer be ignored, no matter how distasteful this would be to be the advocates of social class determinism.[30] Some Gymnasiums were permitted to be established on an experimental basis. A proposal to abolish the universal requirement of Russian language instruction was not adopted. Considered premature before the invasion, afterwards an insistence on such a demand would have qualified as antistate provocation.

Even conservative political forces realized the magnitude of the alienation of the young and their dislike of both the Party and the Soviet mentor. Since 1969, a massive socialization program aimed at regaining the allegiance of the young has been underway. According to the outline of the Ministry of Education:

> In the school year 1969–1970 it is imperative to strengthen instruction in the Marxist-Leninist world outlook, to mold positive political views among the young, in particular, to deepen the indoctrination in socialist patriotism and internationalism. Relations with the USSR and the other socialist countries require particular sensitivity and attention. The Ministry of Education expects all teachers to lead youth toward restoration of the traditional friendship with the Soviet youth and all the people of the USSR.[31]

Implementation of this gigantic task requires thorough changes in the cadre policy, curricula, and indeed any functional and structural aspects of the educational system.[32]

The stand of the teaching profession will be among the crucial variables in this transformation. In formation of attitudes, it is in the education below the college level where the role of the teacher is of utmost significance. In the past, this profession was not immune to autocratic trends of the day. This inclination, along with a conspicuous lack of civic courage, is likely to account for the relatively high percentage of pro-Nazi collaborators among Czech teachers during the war and of ferocious Stalinists since 1948. These educators perhaps epitomized totalitarianism more than the apparatchiks or the STB agents.[33]

Youth Organization

A considerable effort was spent creating a uniform youth organization to complement the uniform school system, as twin structures of socialization of the young. The Soviet Union provided suitable models: the Czechoslovak Youth Organization (CSM) imitated the Komsomol, and the Pioneer Organization (PO) copied its counterpart in everything, including the name. The Pioneers were children between eight and fifteen, and the CSM members were youth between fifteen and twenty-five. Some adjustments were later made in the CSM to accommodate even those over thirty.[34]

The blue shirts of the CSM became the symbol of totalitarianism's failure in socialization. After twenty years of monopoly, the organization collapsed in 1968 and was dissolved. The peak years of CSM activism were those immediately following the Communist ascendancy to power. As with the KSC, the CSM did not aim to become an elitist organization but instead tried to build up a mass following. Lack of adequate data notwithstanding, it is known that this open recruitment policy was not too successful. Whether or not to join the CSM ranks was largely determined by the applicant's stake in the system and the likelihood of punitive sanction for noncompliance. Given their high vulnerability, students were destined to form the major part of CSM ranks. Accordingly, a 100 percent enrollment of high school classes was a rather common occurrence.[35]

The general decline of the political system's capability in the 1960s also affected the youth movement. For one thing, the number of members decreased. According to a 1966 source, CSM membership stood at 1.05 million, i.e., not quite half of the national population in the fifteen- to twenty-five-year-old age group, and most of its members and activities were concentrated in schools. The organization failed to enroll, even if only for nominal membership, three-fourths of the young workers. Lack of interest among the rural youth was even more marked.[36] In 1967, on the eve of the Fifth (and last) CSM Congress, total membership amounted to 983,000, i.e., about 32 percent of the young. Although there were over a million trade unionists under twenty-six, only 200,000 workers belonged to the CSM, and their ranks were dwindling. A million and a half citizens under twenty-six lived in the countryside, but only 91,000, mainly high school students, were organized in CSM village cells.[37]

By 1967 the CSM was an incurably sick organization. A sociological study from Brno diagnosed poor motivation for joining the CSM as the fundamental cause of the illness. Members were no more than passive onlookers in a moribund movement. The majority was unfamiliar with CSM bylaws.[38] The bylaws stated that "the greatest honor for a member of CSM is to be admitted to the Communist Party," and that "CSM is the reserve force of the Communist Party. Its activities are based on the Party's policy." Furthermore, "CSM educates the young people in the spirit of socialist principles ... and actively promotes among them the ideas of socialist patriotism. It guides young people toward mastering

Marxism-Leninism." Among the numerous duties of the members was that of "acquainting oneself with the aims of the Communist Party and of bringing them to life."[39]

CSM was conceived as an antechamber to Party membership, and the structure of both organizations was identical. The CSM comprised district, regional, and central offices, "youth apparatchiks," local organizations and committees, a Central Committee, Presidium, Secretariat, and Secretaries, and a Congress that was the highest ranking component of the organization.

The young, less inhibited or compliant than their elders, found this bureaucratic monster unappealing and its professional personnel unimpressive. As a rule, the CSM apparatus was staffed with bureaucrats neither particularly intelligent nor young. These were the apprentice apparatchiks with an eye on elevation into the KSC structure.

One of the most damaging policies of the CSM was the Party-sponsored hostility toward any form of pluralism. Unity and uniformity in everything was demanded with dogmatic insistence, and purveyors of opposing views were severely punished. University students in Prague were the prime dissenters. As early as 1965 they proposed the federalization of the CSM and a recognition of the diversity of interests among young people. It was argued to no avail that the interests of the fifteen-year-olds differed from those of university graduates and that those of industrial youth were not identical with those of their rural counterpart. The advocates of reform were expelled from the university.[40]

Soon after, it was found that these heretical demands were not radical enough. Because federalization of the CSM was not permitted in 1965, no one in power in 1968 was willing to save the CSM in any form—centralized, federalized, confederalized, or otherwise.

On the other hand, the Pioneer Organization did survive the 1968 turmoil but lost its monopoly over the eight- to fifteen-year-olds. The survival of the PO is all the more surprising in that this was a purely Soviet import that copied even the white shirts, red kerchiefs, and (to a Czech eye) repulsive salutes.

Just as the CSM was designed as the "reserve force" of the Party, so was the PO the "reserve force" of the CSM. Organizationally, the PO was considered a part of the CSM. The CSM Congress elected the top PO organ, the Central Council, which commanded the lower components, known (in approximate translation) as Groups, Detachments, and Units. The principle of centralized command was implemented by a force of 84,000 adult Pioneer leaders.[41]

For a critical analysis of the PO performance we have the best reference source obtainable—Oldrich Krystofek, the head of the entire PO until 1969 and a progressive, liberal Communist. His harsh assessment of the organization's past activities included: enforced rather than voluntary participation, manipulated instead of spontaneous activism, boredom instead of attraction, superficial slogans rather than truth in socialization, and the use of professional bureaucrats rather than volunteers.[42]

In addition, the PO was handicapped in attracting the school children because of the "etatization" of the organization: each school had its own PO unit, and the PO leader was the teacher's alter ego. The authenticity of the enthusiasm among the adult PO professionals who worked with children has always been questionable. When the PO was reconstituted in 1968 as a truly voluntary organization, and the official ties with the school system were severed, PO functionaries were in short supply. In one district, comprising twenty-two grade schools and hence twenty-two full-time PO officials, only three expressed any interest in continuing their youth activities once they became voluntary—and unpaid. Even in the fourth post-invasion year the problem had not been disposed of. As of June 1972, at least 50,000 PO leaders (an estimated 60 percent of the necessary total) "who like children and can afford to spend each year about 500 hours of their free time" had yet to be found.[43]

The PO survived the de-Stalinization crisis of 1968 largely because of its emancipation from both the state and the school. According to Krystofek, no more than 130,000 genuine members were left by the beginning of 1969.[44] Characteristic of the new spirit in the organization, individual units were free to decide whether or not to keep the discredited symbol of the red kerchiefs.

The post-invasion PO had a surprisingly sympathetic attitude toward the Scout movement, revived after twenty years of banishment and persecution. In the understanding of Stalinism,"The Scout movement is one means of the ruling bourgeoisie to divert the attention of the young from the righteous struggle of the workers against exploitation. . . . It misleads youth and, in fact, deprives it of national pride by extolling the Anglo-Saxon culture and way of life."[45] After 1948 the Scouts were persecuted with extraordinary ferocity, with courts sentencing both leaders and teenage rank and file to terms longer than the age of the victims. It was on the ashes of the destroyed Scout movement that the Pioneer Organization was imposed upon the country. In 1968, hostility between the victim and the beneficiary would have been only natural. Yet nothing of this kind happened. Whereas the PO was a product of Stalinism, two decades after its founding its members were not ardent Stalinists. The Pioneers of 1968 demanded the rehabilitation of the Scouts and called for friendly competition. In the best tradition of European romantic youth, evoking the folklore of American Indians, a peace pipe was smoked to seal the good intentions.

Both organizations were handicapped by similar, though not identical, problems of leadership. The Pioneers had never developed a core of volunteers. Scout leaders did exist, but they were mainly old people whose enthusiasm could not fully compensate for their prolonged incarceration and loss of contact with the outside world. Many of them had gone to jail before the present generation of Scouts was born.

While Krystofek presided over the destruction of the PO monopoly, his fellow liberal Communist Zbynek Vokrouhlicky, the head of the CSM, carried through the total liquidation of that organization. The uniform CSM was superseded by a host of independent organizations accommodating special interests, such as the Union of High School Students and Apprentices, the Union of Working Youth, "Juvena" (for rural youth), the Campers' Union, the Union of Youth Clubs, and the Union of University Students. In both the Czech and Slovak republics, respectively, these organizations joined in the Association of Children and Youth Organizations. Unlike the defunct CSM, the Association had only nominal powers, precluding interference with or manipulation of individual organizations.

In 1969 the KSC denounced the destruction of the CSM and the attendant pluralization, and called for reunification of the youth movement. As the first step, the Leninist Youth Union was established. However, it failed to attract a following other than former CSM apparatchiks and some children of

(*Reporter*, April 24, 1969)

prominent Stalinists. With a total membership of 12,000[46] the Leninist Youth Union dissolved itself in the fall of 1970 and fused with the newly created Socialist Union of Youth (SSM), the post-invasion copy of the dismantled CSM. The explanation for this decreed development was predictable:

The act of discrediting and destroying the uniform youth organization after January 1968 was a crime against young people, and also an attempt to divert the youth from socialist perspectives. . . . After a lapse of almost two years, a uniform organization has once again been created—the Socialist Union of Youth. Mindful of past mistakes, it will continue with the correct ideological, political, and organizational principles of the Czechoslovak Union of Youth.[47]

Exhortation about historical continuity was balanced with pledges of flexibility. The spokesmen for the new organization, although emphasizing its link to its unwanted, discredited predecessor, warned against the repetition of such past mistakes as forcible recruitment and "formalism" in its activities. The warnings were both timely and ineffective.

In the meantime, the youth under fifteen were to be reunited in the Pioneer Organization. This plan called for the liquidiation of the Scout movement. As in 1948, the Scouts came under attack during the 1969–1970 school year, being charged with imperialist origin, religious ideology, apolitical orientation, and right-wing leadership. By the beginning of the 1970–1971 school year the Scouts had been outlawed.[48]

The data on recruitment by the SSM are neither complete nor detailed but do give some picture of the trend and its implications. As in the years before 1968, recruitment has been uneven. Thus, by May 1971, of the total 18,469 SSM members in the universities, only 6,355 were in the Czech Republic; the majority was to be found in a more "pacified" Slovakia.[49] More importantly, the SSM has failed to attract youth with a desirable socioeconomic profile, i.e., industrial workers and collective farmers. Instead, students who believe that membership will further their future careers again make up the majority. Students face an offer they cannot refuse: "I know of only two types of students at this institution," one professor stated, "those who will not graduate and those who are members of the SSM."[50]

Under such circumstances, in less than two years there were some 750,000 Pioneers and some 600,000 SSM members. At the First Congress of the SSM, in September 1972, its chairman, Juraj Varholik, announced the recruitment of 900,000 Pioneers and 800,000 SSM members. One out of every four fifteen- to thirty-year-olds belonged to the organization. The highest percentage of recruitment (60 percent) was among high school youth, followed by 43 percent of university students, 42 percent of apprentices in vocational programs, but only 25 percent of industrial workers.[51]

The shortage of volunteers to serve as PO leaders in this suddenly increased organization has already been mentioned. In the SSM, mass recruitment has had an affect on the political orientation of the youth movement and the role of the militant nucleus of the 12,000 former Leninist Youth Union members. The majority of members in the SSM are draftees rather than volunteers. They seem to determine the climate in the SSM, immobilizing the minority of authentic supporters of the post-invasion regime. The basic conflict is that between the militants and their preference for the recruitment of only the committed, and thus for an elitist type of organization, and the school authorities who promote mass recruitment in order to promote themselves as practitioners of successful socialization.

The weekly *Tribuna*, reflecting ultra-conservative opinion within the Party, provided ample space for the promotion of the elitist case. For example, one letter to the editor warned against those who joined the organization only to secure school admission or to be allowed to travel abroad. Another letter charged that "nowadays, under the SSM sponsorship any kind of a long-haired creature can run wild with his guitar, even wearing a [Christian] cross around his neck, a fellow who speaks only English when he opens his mouth."[52] "Yes," another voice adds, "the beatniks are joining the SSM so that they can get their own clubroom because that is the only way how to get it."[53]

The youth publications came under attack for their apolitical, "recreational" tone. Critics noted that in the October and November 1970 issues of *Pionyr*, there was no mention of the 1917 Bolshevik Revolution and that it was perhaps the only publication in the country that ignored the birthdays of Klement Gottwald and Ludvik Svoboda. A lack of political maturity was detected even within the SSM apparatus. In *Tribuna* a correspondent accused a district secretariat official for his statement to a gathering of young people: " 'Don't be afraid of the SSM statutes. You know, you can't write them down in any popular way,' said the functionary, and added, 'we [SSM] are only seemingly a politically oriented organization.' "[54]

The 1968 socialization experience has been a millstone around the neck of Husak in his attempt to achieve spontaneous participation and authentic commitment. The members of the former Leninist Youth Union are outnumbered in the SSM by about fifty to one. The activists, incapable of mobilizing the majority and failing to convert the mass SSM into an elitist phalanx, had no other choice but to establish their own organization. Called "Leninist Clubs of the SSM," it consists of a few thousand of original "Leninists" who engage in socialization efforts and a political style which was planned for the mass SSM but failed to be imposed on it.[55]

Adult Socialization

Even allowing for the persistent practice of the lower echelons to magnify their achievements in reports to higher officials in the socialization structure, the overall effort of the state to mold the minds of the citizenry has been considerable. At the same time this effort has yielded rather disappointing results.

As with the young and their participation in CSM (SSM), the stake of adult citizens in the society, their ambition, and their social and economic vulnerability greatly affect the degree of their political engagement. Party members rather than non-members, white collar rather than blue collar, family men rather than bachelors, and applicants for anything where the favor of the state is involved are the most likely participants. Citizens are expected to fill two roles: that of an object of socialization and that of an active participant assisting other citizens in this process. Whether activist or "passivist," all socialization has been marred by a deficiency known as "formalism", i.e., superficiality as a by-product of involuntary, imposed participation. Totalitarian socialization has been anything but durable.

These remarks are intended to suggest a cautious approach (if not a skeptical one) to some of the very impressive figures which follow.[56] In 1966, 1.29 million members of trade union locals were reported to be engaged in political activity. Almost a quarter of a million citizens have been elected deputies of People's Committees on various levels. In 1969, 260,000 activists were elected to local Party cells. The Czechoslovak-Soviet Friendship League, in the early 1950s 2.5 million strong, also required a host of functionaries. The Circles of Cultural Creativity have attracted half a million citizens. Other "friendship societies," public enlightenment groups, and organizations with at least a covert political mission have each been responsible for a share in the creation of the new socialist man. One rather agile group has been the so-called "long-title society," —i.e., the Society for the Dissemination of Political and Scientific Knowledge, more recently known by the more elegant label of "Socialist Academy." The Academy consists of some 33,000 members of the intelligentsia, who give public lectures on political and popular science topics.[57] Atheistic propaganda has been on the priority list of the organization. In 1966 the political socialization network in Czechoslovakia included 136 "Houses of Enlightenment," over 650 clubs, and more than 5,500 "Red Corners" set up by the trade unions. The annual number of participants in this type of socialization was 55 million, of which half a million completed at least one of a variety of courses.[58]

Functionaries of the higher rank have frequently been guests at local meetings of their organizations—guests who had advisory and supervisory roles. Members of the Party's Central Committee Secretariat reportedly took part in almost 11,000 KSC gatherings in one six-month period.[59] Rank and file attendance varies in accord with the composition, background, and motivation of the membership. The passage of time has also been of importance. For example, the Prague population participated in the work of the People's Committees with this declining fervor: The attendance of 300,000 in public meetings in 1964 dropped to 200,000 in 1965 and to 100,000 in 1966 and 1967. In 1968 attendance was 37,000, and a record low was reached in 1969 with 17,000.[60]

Political education under the auspices of the KSC has been designed predominantly but not exclusively for its members. In 1966 the Party employed 61,000 lecturers in various courses with a total enrollment of 525,000 KSC members and 125,000 nonmembers. This indoctrination was carried out in 87 evening universities of Marxism-Leninism, 6,527 evening schools of Marxism-Leninism, 6,957 seminars, and 7,267 other units (called "circles," "lecture series," etc.).[61] In addition to these programs, the KSC maintained the Party College—referred to in the preceding chapter as the hotbed of revisionism—its Slovak sister institution, along with a number of regional party schools and seminars—some permanent, but most transient or short-term.

The 1968 invasion rendered an unanticipated blow to these socialization activities. "The system of Party education, save for evening universities and a handful of evening schools, completely fell apart."[62] The evening universities suffered a decline in enrollment: in the province of Western Bohemia enrollment was 1,372 in 1966–1967, and 844 in 1968–1969.[63] This decline was attributed to a variety of reasons, notably, the excessive length of the courses (three years), a lack of relevance to professional life and advancement, and an obsolete curriculum focused on dialectical and historical materialism, political economy, and the history of the USSR Communist Party. It was conceded that students preferred sociology, psychology, and business management courses. A demand for facts and an aversion to propaganda further contributed to the mood, "characterized by a *significant decline of interest in the study* of Marxist-Leninist theory and by the shift to factual political information" (original italics).[64]

In the year following the 1968 invasion, Party indoctrination further deteriorated. This was confirmed by a survey undertaken between May and July 1969 in three districts (Sokolov in Western Bohemia, Znojmo in Southern Moravia, and Ceske Budejovice in Southern Bohemia), which probed into the performance of the socialization structures and into their methodological and substantive problems. In some places Party education had been completely abandoned. The vast majority of the "ideological *aktif*" (Party propagandists) took a very critical view of this state of affairs. Only 2.1 percent of the *aktif* in the survey were satisfied with the current situation. The comparatively small number of officials engaged in Party socialization was also stressed. Reportedly, only 9 percent of all apparatchiks on the district level specialized in ideology and indoctrination.[65]

In June 1970 the Party passed a resolution containing the indoctrination curricula for 1970–1971 and a long-range plan (three to five years) for restructuring the education program. In the words of Ladislav Novotny, then head of the Department of Ideology of the Central Committee's Secretariat, it was crucial not to reduce the audience "to a mere object of ideological-political impact."[66]

The most recent information on Party education is the 1972–1973 program as approved by the Politburo.[67] The three-level educational structure was preserved.

(1) The basic grade, involving the majority of Party members, consists of three "study circles": ideological preparation (two years), economics (two years), and current problems of socialist development (one year).

(2) The middle grade, devoted to the education of activists in the primary KSC. Non-Party members from among the intelligentsia may be invited to participate.

(3) The higher grade, intended for the ideological growth of activists in the districts.

The entire program is characterized by a preoccupation with the study of the Party's economic policy. The Politburo, reflecting the old-fashioned craving for total organization, recommended Monday as the day of class meetings.

The post-invasion socialization effort included the revival of mass organizations. For example, the Czechoslovak-Soviet Friendship League (SCSP), once 2.5 million strong, practically collapsed in August 1968 and had to be rebuilt from the debris. In 1972 it was reported that three years of work by the SCSP in the Czech provinces alone had resulted in 100,000 political and educational events of various kinds, with over 10 million persons attending. In the same period the SCSP regained almost a million members, organized in 16,940 cells. The average membership age, however, is 56 years.[68]

Although the next chapter is devoted to social communication and the mass media, some data on this significant source of attitude formation and the prime contributor to man's "cognitive map" would be helpful here. In Czechoslovakia in the late 1960s there was one radio receiver per 4.6 of the population, one television set per 6.7, and one telephone per 11. In 1965 there were 3.72 million radios and 2.11 million television sets in the country. In the same year the total attendance in 3,711 movie houses was 128.4 million and in 84 repertory theaters 10.4 million. As in other countries, television adversely

affected attendance of both the film and theater. While the average television viewing time increased to sixteen to eighteen hours per week, attendance at the movie houses dropped in 1964 to 71.6 percent of that in 1957.[69]

A new form of mass communication, called "cable radio," and not well known in Western countries, has been installed throughout Czechoslovakia. This is a one-station receiver emitting the voice of the system in the closest imitation of Big Brother to date. About 1.2 million boxes of this type have been installed in urban centers, including all district administration towns. However, there are some 11,000 communities with populations of less than 2,000 in which 42.5 percent of all Czechoslovaks live.[70] These areas are serviced by public address systems to spread appropriate messages.

The Stalinist emphasis on quantity rather than on quality applied also to the printed word. As an example of a saturation campaign of prime magnitude, we may refer to the 1951 speech of Gottwald that exposed the Brno apparatchik Otto Sling as an enemy of the people. This speech was printed in an edition of 4.5 million pamphlets (one copy for every adult), and the daily press devoted 2,971,000 lines to the same subject.[71] Of the 61,533,300 books published in 1967, the share of political literature was substantial. Marxism-Leninism accounted for 642,000 titles, economics, 1,218,900, and political enlightenment, 6,487,800.[72]

According to a report to the KSC Central Committee in 1967, the circulation of the Party's main daily, *Rude pravo*, exceeded one million copies a day and was second largest in the world on a per capita basis[73]—the first, presumably being Moscow's *Pravda* (see Table 9.2). Besides imposed uniformity, the price for this achievement was the strangling of the local press. For example, Olomouc, a northern Moravian city with a not negligible cultural tradition and a university more than four centuries old, used to have seven dailies. Since the ascendancy of the Party to power, all have been forced to suspend publication. The totalitarian urge for uniformity was complemented by the high cost of censorship: the maintenance of censors for every periodical in the country proved to be too costly. As a consequence, by April 1967, 236 periodicals published by trade unions and other groups in districts were closed down. This measure did not affect only small towns. In Prague, of 43 journals only 11 survived.[74]

Table 9.2. Annual Circulation of Czechoslovak Periodicals, 1967.

Type	Number	Circulation
Dailies	28	1,359,615,500
Weeklies	266	367,585,700
Biweeklies	108	61,994,200
Monthlies	477	71,347,900
Others	325	6,386,900
Total	1,204	1,866,930,200

Source: *Statisticka rocenka CSSR 1968* (Prague: SNTL, 1968), p. 508.

Censorship has existed continuously since 1948 (with only a short interruption in 1968). However, dullness of the media has declined. In the mid-1960s the KSC recognized, albeit belatedly and with great reluctance, that the "press of opinion" had failed as an instrument of socialization and that some allowance had to be made for the "press of information." In response to a reader who complained about such innovations as crime reports, crossword puzzles, and even classified ads, Jiri Franek, a Stalinist journalist, wrote in *Rude pravo* in 1966: "We are responding to the fact that the people are fed up with empty phrases—they want to know facts."[75] (Neither the complaining reader nor Franek could have anticipated that in a not-too-distant future *Rude pravo* would carry striptease advertisements with photos of nude performers.)[76]

The first exposure to objective facts whetted the readers' appetite. With the growing distaste for the press of pure opinion, the preference was for cognition and not evaluation. Even the readers of *Rude pravo*, who would be least likely to be dissatisfied with the mass media, expressed a clear preference for the press of information, according to the Academy of Sciences survey in February 1968. In response to the question "What do you look for in *Rude pravo*?" 73 percent emphasized "information," 17 percent "entertainment," and 9 percent "indoctrination."[77]

The year 1968 provided an intense political experience for the entire citizenry, and the lion's share of this accomplishment belongs to the mass media. While in Novotny's time television was predominantly a source of entertainment for 89 percent of the viewers, in 1968 it became a powerful instrument of socialization.[78] For the first time the political leaders literally faced the nation, from television studios, and came under the scrutiny of a critical public. Periodicals became the favorite source of political communication. The weekly *Literarni listy* reached a circulation of 300,000—a large number for a journal devoted (at least formally) to literature. The popularity of the press was also reflected in the frequency of communications from readers. According to *Literarni listy*, its average annual volume of such letters was 5,000. In 1968, 3,000 came in within six weeks.[79] This upsurge of activity was experienced by all periodicals of reformist orientation.

The media substituted for nonexistent political forces in many ways. One that was particularly effective was exercising social pressure in cases where the state failed to uphold the law. Newspapers engaged in a program of fostering social ostracism of STB torturers and similar criminals of the Stalinist era—to compensate for a lack of official punitive measures—by publicly identifying them.[80]

The media earned public gratitude as they harvested the wrath of the conservatives. The 1970 "Open Letter of the Central Committee to All Party Members," inaugurating the nationwide purge, stated. "The press, radio, and television interfered with Party life, forcefully demanded publication of internal Party documents, and organized public opinion surveys regarding who should and who should not be elected to the Party's Central Committee."[81]

The post-invasion leadership turned the media into a sacrificial goat, making it responsible for confusing the nation during the revisionist period. A 1968 public opinion survey asked whether the respondents believed that the media meddled in political affairs beyond their rights and competence. The percentage of affirmative responses was as follows: 11 percent among nonmembers of the Party, 32 percent among Party members, and, not too surprisingly, 82 percent among regional and district apparatchiks.[82] The mental processes of the apparatus are echoed in the quote, "As Josef Nemec, one of the regional secretaries of the Party used to say, everything would be in order if it were not for the press, radio, and television."[83]

Reinstitution of strict censorship generated a search for supplementary channels of information. Foreign broadcasts were the most obvious and accessible choice. Fourteen presumably hostile radio stations broadcast in Czech and Slovak from abroad.[84] They are listed in Table 9.3. The impact of these stations on socialization is impossible to determine if only because of the signal-jamming that effectively obliterates reception in entire areas. According to a 1970 survey referred to by the Party monthly *Nova mysl*, older citizens prefer the BBC and Voice of America because of their reputations for reliability gained during World War II. By contrast, the majority of young listeners tune to Radio Free Europe and the West German outlets. In overall popularity, Radio Free Europe is first, followed by Vienna, the BBC, and Deutsche Welle. *Nova mysl* also profiled the most likely type of listener: "Analysis of the sociological composition of respondents shows that a substantially larger number of listeners are young people and those with higher education and interest in acquiring a greater amount of information." This remarkably frank report on a very sensitive subject confirmed that an absence of information in domestic mass media leads to increased popularity of foreign sources. Not more than 16.98 percent of the respondents listened to foreign broadcasts during the censorship-free period in 1968 as opposed to 47.16 percent in June 1967, 61.68 percent in December 1968, and 56.50 percent in March 1969.[85]

Table 9.3.   "Hostile" Radio Stations from Abroad.

Source	Daily output (in minutes)
Radio Free Europe	8,480
Tirana	210
BBC	195
Madrid	180
Voice of America	150
Deutsche Welle	105
Canada	90
Rome	65
Peking	60
Vatican	60
Paris	40
Deutschlandfunk	30
Monte Carlo	15
Vienna	5 (?)

In 1968 one of the achievements of liberalization was the public sale of Western non-Communist periodicals. However, this was short-lived, and restricted to a few urban areas and international hotels.

Tourism provides an important source of information about the outside world. Travel restrictions were eased in the mid-1960s under Novotny. An increasing number of Czechoslovaks were permitted to travel abroad, in both the East and West. Correspondingly, many foreign tourists visited the country. Foreigners, an exciting rarity in the 1950s, became commonplace in the 1960s.

Mutual exposure rendered ineffective the primitive propaganda that purported to compare living standards under capitalism and socialism. In 1967, 2,090,710 Czechoslovaks visited socialist countries, and 303,379 saw capitalism—Austria, West Germany, Italy, and France, in order of frequency.[86] Indirectly the whole nation profited because the propagandists took cognizance of the growing number of witnesses of the quality of life in forbidden lands and abandoned the practice of blatant distortion.

At the same time, 3.7 million foreigners from the East and 830,000 from the West visited Czechoslovakia. It hardly escaped the attention of Walter Ulbricht that over half a million of East Germans (roughly every thirty-second citizen) saw the 1968 Czechoslovak experiment in humanistic socialism in person. By contrast, only 25,700 Soviet tourists were exposed to this germ.

From 1960 to 1965 the number of Czechoslovaks spending their vacations abroad tripled, reaching 1.03 million in 1965, i.e., 7 percent of the total population. In 1967 one in six Czechoslovaks traveled abroad. In the Soviet Union roughly one in 180 enjoyed the same privilege.[87] This, too, added to the vast disparity between the Soviet teacher and its somewhat recalcitrant pupil. The picture, of course, changed in August 1968. At that time, the Czechs, with black humor, hoisted the sign "We do not approve of this kind of tourism," as a defiant welcome to the estimated half a million uninvited guests in arms.

By the fall of 1969 the Western frontier was effectively closed, preventing further exodus of refugees. However, revocation of the right of free travel did not mean a return to the "sealed-door" policy of the 1950s. According to *Rude pravo*, in 1972 a half million Czechoslovaks were scheduled to visit capitalist countries, and about a million tourists from the West were expected to visit Czechoslovakia.[88] Occasional laments, such as that by Jaroslav Toms, District Party Secretary from the West Bohemian spa of Karlovy Vary (Karlsbad), who said that "the worst [effect of tourism] is the importation of petty bourgeois illusions and ideas,"[89] have not been effective enough to generate a change in policy. Economic interests seem to prevail over ideological considerations, and visitors from hard currency areas remain welcome.

Creation of the New Socialist Man—Some Setbacks

The 1960s was a decade of grudging acknowledgment of reality and adjustment to it. Doctrinaire Communists were forced to take into account the Czech national character. For example, shortly after 1948 the two most popular Prague soccer teams, Sparta and Slavia, were renamed Spartak and Dynamo, respectively, in order to conform with the Moscow model. Irrespective of the indoctrination effort, exercised with childish persistence, the public refused to refer to the teams by their new names. After more than a decade of trying, the Party gave up and both clubs resumed their traditional names. Academic degrees went through the same metamorphosis—abolishment and reinstitution—and 1966 graduation ceremonies were once again conducted in Latin.[90]

Probably the most intense socialization effort, and subsequently the most monumental failure, involved the issue of proper comradely etiquette. After 1948, in the best tradition of Stalinist insensitivity, new manners were simply decreed, with instructions posted in public buildings. One old Bolshevik wrote in 1967: "In those days there were signs on doors announcing: 'We are trade unionists. We address each other as "Comrade" and use the greeting "Labor be Honored" [Cest praci]!' Why on earth haven't people got used to it after almost twenty years?"[91]

The nation refused to replace "Good day" with the ludicrous "Labor be honored," or "Mister" with "Comrade." Similarly, use of the familiar form of "you" (ty instead of the more formal vy) was vigorously demanded by the Party but failed to take root. By 1966 several articles had been published touching upon issues of social conduct, including the

politically mature manner of greeting a comrade in a public lavatory.[92] In the final analysis the Party surrendered, but instead of calling defeat by its right name, it was explained that there were progressive features in national tradition after all. It was noted that the Russians, too, did not always use a familiar form of address and that comradely greetings and etiquette were too precious to be wasted on possibly unworthy individuals.

In the 1970s, after a quarter of a century of KSC rule, the nation, and especially its youth, exhibits a remarkable resistance to imposed values and manners. Fellow citizens still fail to call each other "comrade." Even professional soldiers, who are under specific orders to follow prescribed etiquette, adopt bourgeois manners in their off-duty hours.[93]

The Party also failed to invent acceptable substitutes for ceremonies traditionally performed by churches, such as those of baptism, marriage, and especially, burial.

> A Communist passes away. . . . At the grave there is no one to speak up in the name of the Party organization in appreciation of the lifetime work of the deceased, to emphasize that he who is leaving is a member of the Party which made it its mission to change and perfect life on earth. And it is even more painful when the last words are those of a priest. Over the grave of a Communist![94]

In this context it may be useful to assess the degree of surviving religious sentiment in the country, without however, elaborating on the familiar pattern of Stalinist persecution of the churches and the underlying intolerance for any competitive creed. The KSC policy was one of confiscation of church property, banishment of religious orders, mass arrests of the clergy and/or their assignment to manual labor, assorted forms of harassment, curtailment of religious instruction, and a general climate of intimidation that would make a person think twice before attending church services. In view of this effort and of the traditionally lukewarm religious sentiment in the Czech provinces—unlike Slovakia and her devout Catholics—the victory of atheism was expected but did not fully materialize.

The membership of individual churches cannot be ascertained, partly because of the 1954 government order that abolished any reference to religious affiliation in official documents. Although all the

"Mary, there are three kings and some sort of comrade out here."
(*Listy*, December 19, 1968)

churches were subjected to persecution, the Uniate Church was completely destroyed, as were sects with Western ties, such as the Mormons and Jehovah's Witnesses. At present the Roman Catholic Church is the largest denomination, followed by the Czechoslovak Church (which originated with the Hussite movement), and the Evangelical Church of Czech Brethren (some 260,000 followers of what once was the Unitas Fratrum, with Comenius as its last bishop). In Slovakia the Evangelical Church (400,000 strong) is Lutheran in character.[95] The Marxist scholar Vitezslav Gardavsky, whose specialty is the study of Christianity, asserted in 1968 that the slow but continuous liquidation of the churches in Czechoslovakia had reduced the number of Christians to 30 percent of the total population.[96] On the other hand, the head of the Catholic Church, Bishop Frantisek Tomasek claimed that "according to the latest statistics, Catholics constitute 60 percent [of the population], atheists 30 percent, and members of other denominations 10 percent."[97]

Until 1963 the Party did not consider religion worthy of solid research. In that year, a study by Erika Kadlecova was the first to receive official endorsement. The results were published in 1965 and caused a sensation, to put it mildly. The area studied was Northern Moravia, which includes traditional pockets of piety but also the city of Ostrava, which has the largest industrial concentration in the country, a transient population, high wages, a high crime rate and generally little respect for anything spiritual other than distilled spirits.

Kadlecova found that the influence of the Catholic Church, though weakening, remained greater than that of the Protestants, but that there was more stability in the latter's ranks. Of the total adult population in the area, 30 percent were "atheists," 30 percent were "practicing believers," and the remaining 40 percent "undecided." The degree to which the government's anti-religious campaign had been successful was indicated by the data on the religious orientation of different age groups. The highest proportion of declared atheists (35 percent) was in the 30–40-year-old age group, followed closely by the 40–50-year-old group. Religious sentiment was most common among those over 50. The younger generation, brought up under socialism, demonstrated the highest degree of indifference toward both religion and state-sponsored atheism. Just as unexpected was the discovery that the proletariat, the most progressive class in Marxist-Leninist ideology, was more religious than the

Table 9.4. Religious Convictions by Age Group (in percentages).

Age group	Atheists	Believers	Undetermined	Total
18–24	15.6	58.7	25.7	100
25–39	19.1	65.5	18.4	103 (*sic*)
40–54	13.7	75.1	11.2	100
55 up	7.8	82.9	9.3	100

white-collar labor force. As a final point of embarrassment to the state, Kadlecova detected a trend toward further losses for the cause of atheism.[98]

A second study of religious sentiment, conducted in the fall of 1968, used a representative sample of 1,400 residents of Slovakia. The results, published in 1970,[99] confirmed the findings and indication of trends by Kadlecova. As expected, religious sentiment was found to be more profound in Slovakia than in Northern Moravia. After two decades of official atheism, 70.7 percent of the sample remained religious believers. A decline in religious sentiment did not automatically lead to a rise in atheism. A breakdown according to age groups yielded the results shown in Table 9.4.

Twenty years of socialization represented an intense, often ineffective, and, with regard to the young generation, counterproductive process. In the period during which Stalinist crimes were publicized the generational conflict was intensified: it was the youth who castigated their elders for cowardice, hypocrisy, complicity, and for plain stupidity. The Party's emphasis on uniformity and its reluctance even to admit the existence of generational diversity further exacerbated this antagonism. According to youth leader Oldrich Krystofek, "Youth has become a specific social category with its own special problems and its subculture. This situation has arisen out of the marked cultural and historical discontinuity between the postwar generation and its elders. . . ."[100]

Recognition of the existing generational conflict coincided with the official rehabilitation of sociology, which was then utilized for better understanding of the problem. For example, studies of the ethical values of the young showed that their objective and subjective moral criteria did not coincide. Students in one teachers' college were asked the following questions in 1964: "Recently Brigit Bardot posed in a

bathing suit advertising a camera. For this promotion she received 12,000 West German marks. Is it moral for a movie actress to engage in such activities?" (Question A); and, "If you were Brigit Bardot, would you do what she has done?" (Question B).[101] The results are shown in Table 9.5.

Table 9.5. Response to Questionnaire About Bardot.

Question	Yes	No	Don't know
Question A (Is it moral?)	38	77	1
Question B (Would you do it?)	81	34	1

Other surveys revealed a high frequency of noncommitment to official values on the part of the young. Studies of 1965 draftees showed that only a small minority—5.1 percent representing the extreme positive pole, and 2.6 percent the extreme negative pole—had a definite orientation toward official values.[102] Theoretically at least, the socialization of nine out of ten draftees was unfinished.

Right up to the end, the Novotny regime maintained a posture of cheerless acquiescence to the fact that the youth of the 1960s was different from the preceding generation. The authoritative *Nova mysl* conceded in 1967 that total manipulation was not such a good thing after all and that "it appears that hostility toward manipulation, so characteristic of the attitudes of the young, also has some positive features." The journal then, in a conciliatory gesture, evaluated the young:

The opposition to manipulation does not manifest itself only as a certain reserve in behavior. It is also manifested in a desire not to take over finished life forms, but to find and create its own life style. . . . The most characteristic mark of the attitudes of contemporary youth is an aversion toward empty phrases that solve nothing, a strong anti-bombast posture, civility, democratism, and reliance on facts. The established system of political engagement is alien to the young; it appears to them as an unintelligible, purposeless mechanism, which (in the eyes of the young) can only be ignored. Politicization of the youth of today does not and cannot have the same content and form as the politicization of the youth at the end of the 1940s and the beginning of the 1950s.[103]

In 1968 it was also frankly acknowledged that the youthful population constituted a subculture in its own right. Adults split on this issue along strictly political lines. Liberals confessed the failure of their efforts to assimilate the youth to the mainstream of socialist culture, pleaded that the naiveté of the early postwar years, was a mitigating factor, and offered their cooperation. By contrast, the conservatives maintained their morose hostility toward all things young.[104]

The young, who had been persistently reprimanded by the regime for their political passivity, enthusiastically participated in the 1968 experiment. As could be expected, the students were the most susceptible to change. Before January 1968 only 2 percent of a student sample believed socialism was living up to its real potential; a mere 10 percent were politically active. The demise of the Novotny regime was welcomed by 99.6 percent of the students questioned. Their political participation tripled, and their support for the Communist Party grew accordingly. Their positive attitude toward the new leadership and its policies was strengthened by its stress on national emancipation. Students identified freedom and sovereignty as the highest values, whereas friendship and cooperation with the Soviet Union and other socialist countries and their common struggle against imperialism was lowest on the scale of values.[105]

Political generations seem to be formed around "core events." The 1968 invasion was a traumatic experience for the young which no contradictory propaganda will be able to eradicate, and affected their political outlook in much the same way as the Munich Pact and World War II formed and slanted the postwar political perceptions of the preceding generation. The 1968 perfidy, almost coinciding with the thirtieth anniversary of the 1938 betrayal, offers a common denominator and outlook for both the young and old.

The anti-totalitarian sentiment was associated with a strong feeling of patriotism and anti-Sovietism. As one writer remarked, "I saw children crying at the sound of our national anthem—and believe me, this was shocking above anything else."[106] The youth who returned to the classrooms were more mature, tense, cautious, and supremely politicized, prompting the remark that "they will never reach this youth with any demagogy or half-truths."[107]

It was the young, and the university students in particular, who organized the strike in the fall of 1968 as a gesture of protest and of determination to adhere to the democratization program. Surveys showed that the vast majority of the adults—workers, and intellectuals alike—approved of this action.[108]

Student strikes are an uncommon event in Czechoslovakia. It is misleading to equate them with similar happenings in Western countries; and particularly misleading, for example, to draw close parallels between student protests in Prague and, Paris or Berkeley. Czech students themselves resented such comparisons and argued that their movements did not parallel those in the West. First, the Czechoslovak student action was essentially defensive, destroying nothing, but *protecting* the Action Program from outside destruction. Second, these students did not operate in a social vacuum; the industrial proletariat and the trade unions were close allies and active supporters of the striking force. Third, and most important, the Czechoslovak students were free from totalitarian intolerance, messianic self-righteousness, humorless zeal—all of which seemed to permeate the student organizations of the West. "Because we are living in the world of Franz Kafka," it was remarked, "we must above all cultivate humor and tenderness. Lack of love is fatal."[109]

The postures of the Western New Left appear to Eastern Europeans—myself included—as more theatric than real—if not downright phony. The Westerner, it is argued, is handicapped by the absence of tragic experience. He seems to consider that poverty and socialist virtue go hand in hand, as if not realizing that abundance is a basic prerequisite for the ultimate equitable distribution of goods in a socialist society. It is equally naive to ask the East Europeans to be contemptuous of "bourgeois liberties" when their liberties have been in as short supply as their consumer goods. The appearance in Prague of German apostles of intolerance, such as Rudi Dutschke, was a fiasco:

> The pose of Western students as revolutionaries ... generated on the part of our students the indulgent smile of those prematurely grown up rather than any enthusiasm.... Proclaimed violence, with whatever justification, is for them [Czech students] a complete taboo. Herbert Marcuse with his views would have failed before this audience even before August 21 [and the more, since].[110]

The New Left to them is not the promise of the future but the ghost of the unwanted past.

Just as it takes a well-fed society to produce persons with a craving for quasi-revolutionary austerity, so does it take an environment of political tranquility to produce persons with a genuine concern for foreign issues and sympathy for suffering in faraway countries. In Czechoslovakia in 1968, according to a blunt confession, "All social groups of the population lost sympathy for internationalism.... There is a great gap between involvement in the West and the indifference in socialist countries."[111] But there was no indifference to the rediscovered national pride. In one survey, 78 percent of respondents thought Czechoslovakia was the best place to live. Only 17 percent opted for the capitalist system (preferably Swedish or American), and 3.6 percent for other socialist countries (Yugoslavia and Rumania).[112] Simultaneously, the 1968 invasion generated intense anti-Soviet attitudes. The artists of the National Theater in Prague even protested against a staging of the Nutcracker ballet because the music was composed by a Russian.[113] A check of the programs of Prague cinemas in the first week of May 1969 (i.e., under Husak's leadership) showed 28 Czechoslovak, 15 American, 9 West German, 8 French, and a few British and Italian films. There were no Soviet films being shown in the capital.[114] Early post-invasion attempts by pro-Soviet political interests to reach Czechoslovak society with other media had little success. The Soviet News Agency started to publish a Czech-language weekly *Tydenik aktualit* with a printing of 100,000. In Prague, which has the largest consumption of printed material in the country, there were thirty-three subscribers to this journal, three of whom were private citizens.[115]

The gigantic socialization task of obliterating the memories of 1968 seems to be being carried out with the old Stalinist lack of sophistication. A poll taken in 1969 among army draftees showed that 75 percent of the respondents opposed restoration of friendship with the Soviet Union. To this the Party responded: "This demonstrates what can be achieved in a relatively short time by inconsistencies in our own propaganda or by negative foreign propaganda."[116] The citizen continues to be viewed solely as an object of manipulation, a meek and weak creature who needs only to have the right amount of socializing messages pumped into him to transform him into an ardent supporter of the regime. Successive failures having bestowed no wisdom, such a futile undertaking is likely to characterize the attempts to create socialist man in the 1970s.

The society is alienated to a degree unknown since the wartime Nazi occupation. Call for national amnesia is unrealistic and the adopted techniques of socialization are anything but subtle. Echoing Ulbricht's notion of "people not worthy of their leadership," the political diagnosis of the nation revealed that its low resistance to antisocialist infection was the result of a hereditary deficiency prevalent among those without sturdy working class parentage. Based on what he said were the most recent findings of the Academy of Sciences, Jaroslav Kucera published detailed serialized revelations in *Tribuna*, exposing the bourgeois ancestry of a high proportion of the Czechoslovak people.[117] According to Kucera, half a million bourgeois and over four million petty bourgeois lived in the country in 1946–1947. In 1969, 300,000 bourgeois (including children), 380,000 petty bourgeois, and 2,500,000 "former petty bourgeois" still remained. The bourgeoisie had been expropriated, unlike the petty bourgeoisie, whom Kucera identifies as owners of small farms in remote mountainous areas. The majority (200,000) live in Slovakia. The strange category of "*former* petty bourgeois" denotes individuals who, though economically a part of the socialist system, have not adopted socialist values. In other words, two decades of political indoctrination failed to socialize the majority (almost 2.9 million out of 4 million) of the petty bourgeoisie. The magnitude of the ancestral taint was summarized by Kucera:

If we add to those four million members of the petty bourgeoisie who existed before 1948 half a million members of the bourgeoisie from the same period, and further add a substantial part of the representatives of the bourgeois state apparatus, those who were employed by repressive organs of the bourgeois state, and family members of both of these, and so on [sic], we may conclude that almost half of the population of our country was in the past more or less related by class with the petty bourgeois strata or directly with the bourgeoisie.[118]

This analysis makes for strange science but its political message sounds familiar. It is a call to reactivate the command system and to treat the populace with continued suspicion, regardless of the declared 99.9 percent electoral victory. The nation's body, defective at birth, and with little resistance to germs spreading inappropriate attitudes, requires prolonged treatment, ranging from a set of dietary restrictions to shock therapy.

The patient's environment is made antiseptic largely by continuous applications of censorship. The criteria of ideological propriety are more severe than ever before. The antisepsis of censorship includes canceled stage productions, permanent closing of a prominent Prague theater, burning of germ-infested new movies, and stoppage of production on others. Since the purification of the mass media and book publishing will be discussed in some detail in the next chapter, it suffices here to note that the censorship in Czechoslovakia in the 1970s reached unprecedented severity. Molière had to be withdrawn from the stage because of improper reactions by the audience. Parts of Brecht's *Mother Courage* were deleted because the sad end of the Swedish King Gustavus Adolphus might have reminded the audience of that of Gustav Husak. A Soviet hero dies on stage and provokes laughter —"incidents, demonstrations of hostility, drops of poison, hatred, and cowardice,"[119] such are the symptoms of the societal malady.

For both opponents and supporters of the regime, the popularity of Soviet movies has traditionally been a very political issue, as if the box office were a polling place and the admission ticket a surrogate ballot revealing the true popularity of the USSR and its political system. Owing to their low technical and artistic quality, unsophisticated political messages,

and Party pressures for high attendance, the Soviet movies have never been very popular, and in 1968–1969 they disappeared altogether from Czechoslovak screens. Hence, their reintroduction has been viewed as a significant step in the normalization process and the public reaction as a barometer of political mood. In an article, entitled "Revolt of the Petty Bourgeoisie," *Tvorba* reported in 1971 that on a night when the decadent capitalist film *Lady Hamilton* played to a full house the Soviet masterpiece *And Quiet Flows the Don* had only eight viewers. Letters to the editor published in the press praise socialist movies, condemn capitalist products, and accuse state distributors of profit motives. Despite such attacks Prague movie houses in the first week of January 1972 showed 64 productions from capitalist countries (only one with distinctly progressive features), 22 Czechoslovak productions, and 32 productions of other socialist countries. Quite understandably, the report did not include attendance figures.[120]

Another surrogate political contest is being waged in the field of popular music. To an outside observer the political significance of this issue may well be incomprehensible, but it has occupied the attention of Party authorities, the Politburo included. Even this branch of mass culture reflects the revivalistic desires of the leadership, tempered by a grudging acknowledgment of changed times. Some leaders are determined proponents of revolutionary songs in the style of the early 1950s; others concede some legitimacy to popular music provided that its practitioners adopt Czech names for their groups and eliminate all English words from the songs. The penetration of English into the Czech language has been severely criticized, especially in view of the failure of the Russian language to register similar inroads.[121]

Deficiencies in the socialist behavior of the nation—the youth in particular—are juxtaposed with the models of propriety manifested in other socialist countries, notably the USSR and the DDR.[122] Such deficiencies call for shock treatment, and that which the socialization agencies administer to the nation is intended to change the patient's attitude toward the most sensitive issue of recent political experience —the August 1968 invasion, later called "entry," and finally "fraternal international assistance." In short, if the treatment is successful the patient will feel guilty for necessitating the Warsaw Pact expedition and for failing to express adequate gratitude. Thus, *Tvorba*, a weekly with a relatively moderate orientation, wrote in 1971:

> The emotional wave which rose up especially after August 1968 is gone. Nothing is left of it, except the frequent feeling of our shame and also our realization that it has never happened that the Soviet people have by any means whatsoever endangered in the least their ties of friendship with the Czechoslovak people.[123]

The mass media carry stories contrasting Soviet unselfishness with Czechoslovak ingratitude and even rudeness toward Soviet military personnel and their families. Instances of individual repentance are also reported, such as that of an elderly worker apologizing to Leonid Brezhnev in 1971 during a visit to Czechoslovakia: "I, too, blamed you—and now I am so ashamed I would like to cry."[124]

The Party socialization program is impeded by an alienated audience, shattered values, and the low capability of the personnel and the ineffectiveness of the tools they employ in this effort. In universities, completely undistinguished individuals and visiting Soviet educators try to fill the vacuum caused by the thorough purge of the social science faculty, and the discarding of textbooks, which were declared to be ideologically deficient, lacking in adequate class outlook and militancy. Remedial measures have so far produced no adequate results. Official sources acknowledged the lack of social science textbooks but pledged that manuscripts were to be submitted for approval in 1973. In the meantime the gap was to be filled with material "selected from generally valid theoretical topics in foreign textbooks. They have one disadvantage. They do not include Czechoslovak problems. . . ."[125]

The immunity against indoctrination takes a number of forms, perhaps the most common being what is officially termed *faktomanie*—"the obsession with mere facts" without concern for their adequate ideological interpretation. This disdain for ideological commitment may be illustrated by the following episode at Charles University in Prague: Whenever the instructor in Marxism-Leninism called for a vote on any of the issues, no one voted in favor or against, but all abstained. The students explained: "Every year we are taught something different. How can we know what the situation will be like next year? Then perhaps what we are saying nowadays will be held against us. So in order not to have to recant next year, we confess our errors at this moment."[126]

A frank assessment of students' resistance to the lure of the regime is presented by Silvester Novacek, who wrote about his experience as a university teacher in 1970. When he questioned his class—a seminar of twenty-two—about their attitude toward the Soviet Union, only one student declared his love for the USSR, while a majority (thirteen) voted for neutrality of Czechoslovakia; the rest viewed the relationship with the Soviets as a marriage of convenience. "When I tried to make clear the essentially wolfish nature of imperialism," Novacek complained, "they made fun of my words, as if I were telling them the story of little Red Riding Hood."[127]

In view of these findings the overall assessment of the situation as presented by another educator, Ondrej Pavlik from the Slovak Academy of Sciences, seems accurate. Pavlik commented: "The struggle to capture the mind and soul of the people, especially of the young, the struggle to eliminate rightist and antisocialist misconceptions, is still before us, rather than behind us."[128]

10

Political Communication

In a modern society the life of every citizen is affected by the amount and accuracy of information he receives. Earlier we touched upon the role of the mass media and their political impact; in this chapter we intend to discuss the various structures engaged in communication and their effect on the capabilities and performance of the political system. Manipulated information and the manipulated man will remain the focus of our attention.

The gradual exhaustion of totalitarianism in Czechoslovakia during the 1960s was also reflected in the communication realm. The mass media profited from fatigue and ineptitude rather than from any deliberate benevolence of the censors. In 1968, censorship was abolished, and the media experienced an exhilarating (but brief) period of emancipation.

Totalitarianism is determined to create a new man whose mind, ideas, and ideals are shaped by the approved and tested guardians of purity of thought. Josef Spacek, a reformist member of the 1968 Politburo, commented on these matters:

Concealment and secretiveness in connection with Party policy have their roots in a lack of trust in the people. Not that the people are regarded as enemies or that it is thought that they would divulge what they were told. It is simply a lack of faith in their ability to grasp the state of affairs and to draw an independent conclusion about the solution. . . . It is a lack of faith in the ability of the people to govern themselves.[1]

The flood of inflated propaganda contrasted with the stingy dosages of information that was made available. Leaders even kept a veil of secrecy over their personal lives. Czechoslovaks read detailed accounts of the weddings of President Lyndon Johnson's daughters, but were not allowed to know that President Novotny had a son.

The political leadership attempts to control the flow of all information in all directions, not only that to the mass media but that from input structures (such as mass organizations), and from output structures (such as the bureaucracy). Since the system's voracious appetite exceeds its digestive capacity the result is more often than not the production of gaseous effluvium. Rumor substitutes for information.

However, informal face-to-face contacts and traditional socialization units (notably the family) to some degree elude the controlling grip of the monopolist of power. Characteristic of the gap between official and unofficial values is the "dual public opinion" that exists among the distrustful, alienated citizenry.[2] The unauthorized set of values is usually a negation of the messages disseminated by the system. Hence, an unfavorable review of a movie by official reviewers is the most reliable guarantee of box-office success, whereas their praise keeps the public away.

It may be added that Stalinist elites, partly owing to their unspectacular intellectual caliber, shy away from extemporaneous speeches and informal interviews. Ghost-written speeches and prepared answers to predetermined questions rather than spontaneous statements have been the pattern; the few episodes to the contrary have revealed an embarrassing amount of primitivism.

The Language of Stalinism

One very stringent limitation is placed on communication by the language of Stalinism, which is characterized by the absence of the concrete, by vagueness, by a euphemistic, misleading vocabulary, by sophistry and disregard for what are generally regarded as the principles of logical thinking, and by a complete lack of humor. Humor—"the reliable distinguishing mark of humanity and unacceptable in the drilled community of totalitarian high boots"[3] —was not a legitimate ingredient of public expression until 1968, and then for only a few months.

In the black-and-white imagery of Stalinism some words are solely descriptive of the angels, and others are used in discourse only to designate the doomed. No devil (a domestic or foreign enemy) can ever qualify for the adjective "courageous". Only in exceptional cases can he be described as anything but "cowardly"; should he exhibit what in a comrade would be hailed as the highest form of courage, he is "cynical." Similarly, competition within the capitalist orbit is *konkurence*; competition in socialism is *soutezeni*. *Konkurence* accelerates the preordained doom of exploitative societies; *soutezeni* opens the

gate to terrestrial bliss. The armament program of the potential enemy is always a "feverish" one; an incompetent Stalinist bureaucrat is always an "honest" comrade. "Democracy," denoting a pluralistic representative system, is always preceded by such adjectives as "false," "unbridled," "destructive," "sham," or at least "bourgeois."

Concreteness implies definiteness, and definiteness makes a binding commitment of a declaration and increases the difficulty of abrogating it. In Chapter 7 we noted that vagueness and elasticity were the principal characteristics of totalitarian law. The Czech poet Miroslav Holub referred to the abandonment of the concrete as the "killing of words," usually preceding the killing of (equally innocent) people. These are a few examples of the killing of words by translation into Stalinese:[4]

> *arbitrariness, injustice*: subjectivism
> *torture*: improper (use of) administrative methods
> *guilt, innocence*: share of responsibility
> *rise of prices*: popularly acclaimed price adjustment
> *political appointment*: election

An ordinary brick is not a "brick" but a "construction unit." This too, as Holub states, adds to the feeling that one is existing in an imaginary world. Metaphors are codified and the need for defining them and explaining their meaning is missing. For the Stalinist elite "in whose eye the whole universe has been politicized, from boot nails to the star of the most distant galaxy,"[5] a writer becomes a "member of the cultural front" and a janitor a "functionary who also takes care of the house." According to the philosopher Jiri Cvekl, because of the lust for total manipulation, "all human functions are converted into a kind of bureaucratic ritual ... in which concrete objects and real people are transformed into bureaucratic symbols and hieroglyphs." The concrete is absorbed by the abstract and the general. Every disagreeable problem can be disposed of through generalization. An invasion becomes an "event," or "the so-called invasion." In every defeat of a Stalinist cause in an election, the losers refer to the victors as "the so-called numerical majority."[6]

One of the peak examples of Stalinist linguistic pollution was the word "tank" translated as "conveyor belt technique" (*pasova technika*), as awkward in Czech as it is in English. This semantic accomplishment prompted this outcry: "From time immemorial a tank has been a 'tank,' a tractor a 'tractor,' a car a 'car,' and a fork a 'fork'—not a 'dining technique.' We are neither such illiterate fools nor such inarticulate toddlers that it becomes necessary to communicate with us in the secretive language of the generals."[7] The militant mind easily adopts militaristic rhetoric—intolerance is fortified by martial terminology. In Moscow's *Pravda* in one article on ideology the following phrases appeared: "a sector of the antiimperialist struggle," "to take the offensive," "the counterattack of the reactionaries," and an "individual revolutionary detachment."[8]

Absence of the specific is complemented by the absence of the logical and by an abundance of demagogism. The Stalinist Alois Indra defended the Workers' Militia by arguing that "because some want to dispose of the Militia, this is a sufficient proof of the necessity to retain this organization."[9] The old student bon mot "We don't know whether Homer actually lived but we know for certain that he was blind" would easily qualify as an example of Stalinist logic. The post-invasion politicians, Husak included, have on numerous occasions said that though the leaders of the counterrevolutionary conspiracy were unknown, it was certain that they were directed from the West.[10]

Manipulation of thoughts and quotes out of context, indictments and charges with no desire to substantiate them, reliance on vague, empty images such as "struggle," "victory," "people," was something which the country overwhelmingly rejected in 1968. The breakdown of Stalinism meant the breakdown of Stalinese. Among the foremost results of Dubcek's leadership was the rehabilitation of concrete language. "The pre-January political leadership was used to referring to all pivotal problems in general terms," stated Ota Sik, who during the period of reform distinguished himself as a disseminator of very specific information.[11] In a famous series of television talks he informed the nation, accustomed to rosy nondescript messages for twenty years, on the near-economic catastrophe in the land.

Under Dubcek, pompous, verbose, and rather meaningless messages were considered to be not only obsolete but offensive. As the Czech Vladimir Blazek found in a discussion with Soviet academician F. Konstantinov, to effect a useful exchange of views it would have been necessary to reconcile two irreconcilable objects—the liberated and the Stalinist

mind.[12] It was an idle exercise to engage in a dialogue with a spokesman for a party for whom the only acceptable settlement of any conflict was the opponent's total surrender. "The very idea that we might expect something else was regarded as shocking."[13] In the language of Stalinism the truth is not searched for, but stated *ex cathedra*, with the authority of a Papal decree.

Stalinese, with its vagueness, repetitiveness, sacral connotation, alogism, and superficiality leaves as its final imprints boredom, witlessness, humorlessness, an absence of any kindness, and an inability not to take oneself seriously. The Establishment promoted "constructive satire," but this was predictably anemic. *Dikobraz*, the satirical weekly, entertained the toiling masses with such witty sayings as "A man learns by his mistakes but a capitalist does not."[14]

Under Stalinism even the use of authorized language, ideological zeal, the sheer conformity of its disseminators, self-censorship, and a keen sense for survival were not found sufficient guarantees of the purity of communicated messages. In 1953, after five years of leaving to editors-in-chief the role of censors of their own publications, an unpublished governmental decree called for the establishment of a special censorship agency, the Main Administration of Press Supervision (HSTD) under the Ministry of the Interior. The existence of HSTD was kept secret for thirteen years (including the ten years following the Twentieth Congress of the USSR Communist Party, at which Stalin was denounced). In 1966 a new press law was adopted, acknowledging the existence of censorship which by then was administered by an agency called the Central Publication Administration (UPS). Its personnel had to cope with a truly enormous task. Everything—newspapers, periodicals, books, films, even death notices—had to be submitted for prior censorship.[15]

In 1968 the liberal weekly *Reporter*[16] obtained a copy of a HSTD order and published it.

Officially, the censor was the protector of state secrets and social interests.[17] A variety of sources defined the contents of this vague framework, and it became a regular practice for political elites to meddle in all branches of communication. A ranking apparatchik or government official would (and probably still does) issue instructions to HSTD to ban the publication of all writings of an author or the reporting of even such an event as an ordinary fire in the neigh-

Retired censor: "Jesus Christ! What did I find wrong in this?"
(*Dikobraz*, April 11, 1968)

borhood. If any mechanism to check upon the propriety of such instructions exists it has been kept secret.

The interference of censors was capricious, unenlightened, and inconsistent. A good example is provided by the collected articles of Jan Prochazka (a former confidant of Novotny and, then, after the fall of Novotny, one of the most outspoken critics of totalitarianism). Entitled *Politics for Everybody* and published in 1968, this anthology includes the paragraphs, sentences, and single words (in italics), originally deleted by the censors.[18] In retrospect, it is almost impossible to discover the reasons for any given excision.

Little logic and a plenitude of primitivism describe the list of banned books that was compiled and issued in 1953 and was still in force in 1968. For example, the protectors of the nation's ideological health banned numerous medieval tracts from circulation. One hexagonal stamp signified a quarantine for the book, two stamps meant unqualified damnation.[19]

MINISTRY OF INTERIOR
Main Administration of Press Supervision

Prague, April 15, 1964.
TOP SECRET
Copy No.:

TELEPHONE ORDER NO. 219

Issuance of the order requested by:
Enforcement of the order issued by: Deputy Chief, HSTD Lt. Col. J. Kovar
Anticipated term of the order: 2 years
The order to be transmitted to these administrative branches of press supervision:

1. Departments of HSTD
2. STD
3. Departments of press supervision in KS-MV
4. Trustees for press supervision at OO-KV

CONTENTS:

All articles and other material by Ivan Svitak must not be published. Submit at once confiscated material by this author.

You were originally supposed to see this cartoon on February 15, 1968, but it was confiscated by the censors on January 31, 1968 [i.e., three weeks after the January Plenary Session of the Party Central Committee]. Guess why?

(*Rohac*, March 27, 1968)

During the 1950s the censors' insistence upon "constructive messages" was especially narrow-minded, with implications bordering on the supernatural. "World news" from the capitalist orbit consisted solely of disaster reports—airline crashes, hurricanes, earthquakes, mining tragedies, crimes, and the like—so that the reader could not help but conclude that (official atheism notwithstanding) some mysterious force was subjecting the world of the exploiters to a multitude of assorted punishments. One Czech provincial newspaper reported floods in the Ohio Valley while failing to mention the floods that had forced the editors to vacate their desks.

In the 1960s such folly gradually disappeared. The fatigue and indifference of the public prompted the system to enliven the style and content of reporting. In 1963, because of the unappealing life in the kolkhoz and a shortage of women willing to marry cooperative farmers, *Zemedelske noviny* the daily of the Ministry of Agriculture, introduced "get-together" classified ads.[20]

The literary journals, in particular, exhibited courage and imagination. The censorship barrier began to crumble under this impact. In comparison with the rigidly controlled publications of the Husak era, volumes of *Literarni noviny* for the years 1963–1967 read as if they were produced in some distant age of enlightenment.

For the censors, the route from Novotny to Husak was a closed circle. When Dubcek was elected First Secretary of the Party, the UPS structure was paralyzed; though not officially abolished, it ceased to function. *De jure* abolishment was achieved shortly before the August 1968 invasion. Since that event, several steps have been taken toward reinstitution of censorship: first, self-censorship by editors, then post-publication censorship, and finally, in 1969, prior censorship of the standard totalitarian type. The short-lived autonomy of the communication media, free from censors and also free from the domination of the ruling party, ended.

Information as Power

Elaborating on the issue of freedom of information, the daily paper *Zemedelske noviny* stated in 1968 that the only enemies of this freedom were the beneficiaries of the old system: "Sometimes it looks to me as if some officials in the country are jealous of the function of the press, radio, and television. Many have indirectly admitted as much. Formerly, it was they who were kept informed and who knew more than the others."[21] The Stalinists—"in the name of the people"—called for restoration of censorship and considered its abolishment detrimental to everyone except a handful of subversive intellectuals. Illustrative of this mentality was the suggestion of publishing the works of the Soviet novelist Ovechkin in two versions: unabridged for the mature cadres and expurgated for the masses, which "might have lost confidence in the USSR if allowed to read that there are some economic difficulties there."[22]

In a closed system access to information is of great importance. One's place on the political ladder determines the volume of allotted information. When in 1963 the long overdue rehabilitation of the Slansky group took place, the announcement was made in four ways. First, there was a report of several hundred pages, reserved for members of the Central Committee of the Party. Second, a 150-page report was given to the "*Aktif* of the functionaries", i.e., Party officials and activists. Third, a 20-page statement addressed to the million and a half rank and file of the Party. Fourth, a press release of a page or so was issued to inform the nation.[23] This example may serve as a standard yardstick of information rationing in post-1948 Czechoslovakia.

The issue of enlivening the mass media in order to combat public fatigue and apathy, was parallelled by scrutiny of the state of communication within the Party. One provincial apparatchik argued that more information was necessary because of the reluctance of the membership to accept mere generalizations, which did nothing to halt the loss of revolutionary certainty of purpose and of ideological firmness under the impact of the rather discouraging reality. Among the unnecessary malfunctions of the transmission system that were mentioned was the failure of many Party officials to take notes at briefing sessions; as a consequence, these officials presented partial and/or distorted information to lower echelons.[24]

Another critic identified three defects in the Party communication process. First was the notion that *informovanost* ("the level of information available and received") was solely dependent upon individual initiative. Comrades maintaining such a view were

guilty of oversimplification. Second, any demand calling for unlimited information was condemned as "liberalism." Third, and most prevalent, was "sectarianism," the belief that the extent of information available should be in direct proportion to individual political status.[25]

Both within the Party and throughout the nation, demands for more information and criticism of existing practices mushroomed, especially after Novotny's demise. "Surprised public" was an interesting term coined to describe the final product of manipulation—a citizenry that is informed about its own allegedly spontaneous reactions, moods, and demands (i.e., "the public demands, condemns, protests, etc.").[26] For a short time in the late sixties the vertical one-way flow of information from the rulers to the ruled was interrupted and supplemented by a horizontal flow of information among hitherto isolated sources. By 1969, however, any channels of horizontal communication that were unacceptable to the monopolists of power had been closed. The tactic of "surprise" was reintroduced and communication once again traveled along a one-way street leading to a dead end which "all the news from the sphere of politics reaches as a kind of natural catastrophe."[27] Totalitarian norms require that the public be misinformed when it is not completely uninformed—yet the public is urged to participate in "national discussions." As has been pointed out, these can be nothing but pseudo-discussions, creating an image of pseudo-participation about a pseudo-program, approved through pseudo-consent.[28]

Jan Kaspar, Dubcek's head of the information section in the Party Central Committee, addressed himself to the issues of communication in an article published just before the invasion, pleading for professionalism in this Party role.[29] Kaspar argued that the KSC apparatus should offer highly qualified services to elected bodies. This would require setting up a new information network to replace the dysfunctional structure then existing, since the information explosion had thus far inhibited a complex synthetic analysis of societal trends, and only partial, empirical, nonrelated studies had been produced. He distinguished between strategic-tactical information (conceptual) and operative information (specific but incomplete). The Party bureaucracy was severely handicapped by absence of a common terminology, symbols, and coding. Without these, according to Kaspar, a complex utilization of information was impossible. In addition, the majority of data accumulated by the Party structures were not quantifiable.

Earlier we touched upon the dilettantism of Novotny's rule and how its ineptness enabled the man in the street to outwit the system. For example, Stalinists rejected computers as the toys of bourgeois pseudo-science, unworthy of the attention of self-respecting Marxist scholars, and thus postponed for rationalized management and control of the society for several precious years. In his article, Kaspar stressed the need for a computer center, conceding, though, that both programs and programmers were in short supply.

In the *Report on the Current Situation* prepared by the Central Committee of the Party in August 1968, it was asserted that:

> Despite expanded efforts, it was not possible to achieve, even in the Party's regional committees, conditions which would correspond to modern, scientific methods of disseminating information. . . . A permanent deficiency in our activity is that communication networks in the entire Republic are totally obsolete. . . . This near-catastrophic state in communication networks, and in communications in general, is also one of the main reasons why it seems to be impossible to direct, from one center, eighty-five districts in the Czech provinces.[30]

Further recommendations called for improvement in facilities for communication between different Party structures, construction of a teletype network, and, technical conditions permitting, a system of tape recording telephone messages. Construction of communication links on the fundamental level, i.e., between local cells and the district secretariats, was also envisioned.

The article by Jan Kaspar indicated an attempt to establish rational communication within the Party structure. It appears that the Party was well-aware of such cardinal problems as overloading and transmission error. To these problems, which occur in any type of a modern society, must be added some specifically totalitarian handicaps, in particular the timidity of the reporting sources, who feared that they might displease their superiors in the chain of communication; ideological blinds; and rigid adoption of Soviet practices.

There is no evidence to suggest that in its effort to modernize communication processes the Party contemplated any decentralization. Instead, the emphasis was on coordination, standardization, and strict centralism. The Party bureaucracy has traditionally exhibited an insatiable appetite for data, including highly technical data pertaining to the economy. The KSC apparatus is both unable to assimilate the wealth of information it receives and unwilling to share it. Yet it has been officially estimated that not more than 10 percent of all information in the possession of the Party should be kept from the public eye.

It seems unlikely that many of the proposals will be efficiently implemented by the conservative post-invasion leadership. Some suggestions will no doubt be discarded as outright revisionist rubbish, such as the "permanent verification of the popularity, authority, and activity of individual functionaries and Party organs in the structure of the Party system."[31]

Implications of 1968

The ouster of Novotny seriously affected communication processes. Uncertainty and uneasiness among the new power holders and a lack of consensus on how to formulate the political change for the Party rank and file (and consequently for the public at large), were reflected in the minimal amounts of official information that were made available. The political elite left everybody, including the censors, in the dark. The only beneficiary of this state of affairs was the mass media, which fully exploited the censors' paralysis.

The Party rank and file and the lower echelons of activists were very critical of this information blackout. They realized that, against all the logic of one-party rule, the KSC members were more ignorant than outsiders. A typical complaint was how difficult it was for a Communist to retain his prestige when left in a limbo of guesses while the public was kept informed through such channels as Radio Free Europe.[32] "Important information," *Rude pravo* complained, "so to speak, first-hand information, is often first reported in foreign broadcasts. There is nothing pleasant in defending the Party line and having it proved that the truth was with the adversary who was not supposed to be informed at all."[33] The KSC members, less inclined to turn to Western sources of information, and insulated from the distrustful non-Communist majority, thus felt abandoned by the leadership. They were bitter and embarrassed and insisted on improvement. When the KSC monopoly over communication was dismantled in 1968, a bizarre situation developed when the KSC members, at the mercy of tight-lipped apparatchiks, received less political information than the members of the puppet parties. This was reported from the Southern Moravian district of Znojmo, where the Socialist Party had a better record in communicating with its membership than did the ruling Communists.[34]

The new leadership introduced a new style of communication that was widely appreciated. The populace was given its first taste of this by Dubcek at his first public appearance in February 1968, when he addressed the Seventh Congress of the Cooperative Farmers. Instead of the classic ritual of cliched rhetoric, personal detachment, criticism, and veiled threats, the audience was treated with easy informality.[35] The reformers also vowed to change the content of communications. They promised to tell the truth, even if it proved unpleasant. They also recognized that the emancipation of the mass media would make it necessary for them to accustom themselves to criticism from such sources.[36]

However, these changes were neither durable nor thorough. The Party weakened its grip over the mass media but it did not surrender many of its prerogatives. Equal status for Party and non-Party channels of communication was not implemented or even expected. At briefing sessions for editors-in-chief, Central Committee Secretary Cestmir Cisar (one of the most progressive politicians of the time) continued to discriminate between "whites" and "coloreds" as his critics put it. Cisar failed to invite non-Party members, including Stanislav Budin (an expelled, prewar Communist) who was editor-in-chief of *Reporter*, a weekly and the main outlet of the Union of Czechoslovak Journalists.[37]

Experimentation with freedom put the mass media in a state of uneasy exhilaration. The fear that their newly acquired emancipation would be revoked called for cohesion and a uniform front, and as a consequence, prevented them from expressing differences of opinion. Their degree of homogeneity surpassed that in the closing years of the Novotny era. As a paradox of the first magnitude, there was more heterogeneity in the totalitarian period than in the post-totalitarian one! The Writers' Union weekly, *Literarni noviny*, the leading force of

progressivism in the 1960s, was politically further from *Rude pravo* in 1967 than in the year after, when the latter also jumped on the liberals' bandwagon.

Some differences within the reformist camp could still be detected, however. Recognized novelists enjoyed the widest range of permissible behavior (or misbehavior). They capitalized on their public prestige and relative economic independence. Their sources of income ranged from royalties received in hard currency from abroad to lucrative contracts with the movie industry. Staff journalists were in a more vulnerable position and were further handicapped by a past record of persistent docility. As late as October 1967 the Congress of the Union of Czechoslovak Journalists supported Novotny against the rebellious writers. A desire to erase such a blemish accelerated the speed with which the journalists embraced the liberal cause. Conflicts erupted in several editorial offices between journalists and publishers, who took a less daring and at times very conservative stand. In all such conflicts, whether in the press of the puppet parties or in *Rude pravo*, the management invariably lost.

The relative homogeneity of the press in 1968 notwithstanding, some degree of differentiation existed. The publications below are listed in the order of the daring with which they challenged the old system, its structures, processes, and ideological premises.

(1) The weeklies *Literarni listy* (and its Slovak counterpart *Kulturny zivot*), *Student* (published by the university students), and *Reporter*. *Literarni listy* was the most influential (circulation 300,000), *Student* the most daring.

(2) The dailies representing special interests: *Prace* (trade unions), *Mlada fronta* (youth organization), and *Zemedelske noviny* (a farmers' paper, though officially published by the Ministry of Agriculture). These were the only three dailies to publish the famous "Two Thousand-Word Manifesto."

(3) The dailies *Svobodne slovo and Lidova demokracie*, published by Czech puppet parties. Their particular contribution was reporting past Stalinist crimes. With a circulation of 250,000 each, their influence was far greater than that of the moribund press of the Slovak puppet parties.

(4) The Communist Party daily *Rude pravo* and its provincial counterparts. Their contribution was not so much in initiating liberalization as in sanctioning the initiative of others.[38]

Of course, this is not a comprehensive evaluation but merely a general assessment of the press. It is unlikely that an in-depth content analysis of some 1,200 periodicals published in Czechoslovakia has been undertaken, either in Czechoslovakia itself or elsewhere. However, a study of Slovak dailies in 1967 and 1968 was carried out by the Institute for Research in the Mass Communication Media in Bratislava.[39] The story concluded that the nature of Slovak dailies was fundamentally political. This was especially evident in 1968, when politics occupied an average of 39 percent of the newspapers' space. Sport occupied the next largest proportion of space, third was general reporting (disasters, "interesting events"), followed by human-interest stories, essays on culture, education, and art, articles on economics (11 percent), advertising (9 percent), and, last, science and technology (3 percent). These data are of questionable reliability, however, since they were published in August 1969, by which time strict censorship had been reimposed.

Despite accusations by the conservatives, the mass media did not aim at usurping political power in the nation. As Jiri Hochman, one of the most influential reformist commentators, pointed out, the press was not a political movement or a party, but, given the special conditions, was a factor of change.[40] The media's multifunctional role included providing information about the nature of the Stalinist past, serving as a rallying point for the proponents of liberal causes, and contributing greatly to the establishment of national unity, including political cooperation of the intellectuals and the workers. During the invasion, when the political leaders who were not kidnapped by the Soviet forces were in hiding, the mass media, and the radio network in particular, in a magnificent example of human ingenuity and courage, substituted for the paralyzed government, thereby averting chaos and disintegration. This singular achievement postponed the realization of Soviet policies for almost a year.

In the first occupation edition of *Literarni listy* (abridged to mere *Listy* in a symbolic gesture of national impoverishment) the editorial statement emphasized that the "fundamental fact of [the August invasion] is that the press has ceased to play the role of a coarchitect of policy."[41] This was an accurate but premature diagnosis. The initial weakness of the Soviet-installed regime, which was on the defensive against the wrath of a united nation, caused delays in adopting new censorship measures and in taking action against the reformist press, which had been augmented by several new progressive periodicals. Symbols of continuity with the pre-invasion phase were stressed. Some new periodicals went so far as to claim to continue in the tradition of publications that had flourished in the pre-1948 era: the new trade unionist periodical was called *Svet prace*, the name of a long-banned Social-Democratic weekly, the Socialist Party's *Zitrek* carried on the tradition of *Svobodny zitrek*, the People's Party's *Obroda* continued along the path of *Obzory*. In addition, new, old, or revived literary journals, such as *Orientace*, *Tvar*, *Index*, and *Impuls*, fortified the strength of the liberal press.

Incredible as it may seem, by the end of 1968, after almost half a year of occupation, former strongholds of the Stalinist apparatus, such as *Zivot strany*, followed the progressive line. Stalinist journalists remained unemployed; the only periodical articulating Soviet interests was *Zpravy*, published and distributed by the Soviet army. Poorly written, it had little effect.[42]

In 1969 the situation changed drastically, and the circle was once again closed: from the imposed homogeneity of the media in the early Stalinist period to the grudgingly tolerated heterogeneity of the 1960s, then to the uniform front of progressivism in 1968, then back to heterogeneity, and finally back to imposed homogeneity. Near the end of 1968 the Stalinists started the publication of the weekly *Tribuna*, which, under its editor-in-chief Oldrich Svestka, became the rallying point for advocates of totalitarianism. Reflecting the power struggle in the KSC apparatus, a situation developed which was highly irregular for a one-Party state: Communist journals—the Stalinist *Tribuna*, the centrist *Zivot strany*, and the liberal *Politika*—engaged in mutual polemics.[43]

In the early part of 1969 the press still offered informative reading. A copy of the People's Party's daily *Lidova demokracie* selected at random (February 22, 1969) carried on one page three articles on delicate, soon-to-be-forbidden topics: an incident in the town of Semily, where young people protested the gathering of a Stalinist group; a mysterious car accident involving a witness in the investigation into the death of Jan Masaryk; and a case of attempted rape at the Nelahozeves railway station, with shooting and multiple injuries (although the Soviet soldier who was responsible was referred to merely as "a uniformed man"). Of all the dailies, the trade unionist *Prace* remained the most outspoken.

In April, 1969 Husak replaced Dubcek as head of the Party. Among his first acts were the introduction of preliminary censorship and the banning of *Listy* and *Reporter*.[44] (It should be pointed out that Novotny had never dared to ban a periodical without authorizing publication of an alternate by the writers' and journalists' unions.) The new journal *Zitrek*, a shade more outspoken and nationalistic than the banned weeklies, voluntarily ceased publication. By the end of the year an unprecedented number of casualties (e.g., *Cerveny kvet, Filmove a televizni noviny, Arch, Obroda*) had been sent to the graveyard. During the eighteen months of "normalization" all the journals published by the Union of Czech Writers were banned by administrative order: *Listy, Tvar, Sesity, Host do domu, Plamen, Orientace,* and *Analogon.* In addition, the Slovakian publications *Kulturny zivot, Literarny zivot,* and *Mlada tvorba* were banned.

The most massive purge took place in the state-owned radio and television stations. In 1968 these stations were firmly in the hands of the reformist forces. Programs such as the six television talks on the bankrupt economy by Ota Sik, live panel appearances of the old political elite sweating as they attempted to answer pointed questions, and the encounters of political prisoners with their former tormentors, were powerful instruments of socialization. The vital role of the underground radio network during the invasion has already been mentioned.

In the first post-invasion year there was a gradual choking of the communication channels. This was expected, feared, and resented. Along with such complaints as "We are groping in a maze of generalities, we suffer from lack of matter-of-fact information . . ."[45] the determination was expressed "to exhibit the maximum effort to name things by their right name."[46] Soon the amount of rationed information was likened to the tip of an iceberg,

with rumor and speculation providing the only clues to the great mass of material that lay beneath the surface and thus becoming autonomous instruments of socialization.

"The Czechs are sensitive about small things" wrote Jan Prochazka. "In the newspapers they first look at the items in small print informing them about who goes where, who welcomes whom, and who has invited whom to pay us a visit. It is incredible how sensitive we have become lately to men kissing one another. . . ."[47]

In the understanding of the conservatives, "normalization" of the political climate included a socialization offensive in which objective presentation of facts was not in order. One citizen protested: "According to "political reality" I already know that white is not white, but pink; black is not black any more, and not a sign of sorrow but of friendship . . . A wheel I take for a rope, a rope for a banana peel, a peel for myself, and myself for an idiot."[48]

Like the nation at large, the Party suffered from the impoverished flow of information. At the annual local meetings of the KSC in Northern Bohemia 1,737 members talked on this subject. Of these 138 were satisfied with the amount of information received and 832 were not.[49] The closing of the communication channels affected higher echelons of the political elite as well. According to Marie Mikova, a Communist member of Parliament, "The public justly complains because of the lack of information and we, the deputies, are no exception."[50] Public opinion surveys taken in Northern Moravia in September, 1968 and in Slovakia in June, 1969 revealed strong dissatisfaction with the information shortage by respondents from all walks of life.[51]

While the Party was ordering the elimination of several channels of communication, the remaining mass media were subjected to prior censorship. The magnitude of the censors' interference was matched by the punishment meted out to real and imagined violators of imposed restrictions. When in October 1969, the children's monthly *Materidouska* published a seven-line poem with alleged anti-Soviet connotations that had escaped the censor's attention, the Party raised such a hue and cry that the author Jiri Pistora was driven to suicide.

At the same time that the authorities were eliminating communication channels and placing restrictions on messages, they were adding the articulators of the messages to the casualties of "normalization." Less than two years after the invasion the works of some eighty Czech writers had been banned and almost 40 percent of all journalists had been deprived of their livelihood.[52] Inexperienced and unqualified personnel filled the vacancies, further augmented by a high mortality rate among Czechoslovak journalists, whose average life expectancy is about fifty years.[53]

By 1972 the Party had still failed to assemble an editorial team capable of producing a literary journal. The alienation and discontinuity of the literary front has no precedent in modern Czech history, the war years of Nazi occupation included. Mass media personnel—the survivors of the purge and the newcomers—have failed to satisfy the nation as well as the leadership. Control has generated conformity and boredom but has failed to rekindle the desired zeal.

There is no power capable of extirpating from the hearts and minds of the majority of young workers, students, and farmers the ideals of the Czechoslovak spring 1968.[1]

Zbynek Vokrouhlicky, Smena, *October 29, 1968.*

Gentlemen, beware: In the process of raping the nation you beget patriots.

Gabriel Laub, Text, *No. 11–12 (1971).*

The Resulting Political Culture

In 1968 Czechoslovakia celebrated the fiftieth anniversary of her foundation. This half a century consisted of twenty years of a pluralistic democracy (1918–1938), twenty years of a totalitarian dictatorship (1948–1968), six years of Nazi occupation (1939–1945), and four years of transition (1938–1939, 1945–1948). The first experience with political emancipation lasted two decades, the second three years, and the third only eight months. Accordingly, a person born between the two world wars has received the dubious benefit of exposure to an extensive variety of modes of government. The fifty years embrace two generations of political prisoners (the first, foreign-made, the second, home-made) and two traumatic experiences with colossal betrayal. In 1938 Western allies turned the country over to aggressor: in 1968, Eastern allies were the aggressor. At neither time did Czechoslovakia attempt to defend her sovereignty.

The weight of such a heritage would bend the backbone of any nation. In 1968, thorough introspection took place. The Czechs, in their own estimation, are pragmatic rather rather than romantic, with a sense of humor rather than an instinct for heroism. They are among the least chauvinistic peoples of Europe and proud of never having been conquerors.[1]

Regrettably, the shortage of military heroes has been complemented by a shortage of statesmen. Men from the arts and literature have had to fill the vacuum. The aspirations for a national rebirth in the nineteenth century were symbolized by a campaign for donations to build the National Theatre in Prague. University professors founded and ruled the prewar republic. Under Stalinist leadership conformity became the rule, and the leaders exhibited neither statesmanship nor culture. During the changing 1960s, it was men of culture who provided the political imagination that seemed to be leading to the establishment of an independent policy. This appropriate lament was published in the jubilee month of October 1968: "I think that culture is the root of a nation. [Czechoslovakia] has a great culture, great minds, intellect, and character. But, quite frankly, it has no policy whatsoever of its own."[2] Servitude does not promote self-respect—especially if the servant acquiesces in his fate. Continual references to helplessness in the presence of powerful neighbors has encouraged the would-be aggressor, and has lowered the resistance of his target. Although Czechoslovakia is one of the more populous European nations, the pervading feeling that "we are small and weak" has ultimately become a rationalization for defeatist attitudes.[3]

An equally unimpressive corollary is the Panslavic megalomania of the past century, with which the Czechs have attempted to compensate for their national inferiority complex. Adoration of many things Russian (and later, Soviet) survived such perfidious acts as the signing of the Soviet-Nazi Pact and the liquidation of Poland. According to historian Jan Tesar (one of Husak's first political prisoners in 1969), a naive belief in and trust of the great powers has been one of the dominant Czech political sentiments.[4] The sparks of the Reformation, of the Thirty Years' War, of the Cold War, and the ideological challenge of 1968, all of which they consider to have emanated from Prague, have tempted the Czechs to view their actions as having global significance. In exchange for the world's appreciation of such an achievement they tend to delegate moral responsibility for their own national welfare to the great powers.

Equally unique is the Czech talent, nurtured over generations under the Hapsburgs, known as Schweikism—the pretense of naiveté as a way of survival. Schweikism does not preclude a feeling of being superior to the conqueror. Its salient ingredients are a sense of humor and an appreciation of the absurd. Indeed, in Prague in August 1968, a wandering fiddler serenaded the invading tanks—to the puzzlement of their crews.[5] In those tragic days native humor flourished, dumbfounding the invaders and prompting the remark, "There is no way of exterminating a nation which flees under the protective wings of Josef Schweik."[6]

It remains an open and frequently debated question whether this response is commensurate with the magnitude of the nation's disappointment and humiliation. The atypical and unprecedented act of a student setting himself on fire in January 1969 introduced different dimensions to the issue. In the view of many, Jan Palach's sacrifice disqualified Schweikism as an obsolete, cheap form of escapism.

Some may also consider Schweikism irrelevant simply because it is a denial of the tragic, a kind of "optimistic alienation," taking nothing (oneself included) too seriously. Schweikism requires energies that a defeated, exhausted, and embittered nation may not likely possess or not be willing to exert.

In the formative years of Stalinism in Czechoslovakia a hybrid developed, which for lack of a better term we shall call "petty bourgeois totalitarianism." Revolutionary in gesture, and a Schweik in almost everything else, the average citizen claimed to feel class hatred where he really felt envy, and translated Communist Nirvana into the coziness of undisturbed privacy. He acted rather than lived his loyalty to the strange cause. Disliking fanatics he failed to appreciate the heroes.

Time corroded the commitment of a great many authentic totalitarians. Two decades of revolutionary dedication to a cause that gets nowhere leaves the practitioner with strained vocal cords and sore feet. Invocation of a dream that fails to bear tangible results ends in fatigue. It is unrealistic to expect an orgasm to last for twenty years. Determination turns into improvisation, zeal into hypocrisy, and the Marxist Writ becomes as impractical and misplaced a source of inspiration as a Gideon Bible in a brothel.

Disenchanted with the cult of personality, the citizen turned to the "cult of things."[7] Withdrawal from political participation was complemented by a fetish for private possessions as the dominant determinant of both economic and social advancement. Alienation included the previously discussed "legal nihilism" and public sympathy for the law breaker rather than the law enforcer.

The Czechoslovaks have not embraced Stalinism, but neither have they remained untouched by its influence. The origins of brutalization can be traced back to the war years. More compliant than defiant vis-à-vis the Nazi occupation force, the nation resorted to widespread revenge on Germans in 1945. Mob brutality accompanied their expulsion from the country. A lack of civic courage and an abundance of primitive vengeance provided the proper background for the hysteria of the Stalinist trials of the early 1950s. Intolerance and fundamentally undemocratic behavior marred the 1968 political renaissance. Democratization of the system was hardly possible without democratization of the individual citizen.[8]

"After twenty years of hibernation, or revolu-

(*Dikobraz*, reprinted in *Atlas*, U.S.A., October 1967)

tionary certitude, or resignation, or routine work, or internal immigration," the magnitude of the opportunity to terminate the anachronistic oppressive system dizzied the ruler and the ruled alike: "both are trapped and puzzled, like a child who loosened the brakes of a carriage at the top of a hill."[9] It was Soviet armor which stopped the carriage while it was still on the totalitarian slope.

In the Soviet-dictated restoration after the invasion, an insistence on the mental *status quo ante* was unrealistic. When censorship was lifted in 1968, the veil of ignorance of many facets of the nation's Stalinist past was also lifted, leaving a profound effect on the orientation of the citizenry. Objective public opinion surveys confirmed a unique achievement: a ruling Communist Party enjoyed

"Professor, what is democracy?"
(*Rohac*, April 17, 1968)

popular support. The nation was willing—temporarily at least, and for reasons of realistic assessment of the international scene rather than because of genuine preference—to accept KSC rule in exchange for frankness concerning past misdeeds and for an honest attempt to dismantle the outlived system. "The period from January to August [1968] will remain as something magnificent in Czechoslovak history, and we shall always return to it as something unbelievably great," wrote Milan Jungmann, the editor-in-chief of *Listy*.[10]

The Soviet military intervention was less an invasion and occupation in the traditional sense, than it was the ultimate form of political pressure after all other forms of pressure (ranging from exchange of letters to large-scale military maneuvers) had failed.[11] The August event was the culminating factor in the national catharsis of 1968. It was as if a sore festering since 1938 had been lanced removing the poisons of envy, pettiness, jealousy, hypocrisy, egotism, and the like. For several months the pre-invasion assessment of Jiri Hochman seemed accurate: "a return [to the old political system] is not possible. Given our situation, even military intervention would have to lead to twenty years of occupation because we have outgrown somehow the possibility of producing our own set of collaborators [with the Soviets]."[12]

The great unity and the euphoria over recovered national pride and purposeful identity was not permanent. The dismantling of the innovations directed

toward a pluralistic open society was not achieved at once but took a full year. The political leadership regained the confidence of the Soviets by losing the confidence of their own people.

Public opinion surveys taken after the invasion, revealed gloom, withdrawal, and alienation. The Stalinist weekly *Tribuna* conceded in August 1969 (i.e., under conditions of rigid censorship) that there was little enthusiasm for the imposed order.[13] In a poll among young members of the Party, 68.6 percent did not believe that the 1968 reform program could be realized under existing conditions; 57.1 percent had no confidence in the Party leadership; 69.7 percent took a pessimistic view of the future development of society. The negative responses were markedly higher among university students.

A critical appraisal of the younger generation appeared in the Party's theoretical monthly *Nova mysl*.[14] Bretislav Dejdar charged in a no subtle way that the "majority of our youth are at present antisocialist, non-Marxist and anti-Soviet." He conceded that "Yes, there is a crisis. Through an unhappy political strategy, youth have been alienated from the ideals of socialism and communism—but why?" Among the causes of this extraordinary failure of two decades of intense socialization, the author identified "our sinful retreat from the class dialectical understanding of our society," "underestimating the influences of the family," "abolishment of Communist upbringing in schools," "ideological formalism," and "cosmopolitan chauvinism." "Anti-Russian racism" [sic], too, contributed to what Dejdar described as "the tragic results of the present time."

Subsequent events further widened the gap between the Party and the people. Of the Four Musketeers (as they were popularly known) Smrkovsky and Dubcek were removed from office, Svoboda was discredited, and Cernik was first discredited and then removed from office. The nation witnessed Premier Cernik applauding his kid-nappers. Popular individuals on all levels of political engagement were forced to resign and were replaced by unwanted Stalinists. Militant pro-Soviet elements were returned to power and the nation was forced to apologize for every harsh word ever uttered against them. Perhaps the zenith of national humiliation was the award by President Svoboda of the highest Czechoslovak decoration, the Golden Star of the Hero of the Czechoslovak Socialist Republic, to the Soviet military leaders of the invasion. By the end of 1969, the last two vestiges of reform, the right to travel abroad and the rehabilitation of victims of Stalinism, had been done away with.

The impact of the 1968 invasion upon the emotional orientation of the nation was essentially twofold: it imbued it with patriotism and anti-Sovietism. The latter is bound to outlast the former. Little national pride is left, in view of the performance of the political elite after Dubcek; the unifying core is hostility to the Soviet Union, which is considered the primary cause of all sorrows. Propaganda aimed at proving that the invasion was a consequence and not the cause of anti-Sovietism has not been successful. Nor have official demands decreeing love for the occupiers been realized. The weekly Zitrek, in one of the last issues of its short existence, commented:

> For a man with integrity, there certainly are areas through which the road of compromise does not lead—for example, affection imposed by the government. Well, that will not work. And I certainly do not see a compromise in short memory, nor in the idea that certain dates of the past year, notably August 21, ought to be erased from the people's minds.[15]

The amorous approaches were rebuffed. The ideologically decontaminated audience refused to respond to outworn messages presented in the dreary old language. This was not all to the good, however, since alienation and apathy may not only produce an immunity against the adoption of any new values, but also the abandonment of any of the old ones that remain. Philosopher Karel Kosik touched upon this subject in his thoughts about the system of total manipulation:

> [There is] the declining ability of the individual to distinguish truth from lies, good from evil. Under a system of universal manipulation, truth blends with lies, good with evil, and this lack of differentiation, along with indifference, creates the prevailing atmosphere of every day life.[16]

Neither love, nor faith, nor any substantive component of political culture can be decreed. Under conditions of enforced conformity, the overt demonstration of demanded responses is no proof of their authenticity. The post-invasion manipulators face a difficult task. Their designated targets of socialization are too knowledgeable, and a far cry from the frightened and gullible citizenry of 1948.

In the post-invasion period, any attempt at participation designed to affect government policies is not only ineffective but is considered illegitimate. Such an approach is as dead as Jan Palach, who set fire to himself to underline the public demand for the preservation of 1968 reforms. The political elites, loyal to the Soviet Union and their own self-interest, are unresponsive to pressures from below. They are aware of the nation's hostility, but not particularly concerned about it.

It remains a gargantuan task to generate devotion and ideological commitment in a people equipped with the memory of recent events and with cognizance of the transient nature of whatever values are accepted at any given time. For example, the series of transformations that Dubcek went through in August, 1968 is well remembered: on August 3 he was embraced and kissed by Brezhnev in Bratislava; on August 21 he was arrested in Prague; on August 22 he was denounced in Pravda as a rightist opportunist; on August 26 he was a signatory of the Moscow Protocol. While aware of their own political impotence, the Czechoslovaks are also aware of the weakness of the system. For an alienated man, an engineered demonstration of public loyalty, expressed in a 99 percent electoral majority, is totally meaningless. As attested by the developments in the early 1970s, the only authentic overwhelming preference of the public is for insulation from political engagement and for rediscovery of the little private pleasures of life. A country cottage, an automobile, a dachshund—not ideological zeal—have become the characteristic goals of the Czechoslovak citizenry, and the present political system has so far failed to alter this value orientation.[17]

Czechoslovakia is the most peace-loving country on earth. She does not interfere even in her own affairs.

Czechoslovak post-invasion joke.

12

It is not possible for us to predict anything. Fortunately, those who forced us to our knees cannot predict anything either.

Kulturny zivot, *August 30, 1968.*

Conclusion

From the standpoint of the present, the second quote above appears, at least in the short run, as rather obsolete. The post-invasion whirlwind has subsided enough to allow for a clear view of the force that is now shaping Czechoslovak state and society: it is the force of neo-Stalinist counterreformation. For the first time since 1945 foreign troops have been stationed in the country to guarantee the implementation of a decreed political model.

Soviet foreign policy is often based not on analysis of social forces but of leaders, sometimes with disagreeable results as in the cases of Sukarno and Nkrumah. After January 1968, the Soviet leaders failed to reach an agreement with Novotny's successors largely because they failed to recognize that the Czechoslovaks were willing to continue to build socialism and to stay in the socialist camp. Khrushchev's dictum of different roads to socialism was replaced by a neo-Stalinist concept of limited sovereignty and a corresponding international obligation of the USSR to put in order the internal affairs of any member of the socialist family. The

inequality between a Party and non-Party citizen in the domestic setting was projected to the international scene through the unequal partnership between the Soviet and Czechoslovak Communist Party. Fundamental in this relationship is the disadvantage suffered by the weaker partner, a disadvantage not mitigated by the latest tendency toward eventually replacing the concept of a leading country and a leading Party (i.e., the Soviet Union) by the concept of the leading role of several countries and several parties (i.e., those of the Warsaw Pact): the Soviet Union continues to interpret for the entire socialist community the meaning of the term "international"—international duty, responsibility, assistance, violation of trust, and so on.

A large black mark appears after the name Czechoslovakia in the Soviet Book of Judgment, denoting a grossly insubordinate pupil who discarded the Soviet model because he believed it to reflect only one of many possible interpretations of Marxism—an interpretation which simply does not fit the conditions in a small Central European country. The

"Proletarians of the world, unite! Or I shoot!"
(*Literarni listy*, August 28, 1968)

pupil did not underestimate the provocative nature of his views but he did underestimate the schoolmaster's determination to discipline him. One month before the invasion, the political scientist Petr Pithart wrote: "For this is the very logic of the refined Stalinism that continues to exist in many countries. Its basis is to dictate that only a single type of socialism is possible and that any deviation, no matter how restrained, must be regarded a threat to socialism in general, as an opening to counter-revolution."[1] After the August punishment was administered, the nation sought consolation in historical analogies concerning right ideas at the wrong time. Czechs felt this was not the first time they had been set upon by powerful neighbors for prematurely championing the truth.

To conservative Communists the Czechoslovaks were guilty of unpardonable heresies. In their view, policies before January 1968—which included misdeeds ranging from mismanagement of the economy to judicial murders—were merely distortions of socialism. Policies under Dubcek, however, constituted destruction of socialism. The idea of "socialism with a human face" was condemned as anti-Marxist, anti-Soviet, and provocative, as was also the Czech contention that the cause of internationalism would be best served by construction of a kind of socialism that would prove attractive abroad. Not Czechoslovakia but the Soviet Union is supposed to be the center of attraction.

Conservatives restored the old dogmas. Most prominent of these is the concept of the leading role of the Communist Party, which precludes pluralism, the sharing of power, autonomous structures, or secularization of the system. The doctrine of Party infallibility is a serious birth defect of the post-invasion regime. An infallible brain "excludes a priori all control, because admission of control in itself is an admission of the right to doubt the infallibility of the absolute brain. This absolute brain and absolute power are therefore necessarily uncontrolled and uncontrollable."[2]

The government visualized three stages of development in the economic system. First, in 1970, the reimposition of state control. Second, from 1971 to 1974, moderate innovations in, among other things, the wage system, and the expansion of light industries. After a first step backward, and a second step timidly ahead, a great leap forward is scheduled for approximately 1974–1980. This period has been described in somewhat contradictory terms, calling for the development of a "modern economic system, based on central directive planning."[3]

Conservative political restoration (officially termed "normalization") affected the Party, the state, and the citizen. Implied or explicit promises in the Action Program of April 1968 were annulled: pluralism, separation of powers, civil rights, rehabilitation of victims of Stalinism, autonomy of the economy from the state, and autonomy of the state from the Soviet Union. The only reform left was federalization of the country, albeit in a substantially curtailed form.

Husak's regime has managed to establish a continuity with the Novotny regime, erasing the effects of the revisionist interlude of 1968. "Normalization" is conceived as restoration of the pre-1968 order without its defects. Policies of counterreformation prompted the public to rename the "socialism with a human face" of 1968 as "Stalinism with a human face" in the 1970s, or, to acknowledge the role of Gustav Husak (whose surname translates as "goose"), as "socialism with goose pimples."

Normalization does not preclude a power struggle among political elites. Husak is hardly the ideal type to preside over the affairs of an occupied Czechoslovakia. To Moscow's orthodox mentality, this autocratic, nationalistic intellectual is, first of all, a reformed deviationist. On the other hand, one might argue, invoking the northern and southern neighbors of Czechoslovakia as precedents, that a criminal record under Stalinism does not necessarily rule out a durable and successful career in the service of antiliberal aims. Like Wladyslaw Gomulka of Poland and Janos Kadar of Hungary, the former political prisoner Husak was given a new lease on political life; Soviet leaders were undoubtedly aware in 1969 that Husak surpassed all eligible competitors for the office in skill, intelligence, and genuine popularity, even if this popularity was limited to a segment of Slovak nationalists.

Irrespective of his talents, Husak is handicapped by his incarceration for almost a decade and his absence from political life for more than fifteen years. Characteristic of his generation of Communists, Husak is intellectually and emotionally tied to the political experience of the late 1940s—the years of victory and glory. After that came decline: Stalinism, which meant involvement in crimes either as perpetrator or victim, followed by the unintelligent, ineffective rule of Novotny, the uncontrolled national renaissance of 1968, and finally, invasion and a puppet regime. The rhetoric and arguments of Husak's political generation reveals a revivalistic nostalgia for 1948 and the first years of Party rule. These veterans of the KSC triumph persist in a quaint attempt to evoke the past, to restore outworn institutions in the vain hope of reviving the spirit of naive loyalty that has long been dead in the nation.

Whatever may divide the Czechoslovak leaders, they do have this in common: they are all beneficiaries of the invasion and their careers depend upon Soviet tutelage. If there were no invasion they would have to invent one. The national leaders of 1968 did

not call for Soviet military help. Should the improbable happen and the occupation status be lifted, their successors would soon have to call for such assistance.

The responsive capacity of the post-invasion regime is determined by Moscow. In 1970 Czechoslovakia and the USSR signed a new friendship treaty that, according to Minister of Justice Jan Nemec, included a new principle of international law relating to the issue of precarious sovereignty. In the words of Nemec, the new principle implied that "the entry of allied armies [in 1968] was completely legal and was in accordance with international agreements concluded at the highest level."[4] No one was heard to point out that Article 5 of the Moscow Protocol of August 1968 stipulated withdrawal of Soviet forces from Czechoslovakia the moment the danger of counterrevolution was averted, and that this point was presumably reached in November 1971 with the 99 percent electoral victory for the Soviet-approved regime.

The year 1970 was one of massive turnover of personnel in the political, economic, educational, scientific, and artistic fields. Simultaneously, a purge of Communist Party ranks was carried out. After this, in 1971 the leadership was able to convene the Fourteenth Party Congress and to conduct a general election. The Party Congress explicitly approved Brezhnev's doctrine of limited sovereignty under socialist conditions. In 1972 institutional consolidation of the reunified transmission belts took place. Accordingly, youth organizations, trade unions, various friendship societies, and other groups held their first post-invasion congresses.

The Party calls for national amnesia. Socialization structures, discarded in the 1960s, have been restored to carry out the indoctrination tasks. Neo-Stalinism is particularly evident in the sphere of recruitment. The discriminatory concept of "classness" is again the primary criterion for advancement in a career: proletarian background and ideological conformity prevail over ability and achievement. As in the past, these recruitment practices will almost surely lead to promotion of the unworthy, a waste of talent, and the perpetuation of economic malaise. From this perspective the fears of Czechoslovak liberals that their country might duplicate the East German socialist *dolce vita* of well-clad, well-fed robots seem to be rather unsubstantiated.

It is my belief that this neo-Stalinist restoration in

"I know it looks unlikely, but they'll die out!"
(*Dikobraz*, October 8, 1968)

the Czechoslovakia of the 1970s will fail to revive the totalitarian order. Instead, a weakened, exhausted system will emerge, possessing the characteristic of what may be termed a "post-totalitarian system": an involuntary, partial retreat toward classical dictatorship—or, to use the terminology of Almond and Powell, a move toward a conservative authoritarian system. The power of the USSR will prevent the Czechoslovak regime from falling apart, but at the same time, the lack of mass support and the thorough alienation of the populace, especially of the young, will deprive this regime of the fresh totalitarian vigor its predecessor enjoyed shortly after 1948.

The Czechoslovak political situation in August 1968 resembled the situation in Poland in 1956: the nation supported its Communist Party against the Soviet Union. In 1969, Czechoslovakia resembled the Hungary of 1956: the nation stood in opposition to both the Soviet Union and its own discredited Communist Party. The resultant political system, handicapped by the cadre turnover in favor of incompetent opportunists, is likely to exhibit low performance, low capability, and low mobilizational capacity. With its aim being to conserve what it has and to avoid innovation, such a system will hardly be capable of imposing mandatory mobilization and political involvement of the citizenry. As long as political neutrality is not penalized, this, too, will attest to the post-totalitarian character of the state.

Shortly after Husak's appointment as the head of the regime, a rumor circulated in Czechoslovakia to the effect that the country would be permitted to evolve into a kind of socialist *Rechtstaat*—a system that would guarantee legal rights though not political freedoms. This development would be presided over by a man whose legal rights had been violated, and who was no friend of political freedom, Gustav Husak. However, the post-1969 legislative output and the restated concept of "class justice" jeopardized this prospect. In the light of the political trials in 1972 the idea of socialist *Rechstaat* became rather meaningless.

The Czechoslovaks are aware that the fate of their country will be decided by forces other than their own. Victims of limited sovereignty, they welcome any issue and any event that dissipates Soviet energies and distracts Soviet attention from any misbehavior in Prague, be that event a power struggle in the Kremlin or an embroglio in the Far East. The Czechoslovaks speculate, rather facetiously, whether Lenin's dictum about the inevitability of wars among capitalist states should not be updated to include the inevitability of wars among socialist states. For the Czechoslovaks "Chinese is beautiful." Mao aside, attention is paid to such domestic Soviet developments as the minority problem, the growing importance of the technical intelligentsia and their recognition of the heavy-handed, archaic nature of the Soviet system, the conflict between generations, and the like.

In a private talk, Czech philosopher Ivan Svitak suggested that the Soviets were mainly afraid of words. Words imply to them "programs", and programs imply "challenges". Silent deeds are less alarming to them. Debatable as this point may be, it is given credence by comparing the Hungarian success in quietly dismantling the Stalinist economic structure with the failure of the loquacious Czechs to proceed in the same direction.

Hungarians have reforms, Rumanians have sovereignty, and the Czechoslovaks have neither. Czechoslovakia of the 1970s is a political felon on probation. Under the disciplinarian eye of the Soviet probation officer she watches the revisionist Yugoslavs, the patriotic though dogmatic Rumanians, the resourceful Hungarians, and the unpredictable Poles, and entertains the prospect of joining an extended new version of the Little Entente. Eventually, felons like these could manage, before the turn of the century, to reform the entire penal system.

Notes

PREFACE

[1] Ivan Svitak, *Literarni listy*, March 1, 1968 (No. 1). (As a rule, titles of articles in journals will be omitted in all notes.)

[2] Miroslav Jodl, *Literarni listy*, May 16, 1968 (No. 12), p. 4.

[3] See especially Gabriel A. Almond and G. Bingham Powell, Jr., *Comparative Politics: A Developmental Approach* (Boston: Little, Brown, 1966).

CHAPTER ONE
State Building

[1] Zdenek Jisa, *Reporter*, December 25, 1968 (No. 47), pp. 6–7.

[2] In the election of 1946—the only free election in the post-World War II period—the Communist Party was the winner in Bohemia (receiving 43.25 percent of the votes cast) and in Moravia (34.46 percent). See Josef Korbel, *The Communist Subversion of Czechoslovakia* (Princeton, N.J.: Princeton University Press, 1959), pp. 151–155; and for the interwar era, see Hugh Seton-Watson, *Eastern Europe* (Hamden, Conn.: Archon Books, 1962), p. 171ff.

[3] After 1963 the Czechoslovak communications media and some periodicals such as *Literarni noviny* became increasingly candid about the economic facts of life. Admission of failures culminated after the abolition of censorship in 1968. From among the leadership, the most outspoken criticism was presented by the Deputy Prime Minister Ota Sik both in print and in his television series.

[4] *Student*, May 17, 1968; *Literarni listy*, May 30, 1968 (No. 14), p. 2, and August 15, 1968 (No. 25), p. 2.

[5] *Reporter*, 1968 (No. 17), April 24, 1968 (No. 22), and July 3, 1968 (No. 27).

[6] Edo Fris, *Listy*, January 16, 1969 (No. 2), pp. 1, 9.

[7] Pavol Stevcek, *Kulturny zivot*, September 6, 1968 (No. 34).

[8] *Zivot strany*, October 22, 1969 (No. 43). See also *Rude pravo*, September 25, 1969; Gustav Husak, *Rude pravo*, April 16, 1970; Jaroslav Kucera, *Tribuna*, September 22, 1971 (No. 38), p. 9.

[9] *Smena*, April 28, 1968; *Literarni listy*, June 27, 1968, (No. 18), p. 12.

[10] Josef Belda, *Reporter*, October 16, 1968 (No. 40), pp. 7–8.

[11] Zdenek Hradilak, *Reporter*, February 20, 1969 (No. 7), pp. 14–16. See also Jan Mlynarik, *Reporter*, February 27, 1969 (No. 8), pp. 12–13; Miroslav Jodl, *Literarni listy*, April 25, 1968 (No. 9), p. 5.

[12] Jaroslav Kase, *Zivot strany*, June 11, 1969 (No. 24).

[13] Jiri Cvekl, *Nova mysl*, August 1968 (No. 8), pp. 1011–1020.

[14] Robert Kalivoda, *Literarni listy*, May 2, 1968 (No. 10), p. 13.

[15] Jindrich Fibich, *Literarni listy*, August 1, 1968 (No. 23), p. 6.

[16] Jiri Hochman, *Reporter*, January 23, 1969 (No. 3).

[17] Karel Kosik, *Literarni listy*, April 8, 1968 (No. 8), p. 3; April 24, 1968 (No. 9), p. 3; May 2, 1968 (No. 10), p. 3; May 9, 1968 (No. 11), p. 3; May 16, 1968 (No. 12), p. 3.

[18] Karel Kosik, *Literarni noviny*, May 16, 1968 (No. 12), p. 3.

[19] Milan Kundera, *Listy*, December 19, 1968 (No. 7–8), pp. 1, 5.

[20] *Svobodne slovo*, February 8, 1969; *Reporter*, June 5, 1968 (No. 23), pp. xiv–xvi; R. V. Burks, "The Decline of Communism in Czechoslovakia," *Studies in Comparative Communism*, January 1969, p. 31.

[21] K. Hajek, *Rolnicke noviny*, March 25, 1969.

[22] Anna Tuckova, *Reporter*, August 7, 1968 (No. 31), p. 13.

[23] Miroslav Jodl, *Literarni listy*, May 30, 1968 (No. 14), p. 4.

[24] Karel Bartosek, *Reporter*, October 23, 1968 (No. 41), pp. 5–6. It should be added that Ludvik Svoboda, who succeeded Novotny in 1968 hardly constitutes an exception to the rule, given his record of compliance with developments after 1968.

[25] Evzen Loebl, *Literarni listy*, June 20, 1968 (No. 17), p. 14.

[26] Miroslav Holub, *Literarni listy*, June 13, 1968 (No. 16), pp. 7–8. See also Oto Schmidt, *Literarni listy*, May 23, 1968 (No. 13), p. 3.

[27] Vladimir Blazek, *Literarni listy*, May 2, 1968 (No. 10), p. 2; Zdenek Jisa, *Reporter*, December 18, 1968 (No. 46), pp. 5–6; *Rude pravo*, May 31, 1969; *Svet prace*, July 23, 1969, pp. 6–7.

[28] Stanley Zemelka, "The Problem of Specialization in Comecon," *East Europe*, May 1969, p. 11.

[29] Radio Prague, quoted in *FEC Situation Report*, April 14, 1969; see also *Reporter*, May 15, 1969 (No. 19), pp. ix–xii.

[30] *Moravskoslezsky vecernik*, February 24, 1969. For examples of such boasts see *Pravda* (Bratislava), January 3, 1960, quoted by Harry Schwartz, *Prague's 200 Days* (New York: Praeger, 1969), p. 29.

[31] *Svobodne slovo*, February 17, 1966; *Pravda* (Bratislava) April 12, 1967; *Prace*, June 1, 1967; *Reporter*, April 24, 1969 (No. 16), p. 3.

[32] *Rude pravo*, January 31, 1967, and June 4, 1966; *Czechoslovak Life*, January 1969, p. 16; Frantisek Povolny, *Nova mysl*, April 1969 (No. 4), pp. 432–442.

[33] Jaroslav Kapr, "Prague May First Through a Sociologist's Eyes," *Reporter*, May 15, 1968 (No. 20), pp. 12–13. Also interesting is the frequency of key words on the posters:

Key Word	1955	1960	1968
KSC (Communist Party)	9	3	5
Leadership (Headed by . . .)	6	4	–
People	26	24	3
Socialism	30	36	2
Victory	7	4	1
Fatherland	30	36	3
Construction (socialist)	11	5	1
Struggle	24	9	3
Army	10	5	–
Imperialism	5	1	5°
Progress	2	1	2
Freedom	6	3	9
Democracy	15	5	9
Soviet	20	13	–
World	9	5	2
Liberation	8	8	–
Capitalism	3	2	–
Justice (law)	–	1	7
Truth	–	–	3
Government	3	–	6
National Front	7	2	3
Opposition		–	4
Love	–	–	4
Peace	18	23	7
Friendship	6	5	5°

° Carried by foreigners.

[34] *Literarni listy*, June 13, 1968 (No. 16), p. 12.

[35] *Literarni listy*, April 25, 1968 (No. 9), p. 4. See also Evzen Menert, *Literarni listy*, July 4, 1968 (No. 19), p. 12, and Karel Kral, p. 13; *Reporter*, July 10, 1968 (No. 29), pp. 18–19; *Zitrek*, March 12, 1969 (No. 10), p. 2.

[36] Jaroslav Sedivy, *Literarni listy*, April 18, 1968 (No. 8), pp. 10–11.

[37] Ivan Svitak, *Student*, April 10, 1968. English translation in *Studies in Comparative Communism*, July–October 1968 (No. 1–2), p. 185.

[38] Frantisek Samalik, *Politika*, September 1968 (No. 4), pp. 8–13.

[39] Ludvik Vaculik, *Literarni listy*, June 27, 1968 (No. 18), p. 5; Zdenka Stastna, *Reporter*, December 18, 1968 (No. 46), pp. 10–11.

[40] A multinational population does not seem to be tractable under totalitarian rule. Of all the East European socialist countries, Yugoslavia, Czechoslovakia, and Rumania, include more than one nationality in their respective

populations. An essay perhaps could be written on the possible correlation between the multinational populations of these countries and anti-Stalinist and/or anti-Soviet conduct.

CHAPTER TWO
Nation Building

[1] For earlier data, see *Demografie*, February 1968 (No. 2); *Nova mysl*, February 1969 (No. 2), p. 194; *Zivot strany*, August 1966.

[2] Juraj Zvara, *Nova mysl*, November 1968 (No. 11), pp. 1339–1348; *Politika*, October 24, 1968 (No. 9), p. 29; *Rude pravo*, October 18, 1968; *Tribuna*, February 5, 1969; Julius Lorincz, *Tvorba*, July 21, 1971 (No. 29), p. 5.

[3] Jan Prochazka, *Literarni listy*, June 6, 1968 (No. 15), p. 1; Vladimir Gloc, *Listy*, December 5, 1968 (No. 5), p. 5.

[4] Zvara, *op. cit.*, p. 1341.

[5] A remarkable case of socialist gerrymandering took place in 1960 when the predominantly Polish-speaking district of Cesky Tesin was abolished and divided into two districts, each with comfortable Czech majorities. Vilem Hejl, *Listy*, April 3, 1969 (No. 13), p. 6.

[6] Ondrej R. Hagala, *Literarni listy*, June 20, 1968 (No. 17), pp. 6–7. Zdenka Stastna, *Reporter*, March 13, 1969 (No. 10), pp. 9–11: "Because the new Orthodox Church was short of priests, 'Action P' was swiftly organized. Politically mature peasants and teachers were ordered by the [KSC] to enroll in a speedy six-week training program, after which they would be ordained as Orthodox priests. The Soviet Union, too, sent reliable priests for assistance."

[7] *Rude pravo*, October 18, 1968.

[8] Similar antagonism developed in 1968 between two Bratislava papers, the Hungarian language daily *Uj Szo* and the Slovak weekly *Kulturny zivot*.

[9] *Politika*, September 19, 1968 (No. 4), pp. 16–18; *Reporter*, April 10, 1969 (No. 14), pp. 7–8.

[10] Pavel Pokorny, *Reporter*, October 23, 1968 (No. 41), pp. 10–11; Irena Petrinova, *Reporter*, April 17, 1969 (No. 15), pp. 12–13; *Rude pravo*, November 9, 1968.

[11] *Osvetova prace*, 1965 (No. 10); *Hlas ludu*, June 2, 1967. See also Otto Ulč, no. 12 below.

[12] For an extensive discussion of Gypsies, see Otto Ulč, "Communist National Minority Policy: The Case of the Gypsies in Czechoslovakia, *Soviet Studies*, April 1969 (No. 4), pp. 421–443. See also Jan Drapal, *Listy*, January 23, 1969 (No. 3), p. 2; Anna Tuckova and Vladimir Srb, *Reporter*, April 24, 1969 (No. 16), pp. 6–7; *Praca*, June 23, 1969; Eva Davidova, *Sociologicky casopis*, January 1970 (No. 1), pp. 29–41.

[13] Ivan Derer, *Zitrek*, October 23, 1968 (No. 3), pp. 1, 3.

[14] Ladislav Jehlicka, *Obroda*, October 23, 1968 (No. 2), p. 6; Jan Patocka, *Nove knihy*, October 30, 1968 (No. 44), p. 1.

[15] Quoted by Milan Hubl in the important article "Conflict or Unity," *Literarni listy*, March 14, 1968.

[16] *Nove slovo*, January 3, 1969 (No. 1); *Reporter*, February 6, 1969 (No. 5); *Pravda* (Bratislava), November 5, 1968.

[17] Lubos Kohout, *Pravda* (Bratislava), April 14, 1968.

[18] *Rude pravo*, June 5, 1967.

[19] Jaroslav Zima, *Reporter*, March 6, 1969 (No. 9), pp. 9–11.

[20] See articles by Miroslav Kusy, the very influential Slovak liberal, in *Smena*, January 29, 1969; *Vecernik*, February 21, 1969; *Prace*, March 20, 1969.

[21] Julius Vanovic, *Maticne citanie*, April 14, 1969 (No. 8).

[22] *Listy*, May 7, 1969 (No. 18), p. 3.

[23] *Zivot strany*, May 7, 1969 (No. 19), p. 9.

[24] *Lidova demokracie*, May 4, 1968; *Rude pravo*, May 5, 1968.

[25] Anton Hykish, *Plamen*, January 1968.

[26] *Svobodne slovo*, February 1, 1969.

[27] *FEC Situation Report* (irregular publication of Free Europe Committee, Inc., New York), May 26, 1971 (No. 19).

[28] *Tvorba*, October 27, 1971 (No. 43), p. 5, and November 3, 1971, (No. 44), p. 15; *Rude pravo*, August 12, 1971, p. 2.

[29] Jiri Hajek, *Tvorba*, August 26, 1970 (No. 34), p. 2.

[30] See, for example, Jiri Mucha, *Literarni listy*, July 25, 1968 (No. 22), pp. 1–2; Vladimir Blazek, *Listy*, November 21, 1968 (No. 3), p. 4; Ivan Bystrina, *Listy*, April 3, 1969 (No. 13), p. 1.

[31] *Listy*, March 20, 1969 (No. 11), p. 6; see also Miroslav Holub, *Listy*, February 27, 1969 (No. 8), p. 13.

[32] Miroslav Jodl, *Literarni noviny*, January 7, 1967 (No. 1), and *Listy*, March 20, 1969 (No. 11), p. 3.

[33] *Reporter*, December 31, 1968 (No. 47), p. 2; *Svobodne slovo*, July 14, 1968.

[34] Milan Pohanka, *Reporter*, July 3, 1968 (No. 27), p. 13; Milos Ruzicka, *Host do domu*, June 1968 (No. 6). The frankest treatment of the subject, provoking furor in the USSR, is by Milan Hubl, Jan Prochazka, and Vladimir Blazek, "A Trialogue," *Host do domu*, May 1968 (No. 5).

[35] See Otto Ulč, "The Vagaries of Law," *Problems of Communism*, July–October 1969, p. 17ff.

[36] *Revue dejin socialismu*, July 1969 (No. 3).

[37] Frantiska Faktorova, *Literarni listy*, May 2, 1968 (No. 10), p. 10; Karel Tibitanzl, *Pravnik*, March 1970 (No. 2).

[38] Josef Vlastuvka, *Vecerni Praha*, March 11, 1969. For the anti-Semitism of the Stalinists, see *Prace*, May 5, 1968, and

February 1, 1969; Eduard Goldstucker, *Rude pravo*, June 23, 1968; Arnost Lustig, *Literarni listy*, May 23, 1968 (No. 13), pp. 10–11; Pavel Kohout, *Literarni listy*, June 20, 1968 (No. 18), pp. 1–2.

[39] *Czechoslovak Life*, February 1969, pp. 8–9; *Rude pravo*, July 28, 1968; Helena Klimova, *Listy*, February 13, 1969 (No. 6), p. 3; *Pravda* (Bratislava) September 8, 1968.

[40] *Reporter*, September 18, 1968 (No. 36), p. 8.

[41] *Svobodne slovo*, October 25, 1968. Yugoslavs were identified by both Czechs and Slovaks as the nation closest in character and culture.

[42] *Zemedelske noviny*, October 25, 1968.

[43] *Pravda* (Bratislava), December 20, 1968; *Zivot strany*, May 7, 1969 (No. 19), p. 9.

[44] *Pravda* (Bratislava), December 29, 1968; *Rude pravo*, March 20, 1969.

[45] *Rude pravo*, August 18, 1968.

[46] Ladislav Koubek, "Sociological Research into Contemporary Development of Our Politics," *Nova mysl*, January 1969 (No. 1), pp. 78–87, esp. p. 85.

[47] *Reporter*, March 27, 1969 (No. 12), pp. i–v; Zbynek Vokrouhlicky, *Nova mysl*, October 1969 (No. 9–10), pp. 1148–1155.

[48] Ivo Planava, "The Dangerous Gang," *Listy*, April 3, 1969 (No. 13), p. 3.

[49] Miroslav Jodl, *Listy*, March 20, 1969 (No. 11), p. 3.

[50] Vera Kunderova, *Listy*, February 6, 1969 (No. 5), p. 4.

[51] Jiri Jirasek, *Literarni listy*, August 15, 1968 (No. 25), pp. 1–2.

[52] Jiri Sekera, *Rude Pravo*, July 7, 1968.

[53] Josef Vohryzek, *Literarni listy*, August 15, 1968 (No. 25), p. 1.

[54] *Zemedelske noviny*, September 20, 1968.

[55] Interview with Vasily V. Kuznetsov, First Deputy Foreign Minister of the USSR (September 11, 1968), by Josef Smrkovsky, *Der Spiegel*, October 14, 1968 (No. 42), pp. 160–175.

[56] Declaration of Czech writers, *Listy*, November 7, 1968 (No. 1), p. 9.

[57] Vladimir Nepras, *Reporter*, February 27, 1969 (No. 8), p. 16.

[58] Vladimir Nepras, *Reporter*, February 13, 1969 (No. 6), pp. 12–13.

[59] Statement made at the January 1970 plenary session of the KSC Central Committee, quoted in *Rude pravo*, January 31, 1970.

[60] *Rude pravo*, January 20, 1972, p. 5.

CHAPTER THREE
Problems of Participation

[1] Zora Jesenska, "The Rights of the Citizen," *Kulturny zivot*, April 5, 1968.

[2] Petr Lesjuk, *Nova mysl*, May 17, 1966 (No. 10), pp. 9–12.

[3] Josef Belda, *Reporter*, February 20, 1969 (No. 7), p. 26.

[4] Vaclav Pavlicek, *Nova mysl*, March 1968 (No. 3), pp. 337–347; Evzen Erban, *Nova mysl*, October 1968 (No. 9–10), pp. 1096–1101; Petr Pithart, *Literarni listy*, April 18, 1968 (No. 8), pp. 1, 5.

[5] *Host do domu*, June 1968 (No. 6), p. 57.

[6] Antonin Vanek, *Tribuna*, June 17, 1970 (No. 24), p. 1.

[7] Rudolf Slansky, speech to the Ninth Congress of the KSC, *Lidove noviny*, May 27, 1949.

[8] *Rude pravo*, June 12, 1954, and August 31, 1966; *Zivot strany*, August 1966 (No. 16).

[9] V. Mencl and F. Ourednik, *Zivot strany*, July 1968 (No. 15), p. 11.

[10] Slansky (see n. 7 above). According to Karel Havlicek ("The Party's Social Structure and Action Readiness," *Zivot strany*, June 22, 1970, No. 13), the proportion of workers in the party declined even more, to 39.8 percent. Havlicek also offers figures on switches in political affiliation: in Bohemia and Moravia the Communist Party admitted to its ranks 115,099 Czech socialists, 25,278 deserters from the People's Party, and 113, 536 Social Democrats. For Soviet conclusions on this development, as told by a Moscow ideologue to C. L. Sulzberger, see the *New York Times*, December 4, 1968: "The Czechs accepted change in a sly way. The Social Democrats of Benes and Masaryk decided to amalgamate with the Communist Party. There were 300,000 Social Democrats and 400,000 Communists, and they created a joint organization, just as in East Germany, Poland, and Hungary.... When union was achieved, the Communists took control of practical things like the army and industry, but the Social Democrats clung to theoretical things like the press and the unions. Thus, in the structure of the state, the division within the [Communist] Party was maintained."

[11] *Zivot strany*, 1966 (No. 18); *Rude pravo*, June 21, 1966; Leopold Rykl, *Nova mysl*, May 16, 1967 (No. 10), pp. 7–9; Zdenek Valenta, *Nova mysl*, November 1969 (No. 11), pp. 1329–1338; *Zivot strany*, May 28, 1969 (No. 22), p. 6.

[12] *Rude pravo*, August 31, 1966.

[13] *Rude pravo*, July 12, 1966, and October 17, 1968.

[14] *Rude pravo*, February 10, 1967, August 18 and 31, 1966, and September 25, 1969; *Zivot strany*, 1966 (Nos. 16 and 18); 1969 (Nos. 20 and 26); *Zpravodaj KSC, op. cit.; Reporter*, May 1, 1969 (No. 17), pp. 6–7; *Czechoslovak Life*, January 1969, p. 16.

[15] Libuse Hakova, *Nova mysl*, March 8, 1966 (No. 5), pp. 3–5.

[16] *Rude pravo*, May 27, 1949.

[17] Dalimil, *Literarni listy*, May 9, 1968 (No. 11), p. 4. See also Ivan Klima, *Literarni listy*, April 25, 1968 (No. 9), pp. 1, 5, and July 4, 1968 (No. 19); Pavel Kohout, *Literarni listy*, May 16, 1968 (No. 12), pp. 1, 3.

[18] *Rude pravo*, February 8, 1969.

[19] *Ibid.*; *Mlada fronta*, November 13, 1968; *Svedectvi* (Paris), 1969 (No. 34–36), p. 171.

[20] Samalik, *Literarni listy*, July 11, 1968 (No. 20), p. 5.

[21] *Zivot strany*, 1966 (No. 18); *Rude pravo*, September 15, 1966, and June 20, 1967.

[22] *Literarni listy*, July 18, 1968 (No. 21), p. 6.

[23] *Protokol XIII. sjezdu KSC* [Proceedings of the Thirteenth Congress of the KSC] (Prague: 1966), quoted by Frantisek Havlicek, *Nova mysl*, October 3, 1967 (No. 20), pp. 9–11; see also F. Zdobina, *Rude pravo*, March 7, 1967.

[24] Hendrych, *Zivot strany*, 1967 (No. 6).

[25] Spacek, *Nova mysl*, June 27, 1967 (No. 13), p. 5.

[26] *Rude pravo*, April 9, 1968. For Smrkovsky's views see *My*, April 1968.

[27] The draft was published in the last month before the Warsaw Pact occupation (*Rude pravo*, August 10, 1968).

[28] Havel, "On the Subject of Opposition," *Literarni listy*, April 4, 1968 (No. 6). See similar arguments by Pavol Stevcek, writer and member of the Slovak Central Committee, in *Kulturny zivot*, April 12, 1968.

[29] Lakatos, "The Possibilities of the National Front," *Kulturni noviny*, April 5, 1968 (No. 14), p. 8.

[30] Pithart, "Political Parties and Freedom of Speech," *Literarni listy*, June 20, 1968 (No. 17), pp. 1, 3. See also *Literarni listy*, April 18, 1968 (No. 8), pp. 1, 5.

[31] Mlynar, "On the Democratic Political Organization of Society," *Nova mysl*, May 1968 (No. 5), pp. 607–627.

[32] Kalivoda, *Literarni listy*, May 9, 1968 (No. 11), p. 6.

[33] *Mlady svet*, March 22, 1968 (No. 12), p. 10; *Reporter*, October 23, 1968 (No. 41), pp. 12–13. In "An Analysis of the Situation in Czechoslovakia After January 1968," produced by the Jodas group, it was asserted: "This is the first, truly unbelievable case in the history of the workers' movement that a counterrevolution has originated in the Politburo of the central committee of the Party.... It is necessary to realize that in 1948 the Communist Party of Czechoslovakia carried out a democratic revolution and in 1968 carried out a democratic counterrevolution." The article identified three causes of this counterrevolution: (1) the struggle against the cult of personality, (2) the theory of the withering-away of the class struggle, and (3) the absence of class struggle within the party's ranks. Antonin Ostry, *Ceskoslovensky Problem* (Cologne: Society for Czechoslovak Literature Abroad, 1972), pp. 13, 252–3.

[34] *Daily World* (New York), December 17, 1968. See also *Prace*, December 20, 1968; *Reporter*, January 8, 1969 (No. 1), pp. 9–10, and December 25, 1968 (No. 47), p. 16.

[35] *Lidova demokracie*, February 15, 1969, p. 4.

[36] "Report of the Central Committee of the Communist Party," *Tribuna*, February 5, 1969, and *Rude pravo*, July 2, 1969. See also Stefan Moravcik, *Echo*, May 31, 1968 (No. 4), and June 30, 1968 (No. 6).

[37] *Svobodne slovo*, May 19, 1968, p. 1.

[38] Figures are quoted by Z. A. B. Zeman, *Prague Spring* (New York: Hill & Wang, 1969), pp. 125–126.

[39] For background of puppet party elites, see Jiri Jes, *Student*, May 22, 1968.

[40] V. Henzl, *Lidova demokracie*, May 3, 1968.

[41] See, for example, *Lidova demokracie*, March 9 and May 15, 1968; *Svobodne slovo*, March 3 and 22, 1968.

[42] *Der Spiegel*, 1968 (No. 30), quoted in *Svobodne slovo*, August 4, 1968, p. 2. In view of post-1968 developments, it is strange to read praise in *Rude pravo* (February 12, 1972, p. 4) of the current Slovak Minister of Culture, M. Valek, and his support for "healthy *oponentura*" in the field of art.

[43] *Lidova demokracie*, November 19, 1968, p. 2; *Svobodne slovo*, March 9, April 14 and 21, May 19, June 30, July 7 and 28, August 4 and 18, December 14, 1968, and March 1, 1969.

[44] *Svobodne slovo*, April 28, 1968, p. 1.

[45] "Report of the Central Committee," (see n. 36 above); *Svobodne slovo*, April 21, 1968; *Politika*, October 10, 1968 (No. 7); *Lidova demokracie*, February 22 and March 13, 1969. (According to *Zivot strany*, May 14, 1969 (No. 19), during the first quarter of 1969 a mere 4,035 new members were enrolled in the KSC—the lowest figure since 1952.)

[46] "Report of the Central Committee" (see n. 36 above).

[47] *Svobodne slovo*, September 15 and 29, October 19, November 23, 1968, and January 25, 1969.

[48] *Literarni listy*, May 2, 1968 (No. 10), p. 2; June 20, 1968 (No. 17), p. 2; and July 4, 1968 (No. 19), p. 2.

[49] J. Mlynkova and L. Rybacek, *Literarni listy*, April 11, 1968 (No. 7); *Rude pravo*, May 19, 1968.

[50] J. Mlynkova and L. Rybacek, *Literarni listy*, April 11, 1968 (No. 7).

[51] For more details on KAN, see Ludvik Rybacek, *Literarni listy*, April 25, 1968 (No. 9), p. 3; A. J. Liehm, *Literarni listy*, June 27, 1968 (No. 18), p. 1; *Reporter*, July 3, 1968 (No. 27), p. 8; *Svobodne slovo*, July 11, 1968; Arnulf Ivan Simon, "Czechoslovakia's KAN: A Brief Venture in Democracy," *East Europe*, June 1969, pp. 20–22.

[52] A. J. Liehm, *Literarni listy*, June 27, 1968 (No. 18), p. 1.

[53] Arnulf Ivan Simon, *op. cit.*

[54] *Literarni listy*, June 6, 1968 (No. 15), p. 2.

[55] Jaroslav Brodsky, "Czechoslovakia's 231 Club," *East Europe*, June 1969, pp. 23–25. *Lidova demokracie*, April 1 and May 14, 1968; *Svobodne slovo*, May 21, 1968; Karel Taus, *Kulturni noviny*, April 5, 1968 (No. 14), p. 4; Petr Chudozilov, *Literarni listy*, June 6, 1968 (No. 15), p. 2; Vilem Hejl, *Literarni listy*, June 27, 1968 (No. 18), p. 13; *Literarni listy*, August 8, 1968 (No. 24), p. 5; J. Brodsky, *Reporter*, June 26, 1968 (No. 26), pp. 15–16; J. Prasek, *Reporter*, June 12, 1968 (No. 24), pp. 5–7.

[56] According to *Prace*, April 27, 1966, total membership was 5,252,120 as of January 1, 1966.

[57] *Literarni listy*, May 30, 1968 (No. 14), pp. 1, 3.

[58] *Zivot strany*, March 19, 1969 (No. 12), p. 3.

[59] Vlastimil Toman, chairman of the Metal Workers Union, in a television address. Quoted in *Prace*, January 23, 1969. See also *Mlada fronta*, November 12 and 13, 1968; *Svobodne slovo*, December 7, 1968; *Rude pravo*, March 1, 1969. For accounts of the Trade Union Congress, see *Rude pravo*, March 8, 1969; Jiri Lederer, *Reporter*, March 13, 1969 (No. 10), p. 3. According to *Lidova demokracie* (January 24, 1969), of 1,314 delegates to the Congress, 921 were Communists, 11 socialists, 5 members of the People's Party, 366 without party affiliation, and 11 not identified. The leadership was elected by a secret ballot. The lowest number of votes (841 out of 1,242) was received by the Trade Union head, Karel Polacek, an opportunist with a long Stalinist record. For Moscow comment see *Zitrek*, March 19, 1969 (No. 11), pp. 1, 3.

[60] *Lidova demokracie*, March 18, 1969. On the subject of trade unionism, see Frantisek Velek, "Trade Unions One Year After January," *Nova mysl*, March 1969 (No. 3), pp. 270–281.

[61] *Socialisticka zakonnost*, June 1968 (No. 6), pp. 330–336, and August 1968 (No. 8), pp. 475–478; *Literarni listy*, July 25, 1968 (No. 22), p. 2; *Svobodne slovo*, March 29, 1969, p. 3; *Rude pravo*, April 28 and May 26, 1968; *Literarni listy*, August 8, 1968 (No. 24), p. 6; *Lidova demokracie*, April 23, 1969, p. 4. For an example of Stalinist condemnation of activities of a special-interest group, see Jaroslav Sruta, "Destructive Efforts of the Union of Czech Physicians," *Tribuna*, December 29, 1970 (No. 51–52), p. 16.

[62] *Literarni listy*, August 8, 1968 (No. 24), p. 5.

[63] Eduard Goldstucker, president of the Writers Union, quoted in *l'Unità* (Rome), April 25, 1968.

[64] *Zitrek*, March 19, 1969 (No. 11), p. 9.

[65] Drahos Smejc, "What Kind of Election Would Be Welcomed by the Public," *Reporter*, May 15, 1969 (No. 19), pp. v–viii. This article contains a wealth of interesting data from several 1968 polls. The survey results quoted here came under attack in *Rude pravo* (May 24, 1969), where it was charged that "according to the well-known rules of sociological imagination, an attempt was made to prove that the views of some of our politicians and agencies differed from the will of the people." The May 15, 1969, issue of *Reporter* was the last to be published.

[66] *Rude pravo*, June 27, 1968.

[67] Jiri Hanak, "What Did Comrade Chnoupek Mean?" *Reporter*, April 17, 1968 (No. 16), p. 5.

[68] *Literarni listy*, April 25, 1968 (No. 9), May 9, 1968 (No. 11), May 16, 1968 (No. 12), and June 20, 1968 (No. 17).

[69] Vladimir Blazek, *Literarni listy*, May 9, 1968 (No. 11), p. 12. See also Dubcek's speech at the Tesla Works, in *Rude pravo*, October 12, 1968, pp. 1, 3.

[70] *FEC Situation Report*, June 20, 1968 (No. 69), p. 4.

[71] *Rude pravo*, April 29 and May 22, 1969.

[72] *FEC Situation Report*, September 6, 1968 (No. 105), p. 3.

[73] *Obroda*, November 20, 1968 (No. 4), p. 5; *Svobodne slovo*, May 1, 1969, p. 3.

[74] *Zpravy*, October, 1968 (No. 17), p. 3. (This was a Czech-language journal published and distributed by the Soviet occupation force.)

[75] *Rude pravo*, May 24, 1969, p. 2 (attacking *Obroda*, a weekly published by the People's Party); *Tribuna*, February 5, 1969 (No. 4).

[76] *Pravda* (Bratislava), supplement, June 2, 1969.

[77] *Literarni listy*, August 1, 1968 (No. 23), p. 5, and April 25, 1968 (No. 9), p. 3.

[78] *Rude pravo*, November 23, 1968.

[79] *Rude pravo*, September 17, 1969.

[80] *Lidova demokracie*, June 7, 1969; Eduard Vyskovsky, *Reporter*, October 10, 1968 (No. 39), p. 13.

[81] Milos Prosek, *Tvorba*, August 4, 1970 (No. 31), p. 3; Jiri Hajek, *Tvorba*, August 19, 1970 (No. 33), p. 3.

[82] Leopold Rykl, *Tribuna*, August 25, 1971 (No. 34), p. 5.

[83] *Svedectvi* (Paris), 1970 (No. 39), p. 325.

[84] *Rude pravo*, December 15, 1970, p. 3. For appeals against termination of Party membership, see *Rude pravo*, May 27, 1971.

[85] *FEC Situation Report*, May 12, 1971 (No. 18). (Turnover in the Slovak leadership was more substantial; of 12 Politburo members elected in 1968, only two survived.)

[86] Excerpts from this pamphlet, "Results of the December 1970 Plenum of the Central Committee of the Communist Party of Czechoslovakia," appeared in the February 1971 issue of *Ceske slovo*, published in Munich. Exile publications have been known for occasional inaccuracies in reporting,

but this document seems authentic. Prague did not challenge its accuracy, and official Czechoslovak statistics, partial and scattered as they are, support the report in *Ceske slovo*. Milos Jakes, chairman of the Central Controlling and Auditing Commission of the Party and head of the purging effort, reported in *Tribuna*, June 3, 1970 (No. 22), p. 3, that as of January 1, 1970 (prior to the purge), 26.1 percent of all Party members were workers and 5.2 percent were cooperative farmers. Hence, every eighth worker and farmer carried a Party card. The same proportion applied to retired citizens. By contrast, every third member of the intelligentsia and every fifth employee in administration was an organized Communist. Vanek, *Tribuna*, June 17, 1970 (No. 24), p. 1, offers further details on Party membership among the labor force: economic managers, 70–80 percent; employees of social and interest organizations, 80–90 percent; executives in central administration, 85–90 percent; employees in culture and public enlightenment, 70 percent; male teachers up to the high school level, 50–55 percent; university teachers, 60 percent; technical staff in industry and agriculture, 30–40 percent; research personnel, 40–45 percent; physicians, 25–35 percent.

[87] The healthy core is reluctant to be dissolved in the majority of doubtful loyalty. They demand preservation of an elite, organized as an *"aktif* of merited party members." "Only those who joined the Party in 1945 and have remained faithful to class and international principles" would qualify (*Tribuna*, February 11, 1970, No. 6, p. 6). The comment of one functionary is typical of the resentment among the healthy core: "The worst are not the Rightists—because the Party knows very well who they are—but the hundreds of thousands of saboteurs who slipped through the purge." (*Listy* (Rome), March 1972, No. 2, p. 7.) In addition to some laborers, the healthy core consists of individuals (especially in the higher age bracket) in politically sensitive roles. The underground paper of the so-called Revolutionary Socialist Party presented these estimates of the numerical strength of groups loyal to the system: 22,000 apparatchiks; 50,000 personnel of the Ministry of the Interior; 30,000 professional soldiers; 106,000 officials in government administration and the judiciary; and 50,000 bureaucrats in the economy. (*Der Spiegel*, January 26, 1970, No. 5, p. 98.)

[88] *Listy* (Rome), July 1972 (No. 4), pp. 11–13.

[89] *Rude pravo*, August 12, 1972.

CHAPTER FOUR
Problems of Welfare

[1] Jan Hajda, ed., *A Study of Contemporary Czechoslovakia* (Chicago: University of Chicago Press, for the Human Relations Area Files, 1955), pp. 88–101.

[2] *Ibid.*, p. 106: "In prewar Czechoslovakia there were seven to eight workers in production for every one in administra-

tion; in 1946 the ratio changed to three to four in production for every one in administration."

[3] See Karel Kaplan, *Nova mysl*, May 1968 (No. 5), p. 572, and Vaclav Prucha, *Nova mysl*, July 1968 (No. 7), p. 837.

[4] Eduard Vyskovsky, ed., *Deset let lidovedemokratickeho Ceskoslovenska* [*Ten Years of the People's Democratic Czechoslovakia*] (Prague: Orbis, 1955), p. 16.

[5] Nicolas Spulber, *The Economics of Communist Eastern Europe* (Cambridge, Mass.: MIT Press, 1957), p. 56; Alois Rozehnal, *Unfulfilled Promises* (Rome: Academia Cristiana Cecoslovacca, 1961), p. 29; Eduard Taborsky, *Communism in Czechoslovakia, 1948–1960* (Princeton, N.J.: Princeton University Press, 1961), p. 413; *Rude pravo*, September 25, 1952; *Hospodarske noviny*, February 17, 1961.

[6] *Statisticka rocenka CSSR 1968* [*Statistical Yearbook of the CSSR, 1968*] (Prague: SNTL, 1968), p. 93. See also Ladislav Hrzal, *Nova mysl*, May 31, 1966 (No. 11), p. 25.

[7] Prucha, *op. cit.*, p. 842; *Halo-Sobota*, supplement to *Rude pravo*, March 13, 1969, p. 3.

[8] Prucha, *op. cit.*, p. 843.

[9] *Prace*, July 5, 1967.

[10] *Lidova demokracie*, February 14, 1969.

[11] Vladimir Pribsky, *Svet prace*, July 9, 1969 (No. 27), p. 17; *Rude pravo*, February 14, 1969.

[12] *Nova mysl*, January 24, 1967 (No. 2), pp. 14–17. For further data, see *Rude pravo*, March 8, 1972, p. 3.

[13] *Prace*, June 9, 1967; Jaroslav Stoklasa, *Reporter*, May 8, 1969 (No. 18), pp. 6–7.

[14] *Prace*, May 11, 1967.

[15] Vaclav Pacina, *Nova mysl*, March 7, 1967 (No. 5), pp. 22–24.

[16] Marie Kubatova, *Literarni listy*, July 4, 1968 (No. 19), p. 7.

[17] Pribsky, *loc. cit.* According to J. Kupka, *Tribuna*, October 20, 1971 (No. 42), p. 16, the average annual job turnover in the country in the last few years has been 19.3 percent, meaning that a typical employee changes jobs once every five years.

[18] Servus, "The Undernourished City," *Listy*, February 13, 1969 (No. 6), p. 5.

[19] *Nova mysl*, February 21, 1967 (No. 4), pp. 15–19; *Prace*, October 29, 1968; *Zemedelske noviny*, October 17, 1968. (*Rolnicke noviny*, November 7, 1968, published some results of an opinion survey among Slovak farmers. Surprisingly, only 50.3 percent of the respondents felt that cities were exploiting the countryside.)

[20] Josef Beseda, *Reporter*, December 25, 1968 (No. 47) pp. 14–15; Jan Prochazka, *Literarni listy*, May 16, 1968 (No. 12) pp. 10–11.

[21] *Zemedelske noviny*, July 13, 1968; *Vlasta*, May 15, 1968 (No. 20), p. 11.

[22] Oldrich Svestka, *Tribuna*, October 8, 1969 (No. 39).

[23] *Zemedelske noviny*, March 8, 1967; *Nova mysl*, April 19, 1966 (No. 8), p. 47, and October 18, 1966 (No. 21), pp. 18–19; *Rude pravo*, June 3, 1967. See Jan Bauer, *Tvorba*, May 17, 1972 (No. 20), pp. 3–4, for data on the improved educational profile of the rural labor force.

[24] *Rude pravo*, May 19, 1967; *Reporter*, April 24, 1969 (No. 16), p. 27, and May 15, 1969 (No. 19), p. xii; *Prace*, August 5, 1969.

[25] *Literarni listy*, May 30, 1968 (No. 14), p. 5; June 6, 1968 (No. 15), pp. 5–6; and August 15, 1968 (No. 25), p. 6; *Listy*, May 15, 1969 (No. 19), p. 5.

[26] Igor Tomes, *Literarni listy*, July 18, 1968 (No. 21), p. 5. See also *Literarni listy*, July 25, 1968 (No. 22), p. 5.

[27] *Lidova demokracie*, June 7, 1967. Given the nature of the post-invasion regime, these discriminatory practices are likely to be restored.

[28] Supplement to *Rude pravo*, March 8, 1969, pp. 1, 3; Milada Hrda, *Reporter*, December 25, 1968 (No. 47), p. 13.

[29] *Rude pravo*, October 15, 1968.

[30] *Svobodne slovo*, January 17, 1966; *Prace*, July 19, 1967. For recent trends, see *Rude pravo*, May 20 and August 6, 1971, January 18 and March 8, 1972.

[31] *Prace*, March 30, 1966.

[32] *Literarni noviny*, February 26, 1966 (No. 9).

[33] *Prace*, February 21, 1969; *Literarni noviny*, July 15, 1967 (No. 28); *Rude pravo*, February 12, 1966; *Lidova demokracie*, April 7, 1967.

[34] *Osvetova prace*, 1966 (No. 13).

[35] *Prace*, May 6 and June 13, 1967; *Kulturni tvorba*, June 9, 1966 (No. 23).

[36] *Mlada fronta*, January 21, 1969, p. 3.

[37] *Literarni listy*, May 16, 1968 (No. 12), p. 1, and May 30, 1968 (No. 14), pp. 1, 3; Zdenek Valenta, *Nova mysl*, February 1968 (No. 2), pp. 198–210; and, in particular, *Nova mysl*, November 1968 (No. 11), pp. 1329–1338.

[38] *Rude pravo*, May 11, 1967.

[39] Zdenek Valenta, *Nova mysl*, November 1968, p. 1330ff.

[40] *Prace*, October 12, 1966; *Zivot strany*, August 1966 (No. 16).

[41] Oto Schmidt, *Zitrek*, October 30, 1968 (No. 4), pp. 6–7. See also *Zitrek*, February 12, 1969 (No. 6), p. 7; *Nova mysl*, April 1968 (No. 4), pp. 461–465; *Nova mysl*, May 1968 (No. 5), pp. 637–645; *Nova mysl*, February 1969 (No. 2), pp. 184–193.

[42] Frantisek Samalik, *Literarni listy*, June 20, 1968 (No. 17), p. 16, and July 11, 1968 (No. 20), p. 5.

[43] *Prace*, July 18, 1967; *Lidova demokracie*, November 1, 1968; *Rude pravo*, February 15, 1969.

[44] Milan Skaryd, *Czechoslovak Life*, April 1969, pp. 30–31.

[45] *Prace*, March 16, 1966.

[46] *Prace*, November 10, 1966; *Rude pravo*, June 14, 1968.

[47] Pavel Machonin, *Nova mysl*, June 14, 1966 (No. 12), p. 20; *Prace*, May 25, 1966, and June 29, 1967.

[48] Pavel Machonin, *Nova mysl*, April 1968 (No. 4), pp. 466–474, and January, 1969 (No. 1), pp. 67–71; Alena Cechova, *Reporter*, May 15, 1969 (No. 19), pp. 23–24. Miloslav Petrusek, *Sociologicky casopis*, December 1969 (No. 6) p. 574, Jiri Vecernik, *Sociologicky casopis*, 1970 (No. 1), pp. 21–28, stresses that "social differentiation is very strongly reflected also in the structure of consumption values." For condemnation of Pavel Machonin and his book *Ceskoslovenska spolecnost* (1969), see Miloslav Formanek, "Revisionism in the Theory of Social Structure and the Role of Pavel Machonin," *Tribuna*, May 24, 1972 (No. 21), p. 8, and May 31, 1972 (No. 22), p. 8. Machonin, who became head of the Institute of Marxism-Leninism at Charles University in Prague in 1964, was accused of "abandoning the class concept" and "separating internal class relations from global relations and historical connections."

[49] *Reporter*, July 3, 1968 (No. 27), p. 2, and May 15, 1969 (No. 19), pp. 9–10.

[50] *Zemedelske noviny*, July 6, 1967; *Kulturni noviny*, April 26, 1968 (No. 17); *Svet v obrazech*, August 6, 1968 (No. 31), pp. 8–9; *Jihoceska pravda*, August 31, 1968, p. 3; *Lidova demokracie*, November 28, 1968; *Listy*, May 15, 1969 (No. 19), pp. 10–11.

[51] *Literarni listy*, May 23, 1968 (No. 13), pp. 1, 3.

[52] *Ibid.*

[53] Radio Prague, July 23, 1968, quoted in the *FEC Situation Report*, July 24, 1969 (No. 61), p. 3.

[54] *Svobodne slovo*, March 22, 1969, p. 1.

[55] Jiri Cvekl, *Nova mysl*, January 24, 1967 (No. 2), p. 8.

[56] *Reporter*, May 1, 1969 (No. 17), p. 10ff.

[57] *Lidova demokracie*, May 17, 1969, p. 3.

[58] Oldrich Svestka, "Questions About Workers' Policy," *Rude pravo*, July 14, 1968. (His arguments were persuasively demolished by Karel Stregl and Jiri Slama, "The Social Securities of Oldrich Svestka," *Prace*, July 18, 1968.)

[59] *Reporter*, April 3, 1968, pp. 8–9.

[60] Oto Schmidt, *Zitrek*, March 26, 1969 (No. 12), p. 7.

[61] *Tribuna*, August 5, 1970 (No. 31), p. 13; *Rude pravo*, June 10, 1971, p. 5, and July 13, 1972, p. 2.

[62] Zdenek Urbanek, *Rude pravo*, August 13, 1966; Bohumil Simon *et al.*, "Standard of Living," *Nova mysl*, January 1968 (No. 1), pp. 34–45; *Lidova demokracie*, July 26, 1969.

[63] *Rude pravo*, March 15, 1969.

[64] *Listy*, November 14, 1968 (No. 2), p. 5; *Svobodne slovo*,

June 7, 1969, p. 4. Jan Hajny, *Svet prace*, 1972 (No. 9), quoted in *Ceske slovo*, April 1972, p. 7, reports that consumption of alcoholic beverages in the CSSR almost doubled between 1955 and 1969. The average annual consumption per capita reached an estimated 150 liters.

[65] Urbanek, *op. cit.*; Miroslav Zdarsky, "The Way We Live, and Especially the Way We Used to Live," *Tribuna*, July 18, 1971 (No. 30), p. 20, claims an exceptional improvement in housing conditions: In 1970 the number of households with electricity reached 98.6 percent, with gas 30.3 percent, running water 76.7 percent, private bath 57.2 percent, and central heating 29.4 percent. The average apartment consisted of 2.1 rooms with 3.4 occupants.

[66] Zdenek Jisa, "Successes and Problems of Our Cultural Development," *Tvorba*, November 17, 1971 (No. 46), p. 8.

[67] *Lidova demokracie*, June 9, 1967, and November 19, 1968; *Rude pravo*, June 21, 1967; *Halo-Sobota*, February 8 and April 12, 1969.

[68] *Halo-Sobota*, March 8, 1969. According to the Slovak publication *Vyber*, January 1, 1971 (No. 1), the number of registered private cars on June 1, 1969, was 699,700 (576,000 in the Czech provinces and 123,700 in Slovakia).

[69] Miroslav Holub, *Literarni listy*, June 13, 1968 (No. 16), pp. 7–8.

[70] The high price of gasoline, for example, rules out the use of cars for commuting. However, with the gradual saturation of the market, the automobile has to some extent been replaced by foreign travel as a status symbol. The most desirable areas to visit are (in order of increasing preference): the countries of the Socialist bloc, Yugoslavia, developing countries (Soviet-oriented), developing countries (Western-oriented), Western Europe, and overseas capitalist countries, especially the United States.

[71] *Rude pravo*, February 15, 1969, and September 29, 1966. According to *Rude pravo* (October 2, 1971), the average monthly income in Bohemia and Moravia increased in the last five years from Kcs 1,535 to Kcs 1,970 in the production sector, and from Kcs 1,384 to Kcs 1,871 in the nonproduction sector.

[72] Simon, *op. cit.*, p. 38.

[73] *Zemedelske noviny*, January 28, 1967; *Pravda*, January 31, 1967.

[74] *Reporter*, December 18, 1968 (No. 46), pp. 9–10; *Lidova demokracie*, November 19, 1968, p. 4, and May 14, 1969, p. 4; *Rude pravo*, December 30, 1968, p. 2; *Zitrek*, March 26, 1969, p. 2.

[75] According to *Time* magazine (November 6, 1972, p. 65), the estimated amount of Soviet aid is one billion dollars.

[76] *Rude pravo*, April 12, 1972; *Tribuna*, April 5, 1972 (No. 14), p. 16.

CHAPTER FIVE
Policy Making

[1] Vladimir Nepras, *Reporter*, November 6, 1968 (No. 43), p. 5. See also Michal Lakatos, *Zitrek*, November 13, 1968 (No. 6), p. 2; *Lidova demokracie*, February 24, 1969, p. 1; Vl. Jurik, *Rude pravo*, May 4, 1968, p. 4; Venek Silhan, *Prace*, December 22, 1968.

[2] Frantisek Samalik, *Literarni listy*, August 8, 1968 (No. 24), pp. 1, 3.

[3] Kornel Foeldvari, *Listy*, December 5, 1968 (No. 5), p. 9.

[4] Vladimir Blazek, *Literarni listy*, June 13, 1968 (No. 16), p. 12; Jiri Lederer, "Citizens and Leaders," *Reporter*, December 18, 1968 (No. 46), p. 13.

[5] Jiri Mucha, *Listy*, February 13, 1969 (No. 6), p. 2. See also Tomas, *Zitrek*, February 26, 1969 (No. 8).

[6] *FEC Situation Report*, February 17, 1969 (No. 646). (Holecek made the statement at the Bertrand Russell conference in Stockholm, February 1969).

[7] Jan Prochazka, *Literarni listy*, May 9, 1968 (No. 11), p. 1.

[8] Jiri Hochman, *Svet prace*, November 27, 1968 (No. 9), p. 1, and *Reporter*, January 23, 1969 (No. 3), p. 9. See also Ivan Svitak, *Literarni listy*, July 18, 1968 (No. 21), pp. 1, 4; Jiri Ruml, *Pruboj*, August 27, 1968, p. 3.

[9] Jiri Hochman, *Reporter*, March 6, 1969 (No. 9), p. 3. See also *Reporter*, March 27, 1969 (No. 12), pp. i-v; Michal Lakatos, *Zitrek*, November 27, 1968 (No. 8).

[10] *Rude pravo*, June 5, 1966, and August 24, 1968.

[11] Interview with Ota Sik, *Kulturni noviny*, March 29, 1968 (No. 13), pp. 1–2.

[12] *Rude pravo*, April 14, 1968, p. 1.

[13] Lakatos, *loc. cit.*, and *Zitrek*, December 4, 1968 (No. 9).

[14] Lubos Kohout, *Reporter*, April 3, 1969 (No. 13), pp. v–viii; Ludovit Vlasic, *Nove slovo*, November 21, 1968 (No. 25).

[15] Vaclav Kraus, *Prace*, May 2, 1968; Petr Chudozilov, *Literarni listy*, May 30, 1968 (No. 14), pp. 1–2; Jiri Lederer, *Literarni listy*, July 4, 1968 (No. 19), p. 4; Tomas Vor, *Literarni listy*, July 4, 1968 (No. 19), p. 8.

[16] Ludvik Vaculik, *Literarni listy*, April 25, 1968 (No. 9), p. 6. See also Miroslav Strafelda, *Reporter*, March 20, 1969 (No. 11), p. 13.

[17] *Rude pravo*, April 29, 1965, and April 9, 1966; *Pravda*, February 25, 1966; *Lidova demokracie*, April 18, 1966.

[18] Frantisek Cervinka, *Listy*, March 20, 1969 (No. 11), p. 9.

[19] *Rude pravo*, November 9, 1968, p. 2.

[20] Jiri Seydler, *Reporter*, March 20, 1969 (No. 11), p. 14.

[21] Pavel Juracek, *Mlady svet*, March 29, 1968 (No. 13), pp. 8–9.

[22] *Rude pravo*, July 28, 1968, p. 2; *Zivot strany*, September 25, 1968 (No. 20), p. 2.

[23] Gustav Husak, *Rude pravo*, October 11, 1969.

[24] *Zivot strany*, October 8, 1969.

[25] *Moravsky vecernik*, November 20, 1968, p. 3.

[26] Otto Ulč, "The Unknown Revolt," *Problems of Communism*, May-June 1965, pp. 46–49.

[27] *Mlada fronta*, June 6, 1967.

[28] *Mlada fronta*, November 21 and 22, 1968.

[29] Karel Horalek, *Tvorba*, March 17, 1971 (No. 11), p. 1.

[30] *Tribuna*, February 9, 1972 (No. 6), p. 15.

[31] *Listy*, April 17, 1969 (No. 15), p. 3.

[32] Vaclav Kraus, *Czechoslovak Life*, June 1969 (No. 6), pp. 8–9.

[33] *Socialisticka zakonnost*, 1968 (No. 6), pp. 330–336, and 1968 (No. 8), pp. 493–501. (I myself belonged to the legal profession in Czechoslovakia between 1953 and 1959 but never heard of anyone who might have been a member or anything about the activities of JCSP.)

[34] *Socialisticka zakonnost*, 1970 (No. 4), pp. 247–249.

[35] *Literarni listy*, July 25, 1968 (No. 22), p. 2; *Svobodne slovo*, March 29, 1969, p. 3.

[36] *Prace*, October 31, 1968, pp. 4–5.

[37] *Czechoslovak Life*, March 1969 (No. 3), p. 28.

[38] *Rude pravo*, December 7, 1968, p. 2.

[39] *Zivot strany*, July 12, 1971 (No. 14).

[40] *Vestnik Ministerstva skolstvi a Ministerstva kultury CSR*, [*Bulletin of the Ministry of Education and of the Ministry of Culture of CSR*], April 1971 (No. 4).

[41] Jiri Hajek, *Tvorba*, November 4, 1970 (No. 44), p. 5.

[42] *Listy* (Rome), March 1971 (No. 2), p. 24.

[43] Miloslav Bruzek, *Tvorba*, July 28, 1971 (No. 30), p. 10; Vojtech Mihalik, *Nove slovo*, June 10, 1971; Jiri Hajek, *Tvorba*, March 24, 1971 (No. 12), p. 3. Hajek, editor-in-chief of *Tvorba*, published a letter he had written to Jarmila Glazarova, an accomplished novelist of old Communist standing (September 8, 1971, No. 36, p. 10). The lengthy letter is servile and patronizing. Hajek offers forgiveness in exchange for Glazarova's endorsement of the new regime.

[44] *Rude pravo*, July 7 and August 18, 1968.

[45] *Nova mysl*, April, 1969 (No. 4), p. 479.

[46] Vladimir Vesely charged that the STB was "the largest illegal organization in the history of Czechoslovakia!" *Reporter*, May 8, 1968, No. 19, p. viii). For documentation of STB activities, see Otto Ulč, "The Vagaries of Law," *Problems of Communism*, July-October 1969, pp. 17–32, and "Koestler Revisited," *Survey*, Summer 1969 (No. 72), pp. 108–121. Some data on the Workers' Militia have also been made public. According to *Pravda* (February 22, 1969) and *Zivot strany* (March 5, 1969), 75 percent of the militiamen are workers or former workers; the average age is forty. This force of "several tens of thousands" of armed men is subject to 5–8 hours of demanding training each month, in addition to the final exercises. "As a rule," an individual participates in training during his free time. *Tribuna* (February 25, 1970 No. 8, p. 3) reported that over 40 percent of all members of the Workers' Militia joined the KSC between 1945 and 1948. Over half of all militia members are industrial workers.

[47] Karel Hajek, *Reporter*, June 5, 1968 (No. 23), pp. 7–9.

[48] Miroslav Holub, *Literarni listy*, July 11, 1968 (No. 20), p. 2.

[49] *Lidova demokracie*, February 14, 1969, p. 1.

[50] *Svobodne slovo*, January 28, 1967.

[51] *Smena*, November 23, 1968, p. 1.

[52] *Zpravodaj KSC*, No. 16, supplement to *Zivot strany*, 1969 (No. 18). This source and Jan Kaspar, *Nova mysl*, August 1968 (No. 8), pp. 1002–1010, are the only available references regarding UPOS.

[53] However, the "bad practices" of 1968–1969 are contrasted with the current approach. According to *Tribuna*, "The orientation of today's research programs is diametrically different. It is not detached from society; it does not stand above society but serves as one form of feedback in our collection of information" (April 15, 1972, No. 14, p. 16). According to the article, recent public opinion surveys have dealt with such topics as consumer prices, criminality, and punitive policies. *Rude pravo* (July 21, 1972, p. 2) reported that the Sociological Society of the Czechoslovak Academy of Sciences conducted a survey in Northern Bohemia probing into relations among citizens of Czech, Slovak, and German ancestry. "The findings will be put on the agenda of the Commission on Nationalities of the Regional People's Committee [of Northern Bohemia] and will be forwarded to the presidium of the Czech Socialist Republic as well as other state and scientific institutions as a significant background study for work on Law No. 144/68, Nationalities in Czechoslovakia." It would appear that the present leaders, unlike their predecessors in the 1950s, do utilize social research, but that, unlike their immediate predecessors, they do not make public the data.

[54] Vaclav Slavik, *Literarni listy*, July 25, 1968 (No. 22), pp. 1, 3.

[55] *Lidova demokracie*, September 21, 1966; *Rude pravo*, September 23, 1966.

[56] *Literarni listy*, July 11, 1968 (No. 20) p. 2, and July 25, 1968 (No. 22), p. 14.

57 *FEC Situation Report*, June 28, 1968 (No. 72), p. 1. See also *FEC Situation Report*, May 16, 1968 (No. 56), p. 2.

58 *Sloboda*, August 26, 1968, p. 1; *Zitrek*, January 15, 1969 (No. 2), p. 2.

59 Petr Pithart, *Listy*, January 30, 1969 (No. 4), p. 2. See also *Rude pravo*, January 4, 1969, p. 2.

60 *Reporter*, February 20, 1969 (No. 7), pp. 7–8.

61 *Prace*, March 25, 1969; *Rude pravo*, March 18, 1969.

62 *FEC Situation Report*, April 29, 1969 (No. 36), p. 1.

63 *Svet v obrazech*, July 23, 1968 (No. 29), p. 4.

64 *Lidova demokracie*, January 22, 1969, p. 1, and February 22, 1969, p. 1.

65 *Reporter*, May 15, 1969 (No. 19), p. 8. For details in the Groesser case, see *Rude pravo*, April 30, 1969.

66 *Rude pravo*, November 23 and 29, 1971. The reported 99.9 percent unanimity in no way mirrors the actual political outlook of Czechoslovak society. Theoretically, the ultraconservative wing of the party should have viewed this manifest absurdity as a defeat for its demand for further repressive measures. However, the ultraconservatives remained unconvinced. For example, Jaroslav Kucera called for a "correct" evaluation of the electoral victory, charging that the political enemies had quite wickedly voted for the National Front candidates (*Tribuna*, December 22, 1971 (No. 51), p. 5). Also discomforting to both the ultraconservatives and the centrists of Husak's variety is that, according to the Moscow Protocol of 1968, Soviet forces must leave Czechoslovak soil the moment the danger of counterrevolution passes. A 99.9 percent electoral majority therefore makes it quite difficult to claim further counterrevolutionary danger.

67 *Listy* (Rome), March 1972 (No. 2), p. 6.

CHAPTER SIX
Rule Application

1 *Mlada fronta*, January 21, 1969, p. 3. A chart on federal versus provincial jurisdiction appears in *Rude pravo*, April 12, 1969, supplement, p. 3.

2 *Rude pravo*, June 15, 1967; *Statisticka rocenka CSSR 1966* [*Statistical Yearbook of Czechoslovakia*] (Prague: SNTL, 1966), p. 78.

3 *Rude pravo*, June 28, 1969, p. 1; *Svobodne slovo*, August 9, 1969, p. 1.

4 Miloslav Kubes, *Nova mysl*, March 1969 (No. 3), pp. 363–367; Dalimil, *Literarni listy*, July 11, 1968 (No. 20), p. 4.

5 *Praca*, September 23, 1966; *Mlada fronta*, July 26, 1966.

6 *Kulturni tvorba*, February 17, 1965; *Rude pravo*, January 29, 1966, and June 1, 1967.

7 *Rude pravo*, June 1, 1967. See also Tvorba, March 18, 1970 (No. 11), p. 4.

8 *Prace*, April 12, 1970; *Svet prace*, April 8, 1970.

9 Kusy, *Nova mysl*, November 1968 (No. 11), pp. 1319–1320.

10 Vaclav Slavik, *Literarni listy*, July 25, 1968 (No. 22), pp. 1, 3.

11 *Literarni listy*, August 1, 1968 (No. 23), p. 5.

12 *Zivot strany*, April 2 and September 3, 1969.

13 *Zpravodaj KSC* [*KSC Reporter*] No. 18, supplement to *Zivot strany*, June 11, 1969 (No. 24).

14 Ladislav Abraham, Secretary of the Central Committee of the Slovak Communist Party, interviewed by *Zivot strany*, June 11, 1969 (No. 24), p. 6.

15 *Zivot strany*, March 19, 1969 (No. 12), pp. 1–2.

16 Zdenek Eis, *Reporter*, December 25, 1968 (No. 47), p. 5; *Rude pravo*, July 16, 1969.

17 Jaroslav Korinek, *Nova mysl*, April 14, 1967 (No. 10), pp. 3–6; Jiri Rypel, *Nova mysl*, May 30, 1967 (No. 11), pp. 3–6; Vladimir Nemec, *Nova mysl*, August 22, 1967 (No. 17), pp. 9–12.

18 Vaclav Banovsky, *Reporter*, February 6, 1969 (No. 5), pp. 13–14.

19 *Reporter*, February 13, 1969 (No. 6) p. 16.

20 Zdenka Redlova, *Svet prace*, July 2, 1969 (No. 26), pp. 1, 4.

21 Miroslav Holub, *Literarni listy*, June 13, 1968 (No. 16), p. 7.

22 Bohumil Simon *et al.*, *Nova mysl*, December 28, 1967 (No. 26), p. 8.

23 See the charge by the Stalinist Jodas Group that the NEM was a return to capitalism (*Obrana lidu*, June 6, 1968), and the reply by Ota Sik in *Rude pravo*, June 18, 1968.

24 *Prace*, May 21 and July 5, 1968.

25 Petr Pithart, *Literarni listy*, August 1, 1968 (No. 23), p. 4; Vladislav Chlumsky, *Literarni listy*, August 15, 1968 (No. 25), p. 5; Rudolf Slansky, *Reporter*, May 22, 1968 (No. 21), p. 10; Miroslav Jodl, *Reporter*, June 12, 1968 (No. 24), p. 7; Vaclav Klaus, *Reporter*, June 5, 1968 (No. 23), p. 10; Jan Zoubek, *Reporter*, July 24, 1968 (No. 30), p. 9; Otakar Turek and Miroslav Toms, *Reporter*, August 7, 1968 (No. 32), p. 15; Ivan Svitak, *Prace*, May 19, 1968.

26 *Prace*, January 15, 1966; *Czechoslovak Life*, October 1968 (No. 10), p. 2.

27 J. Klofac and V. Tlusty, "Socialism and Just Reward," *Reporter*, November 6, 1968 (No. 43), pp. v–xii.

28 Jiri Camra, *Nova mysl*, December 28, 1967 (No. 26), p. 6.

29 Jaroslav Kolar and Alena Kunstova, *Nova mysl*, April 1969 (No. 4), p. 480.

30 For example, see Jiri Janoska, *Halo Sobota*, December 30, 1968 (No. 13), p. 6.

31 A. Straub, *Reporter*, November 6, 1968 (No. 43), p. 14.

32 Ladislav Koubek, *Nova mysl*, January 1969 (No. 1), p. 80.

33 *Mlada fronta*, July 14, 1967.

34 *Reporter*, February 6, 1969 (No. 5), p. iv.

35 *Ibid*, p. v.

36 *Prace*, August 13, 1968; Dragoslav Slejska, *Reporter*, April 24, 1969 (No. 16), pp. 25–26; *Sociologia*, 1970 (No. 1).

37 *Politika*, October 10, 1968; *Nove slovo*, March 13, 1969.

38 *Rude pravo*, December 18, 1968, and January 11, 1969.

39 Milos Barta, *Reporter*, April 3, 1969 (No. 13), pp. 7–8.

40 *Ibid*.

41 *Ibid*.

42 Slejska, *op. cit*. See also Stanislav Dvorak, *Nova mysl*, April 1969 (No. 4), pp. 466–475.

43 *Prace*, November 15, 1968; *Rude pravo*, October 25, 1968, October 2 and 25, 1969.

44 Jiri Smrcina, *Rude pravo*, May 23, 1969. It appears, however, that the last chapter in the history of the NEM has yet to be written. According to the well-informed *Listy* (May 1972, No. 3, pp. 14–15), proponents of socialist economic orthodoxy went too far in their condemnation of economic experimentation, offending Jozef Lenart and Drahomir Kolder, members of the Politburo who had participated in the preparation of the "little NEM" in 1965. Miroslav Hruskovic, secretary of the central committee and himself an economist, reportedly reprimanded the conservative critics of the NEM by pointing out that the NEM also had its positive features. *Listy* further reported that as of January 1, 1972, an economic "mini-reform" was introduced in Czechoslovakia. According to the new program, profit, not production, will be the criterion for evaluating the performance of individual enterprises.

45 *Rude pravo*, July 23, 24, and 25, 1969.

CHAPTER SEVEN
Adjudication

1 Vaclav Vrabec, *Reporter*, July 24, 1968 (No. 30), pp. ii, 2. See also *Reporter*, June 12, 1968 (No. 24), p. 6.

2 Lakatos, *Svobodne slovo*, June 30, 1968, p. 3.

3 Vrabec, *op. cit*., p. vi; Karel Kaplan, *Nova mysl*, July 1968 (No. 7), p. 915. See also Otto Ulč, "The Vagaries of Law," *Problems of Communism*, July-October 1969, pp. 17–32, and "Koestler Revisited," *Survey*, Summer 1969, pp. 108–121.

4 *Literarni listy*, May 9, 1968 (No. 11), p. 12.

5 K. Hajek, *Rolnicke noviny*, March 26, 1968.

6 As examples of very sharp criticism of the judiciary, see Jiri Krupicka, *Literarni listy*, June 20, 1968 (No. 17); Vaclav Lachout, *Socialisticka zakonnost*, June 1968 (No. 6), pp. 344–345.

7 Bohuslav Kucera, *Svobodne slovo*, August 11, 1968, pp. 1–2.

8 Quoted in Harold J. Berman, *Justice in Russia* (New York: Random House, 1963), p. 36.

9 Alexej Cepicka, *Za nerozbornou obranu vlasti* [*For the Firm Defence of the Fatherland*] (Prague: Nase vojsko, 1954) p. 352.

10 Ferdinand Boura, *Nova mysl*, 1950 (No. 5–6), p. 454.

11 Jan Bartuska, *Socialisticka zakonnost*, 1957 (No. 9), p. 532.

12 For a more detailed explanation, see Otto Ulč, "Class Struggle and Socialist Justice," *American Political Science Review*, (September 1967), LXI, No. 3, pp. 727–743.

13 The outcome of various civil actions, such as custody, divorce, and even paternity, were also affected by defendants' sociopolitical status. The 1958 volume of *Sbirka rozhodnuti ceskoslovenskych soudu* [*Collection of Czechoslovak Court Decisions*], published by the Supreme Court in Prague, provides many examples of applied "class justice."

14 Jan Bartuska, *Socialisticka zakonnost*, 1958 (No. 1), p. 9; Frantisek Stajgr, *Bulletin of Czechoslovak Law*, XVIII (1960), p. 105.

15 Arts. 1, 2. See also Ferdinand Bilek, *Socialisticke soudnictvi*, 1964 (No. 7), pp. 197–203.

16 *Literarni listy*, May 23, 1968 (No. 13), p. 4. Satisfactory laws have yet to be drafted. According to Josef Rubes, a foremost authority in civil law, the revised Code of Civil Procedure of 1969 is inadequate, does not match the standards of the 1950 version, and should be replaced with an entirely new code (*Socialisticka zakonnost*, 1970, No. 4, p. 193).

17 Miroslav Strafelda, *Reporter*, March 20, 1969 (No. 11), p. 13.

18 Peter Zaturecky, *Socialisticka zakonnost*, 1968 (No. 8), pp. 451–457.

19 Frantisek Samalik, *Reporter*, September 26, 1968 (No. 37), pp. 12–13. For arguments against the army's penal battalions and their basis of dubious legality, see *Literarni listy*, May 23, 1968 (No. 13), p. 12; June 6, 1968 (No. 15), p. 5; and June 27, 1968 (No. 18), p. 12; as well as *Svobodne slovo*, May 19, 1968, p. 3.

20 Zaturecky, *op. cit*., p. 453.

21 Frantisek Zoulik, *Socialisticka zakonnost*, 1968 (No. 5), pp. 277–281; Frantisek Samalik, *Socialisticka zakonnost*, 1968 (No. 7), pp. 418–423; Mojmir Kusak, *Socialisticka zakonnost* 1968 (No. 7) pp. 423–425; Vladimir Mrazik, *Pravnik*, 1968

(No. 7), pp. 642–644; Ivan Kulhanek, *Kulturni noviny*, March 29, 1968 (No. 13), p. 1.

22 *Socialisticka zakonnost*, 1968 (No. 5), pp. 257–260; Otomar Bocek, *Socialisticka zakonnost*, 1968 (No. 6), pp. 342–343.

23 Bohuslav Kucera, *Svobodne slovo*, August 11, 1968, pp. 1–2.

24 Josef Elias, *Mlada fronta*, November 8, 1968; *Socialisticka zakonnost*, 1968 (No. 6), pp. 321–324, and 1968 (No. 7) pp. 411–417.

25 Karel Dobes, *Kulturni tvorba*, July 20, 1967 (No. 29); *Vecerni Praha*, May 11, 1967; *Pravda*, February 23, 1966.

26 *Prace*, January 15, 1966.

27 *Pravda*, June 22, 1967. See also *Svobodne slovo*, March 25, 1966.

28 Boris Vybiral and Alfred Kudlik, "The Local People's Courts in the CSSR," *Bulletin of Czechoslovak Law*, XIX (1961), pp. 1, 4.

29 *Statisticka rocenka CSSR 1968* [*Statistical Yearbook of the CSSR, 1968*] (Prague: SNTL, 1968), p. 127; see also *Rude pravo*, March 26, 1966.

30 *Prace*, November 9, 1966.

31 *Statisticka rocenka CSSR 1968*, p. 125.

32 Jan Pelmar, quoted by Otakar Osmancik, *Reporter*, April 24, 1969 (No. 16), p. 11.

33 *Kvety*, January 18, 1969 (No. 2), pp. 25, 27.

34 Osmancik, *op. cit.*, pp. 11–13, and Frantisek Trojacek, *Reporter*, March 20, 1969 (No. 11), pp. 15–16.

35 Osmancik, op. cit., p. 12.

36 *Rude pravo*, May 17, 1969, p. 2.

37 *Svobodne slovo* and *Lidova demokracie*, May 17, 1969. For more recent data, see Oldrich Dolejsi, *Tribuna*, March 10, 1971 (No. 10), p. 3; Josef Ondrej, *Tribuna*, July 21, 1971 (No. 29), p. 8, and July 28, 1971 (No. 30), p. 8; *Rude pravo*, January 29, February 15, and May 29, 1972.

38 Trojacek (see n. 34 above).

39 *Svobodne slovo*, May 17, 1969, p. 10.

40 *Vecerni Praha*, January 10, 1969, p. 2.

41 *Lidova demokracie*, April 18, 1969; *Rude pravo*, June 11, 1969; *Vecerni Praha*, August 22, 1969; *Mlada fronta*, August 26, 1969.

42 See, for example, *Rude pravo*, March 23, June 19, and July 10, 1971.

43 *Svobodne slovo*, April 11, 1970; *Rude pravo*, May 7, 1971.

44 *Rude pravo*, July 22, August 1, 2, 4, and 12, 1972.

45 Zdenka Stastna, *Reporter*, May 15, 1968 (No. 21), pp. 9–10.

46 *Reporter*, July 17, 1968 (No. 29), pp. 9–10; *Lidova demokracie*, June 20, 1968, p. 3.

47 V. Jurankova, *Listy*, November 28, 1968 (No. 4), p. 2.

48 Otto Ulč, "Czechoslovakia's Restive Jurists," *East Europe*, December 1965, pp. 18–25.

49 Ivan Klima, *Literarni noviny*, January 25, 1964.

50 *Socialisticka zakonnost*, 1968 (No. 5), pp. 261–276; (No. 6) pp. 330–341; (No. 8), pp. 466–473; (No. 9/10), pp. 522–548.

51 Demands like these were also heard after the invasion. For example, see O. Novotny and V. Pavlicek, *Lidova demokracie*, November 6, 1968, p. 3; *Svobodne slovo*, November 23, 1968, p. 1, and November 30, 1968, p. 1; M. Schiller, *Vecerni Praha*, January 14, 1969, p. 6.

52 *Reporter*, August 7, 1968 (No. 32), p. 8.

53 For scattered data on rehabilitation proceedings, see *Pravda*, June 10, 1969; *Nove slovo*, December 4, 1969; *Mlada fronta*, June 12, 1969; *Svobodne slovo*, June 7 and December 20, 1969.

54 In one public opinion survey (*Lidova democracie*, May 4, 1968), 58 percent of the respondents demanded prosecution of the Stalinists guilty of past crimes, 37 percent recommended dismissal from jobs, 3 percent opted for forgiveness, and 2 percent had no opinion.

55 For coverage of the trial see especially the January 1969 issues of *Svobodne slovo* and *Lidova demokracie*. An impressive analysis of the case appeared in *Listy*, January 30, 1969 (No. 4), pp. 6–7.

56 *Rude pravo*, April 19, 1969, pp. 1, 3.

57 *Rude pravo*, October 25, 1969.

58 Jiri Ruml, *Reporter*, February 27, 1969 (No. 8), p. 6; in the same issue see Jiri Hochman, p. 3. The Piller Report reached the West and was published in a number of languages. For an English version, see Jiri Pelikan, ed., *The Czechoslovak Political Trials, 1950–1954: The Suppressed Report of the Dubcek Government's Commission of Inquiry, 1968* (Stanford University Press, 1971), 360 pp.

59 Jiri Smrcina, *Rude pravo*, April 23, 1969.

60 Zdenek Zuska, *Rude pravo*, August 23, 1969.

61 The text of the decree is in *Rude pravo*, August 23, 1969.

62 Bohuslav Kucera, *Rude pravo*, January 5, 1970.

63 Dolejsi, *Tribuna*, April 22, 1970 (No. 16), p. 20; Kucera, *Tribuna*, August 5, 1970 (No. 31), p. 18; Jaroslav Tomchyna, *Socialisticka zakonnost*, 1970 (No. 9), p. 483.

64 Jan Nemec, *Socialisticka zakonnost*, 1970 (No. 7–8), p. 386.

65 *Ibid.*, pp. 389–390.

66 *Socialisticka zakonnost*, 1970 (No. 5), p. 261.

67 Josef Ondrej, *Socialisticka zakonnost*, 1971 (No. 1), p. 11.

[68] Jan Nemec, *op. cit.*, p. 5.

[69] *Rude pravo*, April 26, 1972.

[70] *Listy*, (Rome), September 1971, p. 8, and November 1971, p. 7.

[71] *Tribuna*, July 21, 1971 (No. 29), p. 8. See also *Rude Pravo*, July 1, 1972, pp. 1–2.

CHAPTER EIGHT
Political Recruitment

[1] *Literarni listy*, July 4, 1968 (No. 19), p. 4. See also *Literarni listy*, June 20, 1968 (No. 17), p. 17, and July 11, 1968 (No. 20), p. 2; *Reporter*, May 15, 1969 (No. 19), pp. 9–10.

[2] Anton Hykisch, *Kulturny zivot*, May 31, 1968 (No. 22); Oto Schmidt, *Zitrek*, February 12, 1969 (No. 6), p. 7.

[3] This figure given in *Zivot strany*, 1968 (No. 5), quoted in *Ceske slovo* (Munich), April 1968, p. 3.

[4] Bohuslav Krejci, *Literarni listy*, July 25, 1968 (No. 22), p. 6.

[5] For sharp criticism of preferential recruitment, see Vladimir Bosak, *Literarni listy*, June 20, 1968 (No. 17), p. 15; Ota Sik, *Zemedelske noviny*, February 27, 1968; Radoslav Selucky, *Prace*, March 14, 1968; Oto Schmidt, *Zitrek*, October 30, 1968 (No. 4), pp. 6–7.

[6] For examples of these practices, see Pavel Machonin, *Nova mysl*, June 11, 1968 (No. 12), pp. 17–20; Oto Schmidt, *Zitrek*, March 5, 1969 (No. 9), p. 7; *Reporter*, November 6, 1968 (No. 43), pp. 14–15 and pp. v–xii; Alena Cechova, *Reporter*, May 15, 1969 (No. 19), pp. 23–24.

[7] Vladimir Tuma, *Nova mysl*, August 9, 1966 (No. 16), pp. 14–15, 18; Miroslav Lab, *Nova mysl*, September 6, 1966 (No. 18), pp. 10–12; Ladislav Adamec, *Kulturni tvorba*, July 14, 1966 (No. 28).

[8] Jiri Novotny, *Svet v obrazech*, March 26, 1966 (No. 13); *Literarni listy*, April 18, 1968 (No. 8), p. 12; July 18, 1968 (No. 21), p. 2; *Svet v obrazech*, July 23, 1968 (No. 29), p. 2; *Rude pravo*, October 2, 1969.

[9] Bozena Maturova, *Reporter*, July 17, 1968 (No. 29), pp. 11–12.

[10] Bedrich Hajek, *Reporter*, August 14, 1968 (No. 33), pp. 11–12.

[11] Pavel Steiner, *Literarni listy*, August 8, 1968 (No. 24), p. 4.

[12] Petr Prihoda, *Zitrek*, March 26, 1969 (No. 12), pp. 6–7. See also Zdenka Redlova, *Rude pravo*, August 4, 1968, p. 3.

[13] *Rude pravo*, April 14, 1968, p. 2, and May 1, 1969, p. 7.

[14] Prihoda, *op. cit.*; *Reporter*, December 18, 1968 (No. 46), p. 11.

[15] Tomas, *Zitrek*, November 6, 1968 (No. 5), p. 2.

[16] Vitezslav Gardavsky, *Nova mysl*, February 1969 (No. 2), pp. 156–158.

[17] Vladimir Nepras, *Reporter*, November 6, 1968 (No. 43), p. 14.

[18] For a superb portrait of a bourgeois Communist, see Josef Skvorecky, *Host do domu*, May 1968 (No. 5), pp. 38–41.

[19] It was hardly a coincidence that the Soviet leadership recommended that the Czechoslovaks "elitize" the KSC, reducing the size to just within the estimated strength of the surviving Stalinists. Nepras, *op. cit.*; *Literarni listy*, August 8, 1968 (No. 24), p. 4; *New York Times*, October 20, 1968, p. 12.

[20] Miroslav Kusy, *Nove slovo*, February 20, 1969 (No. 8). See also *Reporter*, October 23, 1968 (No. 41), pp. 7–8; and *Nova mysl*, July 1968 (No. 7), p. 805.

[21] Petr Kettner, *Reporter*, June 19, 1968 (No. 25, pp. x-xi; Karel Kral, *Literarni listy*, July 4, 1968 (No. 19), p. 13.

[22] *Rude pravo*, April 11, 1968.

[23] Zdenek Eis, *Reporter*, October 23, 1968 (No. 41), p. 4.

[24] Frantisck Srdinku, *Nova mysl*, November 14, 1967 (No. 23), pp. 3–7.

[25] *Zivot strany*, February 12, 1969 (No. 7), pp. 1, 4; regrettably, the source is not more specific with respect to the time period of these transfers.

[26] Miroslav Kusy, *Nova mysl*, November 1968 (No. 11), p. 1320.

[27] *Zivot strany*, *op. cit.* See also Jiri Hamernik, *Tvorba*, September 2, 1970 (No. 35), pp. 1, 3, for a discussion of the predicament of "professional politicians, comrades devoted to the cause of socialism," who have been removed since the early 1960s because of incompetence.

[28] Milan Hübl, *Mlada fronta*, November 13, 1968, pp. 1–2.

[29] In 1965 a thorough sociological analysis of teachers of Marxism-Leninism was ordered by a suspicious Party. See *Sociologicky casopis*, October 1968 (No. 5), pp. 606–611.

[30] *Rude pravo*, November 25, 1966, and June 17 and July 1, 1967. For laws and other regulations see *Sbirka zakonu a narizeni*, 1953 (Nos. 60 and 97); 1957 (No. 70); 1961 (No. 86); 1964 (No. 53); 1966 (Nos. 7, 19, 26, and 92); 1967 (Nos. 39 and 40).

[31] *Listy*, March 6, 1969 (No. 9), p. 2; Cestmir Kozusnik, *Reporter*, December 25, 1968 (No. 47), p. 3.

[32] According to *Tribuna*, February 25, 1970 (No. 8), p. 2, the toll of the first purge in 1969 was 11 teachers, with 21 others "expected to leave in the very near future." Of these, so far, Hübl was most severely punished, being sentenced to a 6.5 year term for allegedly engaging in antistate activities. (*Rude pravo*, August 2, 1972).

[33] *FEC Research* May 12, 1971 (No. 18), p. 14.

[34] Interview with Jan Fojtik, *Tribuna*, December 22, 1971

(No. 51), p. 3. According to *Rude pravo*, October 1, 1971, p. 1, a new branch of the Party College has opened in Bratislava.

[35] *Nova mysl*, April 18, 1967 (No. 8).

[36] *Nova mysl*, October 17, 1967 (No. 21), p. 2.

[37] *Obrana lidu*, August 23, 1969; Miroslav Starosta, *Tribuna*, August 20, 1969 (No. 32).

[38] *Zpravodaj KSC*, supplement to *Zivot strany*, November 5, 1969 (No. 26).

[39] Miloslav Chlupac, *Nova mysl*, June 14, 1966 (No. 12), p. 23.

[40] *Ibid*. See also Marie Hulakova, *Nova mysl*, July 11, 1967 (No. 14), pp. 8–12.

[41] Stanislav Vodinsky, *Reporter*, April 10, 1969 (No. 14), p. 6.

[42] Vladimir Wynnyczuk, *Zemedelske noviny*, November 25, 1969.

[43] *Rude pravo*, April 23, 1968, reporting on the abolishment of the Governmental Ordinance of January 17, 1962 (No. 42). However, according to *Tribuna*, November 25, 1970 (No. 47), p. 8, the last discriminatory rule (Instruction No. 116 of the Ministry of Education) was issued in 1964.

[44] *Rude pravo*, May 26, 1966; *Prace*, January 25, 1967.

[45] *Zivot strany*, 1966 (Nos. 7, 17, 18, and 20).

[46] Karel Stradal, *Czechoslovak Life*, April 1969, pp. 26–27, 37. According to *Nova mysl*, January 10, 1967 (No. 1), p. 14, the social composition of the deputies elected in 1960 was as follows: 35.5 percent workers, 26.7 percent collective farmers, 19 percent intelligentsia and administrative employees, 5.3 percent public employees, and 13.5 percent others. Hykisch (see n. 2 above) claims that 95 percent of all deputies were members of the Party; however he does not identify the basis for this assertion.

[47] Stradal, *op. cit.*

[48] *Reporter*, May 1, 1969 (No. 17), pp. 6–7.

[49] *Smena*, November 21, 1968, p. 3.

[50] *Rude pravo*, August 10, 1968.

[51] *Rude pravo*, June 24, 1971.

[52] Supplement to *Ucitelske noviny*, cited in *Text* (an exile monthly, published in Munich), August 1971 (No. 8–9), p. 2.

[53] *Tvorba*, April 19, 1972 (No. 16), pp. 4–5.

[54] *Svedectvi* (Paris), 1971 (No. 40), p. 548.

[55] *Tribuna*, April 15, 1970 (No. 15), p. 1.

[56] *Tribuna*, November 25, 1970 (No. 47), p. 1.

[57] For example, see attack by J. Matejka, *Tribuna*, August 4, 1971 (No. 31), p. 4, on Arnost Duschner for his views on the subject in *Socialisticka zakonnost*, 1971 (No. 4), pp. 248–249.

[58] *Rude pravo*, August 17, 1971, p. 2. Sources from the same period refer to the recurrence of old failures in recruitment such as "formalism." Thus, *Tribuna*, May 26, 1971 (No. 21), p. 2, criticizes the case of a young economist whose application for Party membership was turned down with the explanation that the Party needed to improve its proletarian ratio. She would be eligible to join only after three manual laborers willing to join could be found.

[59] *Rude pravo*, September 10, 1971, January 12 and March 4, 1972; *Ucitelske noviny*, April 15 and 22, 1971; *Mlada fronta*, April 29, 1971; Antonin Vanek, "Working Class and Intelligentsia," *Tribuna*, January 20, 1971 (No. 3), p. 4.

CHAPTER NINE
Political Socialization

[1] Jindrich Chalupecky, *Literarni listy*, May 30, 1968 (No. 14), p. 9; Zdenek Eis, *Reporter*, April 3, 1969 (No. 13), pp. i-vi.

[2] Most important speeches delivered at the congress are included in Dusan Hamsik, *Writers Against Rulers* (New York: Random House, 1971).

[3] Vaclav Cerny, *Literarni listy*, May 16, 1968 (No. 12), p. 6. See also Frantisek Sorm, *Rude pravo*, June 5, 1968; Jan Filip, *Svobodne slovo*, May 26, 1968; *Czechoslovak Life*, January 1969, p. 2. For more details of the polemics involving Cerny, see *Literarni listy*, June 13, 1968 (No. 16), p. 3, and July 4, 1968 (No. 19), p. 11, and *Rude pravo*, June 25, 1968.

[4] Eduard Urbanek, *Acta Universitatis Carolinae, Philosophica et Historica*, 1968 (No. 4), pp. 5–12.

[5] *Rude pravo*, October 19, 1966; *Kulturni tvorba*, November 3, 1966 (No. 44); *Prace*, April 27, 1967; Vojtech Tlusty, *Tvorba*, July 22, 1970 (No. 29), p. 3; J. Kapr *et al.*, *Sociologicky casopis*, 1970 (No. 5), pp. 385–399. According to *Tvorba*, June 24, 1970 (No. 25), p. 13, "We [in Czechoslovakia] had about the world's largest sociological society but also the largest share of dilettants in sociology."

[6] *Sociologicky casopis*, October 1968 (No. 5), pp. 609–611.

[7] *Rude pravo*, June 3, 1966.

[8] Vladimir Divis, *Nova mysl*, July 26, 1966 (No. 15).

[9] *Reporter*, January 30, 1969 (No. 4), p. ii.

[10] *Vestnik Ministerstva skolstvi*, November 19, 1956 (No. 30/31). According to *Lidove noviny*, April 27, 1951, Anna Jungwirtova, a Member of the Parliament, stated: "We must endeavor to bring the children of progressive workers and peasants to universities. We want them to be our future intellectuals, who, in their initiative and adherence to the working class, will approach the quality and ideological maturity of the Soviet intellectuals. On the other hand, . . . if the children of bourgeois origin are healthy enough, they should take on manual work, the work in mines and fac-

tories, which their class gladly left to the proletariat in the past."

[11] *Literarni noviny*, May 6, 1967 (No. 18).

[12] *Vecerni Praha*, March 31, 1967.

[13] *Svobodne slovo*, January 17, 1966.

[14] *Rude pravo*, October 10, 1968.

[15] *Reporter*, February 6, 1969 (No. 5), p. 16; *Rude pravo*, February 1, 1969, p. 2.

[16] Blanka Filipcova, *Nova mysl*, January 10, 1967 (No. 1), p. 16.

[17] *Prace*, April 24, 1966.

[18] *Lidova demokracie*, May 14, 1969, p. 4. (The Compulsory Education Act was enacted May 14, 1869.)

[19] Vilibald Bezdicek, *Reporter*, March 27, 1969 (No. 12), p. 5.

[20] Frantisek Hynek, *Nova mysl*, May 17, 1966 (No. 10), pp. 28–30.

[21] Ladislav Buzek, *Svobodne slovo*, March 29, 1969, p. 10.

[22] Jaroslav Havelka, *Nova mysl*, April 4, 1967 (No. 7), p. 12. See also Jiri Hajek, *Nova mysl*, November 3, 1966 (No. 22), pp. 13–15; Frantisek Hynek, *Nova mysl*, December 28, 1966 (No. 26), pp. 21–24; Frantisek Hyhlik, *Nova mysl*, May 3, 1967 (No. 9), pp. 23–26; and Marie Hulakova, *Sociologicky casopis*, 1968 (No. 5), pp. 550–562.

[23] *Rude pravo*, July 5 and August 22, 1972.

[24] Bretislav Dejdar, *Ucitelske noviny*, October 30, 1969 (No. 43). Dejdar added: "We would need Zdenek Nejedly and his progressively revitalized Slavism to recover from that."

[25] *Kulturni tvorba*, November 3, 1966 (No. 44).

[26] Zdenka Neumannova, *Literarni listy*, June 20, 1968 (No. 17), pp. 1–2.

[27] Zdenek Pokorny, *Reporter*, August 14, 1968 (No. 33), pp. 7–8.

[28] *Ibid.*, p. 8.

[29] *Rude pravo*, October 6, 1966; Vaclav Kotek, *Kulturni tvorba*, October 20, 1966 (No. 42); Jaroslav Kladiva, *Nova mysl*, February 21, 1967 (No. 4), pp. 11–14.

[30] Petr Kettner, *Literarni noviny*, May 13, 1967 (No. 19); *Smena*, January 10, 1969; Stanislav Vodinsky, *Lidova demokracie*, May 8, 1969.

[31] *Lidova demokracie*, August 28, 1969. See also "*Manifest pravdy*", "A Manifesto on behalf of Truth," published as a supplement to the teachers' weekly *Ucitelske noviny*, September 11, 1969, and authored by Jaromir Hrbek, professor of medicine and the new Minister of Education.

[32] The Party declared its determination to remove from schools all politically suspect personnel. Minister Hrbek's effort in this respect made him internationally known. Promoting political denunciations as a necessary socialist virtue, he authored a questionnaire for teachers, obligating them to give names of the enemies of the regime. In 1971 Hrbek resigned allegedly upon his own request and was replaced by a colorless bureaucrat, Josef Havlin.

[33] *Literarni listy*, May 2, 1968 (No. 10), p. 4; Milos Hoznauer, *Listy*, February 6, 1969 (No. 5), p. 3.

[34] *Mlada fronta*, June 15, 1967.

[35] *Rude pravo*, April 4, 1967. See also Zdenka Stastna, *Reporter*, January 8, 1969 (No. 11), p. 13.

[36] *Prace*, April 24, 1966.

[37] *Prace*, June 3, 1967.

[38] *Rude pravo*, June 15, 1967, and January 31, 1967.

[39] *Mlada fronta*, June 15, 1967.

[40] *Student*, 1966 (No. 4).

[41] *Nova mysl*, April 19, 1966 (No. 8), p. 45.

[42] Oldrich Krystofek, *Nova mysl*, April 1969 (No. 4), pp. 492–496.

[43] Miloslav Hajek, *Rude pravo*, June 1, 1972, p. 1; Zdenka Stastna, *Reporter*, April 24, 1969 (No. 16), pp. 5–6; *Rude pravo*, March 11 and 13 and June 8, 1972.

[44] Oldrich Krystofek, *Reporter*, January 3, 1969 (No. 3), p. 1.

[45] *Rude pravo*, May 17, 1952.

[46] *Tribuna*, September 16, 1970 (No. 37), p. 15.

[47] Karel Horalek, *Tvorba*, March 7, 1971 (No. 11), p. 1.

[48] For indictment of the scout movement, see *Mlada fronta*, April 29 and 30, 1970; *Rude pravo*, April 27, 1970; *Tribuna*, September 9, 1970 (No. 30), p. 15. *Zivot strany*, July 26, 1971 (No. 15), indignantly reported an incident involving some thirty boys in scout uniforms standing at attention at a railway station before their leader with a poster saying, "Never capitulate, never betray."

[49] *Rude pravo*, October 13, 1971, p. 3.

[50] *Tribuna*, July 28, 1971 (No. 30), p. 15.

[51] *Tribuna*, February 6, 1972 (No. 6), p. 15; Juraj Varholik, *Rude pravo*, June 8, 1971, p. 2. and September 27, 1972, p. 1; March 30, 1972, p. 3.

[52] *Tribuna*, May 19, 1971 (No. 20), p. 17, and May 12, 1971 (No. 19), p. 15.

[53] *Tribuna*, May 12, 1971 (No. 19), p. 15.

[54] *Tribuna*, March 24, 1971 (No. 12), p. 15.

[55] *Tribuna*, June 9, 1971 (No. 23), p. 15; June 23, 1971 (No. 25), p. 15; July 7, 1971 (No. 27), p. 15.

[56] *Prace*, April 24, 1966; *Zivot strany*, June 25, 1969 (No. 26), p. 11; *Nova mysl*, January 10, 1967 (No. 1), p. 17.

[57] *Prace*, December 15, 1966.

[58] *Zivot strany*, September 1966 (No. 17).

[59] *Rude pravo*, April 4, 1967.

[60] Lord Mayor of Prague, Zdenek Zuska, *Tvorba*, March 10, 1971 (No. 10), p. 5.

[61] *Zivot strany*, September 1966 (No. 17).

[62] *Zivot strany*, April 10, 1969 (No. 15), p. 5.

[63] *Zpravodaj KSC*, No. 20, supplement to *Zivot strany*, July 9, 1969 (No. 28).

[64] *Ibid*. See also *Zivot strany*, June 18, 1969 (No. 25), p. 11.

[65] *Zpravodaj KSC*, September 17, 1969 (No. 23); *Zivot strany*, June 11, 1969 (No. 24), p. 6.

[66] *Tvorba*, September 2, 1970 (No. 35), p. 4.

[67] *Rude pravo*, June 9, 1972, p. 3; *Tribuna*, June 7, 1972 (No. 23), pp. 1, 4–5.

[68] *Rude pravo*, March 4, 1972, p. 2; *Tvorba*, June 14, 1972 (No. 24), p. 5, and November 10, 1971 (No. 45), p. 5.

[69] *Mlady svet*, August 1969 (No. 33), p. 8; *Zivot strany*, 1966 (No. 17); *Statisticka rocenka CSSR 1968*, p. 501; *Nova mysl*, January 10, 1967 (No. 1), p. 15.

[70] *Vecerni Praha*, May 30, 1967; *Osvetova prace*, 1966 (No. 13).

[71] V. Brabec, *Revue dejin socialismu*, July 1969 (No. 3).

[72] *Statisticka rocenka CSSR 1968*, p. 508.

[73] *Rude pravo*, February 10, 1967.

[74] *Rude pravo*, March 22, 1969, p. 3; *Zemedelske noviny*, November 15, 1968, p. 2; *Nova mysl*, August 23, 1966 (No. 17), p. 8; *Zivot strany*, March 19, 1969 (No. 12), p. 11.

[75] Jiri Franek, *Rude pravo*, September 17, 1966.

[76] *Halo Sobota*, supplement to *Rude pravo*, January 18, 1969, p. 15.

[77] Jiri Hudecek, *Reporter*, April 10, 1969 (No. 14), p. xiii.

[78] *Nova mysl*, January 10, 1967 (No. 1), p. 15.

[79] *Literarni listy*, May 2, 1968 (No. 10), p. 12.

[80] *Svobodne slovo*, January 4, 1969, p. 3.

[81] *Halo-Sobota* supplement to *Rude pravo*, February 3, 1970.

[82] Hudecek, *op. cit.*, p. xv.

[83] *Literarni listy*, June 16, 1968 (No. 15), p. 2.

[84] Jan Kaspar, *Nova mysl*, May 1970 (No. 5), pp. 743–751.

[85] *Ibid.*, p. 750.

[86] *Statisticka rocenka CSSR 1968*, pp. 379–380; *Pravda*, January 28, 1967.

[87] *Nova mysl*, January 10, 1967 (No. 1), p. 15; *Politika*, September 19, 1968 (No. 4), pp. 28–29.

[88] *Rude pravo*, July 6, 1972, p. 2. See also *Rude pravo*, September 3, 1971, p. 2.

[89] Jaroslav Toms, *Tvorba*, August 11, 1971 (No. 32).

[90] *Prace*, March 12, 1966; *Pravda*, June 21, 1966.

[91] Jaroslav Diblik, *Zivot strany*, 1967 (No. 6).

[92] *Pravda*, March 20 and July 10, 1966.

[93] For criticism of improper social conduct, see *Tribuna*, September 1, 1971 (No. 35), p. 6; January 28, 1972 (No. 4), p. 6; and March 18, 1970 (No. 11), pp. 14–15. See also *Rude pravo*, September 2, 1972, p. 3; *Tvorba*, March 17, 1971 (No. 11), p. 2.

[94] *Zivot strany*, 1966 (No. 20). See also *Tribuna*, February 16, 1972 (No. 7), p. 7.

[95] *Czechoslovak Life*, April 1969, p. 3.

[96] Vitezslav Gardavsky, *Literarni listy*, June 20, 1968 (No. 17), p. 1.

[97] *Kvety*, July 13, 1968.

[98] *Svobodne slovo*, December 4, 1966; *Literarni listy*, July 25, 1968 (No. 22), p. 7. The results of this survey by Erika Kadlecova were published in 1967 in book form under the title *Sociologicky vyzkum religiozity Severomoravskeho kraje* [*Sociological Survey of the Religious Sentiment in the Province of Northern Moravia*].

[99] P. Pursak, *Sociologia*, January 1970 (No. 1).

[100] *Czechoslovak Life*, January 1969, p. 17.

[101] J. Krejci, *Sociologicky casopis*, 1969 (No. 4), p. 468.

[102] Jaromir Dedek, *Sociologicky casopis*, 1968 (No. 6), pp. 676–681.

[103] Jaroslav Stipek, *Nova mysl*, June 13, 1967 (No. 12), p. 27.

[104] For political dialogue between generations, see Vladimir Blazek, *Literarni listy*, June 20, 1968 (No. 17), p. 20; *Reporter*, June 19, 1968 (No. 25), p. 1; *Rude pravo*, January 29, 1968; Jiri Sekera, *Rude pravo*, May 5, 1968, p. 2; D. Blazej, *Rude pravo*, May 19, 1968, p. 2; Milada Bartosova, *Vlasta*, May 15, 1968, p. 5.

[105] Frantisek Povolny, *Nova mysl*, April 1969 (No. 4), pp. 432–442.

[106] *Pruboj*, August 23, 1968, p. 4.

[107] Milos Hoznauer, *Listy*, November 28, 1968 (No. 4), p. 5.

[108] *Svobodne slovo*, January 18, 1969, p. 1. For students' program, see *Mlada fronta*, November 19, 1968, and *Lidova demokracie*, November 21, 1968.

[109] Ilios Jannakakis, *Listy*, November 21, 1968 (No. 3), p. 12.

[110] Jirina Siklova, *ibid.*, p. 3. See also *Literarni listy*, August 8, 1968 (No. 24), p. 14; Stanislav Pekarek, *Zitrek*, January 15, 1969 (No. 2), pp. 1, 3.

[111] Ilios Jannakakis, *Literarni listy*, July 18, 1968 (No. 21), p. 12.

[112] *Zivot strany*, June 11, 1969 (No. 24), p. 12.

[113] *Zivot strany*, May 28, 1969 (No. 22), pp. 4–5.

[114] *Rude pravo*, May 1, 1969, p. 8.

[115] *Svobodne slovo*, December 3, 1968.

[116] Jan Kozic, *Tribuna*, July 9, 1969 (No. 26). See also *Rude pravo*, November 16, 1968, p. 3.

[117] Kucera, *Tribuna*, September 15, 1971 (No. 37), p. 9; *Tribuna*, September 22, 1971 (No. 38), p. 9; *Tribuna*, September 29, 1971 (No. 39), p. 9; *Tribuna*, March 22, 1972 (No. 12), p. 8, based his findings on the book *Socialni struktura CSSR a jeji vyvoj v 60. letech* by F. Charvat *et al.* (Prague, 1971).

[118] Jan Kucera, *Tribuna*, September 15, 1971 (No. 37).

[119] Vlasta Pikrtova, *Zivot strany*, June 21, 1971 (No. 13); *Tvorba*, September 12, 1970 (No. 35), p. 2; *Rude pravo*, June 12 and July 31, 1971; *Listy* (Rome), 1971 (No. 1) and 1971 (No. 4–5).

[120] For details on the role of movies, see *Rude pravo*, January 6, 1972, p. 5; *Rude pravo*, August 24, 1972, p. 5; *Rude pravo*, December 30, 1971, p. 5.; *Tvorba*, August 19, 1970 (No. 33), p. 12; *Tvorba*, February 17, 1971 (No. 7), p. 2; *Tribuna*, May 17, 1972 (No. 20), p. 7. According to *Rude pravo* (February 17, 1972, p. 2), total attendance at Soviet movies in Czechoslovakia since 1945 reached 860 million, which means an average of 60 films seen by each citizen. The figures conceal the fact that school audiences and mandatory student attendance constitute a substantial share of the audience. By contrast, many adults, on principle, have never attended a single Soviet movie. (To be recognized at a showing of a Soviet movie is considered by such people to be as embarrassing as discovery in a brothel.)

[121] A letter to the editor in *Rude pravo* (February 3, 1972, p. 5) criticized usage of such English terms as "lunchmeat," "minced meat," and "crackers" on Czechoslovak products, and added: "In the cultural sphere the situation is the same—"the Sextons," the Hellmen, the Rangers, always with the inevitable "THE." . . ." See also *Rude pravo*, April 26, 1972, p. 5; *Tvorba*, March 8, 1972 (No. 10), p. 5; *Tribuna*, May 12, 1971 (No. 19), p. 6; *Tribuna*, October 6, 1971 (No. 40), p. 7; *Tribuna*, April 12, 1972 (No. 15), p. 15.

[122] See *Tribuna*, October 27, 1971 (No. 43), p. 7, and December 8, 1971 (No. 49), p. 14, for reports on the political maturity of citizens in the GDR, such as the action of the youth activists searching for television antennas adjusted for the reception of Western stations.

[123] *Tvorba*, July 21, 1971 (No. 29), p. 2.

[124] Vlasta Kosnarova, *Tribuna*, June 2, 1971 (No. 22), p. 11. See also *Tribuna*, August 11, 1971 (No. 32), pp. 6–7, and August 18, 1971 (No. 33), pp. 6–7.

[125] *Tvorba*, May 24, 1972 (No. 21), p. 12. (*Tvorba*, No. 10–21, published regular ideological messages in lieu of nonexistent textbooks on themes such as "Materialistic Concept of Human Personality," "Principles of Party Life," "Life Style of

Socialist Personality," and "Struggle of Two World Systems"). See also *Rude pravo*, February 5, 1972, p. 2.

[126] Vitezslav Pravda, pseudonymous regular contributor to the Munich-based *Ceske slovo*, May 1970, p. 7. For "obsession with facts" and similar defects, see Vitezslav Vaculik, "Is It Possible to Teach the Young Generation Communism?" *Tribuna*, September 1, 1971 (No. 35), p. 15, and May 24, 1972 (No. 21), p. 15.

[127] Silvester Novacek, *Vysoka skola*, October 1970, (No. 1).

[128] Ondrej Pavlik, *Ucitelske noviny*, September 24, 1970 (No. 38).

CHAPTER TEN
Political Communication

[1] *Obrana lidu*, February 10, 1968.

[2] Vladimir Stein, *Osvetova prace*, 1966 (No. 6).

[3] Frantisek Nepil, *Zitrek*, March 19, 1969 (No. 11), p. 1. (The author discusses differences between Western and Eastern European political styles and mentality. He hoped that the Americans would be first on the moon because they were not likely to shout, "Long live the United States, the bastion of capitalism in all the world.")

[4] Miroslav Holub, *Literarni listy*, May 2, 1968 (No. 10), pp. 1–2. See also Jaroslav Putik, *Literarni listy*, April 25, 1968 (No. 9), pp. 1–2; Petr Pithart, *Listy*, November 21, 1968 (No. 3), p. 1; Jan Trefulka, *ibid.*, p. 4.

[5] Milan Uhde, *Literarni listy*, August 15, 1968 (No. 25), p. 4.

[6] Jiri Cvekl, *Nova mysl*, August 1968 (No. 8), pp. 1017, 1019.

[7] *Literarni listy*, July 18, 1968 (No. 21), p. 14.

[8] V. Grishin, *Pravda*, April 22, 1968, quoted by Miroslav Jodl, *Literarni listy*, May 16, 1968 (No. 12), p. 4.

[9] Bohuslav Snajder, *Literarni listy*, July 4, 1968 (No. 19), p. 8.

[10] Zdenek Salaquarda, *Listy*, February 27, 1969 (No. 8), p. 1.

[11] Ota Sik, *Rude pravo*, August 2, 1968.

[12] Vladimir Blazek, *Literarni listy*, June 20, 1968, p. 20.

[13] Jiri Mucha, *Literarni listy*, July 25, 1968 (No. 22). See also *Literarni listy*, August 8, 1968 (No. 24), pp. 1, 8, 14.

[14] *Dikobraz*, 1952 (No. 5), quoted by *Svobodne slovo*, December 30, 1968, p. 9 (the entire page was devoted to examples of Stalinist wit).

[15] Rare insight into censorship operations is provided by an anonymous former apparatchik of the Central Committee Secretariat. "Information on Conditions of Totalism and Revolt," *Svedectvi* (Paris), 1971 (No. 42), pp. 193–211.

[16] *Reporter*, March 27, 1968 (No. 13), p. 5. (The word *Pokyn* is translated here as "Order." It is a Stalinese term, literally

meaning "hint" or "suggestion." The various initials denote various censorship branches.)

[17] Z. Vesely, *Lidova demokracie*, June 17, 1968.

[18] Jan Prochazka, *Politika pro kazdeho* (Prague: Mlada fronta, 1968).

[19] Jiri Zahradil, Vilem Herold, *Literarni listy*, April 25, 1968 (No. 9), p. 7.

[20] Jan Varta, *Halo Sobota*, March 15, 1969, p. 3.

[21] J. Jungwirth, *Zemedelske noviny*, June 9, 1968.

[22] Svatopluk Pekarek, *Literarni noviny*, August 6, 1966 (No. 32), p. 1.

[23] Vilem Precan, *Reporter*, March 13, 1969 (No. 10), pp. 5–6.

[24] Josef Herbolt, *Nova mysl*, March 21, 1967 (No. 6), pp. 3–6.

[25] Alexej Ozarcuk, *Nova mysl*, June 14, 1966 (No. 12), pp. 20–22.

[26] Svatopluk Holec, *Nova mysl*, April 1968 (No. 4), p. 521.

[27] Michal Lakatos, *Zitrek*, December 11, 1968 (No. 10). In the following issue of *Zitrek*, Lakatos pointed out the information blackout whereby the public does not even know the names of their own deputies in the Czech Parliament.

[28] Tomas, *Zitrek*, February 12, 1969 (No. 6), p. 2.

[29] Kaspar, *Nova mysl*, August 1968 (No. 8), pp. 1002–1010.

[30] Published in *Tribuna*, February 5, 1969, and *Rude pravo* (supplement), July 2, 1969.

[31] Kaspar, *op. cit.*, p. 1008.

[32] Karel Tanzl, *Zivot strany*, March 1968 (No. 5).

[33] *Rude pravo*, April 23, 1969.

[34] "Report on the Current Situation," *op. cit.*

[35] *Rolnicke noviny*, February 10, 1968.

[36] Zdenek Mlynar, *Rude pravo*, April 7, 1968; Josef Smrkovsky, *Rude pravo*, April 28, 1968.

[37] Jiri Ruml, *Reporter*, April 17, 1968 (No. 16).

[38] For details on this contribution, see *Zivot strany*, March 19, 1969 (No. 12), p. 11.

[39] Josef Belak, *Nove slovo*, August 8, 1969.

[40] Jiri Hochman, *Reporter*, September 26, 1968 (No. 37), pp. 26–27.

[41] Milan Jungmann, *Listy*, November 7, 1968 (No. 1), p. 1.

[42] A total of sixty-one issues of *Zpravy* was published between September 1968 and May 1969. All the Czechoslovaks participating in this venture remained anonymous or used pseudonyms. (Jiri Lukas was later identified as editor-in-chief.) As a sign of the growing power of the pro-Soviet forces the media began to praise *Zpravy* for its unique and historical role. In 1971 the publishing house Svoboda produced a 392-page book called *Zpravy in Struggle Against Counterrevolution* (*Zpravy v boji proti kontrarevoluci*).

[43] *Rude pravo*, too, engaged in the polemics. See its attack in the February 15, 1969, issue on *Tribuna*.

[44] *Rude pravo*, May 16, 1969, p. 1.

[45] Milan Mitosinka, *Nove slovo*, November 21, 1968.

[46] Jiri Lederer, *Reporter*, November 6, 1968 (No. 43), p. 4. See also *Reporter*, December 18, 1968 (No. 46), p. 13.

[47] Jan Prochazka, *My*, February 15, 1969 (No. 2). This sensitivity is bound to grow. Recipients of impoverished messages engage in esoteric communication, rumors, and guesswork. *Tvorba*, April 19, 1972 (No. 16), p. 2, reported the public reaction one evening in Prague when the regular television news was delayed by a few minutes. The viewers ran inappropriately to telephones, called everywhere—to the television studio, but also to the Secretariat of the Party Central Committee, wanting to know what was going on in Prague. The next day in places of work this was a big topic to ponder about and generalize."

[48] *Smer*, September 1, 1968, p. 2.

[49] *Rude pravo*, March 22, 1969, p. 2.

[50] *Prace*, January 23, 1969, p. 3.

[51] *Rude pravo*, November 5, 1968, p. 1; *Pravda* and *Smena*, July 31, 1969.

[52] *Listy* (Rome), March 1971 (No. 2), pp. 21–24; *Tribuna*, September 30, 1970 (No. 39).

[53] Josef Valenta, President of the Union of Czech Journalists, *Tvorba*, April 19, 1972 (No. 16), pp. 4–5. According to Valenta, there were only 160 newsmen in the country who lived long enough to reach retirement age. See also *Rude pravo*, May 18, 1972, p. 2.

CHAPTER ELEVEN
The Resulting Political Culture

[1] Milan Kundera, *Listy*, December 19, 1968 (No. 7–8), pp. 1–2.

[2] Milan Jugmann, *Reporter*, October 16, 1968 (No. 40), p. 27.

[3] Jiri Hanak, *Reporter*, January 30, 1969 (No. 4), p. 4.

[4] Jan Tesar, *Listy*, April 30, 1969 (No. 17), p. 16.

[5] Jaroslav Putik, *Listy*, November 14, 1968 (No. 2), p. 14. See also *Politika*, August 24, 1968, and *Mlada fronta*, August 27, 1968, p. 3.

[6] Frantisek Nepil, *Zitrek*, quoted in *Reporter*, January 30, 1969 (No. 4), p. 8.

[7] Jiri Franek, *Rude pravo*, February 19, 1966; Jan Pilar, *Zemedelske noviny*, March 13, 1966.

[8] Familiarity with democratic procedures was also absent. Characteristic of this handicap was this comment in *Prace* (January 23, 1969, p. 1), reporting on a trade union congress:

"Excuse us, please, these delays—turned a delegate to the platform with the highest officials. 'For twenty years we did nothing but unanimously raise our hands. Once we have twenty years of democratic practice behind us, we shall be experienced.' "

⁹ Bohumil Nuska, *Literarni listy*, June 20, 1968 (No. 17), p. 9.

¹⁰ Jungmann, *op. cit.*, p. 26.

¹¹ Dusan Hamsik, *Listy*, January 30, 1969 (No. 4), pp. 1, 3.

¹² Jiri Hochman, *Reporter*, August 1, 1968 (No. 31), p. 4.

¹³ Frantisek Motycka, *Tribuna*, August 6, 1969 (No. 30).

¹⁴ Bretislav Dejdar, *Nova mysl*, September 1969 (No. 9), pp. 1122–1132.

¹⁵ Tomas, *Zitrek*, March 19, 1969, (No. 11), p. 2.

¹⁶ Kosik, *Listy*, November 7, 1968 (No. 1), p. 1.

¹⁷ For criticism of anemic political commitment, see Jaroslav Jirasek, *Tvorba*, December 2, 1970 (No. 48), pp. 3, 6; Adolf Ginter, *Tvorba*, July 21, 1971 (No. 29), p. 14; *Tribuna*, March 11, 1970 (No. 10), p. 5, attacking "individuals who have achieved their 'private Communism.' They have nice jobs, a house, country cottage, etc.; all they need is time enough to enjoy their possessions. . . ."

CHAPTER TWELVE
Conclusion

¹ Petr Pithart, *Literarni listy*, July 25, 1968 (No. 22).

² Emil Holas, *Prace*, February 11, 1969.

³ Oldrich Svic, *Tvorba*, November 12, 1969 (No. 11). See also "Directives of the Fourteenth Congress of the Communist Party of Czechoslovakia Concerning the Fifth Five-Year Plan of the Development of National Economy in the Years 1971–1972," supplement to *Tribuna*, April 21, 1971 (No. 16), p. 15.

⁴ Jan Nemec, *Socialisticka zakonnost*, 1970 (No. 7–8), p. 392.

Bibliography

DOCUMENTS

Czechoslovak Republic Constitution. Prague: Ministry of Information, 1960.

Dejiny Ceskoslovenska v datech [*History of Czechoslovakia in Dates*]. Prague: Svoboda, 1967.

Ello, Paul, ed. *Czechoslovakia's Blueprint for "Freedom."* Washington, D.C.: Acropolis Press, 1968.

Littel, Robert, ed. *The Czech Black Book*. New York: Praeger, 1969. (Prepared by the Institute of History, Czechoslovak Academy of Sciences.)

O normach stranickeho zivota: Sbornik [*Norms of Party Life: A Collection*]. Prague: SNPL, 1960.

Protokol XIII. sjezdu KSC [*Proceedings of the XIII Congress of the KSC*]. Prague: Svoboda, 1966.

Rok sedesaty osmy v usnesenich a dokumentech UV KSC [*The Year 1968 in the Resolutions and Documents of the KSC Central Committee*]. Prague: Svoboda, 1969.

Rok stranickeho skoleni [*Year of Party Schooling*]. An annual publication by the Propaganda and Agitation department of the KSC Central Committee.

Sbirka rozhodnuti ceskoslovenskych soudu [*Collection of Czechoslovak Court Decisions*]. Prague: Supreme Court (10 issues a year).

Sbirka zakonu CSSR [*Collection of Laws of the Czechoslovak Socialist Republic*]. Prague: Government Printing Office (published irregularly).

Statisticka rocenka CSSR [*Statistical Yearbook of CSSR*]. Prague: SNTL, 1966, 1968.

Strana a spolecnost [*The Party and Society*] Prague: Svoboda 1968.

Uredni list republiky ceskoslovenske [*The Official Gazette of the Czechoslovak Republic*]. Prague: Government Printing Office (publishes irregularly).

IV. Sjezd Svazu ceskoslovenskych spisovatelu: Protokol [*Fourth Congress of the Union of Czechoslovak Writers: Proceedings*]. Prague: Ceskoslovensky spisovatel, 1968.

BOOKS

Bares, Gustav. *Moznosti a meze* [*Possibilities and Limits*]. Prague: Svoboda, 1969.

Bartuska, Jan. *Obrana nasi vlasti a boj za zachovani miru* [*Defense of Our Fatherland and the Struggle for Maintaining Peace*]. Prague: Orbis, 1953.

Bertelman, K. *Vznik narodnich vyboru* [*Creation of the People's Committees*]. Prague: NCSAV, 1956.

Busek, Vratislav, and Nicholas Spulber, eds. *Czechoslovakia*. New York: Praeger, 1957.

Bystrina, Ivan. *Lidova demokracie* [*People's Democracy*]. Prague: NCSAV, 1957.

Cvekl, J., and V. Lokajicek, *Iluze soukromi v moderni spolecnosti* [*The Illusion of Privacy in Modern Society*]. Prague: Nase vojsko, 1969.

Cvekl, Jiri. *Filosofie a soucasnost* [*Philosophy and the Present*]. Prague: SPN, 1968.

Danis, Jaroslav. *O ulohe strany na skolach* [*On the Role of the Party in Schools*]. Bratislava: Epocha, 1968.

Dierer, J. *Masovopoliticka praca v zakladnej organizacii strany* [*The Political Work in the Local Party Cells*], Bratislava: Epocha, 1968.

Dojcak, P. *Pravo a sociologia* [*Law and Sociology*]. Bratislava: SAV, 1967.

Fibich, Jindrich, *K otazkam byrokracie a byrokratismu* [*On Questions of Bureaucracy and Bureaucratism*]. Prague: Academia, 1967.

Filipcova, Blanka. *Clovek—prace—volny cas* [Man—Work—Leisure Time]. Prague: Svoboda, 1966.

Franek, Jiri, and Jiri Stano. *S tebou, zeme: Kronika viteznych let.* [*With You, My Country: Annals of the Victorious Years*]. Prague: SNPL, 1960.

Gadourek, Ivan. *The Political Control of Czechoslovakia.* Leiden (The Netherlands): Kroese, 1953.

Gardavsky, Vitezslav. *Nadeje je skepse* [*Hope is Skepticism*]. Prague: Svoboda, 1969.

Glos, J., et al. *Prava obcanu* [*The Rights of Citizens*]. Prague: Orbis, 1969.

Goldman, Josef, and Karel Kouba. *Economic Growth in Czechoslovakia.* Prague: Academia, 1969.

Gottwald, Klement. *Selected Speeches and Articles, 1929–1953.* Prague: Orbis, 1954.

Hamsik, Dusan. *Spisovatele a moc* [*Writers and Power*]. Prague: Ceskoslovensky spisovatel, 1969.

Havlicek, Miroslav. *Dialektika vnitrostranickych vztahu* [*Dialectics of Interparty Relations*]. Prague: Svoboda, 1968.

Houska, J., and K. Kara, *Otazky lidove demokracie* [*Problems of the People's Democracy*]. Prague: SNPL, 1955.

Hromada, Juraj. *Prehlad ceskoslovenskych statnych organov* [*Review of Czechoslovak State Organs*]. Bratislava: SVPL, 1955.

Janousek, Jaromir. *Socialni komunikace* [*Social Communication*]. Prague: Svoboda, 1968.

Jodl, Miroslav. *Teorie elity a problem elity* [*The Theory of the Elite and the Problem of the Elite*]. Prague: Academia, 1968.

Kabes, Vladimir. *Socialist Legality in Czechoslovakia.* The Hague: International Commission of Jurists, 1953.

Kalivoda, Robert. *Moderni duchovni skutecnost a marxismus* [*Modern Spiritual Reality and Marxism*]. Prague: Ceskoslovensky spisovatel, 1968.

Kapr, J., and Z. Safar. *Sociologie, nebo zdravy rozum?* [*Sociology or Common Sense?*]. Prague: Mlada fronta, 1969.

Karcol, Jaroslav. *Obsah a forma v cinnosti strany* [*Content and Form in the Activities of the Party*]. Prague: Svoboda, 1967.

Klofac, Jaroslav, and Vojtech Tlusty. *Soudoba sociologie* [*Contemporary Sociology*]. Prague: Svoboda, 1967.

Klofac, Jaroslav, Vojtech Tlusty, and Pavel Machonin. *Je u nas socialismus?* [*Do We Live in Socialism?*]. Prague: Svoboda, 1969.

Klokocka, Vladimir. *Volby v pluralitnich demokraciich* [*Elections in Pluralistic Democracies*]. Prague: Svoboda, 1968.

Knapp, Viktor. *Vlastnictvi v lidove demokracii* [*Ownership in a People's Democracy*]. Prague: Orbis, 1952.

Kohout, Jaroslav. *Sociologie a rizeni ekonomiky* [*Sociology and Economic Management*]. Prague: Prace, 1967.

Kolar, Jaroslav. *Sociologie podniku* [*The Sociology of an Enterprise*]. Prague: Prace, 1968.

Koralka, J. *Co je narod?* [*What Is a Nation?*]. Prague: Svoboda, 1969.

Korbel, Josef. *The Communist Subversion of Czechoslovakia, 1938–1948: The Failure of Coexistence.* Princeton, N.J.: Princeton University Press, 1959.

Kouba, Karel, *et al. Uvahy o socialisticke ekonomice* [*Thoughts on Socialist Economies*]. Prague: Svoboda, 1968.

Kral, Miloslav. *Veda a civilizace* [*Science and Civilization*]. Prague: Svoboda, 1969.

Kusy, Miroslav. *Filosofia politiky* [*Philosophy of Politics*]. Bratislava: VPL, 1966.

_____. *Marxisticka filozofia* [*Marxist Philosophy*]. Bratislava: Epocha, 1968.

Lakatos, Michal, *Otazky lidove demokracie v Ceskoslovensku* [*Problems of a People's Democracy in Czechoslovakia*]. Prague: NCSAV, 1957.

_____. *Uvahy o hodnotach demokracie* [*Thoughts on the Values of Democracy*]. Prague: Melantrich, 1969.

Macha, K. *Medziludske vztahy v modernej spolocnosti* [*Human Relations in Modern Society*]. Bratislava: VPL, 1967.

Machonin, Pavel, *et al. Socialni struktura socialisticke spolecnosti* [*The Social Structure of Socialist Society*]. Prague: Svoboda, 1966.

Musil, J. *Sociologie soudobeho mesta* [*The Sociology of a Contemporary City*]. Prague: Svoboda, 1967.

Pavlicek, V. *Politicke strany po unoru* [*Political Parties After (1948) February*]. Prague: Svobodne slovo, 1967.

Prochazka, Jan. *Politika pro kazdeho* [*Politics for Everybody*]. Prague: Mlada fronta, 1968.

Rechcigl, Miloslav, Jr., ed. *The Czechoslovak Contribution to World Culture.* The Hague: Mouton, 1964.

_____. *Czechoslovakia Past and Present.* The Hague: Mouton, 1969.

Reisky Dubnic, Vladimir. *Communist Propaganda Methods*. New York: Praeger, 1960.

Richta, Radovan, *et al. Civilizace na rozcesti* [*Civilization at the Crossroads*]. Prague: Svoboda, 1966.

Rohan, Rene. *Politicke strany* [*Political Parties*]. Prague: Svoboda, 1968.

_____. *Uceni o strane* [*Teachings on the Party*]. Prague: NPL, 1966.

Samalik, Frantisek. *Clovek a instituce* [*Man and Institutions*]. Prague: Svoboda, 1967.

_____. *Pravo a spolecnost* [*Law and Society*]. Prague: CSAV, 1965.

Schwartz, Harry. *Prague's 200 Days*. New York: Praeger, 1969.

Sik, Ota. *Ekonomika a zajmy* [*Economics and Interests*]. Prague: Svoboda, 1968.

_____ *Plan a trh za socialismu* [*Plan and Market in Socialism*]. Prague: Academia, 1967.

Siracky, Andrej. *Sociologia* [*Sociology*]. Bratislava: SAV, 1967.

Steiner, Hanus, *Teoreticke problemy propagandy a spolecenskeho vedomi* [*Theoretical Problems of Propaganda and Social Consciousness*]. Brno: Universita J. E. Purkyne, 1968.

Stuna, Stanislav, *et al. Zaklady prava* [*Principles of Law*]. Prague: Orbis, 1958.

Suda, Zdenek. *The Czechoslovak Socialist Republic*. Baltimore: Johns Hopkins University Press, 1969.

Taborsky, Eduard. *Communism in Czechoslovakia, 1948–1960*. Princeton, N.J.: Princeton University Press, 1961.

Tauber, J. *Kdo zije na vesnici* [*Who Lives in the Countryside*]. Ceske Budejovice: Nakladatelstvi C. Bud., 1965.

Tomasek, Ladislav. *Veduca uloha strany a politicky system* [*The Leading Role of the Party and the Political System*]. Bratislava: VPL, 1968.

Tomasek, L., J. Litera, and J. Vecera. *Strana a dnesek* [*The Party and the Present*]. Prague: Svoboda, 1967.

Vyskovsky, Eduard, ed. *Deset let lidove demokratickeho Ceskoslovenska* [*Ten Years of the People's Democratic Czechoslovakia*]. Prague: Orbis, 1955.

Zeman, Z. A. B. *Prague Spring*. New York: Hill and Wang, 1969.

Zinner, Paul. *Communist Strategy and Tactics in Czechoslovakia*. London: Pall Mall, 1963.

PERIODICALS

Acta Universitatis Carolinae (Prague). Irregular, organ of Charles University.

Czechoslovak Life (Prague). Monthly, in English, published by Orbis.

Dejiny a soucasnost (Prague). Monthly, published by Orbis.

Demografie Prague). Quarterly, State Statistical Office.

Dikobraz (Prague). Satirical weekly, published by the KSC.

Ekonomicka revue (Prague). Monthly, Socialist Academy.

Hospodarske noviny (Prague). Weekly, economic review of the KSC Central Committee.

Host do domu (Brno). Monthly, magazine of literature, published by Ceskoslovensky spisovatel.

Kulturny zivot (Bratislava). Weekly, Union of Slovak Writers.

Kvety (Prague). Illustrated weekly, KSC Central Committee.

Lidova demokracie (Prague). Daily, published by the People's Party.

Literarni noviny (Prague). Weekly, Union of Czechoslovak Writers. Banned and reappeared in 1968 as *Literarni listy*. After August 1968 invasion, returned as *Listy* in November, 1968. Banned in May 1969.

Mlada fronta (Prague). Daily, Czechoslovak Youth Federation.

Mlady svet (Prague). Weekly, Czechoslovak Youth Federation.

My (Prague). Monthly, Czechoslovak Youth Federation.

Nova mysl (Prague). Monthly, journal of the KSC Central Committee.

Obrana lidu (Prague). Weekly, Ministry of National Defense.

Obroda (Prague). Weekly, published by the People's Party. Banned in 1969.

Plamen (Prague). Monthly, Union of Czechoslovak Writers.

Politicka ekonomie (Prague). Monthly, Economics Institute of the Czechoslovak Academy of Sciences.

Prace (Prague). Daily, organ of Central Council of Trade Unions.

Pravda (Bratislava). Daily, published by the Central Committee of the Slovak Communist Party.

Pravnicke studie (Bratislava). Quarterly, Institute of State and Law of the Slovak Academy of Sciences.

Pravnik (Prague). Monthly, Institute of State and Law of the Czechoslovak Academy of Sciences.

Pravny obzor (Bratislava). Monthly, Institute of State and Law of the Slovak Academy of Sciences.

Predvoj (Bratislava). Weekly, published by the Central Committee of the Slovak Communist Party.

Reporter (Prague). Weekly, Union of Czechoslovak Journalists. Banned in 1969.

Rohac (Bratislava). Satirical weekly, published by the Slovak Communist Party.

Rovnost (Brno). Daily, published by the KSC Regional Committee.

Rude pravo (Prague). Daily, published by the KSC Central Committee.

Signal (Prague). Weekly, published by Svazarm.

Smena. (Bratislava). Daily, Slovak Youth Federation.

Socialisticka zakonnost (Prague). Ten issues annually, Ministry of Justice.

Sociologicky casopis (Prague). Bimonthly, Scientific Board for Philosophy and Sociology of the Czechoslovak Academy of Sciences.

Student (Prague). Weekly, University Board of the Central Committee of the Czechoslovak Youth Federation. Defunct since the 1968 invasion.

Svet prace (Prague). Weekly, organ of the Central Council of Trade Unions.

Svet sovetu (Prague). Weekly, Czechoslovak-Soviet Friendship League. Titled *Svet socialismu* since the 1968 invasion.

Svet v obrazech (Prague). Illustrated weekly, Union of Czechoslovak Journalists.

Svoboda (Prague). Daily, published by the KSC Regional Committee.

Svobodne slovo (Prague). Daily, published by the Socialist Party.

Tribuna (Prague). Weekly, published by the KSC Bureau for the Czech provinces.

Tvorba (Prague). Weekly, published by the KSC Central Committee.

Ucitelske noviny (Prague). Weekly, Ministry of Education.

Vecerni Praha (Prague). Daily, published by the KSC Municipal Council.

Vlasta (Prague). Weekly, Committee of Czechoslovak Women.

Zemedelske noviny (Prague). Daily, Ministry of Agriculture.

Zitrek (Prague). Weekly, published by the Socialist Party. Defunct since 1969.

Zivot strany (Prague). Biweekly, published by the KSC Central Committee.

BIBLIOGRAPHIES

Czechoslovak Academy of Sciences. *Bibliography of Czechoslovak Legal Literature, 1945–1958.* Prague: NCSAV, 1959.

Gsovski, Vladimir, ed. *Legal Sources and Bibliography of Czechoslovakia.* New York: Praeger, 1959.

Periodicals from the Czechoslovak Socialist Republic. Prague: Artia, 1967.

Sturn, Rudolf, ed. *Czechoslovakia: A Bibliographical Guide.* Washington, D.C.: Library of Congress, 1967.

Index

Action Program of 1968, 34, 78, 81, 148
Agriculture, 28, 45–46, 47, 49, 88
Arbitrazh, 2, 86, 90
Armed forces, 110
Auersperg, Pavel, 43
Austro-Hungarian Empire, 1, 18, 100

Bacilek, Karol, 16, 53
Barak, Rudolf, 7–8
Bardot, Brigit, 125
Bartuska, Jan, 87
Bata Industries, 48
Benes, Eduard, 2, 8
Bilak, Vasil, 34, 51, 61, 102
Blazek, Vladimir, 132
Bocek, Otomar, 95
Boura, Ferdinand, 86
Brablcova, V., 50
Brecht, Bertolt, 128
Brezhnev, L. I., 17, 129, 145
Bruzek, Miloslav, 67
Budin, Stanislav, 137

Bulgaria, 89
    See also Warsaw Pact countries
Bureaucracy, 60–61, 74–80
    obezlichka, 3, 7, 78
    See also Rule application

Cadre system. *See* Political recruitment
Cakrtova-Sekaninova, Gertruda, 71
Censorship, 121, 128ff, 132ff, 139
Cepicka, Alexej, 86
Cernik, Oldrich, 3, 55, 61, 74, 145
Cerny, Alfred, 44
Charles IV, 20
Cech, Josef, 95–96
Chnoupek, Bohuslav, 39–40
Churches, 13, 123, 124ff
Cisar, Cestmir, 41, 137
Class struggle, *See* Marxism-Leninism
Clementis, Vladimir, 15
Club of Committed Thinking, 109
Comenius, 19
Cominform, 6, 15

Communist Party of Czechoslovakia (KSC)
  aktif,   27, 102–103, 119
  apparatchiks,   29, 75–80, 81–82, 99,
  102ff, 119, 121
  Central Committee,   41, 44, 61
  central organs,   6, 68, 69, 70, 78, 79
  congresses,   15, 44, 51–52, 61, 149
  democratic centralism, 10–11
  history,   2, 3, 6
  leading role of the Party,   6, 16, 30ff, 63ff
  membership,   27–29, 43–44, 105–106
  statutes,   30
Constitution,   3, 6, 14–15, 29, 68, 70, 87
Criminality,   92–93
Cult of personality.   See *Stalinism*
Czech National Council (CNR), 71–72
  See also National Assembly
Czechoslovak Academy of Sciences,   9, 89, 109
Czechoslovak Life,   59, 74
Czechoslovak-Soviet Friendship League
  (SCSP),   119, 120
Czechoslovak Sociological Society,   109
Czechoslovak Youth Organization (CSM; SSM),
  9, 38, 65–66, 105, 114ff
Czemadok,   14

Daily World,   34
Dejdar, Bretislav,   113, 144–145
Derer, Ivan,   14–15
Dictatorship of the proletariat.   *See* Marxism-
  Leninism
Dikobraz,   132
Dolansky, Jaromir,   71
Dolejsi Vojtech,   97
Dubcek, Alexander,   3, 16, 19, 20, 30, 42, 60, 61,
  137, 144
Dutschke, Rudi,   127

Economic reforms.   *See* New Economic Model
Economy,   8–9, 10, 17, 45, 46, 47ff, 54–55, 149
  See also Soviet model
Educational system
  basic,   110ff
  curriculum,   113
  discrimination,   110
  See also Universities
Ekonomicka revue,   45
Elections,   25, 72–73, 149

Family,   110ff
Farmers.   *See* Agriculture
Federalization,   14ff, 71–73
Fierlinger, Zdenek,   36, 71
Fojtik, Jan,   104
Foreign broadcasts,   121–122, 136
Foreign policy,   10, 147ff
Foreign trade,   10, 47
Franek, Jiri,   121

Gardavsky, Vitezslav,   103
German Democratic Republic,   52, 54, 89, 149
  See also Warsaw Pact countries
Gomulka, Wladyslav,   149
Gottwald, Klement,   3, 6, 7, 8, 25, 70, 118
Groesser, Josef,   72

Hacha, Emil,   8
Hajek, Milos,   104
Hanak, Jiri,   39–40
Hanes, Dalibor,   17
Hanzelka, Jiri,   101
Havel, Vaclav,   31–32, 33, 109
Hendrych, Jiri,   30, 63, 71
Hochman, Jiri,   138, 144
Holecek, Lubos,   60
Holub, Miroslav,   57, 131
Holy, Ivan,   83
Horakova, Milada,   85
Hrabal, Bohumil,   109
Hübl, Milan,   39, 103–104
Hungary,   25, 89–90, 150
  See also Warsaw Pact countries
Hus, Jan,   20
Husak, Gustav,   6, 10, 15, 17, 20, 22, 42, 45, 58, 68,
  84, 96, 104, 128, 148–150

Ideology. *See* Marxism-Leninism
Indra, Alois,   61, 122
Intelligentsia
  political engagement,   28
  professional organizations,   38, 41, 66–67, 68
  status,   52, 99
  Writers Union,   38, 67–68, 109
Interest aggregation,   68–70
Interest articulation,   62, 63–68
Interest groups,   37ff, 41, 63–68
  See also Czechoslovak Youth Organization;
  Trade unions; Intelligentsia

Jesenska, Zora, 24
Jicinsky, Zdenek, 104
Jodas, Josef, 33
    See also Stalinists
Jodl, Miroslav, xi, 8, 21
Johnson, L. B., 130
Jungmann, Milan, 144

Kadar, Janos, 23, 149
Kadlec, Vladimir, 9, 113
Kadlecova, Erika, 124
Kalab, Milos, 110
Kalivoda, Robert, 6, 33
KAN, 36–37, 41
Kaplan, Karel, 1
Kaspar, Jan, 70, 135, 136–137
Kempny, Josef, 79, 130
Kennedy, J. F., 60
Khrushchev, N. S., 3, 9, 43, 59
Klima, Ivan, 94, 109
Klub-231, 31, 37, 41
Kodaj, Samuel, 71
Kohout, Pavel, 24
Kohoutek, V., 100
Kolder, Drahomir, 61, 63–64, 102
Komsomol, 9
Konstantinov, F., 132
Kopecky, Vaclav, 63
Kosik, Karel, 7, 32, 145
Kouba, Karel, 104
Kriegel, Frantisek, 30
Krylenko, N. V., 86
Krystofek, Oldrich, 59, 116, 125
Kucera, Bohuslav, 34, 35, 86
Kucera, Jaroslav, 97, 127–128
Kudrna, Jaroslav, 108
Kulturny zivot, 16, 137, 147
Kundera, Milan, 7, 109
Kusy, Miroslav, 29, 75, 78, 101, 102
Kuznetsov, V. V., 59

Labor, 48
    attitudes, 51, 52–53, 54–55
    codes and discipline, 58, 90, 97
    conditions, 50
    Party membership, 28, 51
Lakatos, Michal, 32, 33, 85
Laub, Gabriel, 141
Lastovicka, Bohuslav, 71

Legal system
    adjudication, 91–93
    amnesty, 93
    attorneys, 89–90
    "class justice," 2, 86ff
    codes, 18, 88ff, 94, 96
    judges, 86, 89, 97
    Prokuratura, 2, 86
    Rechtstaat, 96, 150
    rehabilitation, 95ff
Lenart, Jozef, 74
Lenin, V. I., x, 30, 43
Ler, Leopold, 51
Lidova demokracie, 34, 138–139
Literarni noviny (Literarni listy; Listy), x, xi, 3, 12, 20, 24, 108, 121, 134, 137
Lomsky, Bohumir, 71

Machacova, Bozena, 63
Machonin, Pavel, 53
Makarenko, A. S., 112
Mamula, Miroslav, 68, 78
Marx, Karl, 1, 30
Marxism-Leninism, x, 5, 6, 29, 70, 86ff
Masaryk, T. G., 8, 9, 19, 35
Mass media, 32, 34, 38–39, 120, 137ff
Mass organizations.   *See* Interest groups
Materidouska, 139
Matuska, Waldemar, 36
Mikova, Marie, 63, 139
Miller, Arthur, 18
Ministry of Interior, 37, 41, 66, 72, 132–133
    secret police, 68, 90
Mlada fronta, 75, 137
Mlynar, Zdenek, 30, 32, 33
Mlynarik, Jan, 12
Molière, 128
Moravian patriotism, 68
Movies, 127, 128
Mucha, Jiri, 60
Müller, Vaclav, 54
Munich Settlement, 1, 8

National Assembly, 63, 71–73
    See also Rule making
National character, 18–23, 54–55, 56–57, 141ff
National Front, 25ff, 41ff
National minorities, 12–14, 18, 46
Nejedly, Zdenek, 63, 112

Nemcansky, Milos, 32
Nemec, Jan, 85, 96, 97, 149
Neuman, Alois, 71
New Economic Model, 5, 8–9, 80–84, 100
    See also Economy
New York Times, 45
Nova mysl, 1, 30, 122, 125–126, 144
Novacek, Silvester, 129
Novomesky, Laco, 15
Novotny, Antonin
    performance, 3ff, 8–10, 15, 16, 51–52,
    59, 62, 70, 81
    personality, 7–8, 17, 62, 130
Novotny, Ladislav, 120
Novy, Vilem, 71, 104

Ondrej, Josef, 97
Opat, Jaroslav, 12
Ovechkin, V. V., 135

Palach, Jan, 65, 142, 145
Party College, 10, 29, 33, 103–104
Pastyrik, Miroslav, 63
Pavlik, Ondrej, 129
Pelikan, Jiri, 101
Pelisek, Vaclav, 106
Pelnar, Jan, 92
People's Committees, 75, 79–80, 90, 105–106
Pich-Tuma, M., 95–96
Piller, Jan, 61, 96
Pioneer Organization, 66, 114ff, 117
Pionyr, 118
Pistora, Jiri, 139
Pithart, Petr, 32, 72, 148
Planava, Ivo, 20
Plojhar, Josef, 26, 66, 71
Plzen incident, 65
Poland, 35, 52, 89–90, 109, 150
    See also Warsaw Pact countries
Political culture. *See* National character
Political elites
    style, 8, 59–63, 69, 137
    titles and privileges, 10, 29, 53–54, 103
Political participation, 22, 23, 24ff, 41ff
    opposition (*oponentura*), 30, 35, 38, 39
Political recruitment, 8, 27–29, 51, 53, 98ff, 117
    managers, 81–84, 100–101
    nomenklatura, 83, 85, 99ff, 106
Political socialization, 9–10, 108ff
Prace, 75, 137

Prague, 50
Pravda, 38, 42, 132, 145
Prochazka, Jan, 61, 133, 139
Public opinion surveys, 9, 16, 18, 19, 20, 22–23, 39,
    42, 50, 55, 57, 58, 64, 82, 83, 109, 110, 111, 121,
    126, 127, 139, 143–144
Puppet parties, 25ff, 34–36, 42
Purges, 6, 15, 43–44, 98, 106–107
    See also Terror

Razl, Stanislav, 48, 69, 74
Religion. *See* Churches
Reporter, xi, 39–40, 69, 85, 98, 133, 137
Richta, Radovan, 81
Rude pravo, 17, 22, 38, 39, 43, 63, 84, 121,
    130, 136, 137
Rule application, 74ff
    See also Bureaucracy
Rule making, 70ff
    See also National Assembly
Rumania, 32, 127, 151
    See also Warsaw Pact countries

Samalik, Frantisek, 10, 29, 52
Schools. *See* Educational system
Schweikism, 19, 142
    See also National character
Scout movement, 116ff
Seifert, Jaroslav, 68
Sejna, Jan, 63
Sekera, Jiri, 22
Sik, Ota, 83, 139
Simon, Bohumil, 67
Simunek, Otakar, 71
Siroky, Viliam, 16
Skoda Industries, 48, 83
Skutina, Vladimir, 85
Skvorecky, Josef, x
Slansky, Rudolf, 15, 56
Slavik, Vaclav, 78, 104
Sling, Otto, 120
Slovakia
    agencies, 15, 16, 71–72
    economy, 17, 49
    federalization, 14–18
    grievances, 13ff, 79
    Matica Slovenska, 14
Smena, 141
Smrkovsky, Josef, 30, 59, 60, 71, 145
Socialisticka zakonnost, 85

Social security,   49–51, 53, 54–55, 57
Society, class composition of,   45–46, 47, 53, 127–128
Society for the Dissemination of Political and Scientific Knowledge (Socialist Academy),   119
Society for Human Rights,   34, 41, 67
Sociology,   69, 104, 109ff
Sovereignty,   1, 10–11, 19, 42, 59, 144, 147ff
Soviet model,   4, 6, 12–14, 15, 17, 20, 28, 45ff, 79, 83, 112, 147ff
Spacek, Josef,   30
Spiegel,   35
Stalin, J. V.,   3, 15, 30, 43, 86
Stalinism,   3, 5–8, 30
Stalinists,   20–21, 22, 43, 59–63, 64–65, 100–101, 131–134
Standard of living,   8–9, 50–51, 52–53, 55ff
Stefanik, M. R.,   16, 20
Stevcek, Pavol,   16
Strahov incident,   65
Strougal, Lubomir,   61, 74, 79
Student,   34, 137
Students,   41, 104–105, 111ff, 115, 126ff
Stur, Ludovit,   20
Subrt, Jan,   71
Sulety, Ondrej,   63
Svodoctvi,   59
Svestka, Oldrich,   49, 61, 138
Svet prace,   130
Svitak, Ivan,   10, 83, 133, 150
Svoboda, Ludvik,   3, 86, 118, 145
Svobodne slovo,   34, 56, 137

Talich, Vaclav,   63
Terror,   18, 85ff
    See also Purges
Tesar, Jan,   142
Text,   141
Tiso, Jozef,   15
Tito, Josip Broz,   6
Tomasek, Frantisek,   123
Tomes, Igor,   50–51
Tourism,   48, 122

Tribuna,   118, 127, 138, 144
Tvorba,   43, 129
Two Thousand Words Manifesto,   62

Ulbricht, Walter,   127
Union of Czechoslovak Journalists,   137
    See also Mass media
Union of Czechoslovak Lawyers,   66
United Nations Declaration of Universal Human Rights,   36, 67
Universities,   86, 89, 109, 129
    See also Educational system
USSR.   See Soviet model

Vaculik, Ludvik,   62
Varholik, Juraj,   117
Vlcek, Vladislav,   34
Vokrouhlicky, Zbynek,   116, 141
Vyshinsky, A. Y.,   86

Warsaw Pact Countries,   8, 45, 57, 50
Wichterle, Otto,   72
Women
    employment,   9, 48, 111
    motherhood,   50
    political participation,   29
Workers Councils,   81–84
Workers Militia,   3, 69
Work of Council Renewal (DKO),   41
Writers Union.   See Intelligentsia

Youth,   28, 104–106, 116ff
    See also Czechoslovak Youth Organization; Pioneer Organization
Yugoslavia,   32, 89, 127, 151

Zapotocky, Antonin,   3, 6, 8, 36, 62
Zemedelske noviny,   134–135
Zitrek,   139, 145
Zivot strany,   138
Zpravy,   138
Zuska, Zdenek,   96